New Perspectives on Microsoft Excel 2007

Introductory

June Jamrich Parsons | Dan Oja | Roy Ageloff | Patrick Carey

Australia • Brazil • Japan • Korea • Mexico • Singapore • Spain • United Kingdom • United States

CENGAGE
Learning™

New Perspectives on Microsoft Excel 2007: Introductory

Executive Editors:
Maureen Staudt
Michael Stranz

Senior Project Development Manager:
Linda deStefano

Marketing Specialist:
Courtney Sheldon

Senior Production/Manufacturing Manager:
Donna M. Brown

PreMedia Manager:
Joel Brennecke

Sr. Rights Acquisition Account Manager:
Todd Osborne

Cover Image:
Getty Images*

*Unless otherwise noted, all cover images used by Custom Solutions, a part of Cengage Learning, have been supplied courtesy of Getty Images with the exception of the Earthview cover image, which has been supplied by the National Aeronautics and Space Administration (NASA).

Source:

New Perspectives on Microsoft® Office Excel® 2007, Introductory, Premium Video Edition , 1st Edition
June Jamrich Parsons | Dan Oja | Roy Ageloff | Patrick M. Carey
© 2011 Cengage Learning. All rights reserved.

For product information and technology assistance, contact us at
Cengage Learning Customer & Sales Support, 1-800-354-9706

For permission to use material from this text or product,
submit all requests online at **cengage.com/permissions**
Further permissions questions can be emailed to
permissionrequest@cengage.com

This book contains select works from existing Cengage Learning resources and was produced by Cengage Learning Custom Solutions for collegiate use. As such, those adopting and/or contributing to this work are responsible for editorial content accuracy, continuity and completeness.

Compilation © 2010 Cengage Learning

ISBN-13: 978-1-111-63368-4

ISBN-10: 1-111-63368-1

Cengage Learning
5191 Natorp Boulevard
Mason, Ohio 45040
USA

Cengage Learning is a leading provider of customized learning solutions with office locations around the globe, including Singapore, the United Kingdom, Australia, Mexico, Brazil, and Japan. Locate your local office at:
international.cengage.com/region

Cengage Learning products are represented in Canada by Nelson Education, Ltd.
For your lifelong learning solutions, visit **www.cengage.com/custom**
Visit our corporate website at **www.cengage.com.**

Printed in the United States of America

Table of Contents

Objectives

- Explore the programs that comprise Microsoft Office
- Start programs and switch between them
- Explore common window elements
- Minimize, maximize, and restore windows
- Use the Ribbon, tabs, and buttons
- Use the contextual tabs, Mini toolbar, and shortcut menus
- Save, close, and open a file
- Use the Help system
- Print a file
- Exit programs

Getting Started with Microsoft Office 2007

Preparing a Meeting Agenda

Case | Recycled Palette

Recycled Palette, a company in Oregon founded by Ean Nogella in 2006, sells 100 percent recycled latex paint to both individuals and businesses in the area. The high-quality recycled paint is filtered to industry standards and tested for performance and environmental safety. The paint is available in both 1 gallon cans and 5 gallon pails, and comes in colors ranging from white to shades of brown, blue, green, and red. The demand for affordable recycled paint has been growing each year. Ean and all his employees use Microsoft Office 2007, which provides everyone in the company with the power and flexibility to store a variety of information, create consistent files, and share data. In this tutorial, you'll review how the company's employees use Microsoft Office 2007.

Starting Data Files

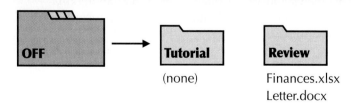

OFF → Tutorial
(none)

Review
Finances.xlsx
Letter.docx

Exploring Microsoft Office 2007

Microsoft Office 2007, or **Office**, is a collection of Microsoft programs. Office is available in many suites, each of which contains a different combination of these programs. For example, the Professional suite includes Word, Excel, PowerPoint, Access, Outlook, and Publisher. Other suites are available and can include more or fewer programs (for additional information about the available suites, go to the Microsoft Web site). Each Office program contains valuable tools to help you accomplish many tasks, such as composing reports, analyzing data, preparing presentations, compiling information, sending e-mail, and planning schedules.

Microsoft Office Word 2007, or **Word**, is a computer program you use to enter, edit, and format text. The files you create in Word are called **documents**, although many people use the term *document* to refer to any file created on a computer. Word, often called a word processing program, offers many special features that help you compose and update all types of documents, ranging from letters and newsletters to reports, brochures, faxes, and even books—all in attractive and readable formats. You can also use Word to create, insert, and position figures, tables, and other graphics to enhance the look of your documents. For example, the Recycled Palette employees create business letters using Word.

Microsoft Office Excel 2007, or **Excel**, is a computer program you use to enter, calculate, analyze, and present numerical data. You can do some of this in Word with tables, but Excel provides many more tools for recording and formatting numbers as well as performing calculations. The graphics capabilities in Excel also enable you to display data visually. You might, for example, generate a pie chart or a bar chart to help people quickly see the significance of and the connections between information. The files you create in Excel are called **workbooks** (commonly referred to as spreadsheets), and Excel is often called a spreadsheet program. The Recycled Palette accounting department uses a line chart in an Excel workbook to visually track the company's financial performance.

Microsoft Office Access 2007, or **Access**, is a computer program used to enter, maintain, and retrieve related information (or data) in a format known as a database. The files you create in Access are called **databases**, and Access is often referred to as a database or relational database program. With Access, you can create forms to make data entry easier, and you can create professional reports to improve the readability of your data. The Recycled Palette operations department tracks the company's inventory in a table in an Access database.

Microsoft Office PowerPoint 2007, or **PowerPoint**, is a computer program you use to create a collection of slides that can contain text, charts, pictures, sound, movies, multimedia, and so on. The files you create in PowerPoint are called **presentations**, and PowerPoint is often called a presentation graphics program. You can show these presentations on your computer monitor, project them onto a screen as a slide show, print them, share them over the Internet, or display them on the World Wide Web. You can also use PowerPoint to generate presentation-related documents such as audience handouts, outlines, and speakers' notes. The Recycled Palette marketing department has created an effective slide presentation with PowerPoint to promote its paints to a wider audience.

Microsoft Office Outlook 2007, or **Outlook**, is a computer program you use to send, receive, and organize e-mail; plan your schedule; arrange meetings; organize contacts; create a to-do list; and jot down notes. You can also use Outlook to print schedules, task lists, phone directories, and other documents. Outlook is often referred to as an information management program. The Recycled Palette staff use Outlook to send and receive e-mail, plan their schedules, and create to-do lists.

Although each Office program individually is a strong tool, their potential is even greater when used together.

Integrating Office Programs

One of the main advantages of Office is **integration**, the ability to share information between programs. Integration ensures consistency and accuracy, and it saves time because you don't have to reenter the same information in several Office programs. The staff at Recycled Palette uses the integration features of Office daily, including the following examples:

- The accounting department created an Excel bar chart on the previous two years' fourth-quarter results, which they inserted into the quarterly financial report created in Word. They included a hyperlink in the Word report that employees can click to open the Excel workbook and view the original data.
- The operations department included an Excel pie chart of sales percentages by paint colors on a PowerPoint slide, which is part of a presentation to stockholders.
- The marketing department produced a mailing to promote its recycled paints to local contractors and designers by combining a form letter created in Word with an Access database that stores the names and addresses of these potential customers.
- A sales representative wrote a letter in Word about an upcoming promotion for new customers and merged the letter with an Outlook contact list containing the names and addresses of prospective customers.

These are just a few examples of how you can take information from one Office program and integrate it with another.

Starting Office Programs

You can start any Office program by clicking the Start button on the Windows taskbar, and then selecting the program you want from the All Programs menu. As soon as the program starts, you can immediately begin to create new files or work with existing ones. If an Office program appears in the most frequently used programs list on the left side of the Start menu, you can click the program name to start the program.

Starting Office Programs | Reference Window

- Click the Start button on the taskbar.
- Click All Programs.
- Click Microsoft Office.
- Click the name of the program you want to start.

or

- Click the name of the program you want to start in the most frequently used programs list on the left side of the Start menu.

You'll start Excel using the Start button.

To start Excel and open a new, blank workbook:

▶ **1.** Make sure your computer is on and the Windows desktop appears on your screen.

Trouble? If your screen varies slightly from those shown in the figures, your computer might be set up differently. The figures in this book were created while running Windows Vista with the Aero feature turned off, but how your screen looks depends on the version of Windows you are using, the background settings, and so forth.

▶ 2. Click the **Start** button 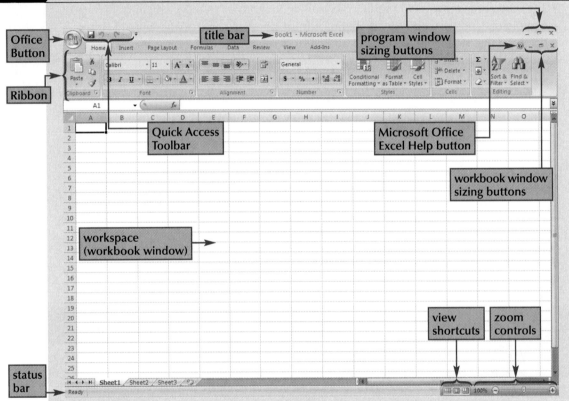 on the taskbar, and then click **All Programs** to display the All Programs menu.

▶ 3. Click **Microsoft Office** on the All Programs list, and then point to **Microsoft Office Excel 2007**. Depending on how your computer is set up, your desktop and menu might contain different icons and commands.

> **Trouble?** If you don't see Microsoft Office on the All Programs list, click Microsoft Office Excel 2007 on the All Programs list. If you still don't see Microsoft Office Excel 2007, ask your instructor or technical support person for help.

▶ 4. Click **Microsoft Office Excel 2007**. Excel starts, and a new, blank workbook opens. See Figure 1.

Figure 1	New, blank Excel workbook

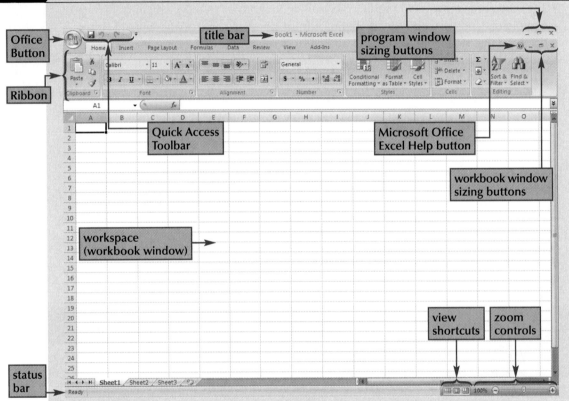

> **Trouble?** If the Excel window doesn't fill your entire screen, the window is not maximized, or expanded to its full size. You'll maximize the window shortly.

You can have more than one Office program open at once. You'll use this same method to start Word and open a new, blank document.

To start Word and open a new, blank document:

▶ 1. Click the **Start** button 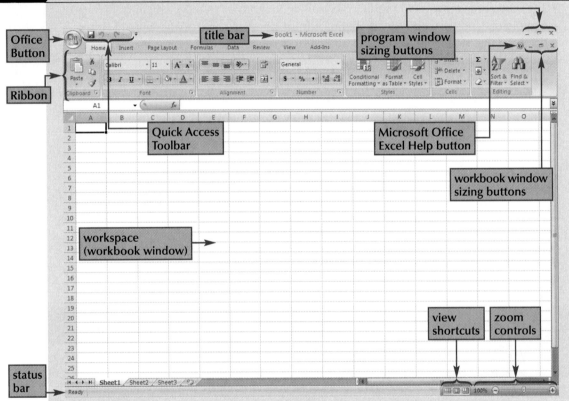 on the taskbar, click **All Programs** to display the All Programs list, and then click **Microsoft Office**.

> **Trouble?** If you don't see Microsoft Office on the All Programs list, click Microsoft Office Word 2007 on the All Programs list. If you still don't see Microsoft Office Word 2007, ask your instructor or technical support person for help.

▶ 2. Click **Microsoft Office Word 2007**. Word starts, and a new, blank document opens. See Figure 2.

New, blank document in Word ◄ **Figure 2**

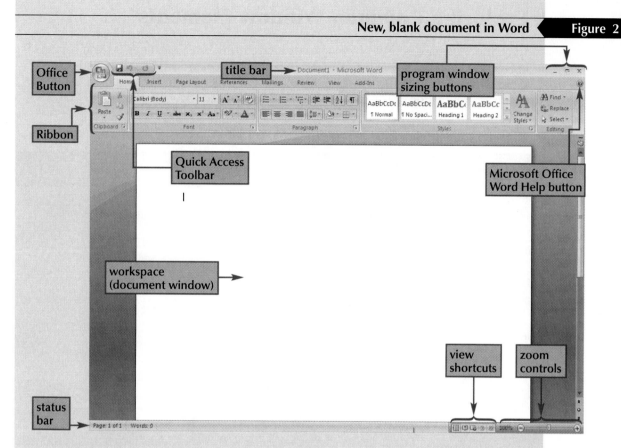

Trouble? If the Word window doesn't fill your entire screen, the window is not maximized. You'll maximize the window shortly.

Switching Between Open Programs and Files

Two programs are running at the same time—Excel and Word. The taskbar contains buttons for both programs. When you have two or more programs running or two files within the same program open, you can use the taskbar buttons to switch from one program or file to another. The button for the active program or file is darker. The employees at Recycled Palette often work in several programs at once.

To switch between Word and Excel files:

▶ 1. Click the **Microsoft Excel – Book1** button on the taskbar. The active program switches from Word to Excel. See Figure 3.

Excel and Word programs opened simultaneously ◄ **Figure 3**

Tip

You can also press the Alt+Tab keys to switch between open files.

▶ 2. Click the **Document1 – Microsoft Word** button on the taskbar to return to Word.

Exploring Common Window Elements

The Office programs consist of windows that have many similar features. As you can see in Figures 1 and 2, many of the elements in both the Excel program window and the Word program window are the same. In fact, all the Office programs have these same elements. Figure 4 describes some of the most common window elements.

Figure 4   Common window elements

Element	Description
Office Button	Provides access to document-level features and program settings
Quick Access Toolbar	Provides one-click access to commonly used commands, such as Save, Undo, and Repeat
Title bar	Contains the name of the open file, the program name, and the sizing buttons
Sizing buttons	Resize and close the program window or the workspace
Ribbon	Provides access to the main set of commands organized by task into tabs and groups
Microsoft Office Help button	Opens the Help window for that program
Workspace	Displays the file you are working on (Word document, Excel workbook, Access database, or PowerPoint slide)
Status bar	Provides information about the program, open file, or current task as well as the view shortcuts and zoom controls
View shortcuts	Change how a file is displayed in the workspace
Zoom controls	Magnify or shrink the content displayed in the workspace

Because these elements are the same in each program, after you've learned one program, it's easy to learn the others. The next sections explore these common features.

Resizing the Program Window and Workspace

There are three different sizing buttons. The Minimize button ▭, which is the left button, hides a window so that only its program button is visible on the taskbar. The middle button changes name and function depending on the status of the window—the Maximize button ▭ expands the window to the full screen size or to the program window size, and the Restore Down button ▭ returns the window to a predefined size. The Close button ✕, on the right, exits the program or closes the file. Excel has two sets of sizing buttons. The top set controls the program window and the lower set controls the workspace. The workspace sizing buttons look and function in exactly the same way as the program window sizing buttons, except the button names change to Minimize Window and Restore Window when the workspace is maximized.

Most often, you'll want to maximize the program window and workspace to take advantage of the full screen size you have available. If you have several files open, you might want to restore down their windows so that you can see more than one window at a time, or you might want to minimize programs or files you are not working on at the moment. You'll try minimizing, maximizing, and restoring down windows and workspaces now.

To resize windows and workspaces:

▶ **1.** Click the **Minimize** button ▬ on the Word title bar. The Word program window reduces to a taskbar button. The Excel program window is visible again.

▶ **2.** If necessary, click the **Maximize** button ☐ on the Excel title bar. The Excel program window expands to fill the screen.

▶ **3.** Click the **Restore Window** button ☐ in the lower set of Excel sizing buttons. The workspace is resized and is now smaller than the full program window. See Figure 5.

Resized Excel window and workspace ◀ **Figure 5**

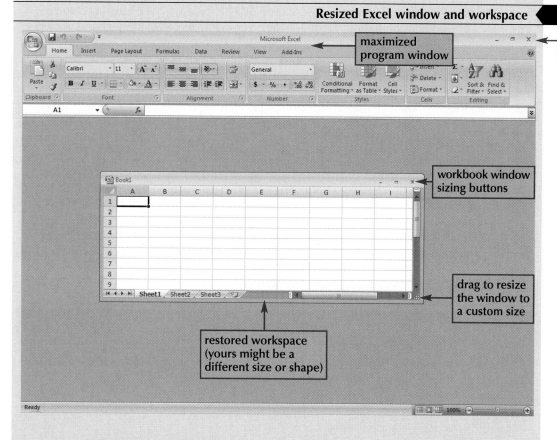

maximized program window

program window sizing buttons

workbook window sizing buttons

drag to resize the window to a custom size

restored workspace (yours might be a different size or shape)

▶ **4.** Click the **Maximize** button ☐ on the Excel workbook window title bar. The Excel workspace expands to fill the program window.

▶ **5.** Click the **Document1 - Microsoft Word** button on the taskbar. The Word program window returns to its previous size.

▶ **6.** If necessary, click the **Maximize** button ☐ on the Word title bar. The Word program window expands to fill the screen.

The sizing buttons give you the flexibility to arrange the program and file windows on your screen to best fit your needs.

Getting Information from the Status Bar

The **status bar** at the bottom of the program window provides information about the open file and current task or selection. It also has buttons and other controls for working with the file and its content. The status bar buttons and information displays are specific to the individual programs. For example, the Excel status bar displays summary information about a selected range of numbers (such as their sum or average), whereas the Word status bar shows the current page number and total number of words in a document. The right side of the status bar includes buttons that enable you to switch the workspace view in Word, Excel, PowerPoint, and Access as well as zoom the workspace in Word, Excel, and PowerPoint. You can customize the status bar to display other information or hide the **default** (original or preset) information.

Switching Views

Each program has a variety of views, or ways to display the file in the workspace. For example, Word has five views: Print Layout, Full Screen Reading, Web Layout, Outline, and Draft. The content of the file doesn't change from view to view, although the presentation of the content will. In Word, for example, Page Layout view shows how a document would appear as the printed page, whereas Web Layout view shows how the document would appear as a Web page. You can quickly switch between views using the shortcuts at the right side of the status bar. You can also change the view from the View tab on the Ribbon. You'll change views in later tutorials.

Zooming the Workspace

Zooming is a way to magnify or shrink the file content displayed in the workspace. You can zoom in to get a closer look at the content of an open document, worksheet, or slide, or you can zoom out to see more of the content at a smaller size. There are several ways to change the zoom percentage. You can use the Zoom slider at the right of the status bar to quickly change the zoom percentage. You can click the Zoom level button to the left of the Zoom slider in the status bar to open the Zoom dialog box and select a specific zoom percentage or size based on your file. You can also change the zoom settings using the Zoom group in the View tab on the Ribbon.

Reference Window	**Zooming the Workspace**

- Click the Zoom Out or Zoom In button on the status bar (or drag the Zoom slider button left or right) to the desired zoom percentage.

or
- Click the Zoom level button on the status bar.
- Select the appropriate zoom setting, and then click the OK button.

or
- Click the View tab on the Ribbon, and then in the Zoom group, click the zoom setting you want.

The figures shown in these tutorials are zoomed to enhance readability. You'll zoom the Word and Excel workspaces.

To zoom the Word and Excel workspaces:

▶ **1.** On the Zoom slider on the Word status bar, drag the **slider button** to the left until the Zoom percentage is **10%**. The document reduces to its smallest size, which makes the entire page visible but unreadable. See Figure 6.

Word document zoomed to 10% **Figure 6**

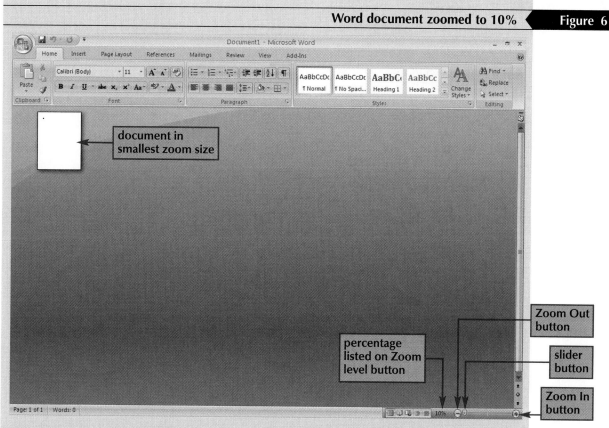

document in
smallest zoom size

percentage
listed on Zoom
level button

Zoom Out
button

slider
button

Zoom In
button

You'll zoom the document so its page width fills the workspace.

2. Click the **Zoom level** button `10%` on the Word status bar. The Zoom dialog box opens. See Figure 7.

Zoom dialog box **Figure 7**

type a custom
zoom percentage

document at
10% zoom

click this
option button

click to accept
the new zoom

3. Click the **Page width** option button, and then click the **OK** button. The Word document magnifies to its page width to match the rest of the Word figures shown in these tutorials.

Now, you'll zoom the workbook to 120%.

▶ **4.** Click the **Microsoft Excel – Book1** button on the taskbar. The Excel program window is displayed.

▶ **5.** Click the **Zoom In** button ⊕ on the status bar two times. The workspace magnifies to 120%. This is the zoom percentage that matches the rest of the Excel figures shown in these tutorials.

▶ **6.** Click the **Document1 – Microsoft Word** button on the taskbar. The Word program window is displayed.

Using the Ribbon

The **Ribbon** at the top of the program window just below the title bar is the main set of commands that you click to execute tasks. The Ribbon is organized into tabs. Each **tab** has commands related to particular activities. For example, in Word, the Insert tab on the Ribbon provides access to all the commands for adding objects such as shapes, pages, tables, illustrations, text, and symbols to a document. Although the tabs differ from program to program, the first tab in each program, called the Home tab, contains the commands for the most frequently performed activities, including cutting and pasting, changing fonts, and using editing tools. In addition, the Insert, Review, View, and Add-Ins tabs appear on the Ribbon in all the Office programs except Access, although the commands they include might differ from program to program. Other tabs are program specific, such as the Design tab in PowerPoint and the Datasheet tab in Access.

To use the Ribbon tabs:

▶ **1.** In Word, point to the **Insert** tab on the Ribbon. The Insert tab is highlighted, though the Home tab with the options for using the Clipboard and formatting text remains visible.

▶ **2.** Click the **Insert** tab. The Ribbon displays the Insert tab, which provides access to all the options for adding objects such as shapes, pages, tables, illustrations, text, and symbols to a document. See Figure 8.

| Figure 8 | Insert tab on the Ribbon |

▶ **3.** Click the **Home** tab on the Ribbon. The Ribbon displays the Home options.

Clicking Button Icons

Each **button**, or icon, on the tabs provides one-click access to a command. Most buttons are labeled so that you can easily find the command you need. For the most part, when you click a button, something happens in your file. If you want to repeat that action, you click the button again. Buttons for related commands are organized on a tab in **groups**. For example, the Clipboard group on the Home tab includes the Cut, Copy, Paste, and Format Painter buttons—the commands for moving or copying text, objects, and formatting.

Buttons can be toggle switches: one click turns on the feature and the next click turns off the feature. While the feature is on, the button remains colored or highlighted to remind you that it is active. For example, in Word, the Show/Hide button on the Home tab in the Paragraph group displays the nonprinting screen characters when toggled on and hides them when toggled off.

Some buttons have two parts: a button that accesses a command and an arrow that opens a menu of all the commands available for that task. For example, the Paste button on the Home tab includes the default Paste command and an arrow that opens the menu of all the Paste commands—Paste, Paste Special, and Paste as Hyperlink. To select a command on the menu, you click the button arrow and then click the command on the menu.

The buttons and groups change based on your monitor size, your screen resolution, and the size of the program window. With smaller monitors, lower screen resolutions, and reduced program windows, buttons can appear as icons without labels and a group can be condensed into a button that you click to display the group options. The figures in these tutorials were created using a screen resolution of 1024 × 768 and, unless otherwise specified, the program and workspace windows are maximized. If you are using a different screen resolution or window size, the button icons on the Ribbon might show more or fewer button names, and some groups might be condensed into buttons.

You'll type text in the Word document, and then use the buttons on the Ribbon.

To use buttons on the Ribbon:

1. Type **Recycled Palette**, and then press the **Enter** key. The text appears in the first line of the document and the insertion point moves to the second line.

   Trouble? If you make a typing error, press the Backspace key to delete the incorrect letters, and then retype the text.

2. In the Paragraph group on the Home tab, click the **Show/Hide** button ¶ . The nonprinting screen characters appear in the document, and the Show/Hide button remains toggled on. See Figure 9.

   Trouble? If the nonprinting characters are removed from your screen, the Show/Hide button ¶ was already selected. Repeat Step 2 to show the nonprinting screen characters.

Button toggled on | **Figure 9**

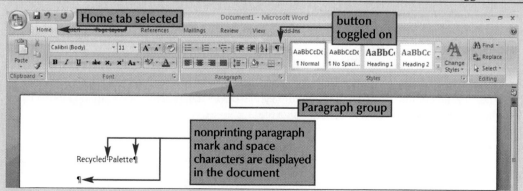

3. Drag to select all the text in the first line of the document (but not the paragraph mark).

4. In the Clipboard group on the Home tab, click the **Copy** button. The selected text is copied to the Clipboard.

▶ **5.** Press the ↓ key. The text is deselected and the insertion point moves to the second line in the document.

▶ **6.** In the Clipboard group on the Home tab, point to the top part of the **Paste** button. Both parts of the Paste button are highlighted, but the icon at top is darker to indicate it will be clicked if you press the mouse button.

▶ **7.** Point to the **Paste button arrow**. The button arrow is now darker.

▶ **8.** Click the **Paste button arrow**. A menu of paste commands opens. See Figure 10. To select one of the commands on the list, you click it.

Figure 10 **Two-part Paste button**

Paste button

click the Paste button arrow to open a menu with additional options

Paste commands

▶ **9.** Click **Paste**. The menu closes, and the text is duplicated in the second line of the document.

As you can see, you can quickly access commands and turn features on and off with the buttons on the Ribbon.

InSight | **Using Keyboard Shortcuts and Key Tips**

Keyboard shortcuts can help you work faster and more efficiently. A **keyboard shortcut** is a key or combination of keys you press to access a tool or perform a command. To quickly access options on the Ribbon, the Quick Access Toolbar, and the Office Button without removing your hands from the keyboard:

1. Press the Alt key. Key Tips appear that list the keyboard shortcut for each Ribbon tab, each Quick Access Toolbar button, and the Office Button.
2. Press the key for the tab or button you want to use. An action is performed or Key Tips appear for the buttons on the selected tab or the commands for the selected button.
3. Continue to press the appropriate key listed in the Key Tip until the action you want is performed.

You can also use keyboard shortcuts to perform specific commands. For example, Ctrl+S is the keyboard shortcut for the Save command (you hold down the Ctrl key while you press the S key). This type of keyboard shortcut appears in ScreenTips next to the command's name. Not all commands have this type of keyboard shortcut. Identical commands in each Office program use the same keyboard shortcut.

Using Galleries and Live Preview

A button can also open a **gallery**, which is a grid or menu that shows a visual representation of the options available for that command. For example, the Bullet Library gallery in Word shows an icon of each bullet style you can select. Some galleries include a More button that you click to expand the gallery to see all the options in it. When you hover the pointer over an option in a gallery, **Live Preview** shows the results you would achieve in your file if you clicked that option. To continue the bullets example, when you hover over a bullet style in the Bullet Library gallery, the current paragraph or selected text previews that bullet style. By moving the pointer from option to option, you can quickly see the text set with different bullet styles; you can then select the style that works best for your needs.

To use a gallery and Live Preview:

▶ **1.** In the Paragraph group on the Home tab, click the **Bullets button arrow** ⊞▾. The Bullet Library gallery opens.

▶ **2.** Point to the **check mark bullet** style. Live Preview shows the selected bullet style in your document, so you can determine if you like that bullet style. See Figure 11.

Live Preview of bullet style ◀ Figure 11

▶ **3.** Place the pointer over each of the remaining bullet styles and preview them in your document.

You don't want to add bullets to your document right now, so you'll close the Bullet Library gallery and deselect the Bullets button.

▶ **4.** Press the **Esc** key on the keyboard. The Bullet Library gallery closes and the Bullets button is deselected.

▶ **5.** Press the **Backspace** key on the keyboard to delete the text "Recycled Palette" on the second line.

Galleries and Live Preview let you quickly see how your file will be affected by a selection.

Opening Dialog Boxes and Task Panes

The button to the right of the group names is the **Dialog Box Launcher**, which you click to open a task pane or dialog box that provides more advanced functionality for that group of tasks. A **task pane** is a window that helps you navigate through a complex task or feature. For example, the Clipboard task pane allows you to paste some or all of the items that have been cut or copied from any Office program during the current work session and the Research task pane allows you to search a variety of reference resources from within a file. A **dialog box** is a window from which you enter or choose settings for how you want to perform a task. For example, the Page Setup dialog box in Word contains options for how you want a document to look. Some dialog boxes organize related information into tabs, and related options and settings are organized into groups, just as they are on the Ribbon. You select settings in a dialog box using option buttons, check boxes, text boxes, lists, and other controls to collect information about how you want to perform a task.

In Excel, you'll use the Dialog Box Launcher for the Page Setup group to open the Page Setup dialog box.

To open the Page Setup dialog box using the Dialog Box Launcher:

▶ 1. Click the **Microsoft Excel – Book1** button on the taskbar to switch from Word to Excel.

▶ 2. Click the **Page Layout** tab on the Ribbon.

▶ 3. In the Page Setup group, click the **Dialog Box Launcher**, which is the small button to the right of the Page Setup group name. The Page Setup dialog box opens with the Page tab displayed. See Figure 12.

Figure 12   Page tab in the Page Setup dialog box

▶ 4. Click the **Landscape** option button. The workbook's page orientation changes to a page wider than it is long.

▶ 5. Click the **Sheet** tab. The dialog box displays options related to the worksheet. You can click a check box to turn an option on (checked) or off (unchecked). You can check more than one check box in a group, whereas you can select only one option button in a group.

▶ 6. In the Print group, click the **Gridlines** check box and the **Row and column headings** check box. Check marks appear in both check boxes, indicating that these options are selected.

You don't want to change the page setup right now, so you'll close the dialog box.

▶ 7. Click the **Cancel** button. The dialog box closes without making any changes to the page setup.

Using Contextual Tools

Some tabs, toolbars, and menus come into view as you work. Because these tools become available only as you might need them, the workspace on your screen remains more open and less cluttered. However, tools that appear and disappear as you work can be distracting and take some getting used to.

Displaying Contextual Tabs

Any object that you can select in a file has a related contextual tab. An **object** is anything that appears on your screen that can be selected and manipulated as a whole, such as a table, a picture, a text box, a shape, a chart, WordArt, an equation, a diagram, a header, or a footer. A **contextual tab** is a Ribbon tab that contains commands related to the selected object so you can manipulate, edit, and format that object. Contextual tabs appear to the right of the standard Ribbon tabs just below a title label. For example, Figure 13 shows the Table Tools contextual tabs that appear when you select a table in a Word document. Although the contextual tabs appear only when you select an object, they function in the same way as standard tabs on the Ribbon. Contextual tabs disappear when you click elsewhere on the screen and deselect the object. Contextual tabs can also appear as you switch views. You'll use contextual tabs in later tutorials.

Table Tools contextual tabs | **Figure 13**

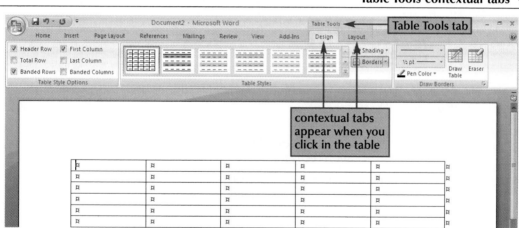

Accessing the Mini Toolbar

The **Mini toolbar** is a toolbar that appears next to the pointer whenever you select text, and it contains buttons for the most commonly used formatting commands, such as font, font size, styles, color, alignment, and indents that may appear in different groups or tabs on the Ribbon. The Mini toolbar buttons differ in each program. A transparent version of the Mini toolbar appears immediately after you select text. When you move the pointer over the Mini toolbar, it comes into full view so you can click the appropriate formatting button or buttons. The Mini toolbar disappears if you move the pointer away from the toolbar, press a key, or press a mouse button. The Mini toolbar can help you format your text faster, but initially you might find that the toolbar disappears unexpectedly. All the commands on the Mini toolbar are also available on the Ribbon. Be aware that Live Preview of selected styles does not work in the Mini toolbar.

You'll use the Mini toolbar to format text you enter in the workbook.

Tip

You can turn off the Mini toolbar and Live Preview in Word, Excel, and PowerPoint. Click the Office Button, click the Options button at the bottom of the Office menu, uncheck the first two check boxes in the Popular category, and then click the OK button.

To use the Mini toolbar to format text:

▶ 1. If necessary, click cell **A1** (the rectangle in the upper-left corner of the worksheet).

▶ 2. Type **Budget**. The text appears in the cell.

▶ 3. Press the **Enter** key. The text is entered in cell A1 and cell A2 is selected.

▶ 4. Type **2008**, and then press the **Enter** key. The year is entered in cell A2 and cell A3 is selected.

You'll use the Mini toolbar to make the word in cell A1 boldface.

▶ 5. Double-click cell **A1** to place the insertion point in the cell. Now you can select the text you typed.

▶ 6. Double-click **Budget** in cell A1. The selected text appears white in a black background, and the transparent Mini toolbar appears directly above the selected text. See Figure 14.

Figure 14	Transparent Mini toolbar

▶ 7. Move the pointer over the Mini toolbar. The Mini toolbar is now completely visible, and you can click buttons.

Trouble? If the Mini toolbar disappears, you probably moved the pointer to another area of the worksheet. To redisplay the Mini toolbar, repeat Steps 5 through 7, being careful to move the pointer directly over the Mini toolbar in Step 7.

Tip

You can redisplay the Mini toolbar if it disappears by right-clicking the selected text.

▶ 8. Click the **Bold** button **B** on the Mini toolbar. The text in cell A1 is bold and the Mini toolbar remains visible so you can continue formatting the selected text. See Figure 15.

Figure 15	Mini toolbar with the Bold button selected

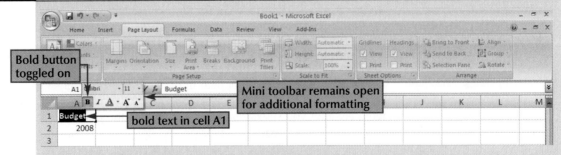

You don't want to make any other changes, so you'll close the Mini toolbar.

▶ 9. Press the **Enter** key. The Mini toolbar disappears and cell A2 is selected.

Opening Shortcut Menus

A **shortcut menu** is a list of commands related to a selection that opens when you click the right mouse button. Each shortcut menu provides access to the commands you'll most likely want to use with the object or selection you right-click. The shortcut menu includes commands that perform actions, commands that open dialog boxes, and galleries of options that provide Live Preview. The Mini toolbar also opens when you right-click. If you click a button on the Mini toolbar, the rest of the shortcut menu closes while the Mini toolbar remains open so you can continue formatting the selection. Using a shortcut menu provides quick access to the commands you need without having to access the tabs on the Ribbon. For example, you can right-click selected text to open a shortcut menu with a Mini toolbar, text-related commands, such as Cut, Copy, and Paste, as well as other program-specific commands.

You'll use a shortcut menu in Excel to delete the content you entered in cell A1.

To use a shortcut menu to delete content:

▶ 1. Right-click cell **A1**. A shortcut menu opens, listing commands related to common tasks you'd perform in a cell, along with a Mini toolbar. See Figure 16.

Shortcut menu with Mini toolbar | Figure 16

You'll use the Clear Contents command to delete the bold text from cell A1.

▶ 2. Click **Clear Contents** on the shortcut menu. The shortcut menu closes, the Mini toolbar disappears, and the formatted text is removed from cell A1.

You'll use the Clear Contents command again to delete the year from cell A2.

▶ 3. Right-click cell **A2**, and then click **Clear Contents** on the shortcut menu. The year is removed from cell A2.

Shortcut menus enable you to quickly access commands that you're most likely to need in the context of the task you're performing.

> **Tip**
>
> Press the Esc key to close an open menu, shortcut menu, list, gallery, and so forth without selecting an option.

Working with Files

The most common tasks you perform in any Office program are to create, open, save, and close files. The processes for these tasks are basically the same in all the Office programs. In addition, there are several methods for performing most tasks in Office. This flexibility enables you to use Office in a way that best fits how you like to work.

The **Office Button** provides access to document-level features, such as creating new files, opening existing files, saving files, printing files, and closing files, as well as the most common program options, called **application settings**. The **Quick Access Toolbar** is a collection of buttons that provide one-click access to commonly used commands, such as Save, Undo, and Repeat.

To begin working in a program, you need to create a new file or open an existing file. When you start Word, Excel, or PowerPoint, the program opens along with a blank file—ready for you to begin working on a new document, workbook, or presentation. When you start Access, the Getting Started with Microsoft Access window opens, displaying options for creating a new database or opening an existing one.

Ean has asked you to continue working on the agenda for the stockholder meeting. You already started typing in the document that opened when you started Word. Next, you will enter more text in the Word document.

To enter text in the Word document:

▶ 1. Click the **Document1 – Microsoft Word** button on the taskbar to activate the Word program window.

▶ 2. Type **Meeting Agenda** on the second line of the document, and then press the **Enter** key. The text you typed appears in the document.

   Trouble? If you make a typing error, press the Backspace key to delete the incorrect letters, and then retype the text.

Saving a File

As you create and modify Office files, your work is stored only in the computer's temporary memory, not on a hard disk. If you were to exit the programs without saving, turn off your computer, or experience a power failure, your work would be lost. To prevent losing work, save your file to a disk frequently—at least every 10 minutes. You can save files to the hard disk located inside your computer, a floppy disk, an external hard drive, a network storage drive, or a portable storage disk, such as a USB flash drive.

Reference Window | **Saving a File**

To save a file the first time or with a new name or location:
• Click the Office Button, and then click Save As (or for an unnamed file, click the Save button on the Quick Access Toolbar or click the Office Button, and then click Save).
• In the Save As dialog box, navigate to the location where you want to save the file.
• Type a descriptive title in the File name box, and then click the Save button.
To resave a named file to the same location:
• Click the Save button on the Quick Access Toolbar (or click the Office Button, and then click Save).

The first time you save a file, you need to name it. This **filename** includes a descriptive title you select and a file extension assigned by Office. You should choose a descriptive title that accurately reflects the content of the document, workbook, presentation, or database, such as "Shipping Options Letter" or "Fourth Quarter Financial Analysis." Your descriptive title can include uppercase and lowercase letters, numbers, hyphens, and spaces in any combination, but not the following special characters: ? " / \ < > * | and :. Each filename ends with a **file extension**, a period followed by several characters that Office adds to your descriptive title to identify the program in which that file was created. The default file extensions for Office 2007 are .docx for Word, .xlsx for Excel, .pptx for PowerPoint, and .accdb for Access. Filenames (the descriptive title and the file extension) can include a maximum of 255 characters. You might see file extensions depending on how Windows is set up on your computer. The figures in these tutorials do not show file extensions.

You also need to decide where to save the file—on which disk and in what folder. A **folder** is a container for your files. Just as you organize paper documents within folders stored in a filing cabinet, you can organize your files within folders stored on your computer's hard disk or a removable disk, such as a USB flash drive. Store each file in a logical location that you will remember whenever you want to use the file again. The default storage location for Office files is the Documents folder; you can create additional storage folders within that folder or navigate to a new storage location.

You can navigate the Save As dialog box by clicking a folder or location on your computer in the Navigation pane along the left side of the dialog box, and then double-clicking folders in the file list until you display the storage location you want. You can also navigate to a storage location with the Address bar, which displays the current file path. Each location in the file path has a corresponding arrow that you can click to quickly select a folder within that location. For example, you can click the Documents arrow in the Address bar to open a list of all the folders in the Documents folder, and then click the folder you want to open. If you want to return to a specific spot in the file hierarchy, you click that folder name in the Address bar. The Back and Forward buttons let you quickly move between folders.

Saving and Using Files with Earlier Versions of Office | InSight

The default file types in Office 2007 are different from those used in earlier versions. This means that someone using Office 2003 or earlier cannot open files created in Office 2007. Files you want to share with earlier Office users must be saved in the earlier formats, which use the following extensions: .doc for Word, .xls for Excel, .mdb for Access, and .ppt for PowerPoint. To save a file in an earlier format, open the Save As dialog box, click the Save as type list arrow, and then click the appropriate 97-2003 format. A compatibility checker reports which Office 2007 features or elements are not supported by the earlier version of Office, and you can choose to remove them before saving. You can use Office 2007 to open and work with files created in earlier versions of Office. You can then save the file in its current format or update it to the Office 2007 format.

The lines of text you typed are not yet saved on disk. You'll do that now.

To save a file for the first time:

Windows XP Tip

To navigate to a location in the Save As dialog box, you use the Save in arrow.

► **1.** Click the **Save** button 🔲 on the Quick Access Toolbar. The Save As dialog box opens because you have not yet saved the file and need to specify a storage location and filename. The default location is set to the Documents folder, and the first few words of the first line appear in the File name box as a suggested title.

► **2.** In the Navigation pane, click the link for the location that contains your Data Files, if necessary.

Trouble? If you don't have the starting Data Files, you need to get them before you can proceed. Your instructor will either give you the Data Files or ask you to obtain them from a specified location (such as a network drive). In either case, make a backup copy of the Data Files before you start so that you will have the original files available in case you need to start over. If you have any questions about the Data Files, see your instructor or technical support person for assistance.

► **3.** Double-click the **OFF** folder in the file list, and then double-click the **Tutorial** folder. This is the location where you want to save the document.

Next, you'll enter a more descriptive title for the filename.

► **4.** Type **Meeting Agenda** in the File name box. See Figure 17.

Figure 17	Completed Save As dialog box

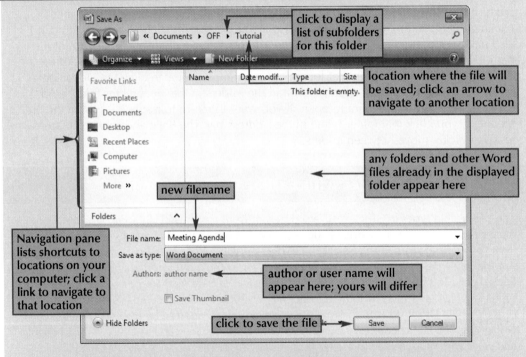

Trouble? If the .docx file extension appears after the filename, your computer is configured to show file extensions. Continue with Step 5.

► **5.** Click the **Save** button. The Save As dialog box closes, and the name of your file appears in the title bar.

The saved file includes everything in the document at the time you last saved it. Any new edits or additions you make to the document exist only in the computer's memory and are not saved in the file on the disk. As you work, remember to save frequently so that the file is updated to reflect the latest content of the document.

Because you already named the document and selected a storage location, the Save As dialog box doesn't open whenever you save the document again. If you want to save a copy of the file with a different filename or to a different location, you reopen the Save As dialog box by clicking the Office Button, and then clicking Save As. The previous version of the file remains on your disk as well.

You need to add your name to the agenda. Then, you'll save your changes.

To modify and save the Word document:

▶ 1. Type your name, and then press the **Enter** key. The text you typed appears on the next line.

▶ 2. Click the **Save** button on the Quick Access Toolbar to save your changes.

Closing a File

Although you can keep multiple files open at one time, you should close any file you are no longer working on to conserve system resources as well as to ensure that you don't inadvertently make changes to the file. You can close a file by clicking the Office Button and then clicking the Close command. If that's the only file open for the program, the program window remains open and no file appears in the window. You can also close a file by clicking the Close button in the upper-right corner of the title bar or double-clicking the Office Button. If that's the only file open for the program, the program also closes.

As a standard practice, you should save your file before closing it. However, Office has an added safeguard: If you attempt to close a file without saving your changes, a dialog box opens, asking whether you want to save the file. Click the Yes button to save the changes to the file before closing the file and program. Click the No button to close the file and program without saving changes. Click the Cancel button to return to the program window without saving changes or closing the file and program. This feature helps to ensure that you always save the most current version of any file.

You'll add the date to the agenda. Then, you'll attempt to close it without saving.

To modify and close the Word document:

▶ 1. Type today's date, and then press the **Enter** key. The text you typed appears below your name in the document.

▶ 2. In the upper-left corner of the program window, click the **Office Button**. A menu opens with commands for creating new files, opening existing files, saving files, printing files, and closing files.

▶ 3. Click **Close**. A dialog box opens, asking whether you want to save the changes you made to the document.

▶ 4. Click the **Yes** button. The current version of the document is saved to the file, and then the document closes. Word is still running.

After you have a program open, you can create additional new files for the open program or you can open previously created and saved files.

Opening a File

When you want to open a blank document, workbook, presentation, or database, you create a new file. When you want to work on a previously created file, you must first open it. Opening a file transfers a copy of the file from the storage disk (either a hard disk or a portable disk) to the computer's memory and displays it on your screen. The file is then in your computer's memory and on the disk.

Reference Window | **Opening an Existing File or Creating a New File**

- Click the Office Button, and then click Open.
- In the Open dialog box, navigate to the storage location of the file you want to open.
- Click the filename of the file you want to open.
- Click the Open button.

or

- Click the Office Button, and then click a filename in the Recent Documents list.

or

- Click the Office Button, and then click New.
- In the New dialog box, click Blank Document, Blank Workbook, Blank Presentation, or Blank Database (depending on the program).
- Click the Create button.

Ean asks you to print the agenda. To do that, you'll reopen the file.

To open the existing Word document:

1. Click the **Office Button** , and then click **Open**. The Open dialog box, which works similarly to the Save As dialog box, opens.

Windows XP Tip

To navigate to a location in the Open dialog box, you use the Look in arrow.

2. Use the Navigation pane or the Address bar to navigate to the **OFF\Tutorial** folder included with your Data Files. This is the location where you saved the agenda document.

3. Click **Meeting Agenda** in the file list. See Figure 18.

Figure 18 | Open dialog box

4. Click the **Open** button. The agenda file opens in the Word program window.

Next, you'll use Help to get information about printing files in Word.

Getting Help

If you don't know how to perform a task or want more information about a feature, you can turn to Office itself for information on how to use it. This information, referred to simply as **Help**, is like a huge encyclopedia available from your desktop. You can get Help in ScreenTips, from the Help window, and in Microsoft Office Online.

Viewing ScreenTips

ScreenTips are a fast and simple method you can use to get help about objects you see on the screen. A **ScreenTip** is a box with the button's name, its keyboard shortcut if it has one, a description of the command's function, and, in some cases, a link to more information. Just position the mouse pointer over a button or object to view its ScreenTip. If a link to more information appears in the ScreenTip, press the F1 key while the ScreenTip is displayed to open the Help window with the appropriate topic displayed.

To view ScreenTips:

▶ **1.** Point to the **Microsoft Office Word Help** button ⓘ. The ScreenTip shows the button's name, its keyboard shortcut, and a brief explanation of the button. See Figure 19.

ScreenTip for the Help button | Figure 19

▶ **2.** Point to other buttons on the Ribbon to display their ScreenTips.

Using the Help Window

For more detailed information, you can use the **Help window** to access all the Help topics, templates, and training installed on your computer with Office and available on Microsoft Office Online. **Microsoft Office Online** is a Web site maintained by Microsoft that provides access to the latest information and additional Help resources. For example, you can access current Help topics, templates of predesigned files, and training for Office. To connect to Microsoft Office Online, you need Internet access on your computer. Otherwise, you see only those topics stored locally.

Reference Window | **Getting Help**

- Click the Microsoft Office Help button (the button name depends on the Office program).
- Type a keyword or phrase in the "Type words to search for" box, and then click the Search button.
- Click a Help topic in the search results list.
- Read the information in the Help window. For more information, click other topics or links.
- Click the Close button on the Help window title bar.

You open the Help window by clicking the Microsoft Office Help button [icon] located below the sizing buttons in every Office program. Each program has its own Help window from which you can find information about all the Office commands and features as well as step-by-step instructions for using them. You can search for information in the Help window using the "Type words to search for" box and the Table of Contents pane.

The "Type words to search for" box enables you to search the Help system using keywords or phrases. You type a specific word or phrase about a task you want to perform or a topic you need help with, and then click the Search button to search the Help system. A list of Help topics related to the keyword or phrase you entered appears in the Help window. If your computer is connected to the Internet, your search results come from Microsoft Office Online rather than only the Help topics stored locally on your computer. You can click a link to open a Help topic with step-by-step instructions that will guide you through a specific procedure and/or provide explanations of difficult concepts in clear, easy-to-understand language. For example, if you type "format cell" in the Excel Help window, a list of Help topics related to the words you typed appears in the Help window. You can navigate through the topics you've viewed using the buttons on the Help window toolbar. These buttons—including Back, Forward, Stop, Refresh, Home, and Print—are the same as those in the Microsoft Internet Explorer Web browser.

You'll use the "Type words to search for" box in the Help window to obtain more information about printing a document in Word.

To use the "Type words to search for" box:

▶ 1. Click the **Microsoft Office Word Help** button [icon] . The Word Help window opens.

▶ 2. Click the **Type words to search for** box, if necessary, and then type **print document**. You can set where you want to search.

▶ 3. Click the **Search button arrow**. The Search menu shows the online and local content available.

4. If your computer is connected to the Internet, click **All Word** in the Content from Office Online list. If your computer is not connected to the Internet, click **Word Help** in the Content from this computer list.

5. Click the **Search** button. The Help window displays a list of topics related to your keywords. See Figure 20.

Search results displaying Help topics   Figure 20

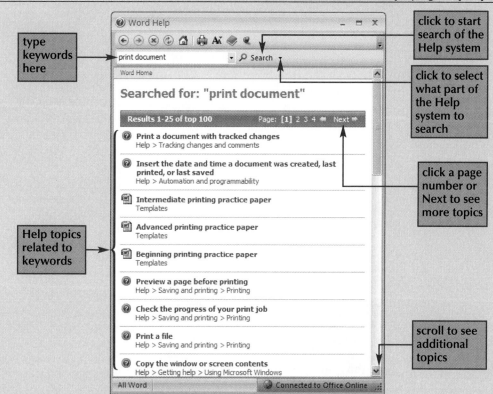

Trouble? If your search results list differs from the one shown in Figure 20, your computer is not connected to the Internet or Microsoft has updated the list of available Help topics since this book was published. Continue with Step 6.

6. Scroll through the list to review the Help topics.

7. Click **Print a file**. The Help topic is displayed in the Help window so you can learn more about how to print a document. See Figure 21.

Figure 21 ▶ **Print a file Help topic**

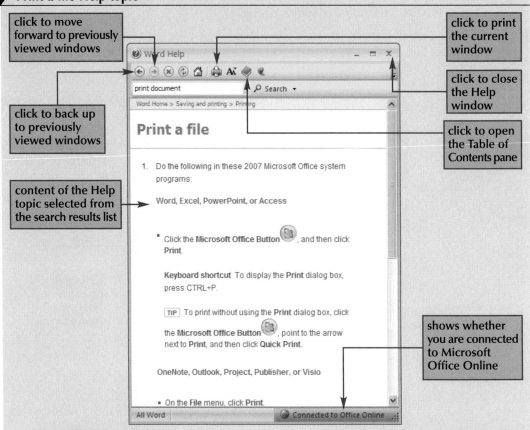

click to move
forward to previously
viewed windows

click to print
the current
window

click to close
the Help
window

click to back up
to previously
viewed windows

click to open
the Table of
Contents pane

content of the Help
topic selected from
the search results list

shows whether
you are connected
to Microsoft
Office Online

Trouble? If you don't see the Print a file Help topic on page 1, its current location might be on another page. Click the Next link to move to the next page, and then scroll down to find the Print a file topic, repeating to search additional pages until you locate the topic.

▶ **8.** Read the information.

Another way to find information in the Help system is to use the Table of Contents pane. The Show Table of Contents button on the Help window toolbar opens a pane that displays a list of the Help system content organized by subjects and topics, similar to a book's table of contents. You click main subject links to display related topic links. You click a topic link to display that Help topic in the Help window. You'll use the Table of Contents to find information about getting help in Office.

To use the Help window table of contents:

▶ **1.** Click the **Show Table of Contents** button 🔷 on the Help window toolbar. The Table of Contents pane opens on the left side of the Help window.

▶ **2.** Click **Getting help** in the Table of Contents pane, scrolling up if necessary. The Getting help "book" opens, listing the topics related to that subject.

▶ **3.** Click the **Work with the Help window** topic, and then click the **Maximize** button 🔲 on the title bar. The Help topic is displayed in the maximized Help window, and you can read the text to learn more about the various ways to obtain help in Word. See Figure 22.

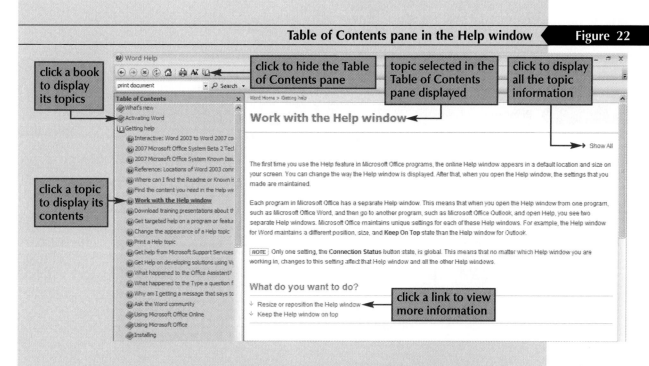

Table of Contents pane in the Help window ◀ **Figure 22**

Trouble? If your search results list differs from the one shown in Figure 22, your computer is not connected to the Internet or Microsoft has updated the list of available Help topics since this book was published. Continue with Step 4.

4. Click **Using Microsoft Office Online** in the Table of Contents pane, click the **Get online Help, templates, training, and additional content** topic to display information about that topic, and then read the information.

5. Click the links within this topic and read the information.

6. Click the **Close** button ⊠ on the Help window title bar to close the window.

Printing a File

At times, you'll want a paper copy of your Office file. The first time you print during each session at the computer, you should use the Print command to open the Print dialog box so you can verify or adjust the printing settings. You can select a printer, the number of copies to print, the portion of the file to print, and so forth; the printing settings vary slightly from program to program. If you want to use the same default settings for subsequent print jobs, you can use the Quick Print button to print without opening the dialog box.

Printing a File	Reference Window

- Click the Office Button, and then click Print.
- Verify the print settings in the Print dialog box.
- Click the OK button.

or

- Click the Office Button, point to Print, and then click Quick Print.

Now that you know how to print, you'll print the agenda for Ean.

To print the Word document:

▶ **1.** Make sure your printer is turned on and contains paper.

▶ **2.** Click the **Office Button** (🔘), and then click **Print**. The Print dialog box opens. See Figure 23.

| Figure 23 | Print dialog box |

Trouble? If a menu of Print commands opens, you clicked the Print button arrow on the two-part Print button. Click Print on the menu to open the Print dialog box.

▶ **3.** Verify that the correct printer appears in the Name box in the Printer group. If necessary, click the **Name** arrow, and then click the correct printer from the list of available printers.

▶ **4.** Verify that **1** appears in the Number of copies box.

▶ **5.** Click the **OK** button to print the document.

Trouble? If the document does not print, see your instructor or technical support person for help.

Exiting Programs

When you finish working with a program, you should exit it. As with many other aspects of Office, you can exit programs with a button or a command. You'll use both methods to exit Word and Excel. You can use the Exit command to exit a program and close an open file in one step. If you haven't saved the final version of the open file, a dialog box opens, asking whether you want to save your changes. Clicking the Yes button saves the open file, closes the file, and then exits the program.

To exit the Word and Excel programs:

▶ **1.** Click the **Close** button ⊠ on the Word title bar to exit Word. The Word document closes and the Word program exits. The Excel window is visible again.

Trouble? If a dialog box opens, asking if you want to save the document, you might have inadvertently made a change to the document. Click the No button.

▶ **2.** Click the **Office Button** , and then click **Exit Excel**. A dialog box opens, asking whether you want to save the changes you made to the workbook. If you click the Yes button, the Save As dialog box opens and Excel exits after you finish saving the workbook. This time, you don't want to save the workbook.

▶ **3.** Click the **No** button. The workbook closes without saving a copy, and the Excel program exits.

Exiting programs after you are done using them keeps your Windows desktop uncluttered for the next person using the computer, frees up your system's resources, and prevents data from being lost accidentally.

Quick Check | Review

1. What Office program would be best to use to create a budget?
2. How do you start an Office program?
3. Explain the difference between Save and Save As.
4. How do you open an existing Office file?
5. What happens if you open a file, make edits, and then attempt to close the file or exit the program without saving the current version of the file?
6. What are two ways to get Help in Office?

Tutorial Summary | Review

You have learned how to use features common to all the programs included in Microsoft Office 2007, including starting and exiting programs; resizing windows; using the Ribbon, dialog boxes, shortcut menus, and the Mini toolbar; opening, closing, and printing files; and getting Help.

Key Terms

Access
application settings
button
contextual tab
database
default
dialog box
Dialog Box Launcher
document
Excel
file extension
filename
folder
gallery
group
Help

Help window
integration
keyboard shortcut
Live Preview
Microsoft Office 2007
Microsoft Office Access 2007
Microsoft Office Excel 2007
Microsoft Office Online
Microsoft Office
   Outlook 2007
Microsoft Office
   PowerPoint 2007
Microsoft Office Word 2007
Mini toolbar
object
Office

Office Button
Outlook
PowerPoint
presentation
Quick Access Toolbar
Ribbon
ScreenTip
shortcut menu
status bar
tab
task pane
Word
workbook
zoom

Practice | **Review Assignments**

Practice the skills you learned in the tutorial.

Data Files needed for the Review Assignments: Finances.xlsx, Letter.docx

You need to prepare for an upcoming meeting at Recycled Palette. You'll open and print documents for the presentation. Complete the following:

1. Start PowerPoint.
2. Use the Help window to search Office Online for the PowerPoint demo "Demo: Up to Speed with PowerPoint 2007." (*Hint*: Use "demo" as the keyword to search for, and make sure you search All PowerPoint in the Content from Office Online list. If you are not connected to the Internet, continue with Step 3.) Open the Demo topic, and then click the Play Demo link to view it. Close Internet Explorer and the Help window when you're done.
3. Start Excel.
4. Switch to the PowerPoint window using the taskbar, and then close the presentation but leave open the PowerPoint program. (*Hint:* Click the Office Button and then click Close.)
5. Open a new, blank PowerPoint presentation from the New Presentation dialog box.
6. Close the PowerPoint presentation and program using the Close button on the PowerPoint title bar; do not save changes if asked.
7. Open the **Finances** workbook located in the OFF\Review folder included with your Data Files.
8. Use the Save As command to save the workbook as **Recycled Palette Finances** in the OFF\Review folder.
9. Type your name, press the Enter key to insert your name at the top of the worksheet, and then save the workbook.
10. Print one copy of the worksheet using the Print button on the Office Button menu.
11. Exit Excel using the Office Button.
12. Start Word, and then open the **Letter** document located in the OFF\Review folder included with your Data Files.
13. Use the Save As command to save the document with the filename **Recycled Palette Letter** in the OFF\Review folder.
14. Press and hold the Ctrl key, press the End key, and then release both keys to move the insertion point to the end of the letter, and then type your name.
15. Use the Save button on the Quick Access Toolbar to save the change to the Recycled Palette Letter document.
16. Print one copy of the document, and then close the document.
17. Exit the Word program using the Close button on the title bar.

Assess | SAM Assessment and Training

If you have a SAM user profile, you may have access to hands-on instruction, practice, and assessment of the skills covered in this tutorial. Log in to your SAM account (**http://sam2007.course.com**) to launch any assigned training activities or exams that relate to the skills covered in this tutorial.

Review | Quick Check Answers

1. Excel
2. Click the Start button on the taskbar, click All Programs, click Microsoft Office, and then click the name of the program you want to open.
3. Save updates a file to reflect its latest contents using its current filename and location. Save As enables you to change the filename and storage location of a file.
4. Click the Office Button, and then click Open.
5. A dialog box opens asking whether you want to save the changes to the file.
6. Two of the following: ScreenTips, Help window, Microsoft Office Online

Ending Data Files

Tutorial

Meeting Agenda.docx

Review

Recycled Palette Finances.xlsx
Recycled Palette Letter.docx

Reality Check

At home, school, or work, you probably complete many types of tasks, such as writing letters and balancing a checkbook, on a regular basis. You can use Microsoft Office to streamline many of these tasks.

Note: Please be sure *not* to include any personal information of a sensitive nature in the documents you create to be submitted to your instructor for this exercise. Later on, you can update the documents with such information for your own personal use.

1. Start Word, and open a new document, if necessary.
2. In the document, type a list of all the personal, work, and/or school tasks you do on a regular basis.
3. For each task, identify the type of Office file (document, workbook, presentation, or database) you would create to complete that task. For example, you would create a Word document to write a letter.
4. For each file, identify the Office program you would use to create that file, and explain why you would use that program. For example, Word is the best program to use to create a document for a letter.
5. Save the document with an appropriate filename in an appropriate folder location.
6. Use a Web browser to visit the Microsoft Web site at *www.microsoft.com* and research the different Office 2007 suites available. Determine which suite includes all the programs you need to complete the tasks on your list.
7. At the end of the task list you created in your Word document, type which Office suite you decided on and a brief explanation of why you chose that suite. Then save the document.
8. Double-click the Home tab on the Ribbon to minimize the Ribbon to show only the tab names and extend the workspace area. At the end of the Word document, type your opinion of whether minimizing the Ribbon is a helpful feature. When you're done, double-click the Home tab to display the full Ribbon.
9. Print the finished document, and then submit it to your instructor.

Objectives

Session 1.1
- Understand the use of spreadsheets and Excel
- Learn the parts of the Excel window
- Scroll through a worksheet and navigate between worksheets
- Create and save a workbook file
- Enter text, numbers, and dates into a worksheet
- Resize, insert, and remove columns and rows

Session 1.2
- Select and move cell ranges
- Insert formulas and functions
- Insert, delete, move, and rename worksheets
- Work with editing tools
- Preview and print a workbook

Getting Started with Excel

Creating an Order Report

Case | RipCity Digital

When Amanda Dunn purchased a DVD burner a few years ago, one of her first tasks was to convert her home videos into DVDs. After she saw how simple it was, she upgraded her hardware and software and proceeded to create DVDs from home movies and slides for her parents and friends. Based on her success, Amanda decided to make a business out of her hobby and founded RipCity Digital, an online service specializing in creating DVDs from the home movies, photos, and slides sent to her from customers. Amanda wants to list the weekly orders from her customers, tracking the names and addresses of her clients, the number of DVDs that she creates, and finally the cost of creating and shipping the DVDs.

Amanda is so busy creating DVDs that she asks you to record her orders. You'll do this in **Microsoft Office Excel 2007** (or **Excel**), a computer program used to enter, analyze, and present quantitative data. You'll also enter the latest orders she received for her new business.

Starting Data Files

Tutorial.01 →

Tutorial	Review	Case1	Case2	Case3	Case4
(none)	(none)	Altac.xlsx	Halley.xlsx	Global.xlsx	(none)

Session 1.1

Introducing Excel

Before you begin working in Excel, Amanda asks you to review some of the features, key terms, and concepts associated with spreadsheets. Understanding spreadsheets and how they work in Excel will help you as you enter RipCity Digital customer orders.

Understanding Spreadsheets

A **spreadsheet** is a collection of text and numbers laid out in a rectangular grid. Spreadsheets are often used in business for budgeting, inventory management, and decision making. They can also be used to manage personal budgets and track household assets. For example, the paper-based spreadsheet shown in Figure 1-1 shows a cash flow report. The spreadsheet records the estimated and actual cash flow for the month of January. Each line, or row, displays a different value, such as the starting cash balance or cash sales for the month. Each column displays the budgeted or actual numbers or text that describes those values. The total cash expenditures, net cash flow, and closing cash balance for the month are not entered directly, but calculated from other numbers in the spreadsheet. For example, the total cash expenditure is equal to the expenditures on advertising, wages, and supplies. For paper spreadsheets, these calculations are done using a hand calculator and then entered into the spreadsheet.

Figure 1-1	Sample paper spreadsheet

Cash Flow Comparison Budgeted vs. Actual		Jan–10
	Budgeted	Actual
Cash balance (start of month)	$4,500.00	$4,500.00
Cash receipts		
Cash sales	12,600.00	14,688.00
Cash expenditures		
Advertising	1,200.00	1,425.00
Wages	7,200.00	7,850.00
Supplies	3,600.00	4,350.00
Total cash expenditures	12,000.00	13,625.00
Net cash flow	600.00	1,063.00
Cash balance (end of month)	$5,100.00	$5,563.00

Excel is a computer program used to create electronic versions of these paper spreadsheets. Figure 1-2 shows the data from Figure 1-1 as it might appear in Excel. As with paper spreadsheets, Excel uses a rectangular grid to lay out the financial information in rows and columns. As you'll see later, values such as total cash expenditures can be calculated automatically rather than entered manually into the spreadsheet. This allows you to use Excel to perform a **what-if analysis** in which you change one or more values in a spreadsheet and then assess the effect those changes have on the calculated values.

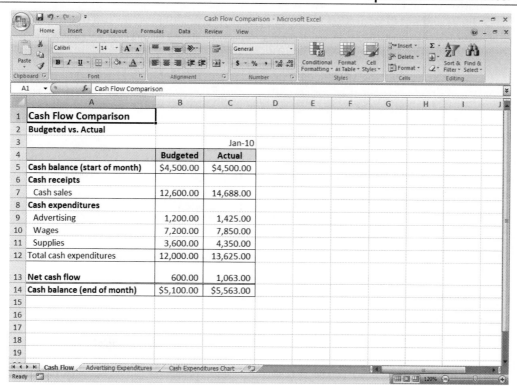

An Excel spreadsheet is more flexible than paper spreadsheets. In fact, it is no longer just an electronic substitute for paper spreadsheets. Excel is now often used for data storage, report generation, and as a tool to access data from the Internet.

Exploring the Excel Window

Before entering Amanda's data, you'll review the different parts of the Excel window. The Excel window contains many of the elements that you find in other Office 2007 programs, including a title bar, the Ribbon, scroll bars, and a status bar. The Excel window also contains features that are unique to Excel. You'll review these features after you start Excel.

To start Excel:

▶ **1.** Click the **Start** button ⊛ on the Windows taskbar, click **All Programs**, click **Microsoft Office**, and then point to **Microsoft Office Excel 2007**.

   Trouble? If you don't see Microsoft Office Excel 2007 on the Microsoft Office submenu, look for it on a different submenu or on the All Programs menu. If you still cannot find Microsoft Office Excel 2007, ask your instructor or technical support person for help.

▶ **2.** Click **Microsoft Office Excel 2007**. The Excel window opens.

   All the figures showing the Excel window in these tutorials are zoomed to 120% for better readability. If you want to zoom your Excel window to match the figures, complete Step 3. If you prefer to work in the default zoom of 100% or at another zoom level, continue with Step 4; you might see more or less of the worksheet on your screen, but this does not affect your work in the tutorials.

3. If you want your Excel window zoomed to match the figures, click the **Zoom In** button ⊕ on the status bar twice to increase the zoom magnification to **120%**. The worksheet is magnified to 120%, which increases the screen size of each cell, but reduces the number of worksheet cells visible in the workbook window.

4. If necessary, click the **Maximize** button 🗖 on the Excel window title bar. The Excel window fills the screen, as shown in Figure 1-3. Depending on your installation of Excel and your monitor resolution, your Excel window might look different from the one shown in Figure 1-3.

Figure 1-3	Parts of the Excel window

Trouble? If your screen varies slightly from those shown in the figures, your computer might be set up differently. The figures in this book were created while running Windows Vista in the Windows Vista Basic settings, but how your screen looks depends on a variety of things, including the version of Windows, background settings, and so forth.

Excel stores spreadsheets in files called **workbooks**. The contents of a workbook are shown in a **workbook window**. You can open more than one workbook window at a time to display the contents of different workbooks. You can also open multiple workbook windows for one workbook to display different views of the workbook's contents. The workbook that is currently being used is the **active workbook** and is displayed in the **active workbook window**. The name of the active workbook appears in the title bar of the Excel window. By default, Excel starts with a blank workbook named "Book1" in the workbook window, maximized to fill the entire Excel window.

Each workbook is made up of individual **sheets**, just as a notebook an accountant might use is made up of sheets of paper. Excel supports two kinds of sheets: worksheets and chart sheets. A **worksheet** contains data, laid out in rows and columns. A **chart sheet** contains an Excel chart that provides a visual representation of spreadsheet data. Charts can also be embedded within worksheets, allowing you to view both the data and charts in one sheet.

Each sheet is identified by a sheet name. The sheet names are displayed in **sheet tabs** located at the lower-left corner of the workbook window. The sheet currently displayed in the workbook window is the **active sheet**, and its sheet tab is white. In Figure 1-3, the active sheet is named "Sheet1." Other sheets included in the workbook shown in Figure 1-3, but not currently visible, are named "Sheet2" and "Sheet3." The sheet tabs for inactive sheets are gray and stacked behind the Sheet1 tab. An inactive sheet becomes active when you click its worksheet tab. By default, all new Excel workbooks are created with these three worksheets.

Each worksheet is laid out in rows and columns. **Row headings** identify each row by a different number. Row numbers range from 1 to 1,048,576. **Column headings** identify each column by a different letter. The first 26 column letters range in alphabetical order from A to Z. After Z, the next column headings are labeled AA, AB, AC, and so forth. Excel allows a maximum of 16,385 columns in a worksheet (the last column has the heading XFD).

Rows and columns intersect in a single **cell**; all the data entered in a worksheet is placed in different cells. You can have more than 17 billion cells in each worksheet. Each cell is identified by a **cell reference**, which indicates its column and row location. For example, the cell reference B6 indicates the cell located where column B intersects row 6. The column letter always appears before the row number in any cell reference. The cell in which you are working is the **active cell**. Excel distinguishes the active cell by outlining it with a thick border. In Figure 1-3, cell A1 is the active cell. The cell reference for the active cell appears in the **Name box** located in the upper-left corner of the worksheet.

Figure 1-4 describes the different parts of the Excel window, which are labeled in Figure 1-3.

Description of the Excel window elements ◀ **Figure 1-4**

Feature	Description
Office Button	A button that provides access to workbook-level features and program settings
Quick Access Toolbar	A collection of buttons that provide one-click access to commonly used commands, such as Save, Undo, and Repeat
Title bar	A bar that displays the name of the active workbook and the Excel program name
Ribbon	The main set of commands organized by task into tabs and groups
Column headings	The letters that appear along the top of the worksheet window to identify the different columns in the worksheet
Workbook window	A window that displays an Excel workbook
Vertical scroll bar	A scroll bar used to scroll vertically through the workbook window
Horizontal scroll bar	A scroll bar used to scroll horizontally through the workbook window
Zoom controls	Controls for magnifying and shrinking the content displayed in the active workbook window
View shortcuts	Buttons used to change how the worksheet content is displayed—Normal, Page Layout, or Page Break Preview view
Sheet tabs	Tabs that display the names of the worksheets in the workbook
Sheet tab scrolling buttons	Buttons to scroll the list of sheet tabs in the workbook
Row headings	The numbers that appear along the left of the worksheet window to identify the different rows in the worksheet
Select All button	A button used to select all of the cells in the active worksheet
Active cell	The cell currently selected in the active worksheet
Name box	A box that displays the cell reference of the active cell
Formula bar	A bar that displays the value or formula entered in the active cell

When Excel starts, it opens a blank workbook with Sheet1 as the active sheet and cell A1 as the active cell.

Navigating a Worksheet

Excel provides several ways to navigate a worksheet. You can use your mouse to click a cell to make it the active cell, or you can use the keyboard to move from one cell to another. Figure 1-5 describes some of the default keyboard shortcuts you can use to move between worksheet cells.

| Figure 1-5 | Excel navigation keys |

Press	To move the active cell
↑, ↓, ←, →	Up, down, left, or right one cell
Home	To column A of the current row
Ctrl+Home	To cell A1
Ctrl+End	To the last cell in the worksheet that contains data
Enter	Down one row or to the start of the next row of data
Shift+Enter	Up one row
Tab	One column to the right
Shift+Tab	One column to the left
Page Up, Page Down	Up or down one screen
Ctrl+Page Up, Ctrl+Page Down	To the previous or next sheet in the workbook

You'll use both your mouse and keyboard to change the active cell in Sheet1.

To change the active cell:

1. Move your mouse pointer over cell **A5**, and then click the mouse button. The active cell moves from cell A1 to cell A5, and the cell reference in the Name box changes from A1 to A5. The column heading for column A and the row heading for row 5 are both highlighted.

2. Press the → key on your keyboard. The active cell moves one cell to the right to cell B5.

3. Press the **Page Down** key. The active cell moves down one full screen to cell B25.

   Trouble? If the active cell in your workbook is not cell B25, your monitor size and screen resolution might be different from those used for the figures in these tutorials. Continue with Step 4.

4. Press the **Page Up** key. The active cell moves up one full screen back to cell B5.

5. Press the **Ctrl+Home** keys. The active cell returns to the first cell in the worksheet, cell A1.

The mouse and keyboard provide quick ways to navigate the active worksheet. For larger worksheets that span several screens, you can move directly to a specific cell using the Go To dialog box or by typing a cell reference in the Name box. You'll try both of these methods.

To use the Go To dialog box and Name box:

1. Click the **Home** tab on the Ribbon, if necessary. The button to open the Go To dialog box is in the Editing group.

2. In the Editing group, click the **Find & Select** button. A menu of options opens.

3. Click **Go To**. The Go To dialog box opens.

4. Type **C14** in the Reference text box.

5. Click the **OK** button. Cell C14 is the active cell and its cell reference appears in the Name box. You'll use the Name box to make a different cell active.

6. Click in the **Name** box, type **A1**, and then press the **Enter** key. Cell A1 is once again the active cell.

Tip

You can also open the Go To dialog box by pressing the Ctrl+G keys.

To view more of the active worksheet, you can use the horizontal and vertical scroll bars, located at the bottom and right side of the workbook window, respectively, to move through the worksheet horizontally and vertically. Scrolling through the worksheet does not change the location of the active cell.

To scroll the worksheet:

1. Click the **down arrow** on the vertical scroll bar three times. The worksheet scrolls down three rows, but the active cell remains cell A1.

2. Click the **right arrow** on the horizontal scroll bar twice. The worksheet scrolls two columns to the right. The active cell still remains cell A1, although that cell is scrolled out of view.

   You can scroll several rows and columns by dragging the vertical and horizontal scroll boxes.

3. Drag the vertical scroll box up until you can see the first row in the worksheet.

4. Drag the horizontal scroll box to the left until you can see the first column in the worksheet.

Navigating Between Worksheets

Recall that each workbook can contain multiple worksheets and chart sheets. This enables you to better organize data and focus each worksheet on one area of data. For example, a sales report workbook might have a different worksheet for each sales region and another worksheet that summarizes the results from all the regions. A chart sheet might contain a chart that graphically compares the sales results from all of the regions. To move from one sheet to another, you click the sheet tabs at the bottom of the workbook window.

Some workbooks contain so many worksheets and chart sheets that their sheet tabs cannot all be displayed at the same time in the workbook window. For these workbooks, you can scroll through the sheet tabs using the sheet tab scrolling buttons. Similar to the horizontal and vertical scroll bars and the active cell, scrolling through the sheet tabs does not change the active sheet in the workbook window. To change the active worksheet, you must click a sheet tab.

To change the active sheet:

1. Click the **Sheet2** sheet tab. The Sheet2 worksheet, which is also blank, becomes the active worksheet. The Sheet2 tab is white, indicating that this is the active worksheet.

▶ **2.** Click the **Sheet3** sheet tab. The Sheet3 worksheet becomes the active worksheet.

▶ **3.** Click the **Sheet1** sheet tab to return to the first worksheet.

Now that you've had some experience moving around a blank workbook, you are ready to start working on Amanda's workbook.

InSight	**Creating Effective Workbooks**

Effective workbooks are well planned and carefully designed. This helps you avoid errors and makes the workbook readable to others. A well-designed workbook should clearly identify its overall goal, and present information in a well-organized format. The process of developing a good workbook includes the following steps:
- Determine the workbook's purpose, content, and organization before you start entering data.
- Create a list of the sheets used in the workbook, making note of each sheet's purpose.
- Insert a documentation sheet into the workbook that describes the workbook's purpose and organization. Include the name of the workbook author, the date the workbook was created, and any additional information that will help others to track the workbook to its source.
- Enter all of the data in the workbook. Add text to indicate what the values represent and, if possible, where they originated. Other users might want to view the source of your data.
- Enter formulas for calculated items rather than entering the calculated values into the workbook. For more complicated calculations, provide documentation explaining them.
- Test the workbook with a variety of values to weed out any errors in your calculations. Edit the data and formulas to correct any errors.
- Save the workbook and create a backup copy when the project is completed. Print the workbook's contents if you need a hard-copy version for your files.

Planning a Workbook

Before you begin to enter data into a workbook, you should develop a plan. You can do this by using a **planning analysis sheet**, which includes a series of questions that help you think about the purpose of the workbook and how to achieve your desired results. In the planning analysis sheet, you answer the following questions:

- What problems do you want to solve? The answer defines the goal or purpose of the workbook.
- What data is needed to solve your problem? The answer defines the type of data that you have to collect and enter into the workbook.
- What calculations are required to solve your problem? The answer defines the formulas you need to apply to the data you've collected and entered.
- What form should the solution take? The answer defines the appearance of the workbook content and how it should be presented to others.

Amanda carefully considered these questions and developed the planning analysis sheet shown in Figure 1-6. You'll use this plan to create the workbook for Amanda.

Planning Analysis Sheet
Author: Amanda Dunn
Date: 4/1/2010

What problems do I want to solve?
• I need to have contact information for each RipCity Digital customer.
• I need to track how many DVDs I create for my customers.
• I need to record how much I charge my customers for my service.
• I need to determine how much revenue RipCity Digital is generating.

What data do I need?
• Each customer's name and contact information
• The date each customer order was placed
• The number of DVDs created for each customer
• The cost of creating each DVD

What calculations do I need to enter?
• The total charge for each order
• The total number of DVDs I create for all orders
• The total revenue generated from all orders

What form should my solution take?
• The customer orders should be placed in a grid with each row containing data on a different customer.
• Information about each customer should be placed in separate columns.
• The last column should contain the total charge for each customer.
• The last row should contain the total number of DVDs created and the total revenue from all customer orders.

Entering Text, Numbers, and Dates in Cells

Now that you have Amanda's plan for the workbook, your next step is to enter the data she's collected. You enter data by selecting a cell in the worksheet to make it the active cell, and then typing the content you want to enter in the active cell. When you finish typing, you can press the Enter key or the Tab key to complete the data entry and move to the next cell in the worksheet. As you enter data into the worksheet, the data entry appears in two locations: within the active cell and within the formula bar. The **formula bar** displays the content of the active cell and, as you'll see later, shows any formulas used to create calculated values.

In Excel, data falls into three general categories: text, numbers, and dates and times. **Text data** is a combination of letters, numbers, and some symbols that form words and sentences. Text data is often referred to as a **text string** because it contains a string of text characters. **Number data** is any numerical value that can be used in a mathematical calculation. **Date** and **time data** are commonly recognized formats for date and time values. For example, Excel interprets the cell entry "April 15, 2010" as a date and not as text. By default, text is left-aligned in cells, whereas numbers, dates, and times are right-aligned.

Entering Text

Amanda wants you to enter some of the information from the planning analysis sheet into the first sheet of the workbook. The first sheet will document the purpose and content of the workbook and the sheets that follow. This documentation sheet will contain the name of the workbook, the workbook's author, the date the workbook was created, and a description of the workbook's purpose.

To enter the text for the documentation sheet:

1. Press the **Ctrl+Home** keys to make cell A1 the active cell on the Sheet1 worksheet, if necessary.

2. Type **RipCity Digital Customer Orders** in cell A1. As you type, the text appears both in cell A1 and in the formula bar.

3. Press the **Enter** key twice. Excel enters the text into cell A1 and moves the active cell down two cells to cell A3.

4. Type **Author** in cell A3, and then press the **Tab** key. The text is entered and the active cell moves one cell to the right to cell B3.

5. Type your name in cell B3, and then press the **Enter** key. The text is entered and the active cell moves one cell down and to the left to cell A4.

6. Type **Date** in cell A4, and then press the **Tab** key. The text is entered and the active cell moves one cell to the right to cell B4, where you would enter the date you created the worksheet. For now, you'll leave the cell for the date blank. You'll enter this date soon.

7. Click cell **A5** to make it the active cell, type **Purpose** in the cell, and then press the **Tab** key. The active cell moves one cell to the right to cell B5.

8. Type **To record orders from RipCity Digital customers** in cell B5, and then press the **Enter** key. Figure 1-7 shows the text entered in the Sheet1 worksheet.

Figure 1-7 | **Documentation sheet**

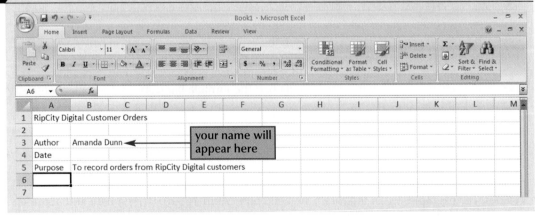

The text you entered in cell A1 is so long that it seems to overflow into cells B1 and C1. The same is true for the text you entered in cells B3 and B5. When you enter more text than can fit in a cell, Excel displays the additional text in the adjacent cells as long as they are empty. If the adjacent cells also contain data, Excel displays only as much text as fits into the cell, cutting off, or **truncating**, the rest of the text entry. The text itself is not affected. The complete text is still entered in the cell, it's just not displayed. To display all of the text, you must increase the cell's width, which you'll learn about in the next session.

Next, you'll enter the RipCity Digital customer orders. As shown in Figure 1-8, the orders will contain the name and address of each customer, the order date, the number of DVDs created from the customer's home videos, and the price per DVD. Amanda's price per DVD decreases for larger orders.

Customer orders | °Figure 1-8

Last	First	Address	Date	DVDs	Price per DVD
Dawes	Gregory	402 Elm St. Merrill, MI 48637	3/13/2010	7	$17.29
Garcia	Susan	1025 Drake Ave. Exeter, NH 03833	3/14/2010	25	$15.79
Torbet	Dr. Lilla	5 North Ln. Oswego, NY 13126	3/17/2010	32	$12.99
Rhoden	Tony	24 Mountain Dr. Auburn, ME 04210	3/24/2010	20	$15.79

You'll enter this data in the Sheet2 worksheet.

To enter the text labels and customer names:

▶ 1. Click the **Sheet2** sheet tab. Sheet2 becomes the active worksheet. You'll enter the column labels in cells A1, B1, C1, D1, E1, and F1.

▶ 2. Type **Last** in cell A1, and then press the **Tab** key. The label is entered in cell A1 and the active cell moves to cell B1.

▶ 3. Type **First** in cell B1, and then press the **Tab** key. The label is entered in cell B1 and the active cell moves to cell C1.

▶ 4. Type **Address** in cell C1, and then press the **Tab** key.

▶ 5. Type **Date** in cell D1, and then press the **Tab** key.

▶ 6. Type **DVDs** in cell E1, press the **Tab** key, and then type **Price per DVD** in cell F1. You've typed all the labels for the customer orders.

▶ 7. Press the **Enter** key. The active cell moves to cell A2, the start of the next row where you want to begin entering the customer data.

▶ 8. Type **Dawes** in cell A2, press the **Tab** key, type **Gregory** in cell B2, and then press the **Tab** key. You've entered the first customer's name and moved the active cell to cell C2. Figure 1-9 shows the text you've entered so far.

Text entered for the customer orders | Figure 1-9

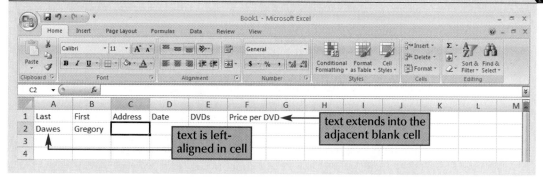

As you enter text in a worksheet, Excel tries to anticipate the text you are about to enter by displaying text that begins with the same letters as a previous entry in the same column. This feature, known as **AutoComplete**, helps make entering repetitive text easier. To accept the suggested text, press the Tab or Enter key. To override the suggested text, continue to type the text you want to enter in the cell. AutoComplete does not work with dates or numbers or when a blank cell is between the previous entry and the text you're typing.

Entering Multiple Lines of Text Within a Cell

The next cell in the Sheet2 worksheet contains the address of the first customer. Addresses are often entered on two or more separate lines. Amanda wants you to follow that convention with her customers' addresses. To place text on separate lines within the same cell, you press and hold the Alt key while you press the Enter key. This creates a line break within the cell.

Reference Window | **Entering Multiple Lines of Text Within a Cell**

- Click the cell in which you want to enter the text.
- Type the first line of text.
- For each additional line of text, press the Alt+Enter keys (that is, hold down the Alt key as you press the Enter key), and then type the text.

You'll enter the address for the first RipCity Digital customer, which will occupy two lines within the same cell.

To enter two lines of text within a cell:

1. Type **402 Elm St.** in cell C2, but do not press the Tab or Enter key. Instead, you'll insert a new line break.

2. Hold down the **Alt** key and press the **Enter** key, and then release both keys. The insertion point moves to a new line within cell C2.

3. Type **Merrill, MI 48637** on the new line, and then press the **Tab** key. The two lines of text are entered in cell C2, and cell D2 becomes the active cell. See Figure 1-10.

Figure 1-10 ▶ **Two lines of text entered within a cell**

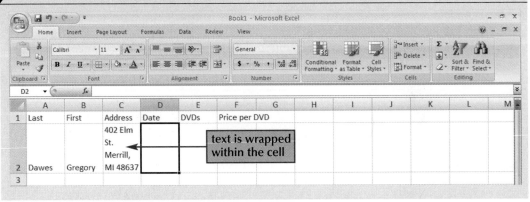

One impact of entering multiple lines of text within a cell is that it changes how text flows within the cell. Excel wraps the text within the cell, increasing the cell's height, if necessary, to show all of the text. As you can see, the text in cell C2 appears on four lines even though you entered the address on two lines. If the cell's width were increased, the text would then appear on two lines as Amanda wants. You'll do this in the next session.

Entering Dates

The next cell will contain the date of the order. You can enter dates in any of the standard formats. For example, you can enter the date April 6, 2010 in any of the following date formats (and many others) and Excel recognizes each format as representing the same date:

- 4/6/2010
- 4/6/10
- 4-6-2010
- April 6, 2010
- 6-Apr-10

In Excel, dates are actually numbers that are formatted to appear as text. This allows you to perform calculations with dates, such as determining the elapsed time between one date and another.

Sometimes Excel alters the date format you've chosen. For example, if you enter the date 4/6/10, Excel displays the date with the four-digit year value, 4/6/2010. Also, if you enter the text April 6, 2010, Excel converts the date format to 6-Apr-10. You'll enter the dates in the format *mm/dd/yyyy*, where *mm* is the month number, *dd* is the day number, and *yyyy* is the four-digit year number.

To enter the dates for the customer orders:

▶ **1.** Type **3/13/2010** in cell D2, and then press the **Tab** key to move to cell E2. The date of Gregory Dawes's order appears in cell D2 and cell E2 is the active cell.

You also need to enter the current date in the Sheet1 worksheet so you can document when you started working on this project.

▶ **2.** Click the **Sheet1** sheet tab. The Sheet1 worksheet is the active worksheet.

▶ **3.** Click cell **B4** to make it active, type today's date using the format *mm/dd/yyyy*, and then press the **Enter** key.

▶ **4.** Click the **Sheet2** sheet tab. The Sheet2 worksheet is the active worksheet, and cell E2 is still the active cell.

Entering Numbers

In the next two cells, you'll enter the number of DVDs that Amanda has created for Gregory Dawes and the price she will charge him for making each DVD. In both cases, you'll be entering numbers. In Excel, numbers can be integers such as 378, decimals such as 1.95, or negative such as –5.2. In the case of currency and percentages, you can include the currency symbol and percent sign when you enter the value. Excel treats a currency value such as $87.25 as the number 87.25 and a percentage such as 95% as the decimal number 0.95. Currency and percentages, like dates, are formatted in a convenient way for you to read. Excel right-aligns numbers within cells.

Tip

If a number exceeds its cell size, you see ###### for the truncated numeric value. You can display the entire number by increasing the column width.

You'll complete the information for Gregory Dawes's order by entering the number of DVDs Amanda created for him and the price she charged him for each DVD.

To enter the numbers for the first customer order:

▶ 1. Type **7** in cell E2, and then press the **Tab** key. The order quantity for Gregory Dawes is entered and the active cell is cell F2.

▶ 2. Type **$17.29** in cell F2, and then press the **Enter** key. The currency value is entered in cell F2, and the active cell moves to cell F3.

▶ 3. Click cell **A3**, which is where you want to enter the information for the next customer. See Figure 1-11.

Figure 1-11 | First customer order completed

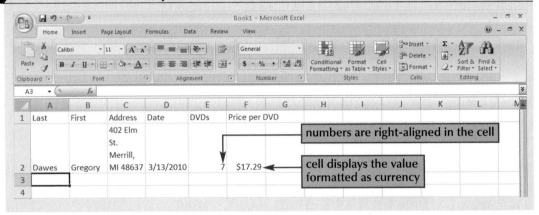

You've completed the data entry for Amanda's first customer. You still need to enter the data for three more customers into the worksheet. You'll use the same techniques you used to enter Gregory Dawes's order to enter their data.

To enter the remaining customer order data:

▶ 1. Type **Garcia** in cell A3, press the **Tab** key, type **Susan** in cell B3, and then press the **Tab** key. The second customer name is entered.

▶ 2. Type **1025 Drake Ave.** in cell C3, press the **Alt+Enter** keys, type **Exeter, NH 03833** on the next line, and then press the **Tab** key. The second customer's address is entered in the cell on two lines.

▶ 3. Type **3/14/2010** in cell D3, press the **Tab** key, type **25** in cell E3, press the **Tab** key, type **$15.79** in cell F3, and then press the **Enter** key. The rest of the second customer's data is entered.

▶ 4. Enter the following data for the remaining two customers in rows 4 and 5, making sure that you press the Alt+Enter keys to enter the addresses on two lines. See Figure 1-12.

Torbet, Dr. Lilla	**Rhoden, Tony**
5 North Ln.	**24 Mountain Dr.**
Oswego, NY 13126	**Auburn, ME 04210**
3/17/2010, 32, $12.99	**3/24/2010, 20, $15.79**

	A	B	C	D	E	F	G
1	Last	First	Address	Date	DVDs	Price per DVD	
2	Dawes	Gregory	402 Elm St. Merrill, MI 48637	3/13/2010	7	$17.29	
3	Garcia	Susan	1025 Drake Ave. Exeter, NH	3/14/2010	25	$15.79	
4	Torbet	Dr. Lilla	5 North Ln. Oswego, NY 13126	3/17/2010	32	$12.99	
5	Rhoden	Tony	24 Mountain Dr. Auburn, ME	3/24/2010	20	$15.79	
6							
7							

Working with Columns and Rows

Amanda has reviewed the customer order data you entered in the worksheet. She asks you to modify the worksheet to make it easier to read and include more data. To do this, you'll need to change the column widths and row heights, insert columns and rows, and delete columns and rows.

Changing Column Width and Row Height

The default sizes of the columns and rows in a worksheet might not always accommodate the information you need to enter. For example, the addresses you entered in the worksheet on two lines wrapped within the cell to display all the text. Other times, long cell content might be truncated. To make the cell content easier to read or fully visible, you can resize the columns and rows in the worksheet.

New workbooks use the default sizes for column widths and row heights. Column widths are expressed either in terms of the number of characters the column can contain or the size of the column in pixels. A **pixel** is a single point on a computer monitor or printout. The default column width is 8.38 standard-sized characters. This means that, in general, you can type about 8 or 9 characters in a cell before that entry is either truncated or overlaps the adjacent cell. Of course, if you decrease the font size of characters, you can fit more text within a given cell. Row heights are expressed in points or pixels, where a **point** is $1/72$ of an inch. The default row is 15.75 points high.

Setting Column Widths | InSight

You should set column widths based on the maximum number of characters you want to display in the cells rather than pixel size. Pixel size is related to screen resolution and a cell might be too narrow under a different resolution. This might come into play if you work on multiple computers or share your workbooks with others.

Reference Window | **Changing the Column Width or Row Height**

- Drag the right border of the column heading left to decrease the column width or right to increase the column width.
- Drag the bottom border of the row heading up to decrease the row height or down to increase the row height.

or

- Double-click the right border of a column heading or the bottom border of a row heading to AutoFit the column or row to the cell contents (or select one or more columns or rows, click the Home tab on the Ribbon, click the Format button in the Cells group, and then click AutoFit Column Width or AutoFit Row Height).

or

- Select one or more columns or rows.
- Click the Home tab on the Ribbon, click the Format button in the Cells group, and then click Column Width or Row Height.
- Enter the column width or row height you want, and then click the OK button.

Amanda suggests you increase the width of the Address column to allow the addresses to appear on two lines in the cells without additional line wrapping.

To increase the width of column C:

▶ **1.** Move the mouse pointer over the right border of the column C column heading until the pointer changes to ✛.

▶ **2.** Click and drag to the right until the width of the column heading reaches **20** characters, but do not release the mouse button. The ScreenTip shows the measurements of the new column width first as the numbers of characters and second in parentheses as pixels for the current screen resolution.

▶ **3.** Release the mouse button. The width of column C expands to 20 characters and all the addresses in column C fit on two lines with no extra line wrapping. See Figure 1-13.

Figure 1-13 | **Increased column width**

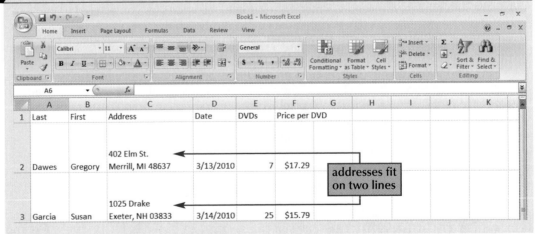

Amanda wants you to increase the widths of columns A and B to 15 characters to accommodate longer names. Rather than resizing each column separately, you can select both columns and adjust their widths at the same time. To select an entire column, you click its column heading. Likewise, to select an entire row, you click its row heading. You can drag across multiple column headings or row headings to select adjacent columns or rows. You can also press the Ctrl key as you click column or row headings to select non-adjacent columns or rows. You can select all the columns and rows in a worksheet by clicking the Select All button in the upper-left corner of the worksheet.

To increase the widths of columns A and B:

▶ 1. Click the **column A** column heading. The entire column is selected.

▶ 2. Hold down the **Ctrl** key, click the **column B** column heading, and then release the **Ctrl** key. Both columns A and B are selected.

▶ 3. Move the mouse pointer to the right border of the column B column heading until the pointer changes to ⬌ .

▶ 4. Drag to the right until the column width changes to **15** characters, and then release the mouse button. Both columns are wide enough to display longer names.

The text in cell F1, "Price per DVD," overflows the cell borders. This column would look better if you increased the width of column F to 12 characters. Rather than use the mouse, you can set the column width using the Format command on the Home tab. The Format command gives you precise control in setting column widths and row heights.

To set the width of column F to 12 characters:

▶ 1. Click the **column F** column heading. The entire column is selected.

▶ 2. In the Cells group on the Home tab, click the **Format** button, and then click **Column Width**. The Column Width dialog box opens.

▶ 3. Type **12** in the Column width box, and then click the **OK** button. The width of column F changes to 12 characters, placing the text in cell F1 entirely within the borders of the cell.

The row heights didn't change after you resized the columns, which leaves a lot of blank space in the four rows of customer data. This extra blank space makes the data difficult to read and extends the content out of view. You'll reduce the heights of all these rows.

Row heights are set in the same way as column widths. You can drag the bottom border of the row or define a specific row height using the Format command on the Home tab. Another option is to autofit a column or row to its content. **Autofitting** eliminates any empty space by matching the column to the width of its longest cell entry or the row to the height of its tallest cell entry. If the column or row is blank, Excel restores the column or row to its default width or height. The simplest way to autofit a row or column is to double-click its border. You can also use the AutoFit commands.

Because you want to remove empty space from the four worksheet rows, you'll autofit the rows to their content rather than specify a particular row height.

To autofit row 2 to its content:

▶ **1.** Move the mouse pointer over the bottom border of the row 2 row heading until the pointer changes to ╪ .

▶ **2.** Double-click the bottom border of row 2. The height of row 2 shrinks to match the content of cell C2, which is the tallest entry in the row with two lines of text.

You could continue to resize the remaining rows one at a time, but a quicker way is to select the rows you want to resize and then autofit all the selected rows simultaneously. Instead of double-clicking the row border, you'll use the AutoFit Row Height command.

To autofit the height of rows 3 through 5:

▶ **1.** Drag the pointer across the row headings for rows 3, 4, and 5. The contents of rows 3 through 5 are selected.

▶ **2.** In the Cells group on the Home tab, click the **Format** button. A menu of commands opens.

▶ **3.** Click **AutoFit Row Height**. The height of each of the three rows autofits to its contents, and all the empty space is removed.

▶ **4.** Click cell **A1** to make it the active cell. The other cells in the worksheet are deselected. Figure 1-14 shows the worksheet with the revised row heights.

| Figure 1-14 | Autofitted row heights |

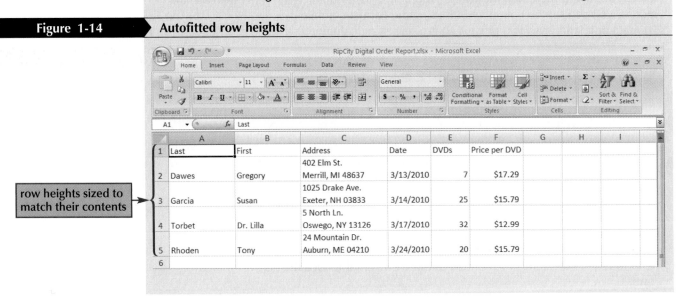

row heights sized to match their contents

Inserting a Column or Row

Amanda notices that the worksheet doesn't include a column containing customer phone numbers. She wants you to insert a column for the customer phone numbers between the Address column and the Date column.

You can insert a new column or row anywhere within a worksheet. When you insert a new column, the existing columns are shifted to the right and the new column has the same width as the column directly to its left. When you insert a new row, the existing rows are shifted down and the new row has the same height as the row above it.

Inserting a Column or Row

- Select the column(s) or row(s) where you want to insert the new column(s) or row(s); Excel will insert the same number of columns or rows as you select.
- In the Cells group on the Home tab, click the Insert button (or right-click a column or row heading or selected column and row headings, and then click Insert on the shortcut menu).

You'll insert a column and enter the customer phone numbers in the new column.

To insert a new column:

▶ **1.** Click the **column D** column heading to select the entire column.

▶ **2.** In the Cells group on the Home tab, click the **Insert** button. A new column D is inserted into the worksheet and the rest of the columns shift to the right. The new column has the same width as column C.

▶ **3.** Reduce the width of column D to **15** characters.

▶ **4.** Click cell **D1** to make it the active cell, type **Phone** as the label, and then press the **Enter** key. The new column label is entered in cell D1, and cell D2 becomes the active cell.

▶ **5.** Enter the phone numbers in cells D2, D3, D4, and D5, as shown in Figure 1-15, pressing the **Enter** key after each entry.

New column inserted in the worksheet ◀ Figure 1-15

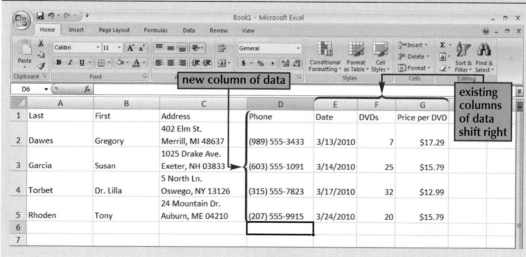

Amanda neglected to include a customer. Because the customer was RipCity Digital's first customer, he should be inserted at the top of the list. To add this new order, you need to insert a new row in the worksheet below the column labels.

To insert a new row:

▶ **1.** Click the **row 2** row heading. The entire second row is selected.

▶ **2.** In the Cells group on the Home tab, click the **Insert** button. A new row 2 is inserted, and the remaining rows shift down.

▶ **3.** Enter the new customer order shown in Figure 1-16 into row 2.

| Figure 1-16 | New row inserted in the worksheet |

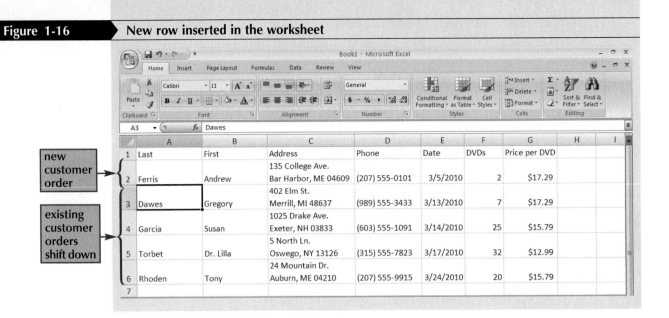

Deleting and Clearing a Row or Column

Adding new data to a workbook is common, as is removing old or erroneous data. Amanda just learned that her second customer, Gregory Dawes, canceled his order. She wants you to remove this order from the worksheet.

You can remove data in two ways: clearing and deleting. **Clearing** data from a worksheet removes the data but leaves the blank cells. **Deleting** data from the worksheet removes both the data and the cells. When you delete a column, the columns to the right shift left to fill the vacated space. Similarly, the rows below a deleted row shift up to fill the vacated space. Deleting a column or row has the opposite effect from inserting a column or row.

You'll first clear Gregory Dawes's data from the worksheet and then delete the row that contained the data. Usually, you would do this in one step by simply deleting the row, but this highlights the difference between clearing and deleting.

To clear and delete row 3:

1. Click the **row 3** row heading. The entire row 3 with Gregory Dawes's order is selected.

2. Right-click the **row 3** row heading, and then click **Clear Contents** on the shortcut menu. Excel clears the values in the third row, but leaves the blank row in that space.

3. Verify that the third row is still selected.

4. In the Cells group on the Home tab, click the **Delete** button. The third row is deleted, and the rows below it shift up. Only four customers remain in the worksheet.

Before proceeding, you'll save your workbook with the name "RipCity Digital Orders" in the default Excel workbook format.

To save the current workbook:

1. Click the **Save** button 🖫 on the Quick Access Toolbar. Because this workbook has not yet been saved, the Save As dialog box opens.

2. Navigate to the **Tutorial.01\Tutorial** folder included with your Data Files. You'll replace the default filename "Book1" with a more descriptive one.

   Trouble? If you don't have the starting Data Files, you need to get them before you can proceed. Your instructor will either give you the Data Files or ask you to obtain them from a specified location (such as a network drive). In either case, make a backup copy of the Data Files before you start so that you will have the original files available in case you need to start over. If you have any questions about the Data Files, see your instructor or technical support person for assistance.

3. Select **Book1** in the File name box, and then type **RipCity Digital Orders**.

4. Verify that **Excel Workbook** appears in the Save as type box.

5. Click the **Save** button. The Save As dialog box closes and the workbook file is saved with its descriptive filename.

Tip

You can reopen the Save As dialog box to save a workbook with a new filename, to a different location, or in another file format; click the Office Button and then click Save As.

You've entered and saved the customer order data. In the process, you worked with rows and columns. In the next session, you'll learn how to work with individual cells and groups of cells. You will also add calculations to the worksheet to determine how much revenue Amanda will generate from these orders.

Session 1.1 Quick Check | Review

1. What are the two types of sheets used in a workbook?
2. List two ways of identifying the active cell in the worksheet.
3. What is the cell reference for the cell located in the third column and fifth row of a worksheet?
4. What keyboard shortcut moves the active cell to cell A1?
5. What is text data?
6. How do you enter two lines of text within a cell?
7. Cell A4 contains "May 3, 2010"; why doesn't Excel consider this entry a text string?
8. Explain the difference between clearing a row and deleting a row.

Session 1.2

Working with Cells and Cell Ranges

A group of cells is called a **cell range** or **range**. Ranges can be either adjacent or nonadjacent. An **adjacent range** is a single rectangular block of cells. For example, all the customer order data you've entered in cell A1 through cell G5 is an adjacent range because it forms one rectangular block of cells. A **nonadjacent range** consists of two or more distinct adjacent ranges. All the last names in cell A1 through cell A5 and all the numbers in cells F1 through G5 together are a nonadjacent range because they are two distinct blocks of cells. A nonadjacent range can include as many adjacent ranges as you want.

Just as a cell reference indicates the location of an individual worksheet cell, a **range reference** indicates the location and size of a cell range. For adjacent ranges, the range reference specifies the locations of the upper-left and lower-right cells in the rectangular block separated by a colon. For example, the range reference A1:G5 refers to all the cells from cell A1 through cell G5. The range reference for nonadjacent ranges separates each adjacent range reference by a semicolon. For example, A1:A5;F1:G5 is the range reference for cells A1 through A5 and cells F1 through G5.

Selecting a Cell Range

You select adjacent and nonadjacent ranges of cells with your mouse, just as you selected individual cells. Selecting a cell range enables you to work with all of the cells in the range as a group. This means you can do things like move the cells, delete them, or clear all their contents at the same time.

Reference Window | **Selecting Cell Ranges**

To select an adjacent range:
- Click the cell in the upper-left corner of the adjacent range, drag the pointer to the cell in the lower-right corner of the adjacent range, and then release the mouse button.

or
- Click the cell in the upper-left corner of the adjacent range, press the Shift key as you click the cell in the lower-right corner of the adjacent range, and then release the Shift key.

To select a nonadjacent range of cells:
- Select a cell or an adjacent range, press the Ctrl key as you select each additional cell or adjacent range, and then release the Ctrl key.

To select all the cells in a worksheet:
- Click the Select All button located at the intersection of the row and column headings (or press the Ctrl+A keys).

You'll use the mouse pointer to select the adjacent range A1:G5, which includes all the content you entered in the worksheet so far.

To select the adjacent range A1:G5:

▶ 1. If you took a break at the end of the previous session, make sure the RipCity Digital Orders workbook is open and the Sheet2 worksheet is active.

▶ 2. Click cell **A1** to select the cell in the upper-left corner of the range A1:G5.

▶ 3. Drag the pointer to cell **G5**, which is the cell in the lower-right corner of the range A1:G5.

▶ 4. Release the mouse button. As shown in Figure 1-17, all cells in the adjacent range A1:G5 are selected. The selected cells are highlighted with color and surrounded by a black border. The first cell you selected, cell A1, is still the active cell in the worksheet.

Adjacent range A1:G5 selected   **Figure 1-17**

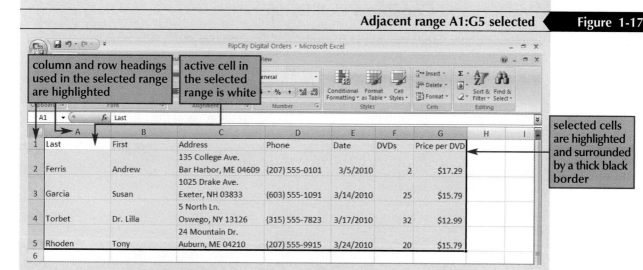

5. Click any cell in the worksheet to deselect the range.

Next, you'll select the nonadjacent range A1:A5;F1:G5.

To select the nonadjacent range A1:A5;F1:G5:

1. Select the adjacent range **A1:A5**.

2. Hold down the **Ctrl** key, and then select the adjacent range **F1:G5**.

3. Release the **Ctrl** key. As shown in Figure 1-18, all the cells in the nonadjacent range A1:A5;F1:G5 are selected.

Nonadjacent range A1:A5;F1:G5 selected   **Figure 1-18**

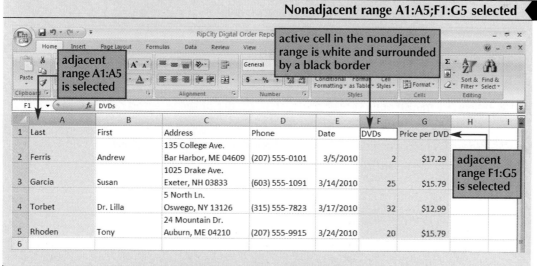

4. Click any cell in the worksheet to deselect the range.

Moving and Copying a Cell Range

Amanda wants you to insert titles that describe the customer order data you've entered. Including the company name, a descriptive title, and the date is part of good worksheet design, enabling others to quickly see the *who*, *what*, and *when* of the data. The current worksheet has no space to add this information. You could insert several blank rows at the top of the worksheet for this information. Another option is to select and then move the customer data lower in the worksheet, freeing up the rows at the top for the new text.

Reference Window	**Moving or Copying a Cell or Range**

- Select the cell or range you want to move or copy.
- Move the mouse pointer over the border of the selection until the pointer changes shape.
- To move the range, click the border and drag the selection to a new location (or to copy the range, hold down the Ctrl key and drag the selection to a new location).

or

- Select the cell or range you want to move or copy.
- In the Clipboard group on the Home tab, click the Cut button or the Copy button (or right-click the selection, and then click Cut or Copy on the shortcut menu).
- Select the cell or upper-left cell of the range where you want to move or copy the content.
- In the Clipboard group, click the Paste button (or right-click the selection, and then click Paste on the shortcut menu).

Tip

You can drag and drop to a range not currently visible. Drag the selection to the edge of the worksheet in which you want to scroll. When the new location is visible, drop the selection.

One way to move a cell or range is to select it, position the mouse pointer over the bottom border of the selection, and then drag the selection to a new location. This technique is called **drag and drop** because you are dragging the range and dropping it in a new location. You can also use the drag-and-drop technique to copy cells by pressing the Ctrl key as you drag the selected range to its new location. A copy of the original range is placed in the new location without removing the original range from the worksheet.

You'll use the drag-and-drop method to move data.

To drag and drop the customer orders:

▶ 1. Select the range **A1:G5**.

▶ 2. Move the mouse pointer over the bottom border of the selected range so that the pointer changes to ⁺⃕ .

▶ 3. Press and hold the mouse button to change the pointer to ⃕ , and then drag the selection down four rows. Do not release the mouse button. A ScreenTip appears, indicating the new range reference of the selected cells. See Figure 1-19.

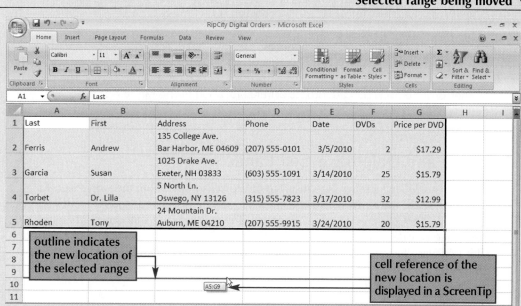

4. When the ScreenTip displays the range A5:G9, release the mouse button. The selected cells move to their new location.

5. Enter the title information shown in Figure 1-20 in the range A1:A3, pressing the **Enter** key after each entry.

	A	B	C	D	E	F	G	H
1	RipCity Digital							
2	Customer Orders							
3	3/31/2010							
4								

Some people find drag and drop a difficult and awkward way to move a selection, particularly if the worksheet is large and complex. In those situations, it's often more efficient to cut and paste the cell contents. **Cutting** places the cell contents into computer memory or on the Clipboard. The contents can then be pasted from the Clipboard into a new location in the worksheet. You'll cut and paste now.

To cut and paste cell contents:

1. With the range **A5:G9** selected, in the Clipboard group on the Home tab, click the **Cut** button. The selected range is surrounded by a blinking border, which indicates that its contents are stored on the Clipboard.

2. Click cell **A11**. This cell is the upper-left corner of the range where you want to paste the data.

> **3.** In the Clipboard group, click the **Paste** button. Excel pastes the contents of the range A5:G9 into the new range A11:G15. The blinking border disappears as a visual clue that the Clipboard is now empty.
>
> **4.** Select the range **A11:G15**, and then, in the Clipboard group, click the **Cut** button ✄.
>
> **5.** Click cell **A5**, and then, in the Clipboard group, click the **Paste** button. The customer order data is pasted into its original location in the range A5:G9.

Inserting and Deleting a Cell Range

Another use of selecting a range is to insert or delete cells from within the worksheet. To insert a range, select the range where you want the new cells inserted, and then click the Insert button in the Cells group on the Home tab. The existing cells shift down when the selected range is wider than it is long, and they shift right when the selected range is longer than it is wide (as illustrated in Figure 1-21). The Insert Cells command located on the Insert button menu lets you specify whether you want to shift the existing cells right or down, or whether to insert an entire row or column into the new range.

Figure 1-21 ▸ **Cells inserted within a cell range**

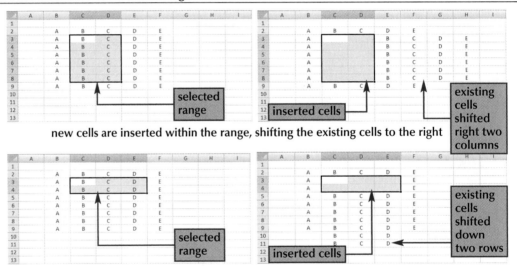

new cells are inserted within the range, shifting the existing cells to the right

new cells are inserted within the range, shifting the existing cells down

If you no longer need a specific cell or range in a worksheet, you can delete those cells and any content they contain. To delete a range, select the range, and then click the Delete button in the Cells group on the Home tab. As with deleting a row or column, cells adjacent to the deleted range either move up or left to fill in the vacancy left by the deleted cells. The Delete Cells command located on the Delete button menu lets you specify whether you want to shift the adjacent cells left or up, or whether to delete the entire column or row.

Inserting or Deleting a Cell Range | Reference Window

- Select a range that matches the range you want to insert or delete.
- In the Cells group on the Home tab, click the Insert button or the Delete button.
or
- Select the range that matches the range you want to insert or delete.
- In the Cells group, click the Insert button arrow and then click the Insert Cells button or click the Delete button arrow and then click the Delete Cells command (or right-click the selected range, and then click Insert or Delete on the shortcut menu).
- Click the option button for the direction in which you want to shift the cells, columns, or rows.
- Click the OK button.

You do not need to insert or delete any cells in the worksheet at this time.

Working with Formulas

Up to now you have entered only text, numbers, and dates in the worksheet. However, the main reason for using Excel is to perform calculations on data. Amanda wants the workbook to determine the number of DVDs she has to create for her customers and how much revenue will be generated by completing these orders. Such calculations are added to a worksheet using formulas and functions.

Entering a Formula

A **formula** is an expression that returns a value. In most cases, this is a number. You can also create formulas in Excel that return text strings. Every Excel formula begins with an equal sign (=) followed by an expression that describes the operation to be done. A formula is written using **operators** that combine different values, returning a single value that is then displayed in the cell. The most commonly used operators are **arithmetic operators** that perform addition, subtraction, multiplication, division, and exponentiation. For example, the following formula adds 5 and 7, returning a value of 12.

=5+7

However, formulas in Excel most often use numbers stored within cells. For example, the following formula returns the result of adding the values in cells A1 and B2.

=A1+B2

So, if the value 5 is stored in cell A1 and the value 7 is stored in cell B2, this formula would also return a value of 12. Figure 1-22 describes the different arithmetic operators and provides examples of formulas.

Figure 1-22 ▶ **Arithmetic operators**

Operation	Arithmetic Operator	Example	Description
Addition	+	=10+A1 =B1+B2+B3	Adds 10 to the value in cell A1 Adds the values in cells B1, B2, and B3
Subtraction	–	=C9–B2 =1–D2	Subtracts the value in cell B2 from the value in cell C9 Subtracts the value in cell D2 from 1
Multiplication	*	=C9*B9 =E5*0.06	Multiplies the values in cells C9 and B9 Multiplies the value in cell E5 by 0.06
Division	/	=C9/B9 =D15/12	Divides the value in cell C9 by the value in cell B9 Divides the value in cell D15 by 12
Exponentiation	^	=B5^3 =3^B5	Raises the value of cell B5 to the third power Raises 3 to the value in cell B5

If a formula contains more than one arithmetic operator, Excel performs the calculation using the same order of precedence you might have already seen in math classes. The **order of precedence** is a set of predefined rules used to determine the sequence in which operators are applied in a calculation—first exponentiation (^), second multiplication (*) and division (/), and third addition (+) and subtraction (–). For example, consider the formula below:

=3+4*5

This formula returns the value 23 because multiplication (4*5) takes precedence over addition. If a formula contains two or more operators with the same level of precedence, the operators are applied in order from left to right. Note the formula below:

=4*10/8

This formula first calculates the leftmost operation (4*10) and then divides that result of 40 by 8 to return the value 5.

To change the order of operations, you can enclose parts of the formula within parentheses. Any expression within a set of parentheses is calculated before the rest of the formula. Note the following formula:

=(3+4)*5

This formula first calculates the value of the expression (3+4) and then multiplies that total of 7 by 5 to return the value 35. Figure 1-23 shows how slight changes in a formula affect the order of precedence and the result of the formula.

Figure 1-23 ▶ **Order of precedence rules**

Formula (A1=50, B1=10, C1=5)	Order of Precedence Rule	Result
=A1+B1*C1	Multiplication before addition	100
=(A1+B1)*C1	Expression inside parentheses executed before expression outside	300
=A1/B1–C1	Division before subtraction	0
=A1/(B1–C1)	Expression inside parentheses executed before expression outside	10
=A1/B1*C1	Two operators at same precedence level, leftmost operator evaluated first	25
=A1/(B1*C1)	Expression inside parentheses executed before expression outside	1

Entering a Formula | Reference Window

- Click the cell in which you want the formula results to appear.
- Type = and an expression that calculates a value using cell references and arithmetic operators.
- Press the Enter key or press the Tab key to complete the formula.

Amanda wants the worksheet to include the total amount she charged for creating each customer's DVDs. The charge is equal to the number of DVDs created multiplied by the price per DVD. You've already entered this information for each customer in columns F and G. You'll enter a formula to calculate the charge for each customer in column H.

To enter the formula in column H:

▶ 1. Click cell **H5** to make it the active cell, type **Charge** for the column label, and then press the **Enter** key. The column label is entered in cell H5. Cell H6, where you want to enter the formula, is the active cell.

▶ 2. Type **=F6*G6** (the number of DVDs created multiplied by the price per DVD). As you type the formula, a list of Excel function names appears in a ScreenTip, which provides a quick method for entering functions. The list will close when you complete the formula. You'll learn more about Excel functions shortly.

▶ 3. Press the **Enter** key. The formula is entered in cell H6, which displays the value $34.58. The result is displayed as currency because cell G6 referenced in the formula contains a currency value.

After a formula has been entered into a cell, the cell displays the results of the formula and not the formula itself. If the results are not what you expect, you might have entered the formula incorrectly. You can view the formula by selecting the cell and reviewing the expression displayed in the formula bar. One challenge with formulas, particularly long formulas, is interpreting the cell references. Excel makes this simpler by color coding each cell reference in the formula and its corresponding cell in the worksheet. You'll see this when you view the formula you just entered.

To view the formula:

▶ 1. Click cell **H6** to make it the active cell. The formula you entered appears in the formula bar, whereas the value returned by the formula appears in the cell.

▶ 2. Click in the formula bar. As shown in Figure 1-24, each cell used in the formula has a different colored border that matches the color of its cell reference in the formula. This provides a visual cue to the formula, enabling you to quickly match cell references with their locations in the worksheet.

Figure 1-24 ▸ **Formula references color coded**

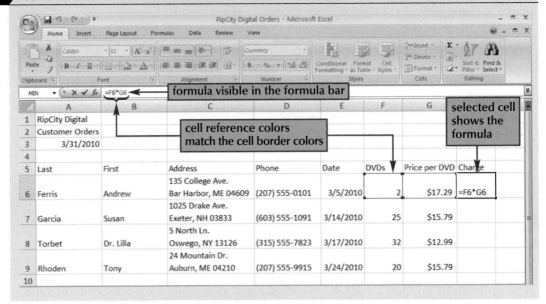

For Amanda's first customer, you entered the formula by typing each cell reference. You can also enter a cell reference by clicking the cell as you enter the formula. This technique reduces the possibility of error caused by typing an incorrect cell reference. You'll use this method to enter the formula to calculate the charge for the second customer.

To enter a cell reference in the formula using the mouse:

▸ 1. Click cell **H7** to make it the active cell, and then type **=**. When you type the equal sign, Excel knows that you're entering a formula. Any cell that you click from now on causes Excel to insert the cell reference of the selected cell into the formula until you complete the formula by pressing the Enter or Tab key.

▸ 2. Click cell **F7**. The cell reference is inserted into the formula on the formula bar. At this point, any cell you click changes the cell reference used in the formula. The cell reference isn't "locked" until you type an operator.

▸ 3. Type ***** to enter the multiplication operator. The cell reference for cell F7 is "locked" in the formula, and the next cell you click will be inserted after the operator.

▸ 4. Click cell **G7** to enter its cell reference in the formula, and then press the **Enter** key. Cell H7 displays the value $394.75, which is the total charge for the second customer.

Copying and Pasting Formulas

Sometimes, you'll need to repeat the same formula for several rows of data. Rather than retyping the formula, you can copy the formula and then paste it into the remaining rows. You'll copy the formula you just entered in cell H7 to cells H8 and H9 to calculate the charges for Amanda's two remaining customers.

To copy the formula in cell H7:

▸ 1. Click cell **H7** to select the cell that contains the formula you want to copy.

2. In the Clipboard group on the Home tab, click the **Copy** button 🔳 . The formula is copied to the Clipboard.

3. Select the range **H8:H9**, the cells in which you want to paste the formula.

4. In the Clipboard group, click the **Paste** button. Excel pastes the formula into the selected range. See Figure 1-25.

Formula copied and pasted ◄ **Figure 1-25**

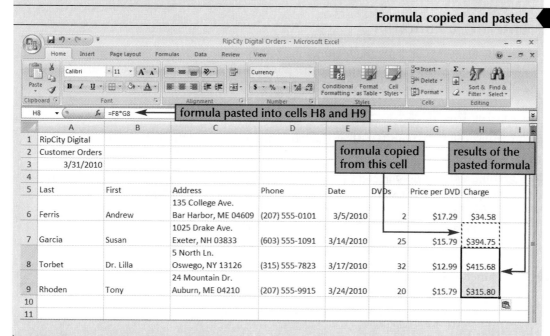

5. Click cell **H8** and verify that the formula =F8*G8 appears in the formula bar, and then click cell **H9** and verify that the formula =F9*G9 appears in the formula bar.

Pasting a formula is different from pasting a value. With the customer order data, Excel pasted the same values in a new location. With formulas, Excel adjusts the formula's cell references to reflect the new location of the formula in the worksheet. This is because you want to replicate the actions of a formula rather than duplicate the specific value the formula generates. In this case, the formula's action is to multiply the number of DVDs Amanda created for the customer by the price she charged for creating each DVD. By copying and pasting that formula, that action is replicated for every customer in the worksheet.

Introducing Functions

In addition to cell references and operators, formulas can also contain functions. A **function** is a named operation that returns a value. Functions are used to simplify formulas, reducing what might be a long expression into a compact statement. For example, to add the values in the range A1:A10, you could enter the following long formula:

=A1+A2+A3+A4+A5+A6+A7+A8+A9+A10

Or, you could use the SUM function to accomplish the same thing:

=SUM(A1:A10)

In both cases, Excel adds the values in cells A1 through A10, but the SUM function is faster and simpler to enter and less prone to a typing error. You should always use a function, if one is available, in place of a long, complex formula.

Excel supports over 300 different functions from the fields of finance, business, science, and engineering. Functions are not limited to numbers. Excel also provides functions that work with text and dates.

Entering a Function

Amanda wants to calculate the total number of DVDs she needs to create for her customers. To do that, you'll use the SUM function to add the values in the range F6:F9.

To enter the SUM function:

1. Click cell **E10**, type **TOTAL** as the label, and then press the **Tab** key. The label is entered in cell E10, and cell F10 is the active cell.

Tip

You can also insert a range reference into a function by selecting the range with your mouse.

2. Type **=SUM(F6:F9** in cell F10. As you begin to type the SUM function, a ScreenTip lists the names of all functions that start with the letter "S." When you type the cell references, Excel highlights all the cells in the specified range to provide a visual reminder of exactly which cells the SUM function is using. See Figure 1-26.

Figure 1-26 | **SUM function being entered**

3. Type **)** to complete the function, and then press the **Tab** key. The value of the SUM function appears in cell F10, indicating that Amanda has to create 79 DVDs to meet all of her current orders.

Entering Functions with AutoSum

A fast and convenient way to enter the SUM function is with the Sum button in the Editing group on the Home tab. The **Sum** button (also referred to as the **AutoSum** feature) quickly inserts Excel functions that summarize all the values in a column or row using a single statistic. With the Sum button, you can insert the SUM, AVERAGE, COUNT, MIN, and MAX functions to generate the following:

- Sum of the values in the column or row
- Average value in the column or row
- Total count of numeric values in the column or row
- Minimum value in the column or row
- Maximum value in the column or row

The Sum button inserts both the name of the function and the range reference to the row or column of data to which the summary function is being applied. Excel determines the range reference by examining the layout of the data and choosing what seems to be the most likely cell range. For example, if you use the Sum button in a cell that is below a column of numbers, Excel assumes that you want to summarize the values in the column. Similarly, if you use the Sum button in a cell to the right of a row of values, Excel summarizes the values in that row. When you use the Sum button, Excel highlights the range it "thinks" you want to use. You can change that range by typing a different range reference or selecting a different range with your mouse.

Understanding How the AutoSum Feature Works		InSight

Make sure to always verify the range selected by AutoSum, especially when a worksheet's column or row titles contain numbers. AutoSum cannot differentiate between numbers used as titles (such as years) and numbers used as data for the calculation.

Amanda wants to calculate the total revenue she'll generate by fulfilling her customer orders. You'll use the AutoSum feature to enter the SUM function.

To use AutoSum to calculate the total revenue:

▶ 1. Click cell **H10** to make it the active cell.

▶ 2. In the Editing group on the Home tab, click the **Sum button arrow** $\boxed{\Sigma \; \cdot}$. The button's menu opens and displays five common summary functions: Sum, Average, Count Numbers, Max (for maximum), and Min (for minimum).

▶ 3. Click **Sum** to enter the SUM function. See Figure 1-27.

| Figure 1-27 | SUM function entered with AutoSum |

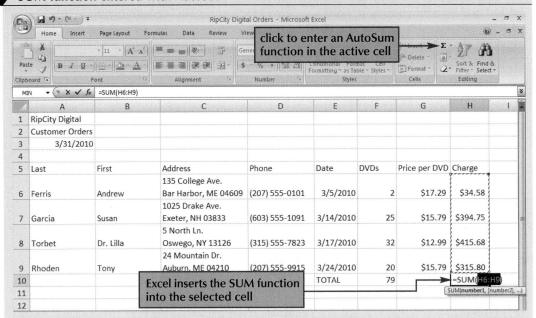

4. Verify that the range H6:H9 appears in the SUM function and is highlighted with a dotted border. The dotted border provides a visual reminder that this is where the SUM function will be applied.

5. Press the **Enter** key to accept the automatically generated formula. The total charge for all of Amanda's customers, shown in cell H10, is $1,160.81.

| InSight | **Creating Effective Formulas** |

You can use formulas to quickly perform calculations on business, science, and engineering data. To use formulas effectively:

• Do not place important data in a formula because the worksheet displays the formula result rather than the actual formula. For example, the formula =0.05*A5 calculates a 5% sales tax on a price in cell A5, but hides the 5% tax rate. Instead, enter the tax rate in another cell, such as cell A4, with an appropriate label and use the formula =A4*A5 to calculate the sales tax. Readers can see the tax rate as well as the resulting sales tax.

• Keep formulas simple. Use functions in place of long, complex formulas whenever possible. For example, use the SUM function instead of entering a formula that adds individual cells.

• Break up formulas to show intermediate results. For example, the formula =SUM(A1:A10)/SUM(B1:B10) calculates the ratio of two sums, but hides the two sum values. Instead, enter each SUM function in a separate cell, such as cells A11 and B11, and use the formula =A11/B11 to calculate the ratio. Readers can see both sums and the value of their ratio in the worksheet.

Working with Worksheets

Recall that new workbooks contain three worksheets labeled Sheet1, Sheet2, and Sheet3. You can add new worksheets to the workbook and remove unneeded ones. You can also give worksheets more descriptive and meaningful names. For Amanda's workbook, you'll remove unused worksheets from the workbook, and you'll rename the two worksheets in which you entered data.

Inserting and Deleting a Worksheet

Although each workbook includes three worksheets to start, sometimes you'll need more or fewer worksheets. You can add worksheets or delete unneeded ones. To insert a new worksheet into the workbook, right-click a sheet tab, click Insert on the shortcut menu, select a sheet type, and then click the OK button. Excel inserts the new sheet directly to the left of the active sheet. You can insert a new worksheet at the end of the workbook by clicking the Insert Worksheet tab located to the right of the last sheet tab in the workbook. The new worksheet is named with the next consecutive sheet number, such as Sheet4. You'll insert a new, blank worksheet at the end of your workbook.

To insert a new worksheet:

▶ 1. Click the **Insert Worksheet** tab 📇 to the right of the Sheet3 sheet tab. Excel inserts a new worksheet named "Sheet4" at the end of the workbook.

The workbook now includes two empty worksheets: Sheet3 and Sheet4. Because you don't plan to use these sheets, it's a good idea to remove them. You can delete a worksheet from a workbook in two ways. You can right-click the sheet tab of the worksheet you want to delete, and then click Delete on the shortcut menu. You can also click the Delete button arrow in the Cells group on the Home tab, and then click Delete Sheet. You'll use both of these methods to delete the Sheet3 and Sheet4 worksheets.

To delete the Sheet3 and Sheet4 worksheets:

▶ 1. Right-click the **Sheet3** sheet tab, and then click **Delete** on the shortcut menu. Excel removes the Sheet3 worksheet.

▶ 2. If necessary, click the **Sheet4** sheet tab to make it the active sheet.

▶ 3. In the Cells group on the Home tab, click the **Delete button arrow**, and then click **Delete Sheet**. Excel removes Sheet4 from the workbook.

Renaming a Worksheet

The remaining worksheet names, Sheet1 and Sheet2, are not very descriptive. Amanda suggests that you rename Sheet1 as "Documentation" and rename Sheet2 as "Customer Orders." To rename a worksheet, you double-click the sheet tab to select the sheet name, type a new name for the sheet, and then press the Enter key. Sheet names cannot exceed 31 characters in length, including blank spaces. The width of the sheet tab adjusts to the length of the name you enter.

To rename the two worksheets:

▶ **1.** Double-click the **Sheet2** sheet tab. The sheet name is selected in the sheet tab.

▶ **2.** Type **Customer Orders**, and then press the **Enter** key. The width of the sheet tab expands to match the longer sheet name.

▶ **3.** Double-click the **Sheet1** sheet tab, type **Documentation**, and then press the **Enter** key. Both sheets are renamed.

Moving and Copying a Worksheet

You can change the placement of the worksheets in a workbook. A good practice is to place the most important worksheets at the beginning of the workbook (the leftmost sheet tabs), and less important worksheets toward the end (the rightmost tabs). To reposition a worksheet, you click and drag the sheet tab to a new location relative to other worksheets in the workbook. You can use a similar method to copy a worksheet. Just press the Ctrl key as you drag and drop the sheet tab. The new copy appears where you drop the sheet tab, while the original worksheet remains in its initial position. You'll move the Documentation sheet to the end of the workbook and then return it to the beginning.

To move the Documentation worksheet:

▶ **1.** If necessary, click the **Documentation** sheet tab to make that worksheet active.

▶ **2.** Press and hold the mouse button so the pointer changes to ⬚ and a small triangle appears in the upper-left corner of the tab.

▶ **3.** Drag the pointer to the right of the Customer Orders sheet tab, and then release the mouse button. The Documentation sheet is now the second sheet in the workbook.

▶ **4.** Drag the Documentation sheet back to be the first sheet in the workbook.

Editing Your Work

As you work, you might make mistakes that you want to correct or undo, or you might need to replace a value based on more current information. Amanda realizes that the price per DVD for Andrew Ferris's order should be $18.29 not $17.29 as entered in cell G6. You could simply clear the value in the cell and then type the correct value. However, sometimes you need to edit only a portion of an entry rather than change the entire contents of a cell, especially if the cell contains a large block of text or a complex formula. To edit the cell contents, you can work in **editing mode**.

You can enter editing mode in several ways: (1) double-clicking the cell, (2) selecting the cell and pressing the F2 key, or (3) selecting the cell and clicking anywhere within the formula bar. When you work in editing mode, some of the keyboard shortcuts you've been using work differently because now they apply only to the text within the selected cell. For example, the Home, End, Backspace, Delete, and arrow keys now move the insertion point to different locations within the cell. The Home key moves the insertion point to the beginning of the cell's content. The End key moves the insertion point to the end of the cell's content. The left and right arrow keys move the insertion point backward and forward through the cell's content. The Backspace key deletes the character immediately to the left of the insertion point, and the Delete key deletes the character to the right of the insertion point. To exit editing mode and accept the changes you made, press the Enter key.

Tip

If you make a mistake as you type in editing mode, you can press the Esc key or click the Cancel button on the formula bar to cancel all of the changes you made while in editing mode.

You'll see how keyboard commands differ when you're in editing mode as you change one digit of the value in cell G6.

To edit the value in cell G6:

▶ **1.** Click the **Customer Orders** sheet tab.

▶ **2.** Double-click cell **G6**. The mode indicator in the status bar switches from Ready to Edit to indicate that you are in editing mode.

▶ **3.** Press the **End** key. The insertion point moves to the end of the cell.

▶ **4.** Press the ← key three times. The insertion point moves to the right of the 7.

▶ **5.** Press the **Backspace** key to delete the 7, and then type **8**. The value in cell G6 changes to 18.29. See Figure 1-28.

Working in editing mode   Figure 1-28

	A	B	C	D	E	F	G	H	I
1	RipCity Digital								
2	Customer Orders								
3	3/31/2010								
4									
5	Last	First	Address	Phone	Date	DVDs	Price per DVD	Charge	
6	Ferris	Andrew	135 College Ave. Bar Harbor, ME 04609	(207) 555-0101	3/5/2010	2	18.29	$34.58	
7	Garcia	Susan	1025 Drake Ave. Exeter, NH 03833	(603) 555-1091	3/14/2010	25	$15.79	$394.75	
8	Torbet	Dr. Lilla	5 North Ln. Oswego, NY 13126	(315) 555-7823	3/17/2010	32	$12.99	$415.68	
9	Rhoden	Tony	24 Mountain Dr. Auburn, ME 04210	(207) 555-9915	3/24/2010	20	$15.79	$315.80	
10					TOTAL	79		$1,160.81	
11									
12									
13									
14									
15									
16									
17									

Cell reference: G6 — 18.29

insertion point to edit the text within the cell

status bar indicates Excel is in editing mode

Documentation | Customer Orders

Edit

▶ **6.** Press the **Enter** key to accept the edit in cell G6. The value $18.29 appears in cell G6, the active cell is cell G7, and the mode indicator in the status bar changes from Edit to Ready to indicate that you are no longer in editing mode.

Undoing and Redoing an Action

As you revise a workbook, you might find that you need to undo one of your previous actions. To undo an action, click the Undo button on the Quick Access Toolbar. As you work, Excel maintains a list of your actions, so you can undo most of the actions you perform in a workbook during the current session. To reverse more than one action, click the Undo button arrow and click the earliest action you want to undo from the list. All actions subsequent to that action will also be undone.

You'll undo the action you just performed, removing the edit to cell G6.

To undo your last action:

▶ **1.** On the Quick Access Toolbar, click the **Undo** button ↶ .

▶ **2.** Verify that $17.29 appears again in cell G6, indicating that your last action—editing the value of this cell—has been undone.

If you find that you have gone too far in undoing previous actions, you can go forward in the action list and redo those actions. To redo an action, you click the Redo button on the Quick Access Toolbar. As with the Undo button, you can click the Redo button arrow to redo more than one action at a time. You'll use Redo to restore the value of cell G6.

To redo your last action:

▶ **1.** On the Quick Access Toolbar, click the **Redo** button ↷ .

▶ **2.** Verify that the value in cell G6 returns to $18.29.

Using Find and Replace

Amanda wants to you to replace all the street title abbreviations with their full names. Specifically, she wants you to use "Avenue" in place of "Ave.", "Lane" in place of "Ln.", and "Drive" in place of "Dr." Although you could read through the worksheet to locate each occurrence, this becomes a cumbersome process with larger workbooks. For greater speed and accuracy, you can use the **Find** command to locate numbers and text in the workbook and the **Replace** command to overwrite them. You'll replace each occurrence of a street title abbreviation.

To use the Find and Replace commands:

▶ **1.** In the Editing group on the Home tab, click the **Find & Select** button, and then click **Replace**. The Find and Replace dialog box opens.

▶ **2.** Type **Ave.** in the Find what box, press the **Tab** key, and then type **Avenue** in the Replace with box.

You can limit the search to the current worksheet or search the entire workbook. You can specify whether to match the capitalization in the Find what box and whether the search text should match the entire cell contents or part of the cell contents.

▶ **3.** Click the **Options** button to display additional Find and Replace options. See Figure 1-29.

Figure 1-29 ▶ **Find and Replace dialog box**

You can choose to review each occurrence of the search value and decide whether to replace it, or you can click the Replace All button to replace all occurrences at once.

▶ **4.** Click the **Replace All** button. A dialog box opens, indicating that Excel has completed its search and made two replacements.

▶ **5.** Click the **OK** button to close the dialog box.

▶ **6.** Type **Ln.** in the Find what box, press the **Tab** key, type **Lane** in the Replace with box, click the **Replace All** button, and then click the **OK** button to close the dialog box that indicates Excel has completed its search and made one replacement.

Next, you want to replace the street abbreviation "Dr." with "Drive." Because "Dr." is also used as the abbreviation for "Doctor" for one customer, you must review each "Dr." abbreviation and make the replacement only in the addresses.

▶ **7.** Type **Dr.** in the Find what box, press the **Tab** key, type **Drive** in the Replace with box, and then click the **Find Next** button. The next occurrence of "Dr." in the worksheet occurs in cell B8 with the text, "Dr. Lilla."

▶ **8.** Click the **Find Next** button to ignore this occurrence. The next occurrence of "Dr." is in the mailing address for Tony Rhoden.

▶ **9.** Click the **Replace** button to replace this text. You've finished finding and replacing text in the worksheet.

▶ **10.** Click the **Close** button to close the Find and Replace dialog box. See Figure 1-30.

Revised customer orders   Figure 1-30

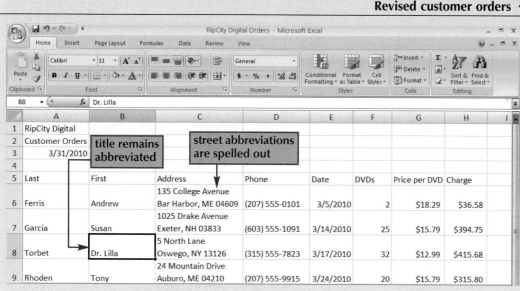

Using the Spelling Checker

Another editing tool is the spelling checker. The **spelling checker** verifies the words in the active worksheet against the program's dictionary. Although the spelling checker's dictionary includes a large number of words, as well as common first and last names and places, many words you use in workbooks might not be included. If the spelling checker finds a word not in its dictionary, the word appears in a dialog box along with a list of suggested replacements. You can replace the word with one from the list, or you can ignore the word and go to the next possible misspelling. You can also add words to the dictionary to prevent them from being flagged as misspellings in the future. Note that the spelling checker will not find a correctly spelled word used incorrectly, such as "there" instead of "their" or "your" instead of "you're." The best way to catch these types of errors is to proofread your worksheets.

Before giving the customer orders workbook to Amanda, you'll check the spelling.

To check the spelling in the worksheet:

▶ **1.** Click cell **A1**, click the **Review** tab on the Ribbon, and then, in the Proofing group, click the **Spelling** button. The Spelling dialog box opens and flags "RipCity" as a possible spelling error. Excel suggests two alternatives. See Figure 1-31.

| Figure 1-31 | Spelling dialog box |

Because RipCity is the name of Amanda's company, you'll ignore all the occurrences of this spelling.

▶ **2.** Click the **Ignore All** button. The spelling checker flags "Torbet," a last name that is not in the program's dictionary.

▶ **3.** Click the **Ignore All** button to ignore the spelling of this name. The next potential spelling error is the name "Lilla" in cell B8. Amanda tells you the name should have been entered as "Lila," a first name that the spelling checker recognizes.

▶ **4.** Click **Lila** in the list of suggestions, if necessary, and then click the **Change** button. The text is changed within the cell. The spelling checker doesn't find any other errors.

Trouble? If the spelling checker finds another error, you might have another typing error in your worksheet. Use the spelling checker to find and correct any other errors in your workbook, and then continue with Step 5.

▶ **5.** Click the **OK** button to close the Spelling dialog box.

▶ **6.** Proofread the worksheet and correct any other spelling errors you find. You do not have to check the spelling in the Documentation worksheet.

Previewing and Printing a Worksheet

Now that you have finished the final edit of the workbook, you are ready to print a hard copy of the customer orders list for Amanda. However, before you print the workbook, you should preview it to ensure that it will print correctly.

Changing Worksheet Views

You can view a worksheet in three ways. **Normal view**, which you've been using throughout this tutorial, simply shows the contents of the worksheet. **Page Layout view** shows how the worksheet will appear on the page or pages sent to the printer. **Page Break Preview** displays the location of the different page breaks within the worksheet. This is particularly useful when a worksheet will span several printed pages.

You'll switch between these views to see how the Customer Orders worksheet will appear on printed pages.

To switch the worksheet views:

▶ **1.** Click the **Page Layout** button 🔲 on the status bar. Excel displays the page layout of the worksheet. You want to see the rest of the data, which extends to a second page.

▶ **2.** Reduce the zoom level to **60%**. See Figure 1-32.

Worksheet displayed in Page Layout view ◀ Figure 1-32

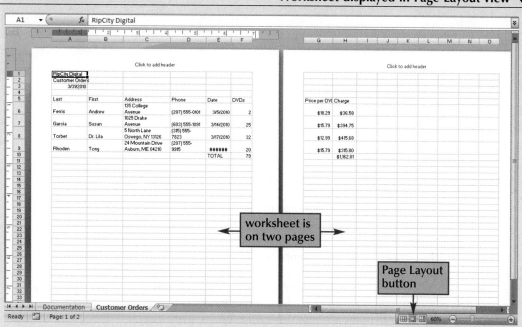

Tip

You can view the workbook in the full screen space (which hides the Ribbon); in the Workbook Views group on the View tab, click Full Screen.

▶ **3.** Click the **Page Break Preview** button 🔲 on the status bar. The view switches to Page Break Preview, which shows only those parts of the current worksheet that will print. A dotted blue border separates one page from another.

Trouble? If the Welcome to Page Break Preview dialog box opens, this is the first time you've switched to Page Break Preview. Click the OK button to close the dialog box and continue with Step 4.

▶ **4.** Zoom the worksheet to **120%** so that you can more easily read the contents of the worksheet. See Figure 1-33.

Figure 1-33 | **Worksheet displayed in Page Break Preview**

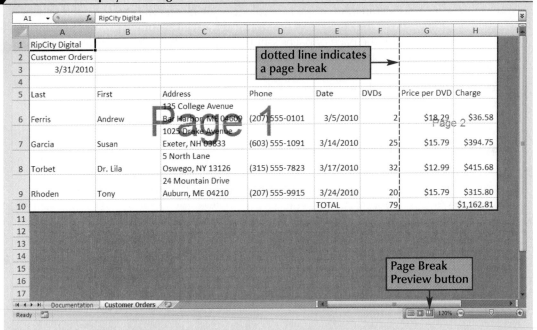

5. Click the **Normal** button 🔳 on the status bar. The worksheet returns to Normal view. A dotted black line indicates where the page break will be placed when the worksheet is printed.

Working with Portrait and Landscape Orientation

As you saw in Page Layout view and Page Break Preview, the Customer Orders worksheet will print on two pages—columns A through F will print on one page and columns G and H will print on a second page. Amanda wants the entire worksheet printed on a single page. The simplest way to accomplish this is to change the page orientation. In **portrait orientation**, the page is taller than it is wide. In **landscape orientation**, the page is wider than it is tall. By default, Excel displays pages in portrait orientation. In many cases, however, you will want to print the page in landscape orientation.

You'll change the orientation of the Customer Orders worksheet.

To change the page orientation:

1. Click the **Page Layout** tab on the Ribbon.

2. In the Page Setup group, click the **Orientation** button, and then click **Landscape**. The page orientation switches to landscape, and the Customer Orders worksheet contents fit on one page.

3. Click the **Page Layout** button 🔳 on the status bar, and then verify that all the worksheet contents fit on one page.

Changing the page orientation affects only the active worksheet. The Documentation sheet remains in portrait orientation.

▶ **4.** Click the **Documentation** sheet tab, and then click the **Page Layout** button 🔲. The entire contents of the Documentation worksheet fit on one page in portrait orientation.

Printing the Workbook

You can print the contents of your workbook by using the Print command on the Office Button. The Print command provides three options. You can open the Print dialog box from which you can specify the printer settings, including which printer to use, which worksheets to include in the printout, and the number of copies to print. You can perform a Quick Print using the print options currently set in the Print dialog box. Finally, you can preview the workbook before you send it to the printer to see exactly how the worksheet will look on the printer you selected with the print settings you've chosen. In general, you should always preview the printout before sending it to the printer.

You'll preview and print Amanda's workbook now.

To preview and print the workbook:

▶ **1.** Click the **Office Button** 🔘, point to **Print**, and then click **Print**. The Print dialog box opens.

▶ **2.** Click the **Name** box, and then click the printer to which you want to print if it is not already selected.

Next, you need to select what to print. You can choose to print only the selected cells, the active sheet (or sheets), or all the worksheets in the workbook that contain data.

▶ **3.** If necessary, click the **Entire workbook** option button to print both of the worksheets in the workbook.

▶ **4.** Make sure **1** appears in the Number of copies box because you only need to print one copy of the workbook. Next, you'll preview how the worksheet will appear on the printed page with these settings.

▶ **5.** Click the **Preview** button. Print Preview displays a preview of the full first page of the printout—the Documentation sheet printed in portrait orientation. The status bar shows that this is the first of two pages that will print.

▶ **6.** In the Preview group on the Print Preview tab, click the **Next Page** button. Print Preview shows the second page of the printout.

The printout will include only the data in the worksheet. The other elements in the worksheet, such as the row and column headings and the gridlines around the worksheet cells, will not print.

▶ **7.** In the Print group, click the **Print** button. The workbook is sent to the printer and Print Preview closes.

Viewing and Printing Worksheet Formulas

Amanda notices that the printout displays only the worksheet values and none of the formulas. Most of the time, you will be interested in only the final results of the worksheet, not the formulas used to calculate those results. In some cases, you might want to view the formulas used to develop the workbook. This is particularly useful when you encounter unexpected results and you want to examine the underlying formulas. You can view the formulas in a workbook by switching to **formula view**, a view of the workbook contents that displays formulas instead of the resulting values. You'll switch to formula view now.

To view the worksheet formulas:

Tip

To toggle in and out of formula view, press the Ctrl+` keys. The ` grave accent symbol is usually located above the Tab key on your keyboard.

▶ 1. Click the **Customer Orders** sheet tab, if necessary, and then click the **Normal** button ⊞ on the status bar. The Customer Orders worksheet is active and displayed in Normal view.

▶ 2. Press the **Ctrl+`** keys. The worksheet changes to formula view.

▶ 3. Scroll the worksheet to the right to view the formulas in columns F and H. The column widths are wider to display the entire formula in each cell. As long as you don't resize the column widths while in formula view, they remain unchanged in other views. See Figure 1-34.

Figure 1-34 ▶ **Worksheet in formula view**

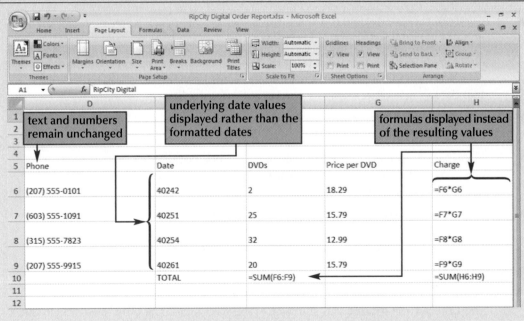

Amanda wants a printout of the formula view. The Customer Orders worksheet will not fit on one page because of the expanded column widths. You can scale the worksheet to force the contents to fit on a single page. **Scaling** a printout reduces the width and the height of the printout to fit the number of pages you specify by shrinking the text size as needed. You can also scale a printout proportionally to a percentage of its actual size. You'll scale the Customer Orders worksheet to a width and height of one page.

To scale the worksheet formulas to print on one page:

▶ **1.** In the Scale to Fit group on the Page Layout tab, click the **Width arrow**, and then click **1 page**.

▶ **2.** In the Scale to Fit group, click the **Height arrow**, and then click **1 page**. You'll verify that the worksheet formula view fits on a single page.

▶ **3.** Click the **Page Layout** button 🔲 on the status bar, and then zoom the worksheet to **50%**. The formula view of the worksheet fits on one page. See Figure 1-35.

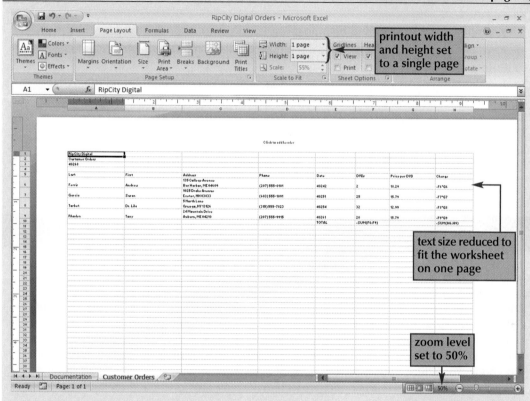

▶ **4.** Click the **Office Button** 🔵, point to **Print**, and then click **Print**. The Print dialog box opens. You'll specify that only the active worksheet will be printed.

▶ **5.** Click the **Active sheet(s)** option button to print only the Customer Orders worksheet.

▶ **6.** Click the **Preview** button. Print Preview displays a preview of the one-page printout of the Customer Orders worksheet in formula view.

▶ **7.** In the Print group on the Print Preview tab, click the **Print** button. The workbook is sent to the printer and Print Preview closes.

At this point, you've completed your work for Amanda. Before closing the workbook, you'll change the view of the workbook contents back to Normal view.

To save and close the workbook:

▶ **1.** Press the **Ctrl+`** keys to switch the worksheet back to Normal view.

▶ **2.** Save your changes to the workbook, and then close it.

Amanda is pleased with the job you've done for her. She will review the workbook you've created and let you know if she has any changes that she wants you to make.

Review | **Session 1.2 Quick Check**

1. Describe the two types of cell ranges in Excel.
2. What is the range reference for the block of cells from A3 through G5 and J3 through M5?
3. What formula would you enter to add the values in cells B4, B5, and B6? What function would you enter to achieve the same result?
4. How do you rename a worksheet?
5. Describe four ways of viewing the content of an Excel workbook.
6. Why would you scale a worksheet?
7. How do you display the formulas used in a worksheet?
8. How are page breaks indicated in Page Break Preview?

Review | **Tutorial Summary**

In this tutorial, you learned the basics of spreadsheets and Excel. After reviewing the major components of the Excel window, you navigated between and within worksheets. You entered text, dates, values, and formulas, and used the AutoSum feature to quickly insert the SUM function. You inserted and deleted rows, columns, and worksheet cells. You selected cell ranges and moved cell contents using drag and drop or cut and paste. You also created new worksheets, renamed worksheets, and moved worksheets within the workbook. You edited your work by using editing mode, finding and replacing text, and using the spelling checker to correct errors. Finally, you previewed and then printed the contents of the workbook.

Key Terms

active cell
active sheet
active workbook
active workbook window
adjacent range
arithmetic operator
AutoComplete
autofit
AutoSum
cell
cell range
cell reference
chart sheet
clear
column heading
cut
date data
delete
drag and drop

editing mode
Excel
Find
formula
formula bar
formula view
function
landscape orientation
Microsoft Office Excel 2007
Name box
nonadjacent range
Normal view
number data
operator
order of precedence
Page Break Preview
Page Layout view
pixel
planning analysis sheet

point
portrait orientation
range
range reference
Replace
row heading
scale
sheet
sheet tab
spelling checker
spreadsheet
text data
text string
time data
truncate
what-if analysis
workbook
workbook window
worksheet

Practice		Review Assignments

Practice the skills you learned in the tutorial using the same case scenario.

There are no Data Files needed for the Review Assignments.

Amanda reviewed your work on the Customer Orders worksheet, and has another set of orders she wants you to enter. The data for the new customer orders is shown in Figure 1-36. In addition to calculating the charge for creating the DVDs, Amanda also wants to include the cost of shipping in the total charged to each customer.

Figure 1-36

Date	Last	First	Address	Phone	DVDs	Price per DVD	Shipping Charge
3/27/2010	Fleming	Doris	25 Lee St. Bedford, VA 24523	(540) 555-5681	7	$18.29	$7.49
4/4/2010	Ortiz	Thomas	28 Ridge Ln. Newfane, VT 05345	(802) 555-7710	13	$16.55	$9.89
4/8/2010	Dexter	Kay	150 Main St. Greenbelt, MD 20770	(301) 555-8823	25	$15.79	$7.23
4/9/2010	Sisk	Norman	250 East Maple Ln. Cranston, RI 02910	(401) 555-3350	15	$16.55	$10.55
4/17/2010	Romano	June	207 Jackston Ave. Westport, IN 47283	(812) 555-2681	22	$15.79	$13.95

Complete the following:

1. Open a blank workbook, and then save the workbook as **Order Report** in the Tutorial.01\Review folder.
2. Rename Sheet1 as **Documentation**, and then enter the following data into the worksheet:

Cell	Data	Cell	Data
A1	**RipCity Digital**		
A3	**Author**	B3	*your name*
A4	**Date**	B4	*the current date*
A5	**Purpose**	B5	**To track customer orders for RipCity Digital**

3. Rename Sheet2 as **Customer Orders**.
4. Delete Sheet3.
5. On the Customer Orders worksheet, in cell A1, enter **RipCity Digital**. In cell A3, enter **Customer Orders Report**. In cell A4, enter **March 27 to April 17, 2010**.
6. In cells A5 through H10, enter the data from Figure 1-36. In column D, enter the address text on two lines within each cell.
7. Set the width of column A to 10 characters, columns B and C to 12 characters, column D to 20 characters, and columns E, G, and H to 16 characters.
8. Autofit all of the rows in the worksheet to the cell contents.
9. In cell I5, enter **Total**. In cell I6, insert a formula that calculates the total charge for the first customer (the number of DVDs created multiplied by the price per DVD and then added to the shipping charge). Increase the width of column I to 11 characters.
10. Copy the formula in cell I6 and paste it into the cell range I7:I10.

11. In cell E11, enter **Total**. In cell F11, use the SUM function to calculate the total number of DVDs created for all customers. In cell I11, use AutoSum to insert the SUM function to calculate the total charges for all of the customer orders.

12. Use editing mode to make the following corrections:
    - In cell D6, change the street address from 25 Lee St. to **2500 Lee St.**
    - In cell F9, change the number of DVDs from 15 to **17**.
    - In cell H8, change the shipping charge from $7.23 to **$8.23**.

13. Use the Find and Replace commands to replace all occurrences of St. with **Street**, Ln. with **Lane**, and Ave. with **Avenue**.

14. Change the page layout of the Customer Orders worksheet to print in landscape orientation on a single page.

15. Preview and print the contents of the entire workbook.

16. Change the Customer Orders worksheet to formula view, landscape orientation, and scaled to fit on a single page. Preview and print the Customer Orders worksheet.

17. Return the view of the Customer Orders worksheet to Normal view, save your changes to the Order Report workbook, and then save the current workbook as **Revised Report** in the Tutorial.01\Review folder. (*Hint:* Use the Save As command on the Office Button to save the existing workbook with a new name.)

18. Kay Dexter has canceled her order with RipCity Digital. Remove her order from the Customer Orders worksheet.

19. Add the following order directly after the order placed by June Romano: date **4/22/2010**; name **Patrick Crawford**; address **200 Valley View Road, Rome, GA 30161**; phone **(706) 555-0998**; DVDs **14**; price per DVD **$16.55**; shipping charge **$12.45**

20. Verify that Excel automatically updates the formulas and functions used in the workbook so they properly calculate the total charge for this order and for all the orders.

21. Edit the title in cell A4, changing the ending date of the report from April 17 to **April 22**.

22. Save the workbook, preview and print the contents and formulas of the revised Customer Orders worksheet, close the workbook, and then submit the finished workbook and printouts to your instructor.

Apply | **Case Problem 1**

Use the skills you learned to complete an income statement for a bicycle company.

Data File needed for this Case Problem: Altac.xlsx

Altac Bicycles Deborah York is a financial consultant for Altac Bicycles, an online seller of bicycles and bicycle equipment based in Silver City, New Mexico. She has entered some financial information in an Excel workbook for an income statement she is preparing for the company. She asks you to enter the remaining data and formulas.

Complete the following:

1. Open the **Altac** workbook located in the Tutorial.01\Case1 folder, and then save the workbook as **Altac Bicycles** in the same folder.

2. Insert three new rows at the top of the Sheet1 worksheet, and then enter the following text on two lines within cell A1:
   Altac Bicycles
   Income Statement*

3. In cell A2, enter **For the Years Ended December 31, 2007 through December 31, 2009**.

4. In the range C6:E7, enter the following net sales and cost of sales figures:

	2009	2008	2007
Net Sales	**12,510**	**10,981**	**9,004**
Cost of Sales	**4,140**	**3,810**	**3,011**

5. In the range C11:E14, enter the following expense figures:

	2009	2008	2007
Salaries and Wages	**1,602**	**1,481**	**1,392**
Sales and Marketing	**2,631**	**2,012**	**1,840**
Administrative	**521**	**410**	**324**
Research and Development	**491**	**404**	**281**

6. Select the nonadjacent range C18:E18;C20:E20;C24:E24, and then enter the following values for Other Income, Income Taxes, and Shares, pressing the Enter or Tab key to navigate from cell to cell in the selected range:

	2009	2008	2007
Other Income	**341**	**302**	**239**
Income Taxes	**1,225**	**1,008**	**781**
Shares	**3,581**	**3,001**	**2,844**

7. In the range C8:E8, enter a formula to calculate the gross margin for each year, where the gross margin is equal to the net sales minus the cost of sales.

8. In the range C15:E15, enter the SUM function to calculate the total operating expenses for each year, where the total operating expenses is the sum of the four expense categories.

9. In the range C17:E17, enter a formula to calculate the operating income for each year, where operating income is equal to the gross margin minus the total operating expenses.

10. In the range C19:E19, enter a formula to calculate the pretax income for each year, where pretax income is equal to the operating income plus other income.

11. In the range C22:E22, enter a formula to calculate the company's net income for each year, where net income is equal to the pretax income minus income taxes.

12. In the range C25:E25, enter a formula to calculate the earnings per share for each year, where earnings per share is equal to the net income divided by the number of shares outstanding.

13. Use the spelling checker to correct and replace any spelling errors in the worksheet. Ignore the spelling of Altac.

14. In cell A18, use editing mode to capitalize the word *income*.

15. Increase the width of column A to 18 characters and increase the width of column B to 25 characters. Autofit the height of row 1.

16. Rename Sheet1 as **Income Statement**; rename Sheet2 as **Documentation** and move it to the beginning of the workbook; and then delete the Sheet3 worksheet.

17. In the Documentation worksheet, enter the following text and values:

Cell	Data	Cell	Data
A1	**Altac Bicycles**		
A3	**Author**	B3	*your name*
A4	**Date**	B4	*the current date*
A5	**Purpose**	B5	**Income statement for Altac Bicycles for 2007 through 2009**

18. Save the workbook, preview the workbook and make sure each worksheet in portrait orientation fits on one page in the printout, and then print the entire workbook. Close the workbook, and then submit the finished workbook and printouts to your instructor.

Apply | Case Problem 2

Use the skills you learned to complete a balance sheet for a food retailer.

Data File needed for this Case Problem: Halley.xlsx

Halley Foods Michael Li is working on the annual financial report for Halley Foods of Norman, Oklahoma. One part of the financial report will be the company's balance sheet for the previous three years. Michael has entered some of the labels for the balance sheet but wants you to finish the job by entering the actual values and formulas.

Complete the following:

1. Open the **Halley** workbook located in the Tutorial.01\Case2 folder, and then save the workbook as **Halley Foods** in the same folder.
2. Rename the Sheet1 worksheet as **Balance Sheet**, and then delete the Sheet2 and Sheet3 worksheets.
3. Insert three new rows at the top of the sheet, and then enter the following text on four lines within cell A1:
   Halley Foods
   Balance Sheet
   As of December 31
   For the Years 2007 through 2009
4. Change the width of column A to 30 characters, the width of column B to 20 characters, and the width of column C to 26 characters. Autofit the height of row 1.
5. Enter the assets and liability values shown in Figure 1-37 into the corresponding cells in the Balance Sheet worksheet for each of the last three years.

Figure 1-37

		2009	2008	2007
Current Assets	Cash and equivalents	796	589	423
	Short-term investments	1,194	1,029	738
	Accounts receivable	1,283	1,151	847
	Net inventories	683	563	463
	Deferred taxes	510	366	332
	Other current assets	162	137	103
Other Assets	Investments	7,077	5,811	4,330
	Restricted investments	910	797	681
	Property and equipment	779	696	420
	Other assets	1,178	484	485
Current Liabilities	Accounts payable	350	293	182
	Income taxes payable	608	442	342
	Accrued payroll	661	564	384
	Other accrued liabilities	1,397	1,250	775
Minority Interest		44	43	36
Shareholders' Equity	Preferred and common stock	5,557	4,821	3,515
	Retained earnings	5,666	4,007	3,401
	Other comprehensive income	289	203	187

6. Use AutoSum to calculate the total current assets, other assets, current liabilities, and shareholders' equity in the ranges D11:F11, D17:F17, D25:F25, and D33:F33, respectively, for each of the previous three years.

7. Insert a formula in the range D19:F19 to calculate the total assets (current plus other) for each year.

8. Insert a formula in the range D36:F36 to calculate the value of the total current liabilities plus the minority interest plus the total shareholders' equity for each year.

9. Use the spelling checker to correct any spelling mistakes in the Balance Sheet worksheet, and then proofread the worksheet.

10. Change the zoom level of the Balance Sheet worksheet to 70% in Normal view to view the entire contents of the sheet in the workbook window.

11. View the Balance Sheet worksheet in Page Layout view zoomed to 80%, and then scale the height and width of the worksheet to fit on one page.

12. Insert a new worksheet named **Documentation** at the beginning of the workbook.

13. In the Documentation worksheet, enter the following data:

Cell	Data	Cell	Data
A1	**Halley Foods**		
A3	**Author**	B3	*your name*
A4	**Date**	B4	*the current date*
A5	**Purpose**	B5	**Balance sheet for Halley Foods for 2007 through 2009**

14. Save, preview, and then print the entire Halley Foods Balance Sheet workbook.

15. Print the formula view of the Balance Sheet worksheet on two pages in landscape orientation. Return the Balance Sheet worksheet to Page Layout view when you're finished.

16. Save and close the workbook, and then submit the finished workbook and printouts to your instructor.

| Challenge | **Case Problem 3** |

Explore using Auto-Sum to calculate production statistics.

Data File needed for this Case Problem: Global.xlsx

Global Site GPS Kevin Hodge is a production assistant at Global Site GPS, a leading manufacturer of GPS devices located in Crestwood, Missouri. One of Kevin's jobs is to monitor output at the company's five regional plants. He wants to create an Excel workbook that reports the monthly production at the five sites, including the monthly average, minimum, and maximum production and total production for the previous year. He asks you to create the workbook that reports these statistics.

Complete the following:

1. Open the **Global** workbook located in the Tutorial.01\Case3 folder, and then save the workbook as **Global Site** in the same folder.

2. Rename the Sheet1 worksheet as **Production History**, and then insert 12 new rows at the top of the worksheet.

3. Increase the width of column A to 23 characters and the width of columns B through F to 14 characters.

4. In the range B7:F7, enter the titles **Plant1**, **Plant2**, **Plant3**, **Plant4**, and **Plant5**, respectively.

5. In the range A8:A11, enter **Total Units Produced**, **Average per Month**, **Maximum**, and **Minimum**, respectively.

⊕ **EXPLORE** 6. Select the range B26:F26, use AutoSum to calculate the sum of the production values for each of the five plants, and then drag and drop the selected cells to the range B8:F8.

⊕ **EXPLORE** 7. Select the range B26:F26, use AutoSum to calculate the average of the production values for each of the five plants, and then drag and drop the selected cells to the range B9:F9.

⊕ **EXPLORE** 8. Repeat Step 7 to calculate the maximum values for each of the five plants and then move those calculated values to the range B10:F10, and then repeat to calculate the minimum production values and drag and drop those calculated values to the range B11:F11.

9. In the Production History worksheet, enter the following data:

Cell	Data	Cell	Data
A1	**Global Site GPS**		
A2	**Production Report**		
A3	**Model**	B3	**MapTracker 201**
A4	**Year**	B4	**2010**
A5	**Total Units Produced**		

10. In cell B5, use the SUM function to add the values in the range B8:F8.

11. Insert a new worksheet named **Plant Directory** as the first worksheet in the workbook.

12. In cells A1 and A2, enter **Global Site GPS** and **Plant Directory**, respectively, and then enter the text shown in Figure 1-38 in the range A4:D9, making sure that the address is entered on two lines within the cell.

Figure 1-38

Plant	Plant Manager	Address	Phone
1	Karen Brookers	300 Commerce Avenue Crestwood, MO 63126	(314) 555-3881
2	Daniel Gomez	15 North Main Street Edison, NJ 08837	(732) 555-0012
3	Jody Hetrick	3572 Howard Lane Weston, FL 33326	(954) 555-4817
4	Yong Jo	900 South Street Kirkland, WA 98033	(425) 555-8775
5	Sandy Nisbett	3771 Water Street Helena, MT 59623	(406) 555-4114

13. Set the width of column B to 15 characters, the width of column C to 30 characters, and the width of column D to 16 characters. Autofit the height of each row to its content.

14. Insert a new worksheet named **Documentation** as the first worksheet in the workbook, and then enter the following data:

Cell	Data	Cell	Data
A1	**Global Site GPS**		
A3	**Author**	B3	*your name*
A4	**Date**	B4	*the current date*
A5	**Purpose**	B5	**Production report for Global Site GPS**

15. Switch the Production History worksheet to Page Layout view, change the orientation to landscape, and then verify that the worksheet fits on a single page.

16. Save your workbook, preview and print the workbook, close the workbook, and then submit the finished workbook and printouts to your instructor.

| Create | | **Case Problem 4** |

Create an Excel workbook to record service calls for a lawn service agency.

There are no Data Files needed for this Case Problem.

Green Lawns Green Lawns provides yard service and maintenance for homes in and around Mount Vernon, Ohio. Gary Taylor manages the accounts for Green Lawns and wants to use Excel to record weekly service calls made by the company. He asks you to create the workbook for him. Gary provides you the list of service calls made in the first week of August shown in Figure 1-39.

Figure 1-39

Customer	Address	Phone	Last Service	Hours	Base Fee	Hourly Rate
David Lane	391 Country Drive Mount Vernon, OH 43050	(740) 555-4439	8/2/2010	3	$35	$15.50
Robert Gomez	151 Apple Lane Mount Vernon, OH 43051	(740) 555-0988	8/2/2010	3.5	$35	$15.50
Sandra Lee	112 Main Street Mount Vernon, OH 43050	(740) 555-3773	8/3/2010	1.5	$20	$12.50
Gregory Sands	305 Country Drive Mount Vernon, OH 43050	(740) 555-4189	8/3/2010	4	$35	$17.50
Betty Oaks	205 Second Street Mount Vernon, OH 43049	(740) 555-0088	8/3/2010	1	$20	$12.50

Complete the following:

1. Open a blank workbook, and then save it as **Green Lawns** in the Tutorial.01\Case4 folder included with your Data Files.

2. Rename Sheet1 as **Documentation**, and then enter information documenting the workbook. Include the name of the company, your name, the current date, and a brief description of the purpose of the workbook. The layout and appearance of the worksheet is up to you.

3. In Sheet2, enter the service calls shown in Figure 1-39, and then enter appropriate formulas and functions to calculate the service charge for each customer. Green Lawns charges each customer a base fee plus a working fee that is equal to the hourly rate multiplied by the number of hours worked. Also, enter a formula to calculate the total charges for all customer calls. The layout and appearance of the page is up to you.

4. Rename Sheet2 as **Service Calls**, and then delete any unused sheets in the workbook.

5. Check the spelling in the workbook, correcting any spelling errors, and then proofread the workbook.

6. Save your workbook, preview the worksheets to ensure that each fits onto a single page, and then print the entire workbook. Close the workbook, and then submit the finished workbook and printouts to your instructor.

Research | **Internet Assignments**

Use the Internet to find and work with data related to the topics presented in this tutorial.

The purpose of the Internet Assignments is to challenge you to find information on the Internet that you can use to work effectively with this software. The actual assignments are updated and maintained on the Course Technology Web site. Log on to the Internet and use your Web browser to go to the Student Online Companion for New Perspectives Office 2007 at **www.course.com/np/office2007**. Then navigate to the Internet Assignments for this tutorial.

Assess | **SAM Assessment and Training**

If you have a SAM user profile, you may have access to hands-on instruction, practice, and assessment of the skills covered in this tutorial. Log in to your SAM account (**http://sam2007.course.com**) to launch any assigned training activities or exams that relate to the skills covered in this tutorial.

Review | **Quick Check Answers**

Session 1.1

1. chart sheets and worksheets
2. The active cell is surrounded by a thick border and its cell reference appears in the Name box.
3. C5
4. the Ctrl+Home keys
5. a combination of alphanumerical characters that form words and sentences (called a text string)
6. Enter the first line of text, press the Alt+Enter keys, and then type the second line of text.
7. Because it's a date; all dates are numbers formatted to appear in standard date formats.
8. Clearing a row removes only the contents of the row, deleting a row removes the contents and the row.

Session 1.2

1. Adjacent cell ranges contain a rectangular block of cells; nonadjacent cell ranges contain a collection of adjacent cell ranges.
2. A3:G5;J3:M5
3. =B4+B5+B6; =SUM(B4:B6)
4. Double-click the sheet tab, and then type a new name on the sheet tab.
5. Normal view shows the columns and rows of the worksheet. Page Layout view shows the layout of the worksheet as it appears on a page. Page Break Preview shows the page breaks within the worksheet. Formula view shows formulas rather than the values returned by the formulas.
6. to force a worksheet to print on one page
7. Press the Ctrl+` keys to switch to formula view.
8. as dotted lines

Ending Data Files

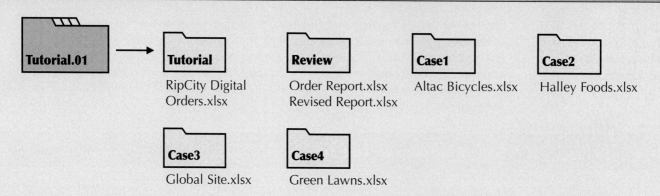

Formatting a Workbook

Formatting a Financial Report

Case | ExerComp Exercise Equipment

ExerComp, based in Mason, Ohio, manufactures electronic and computer components for fitness machines and sporting goods. At the upcoming annual sales meeting, sales managers will present reports that detail the sales history of different ExerComp products. Sales manager Tom Uhen will report on the recent sales history of the X310 heart rate monitor.

Tom has already created a workbook and entered the sales figures for the past two years. He wants you to make that data more readable and informative. To do this, you will work with formatting tools to modify the appearance of the data in each cell, the cell itself, and the entire worksheet. Because much of Tom's data has been stored in tables, you will also use some special formatting tools designed for tables.

Starting Data Files

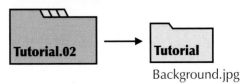

Tutorial.02 →

Tutorial	Review	Case1	Case2	Case3	Case4
Background.jpg	Paper.jpg	Frosti.xlsx	GrillRite.xlsx	Iowa.xlsx	Life.xlsx
ExerComp.xlsx	X410.xlsx				

Session 2.1

Formatting Workbooks

Tom already entered the data and some formulas in the worksheets, but the workbook is only a rough draft of what he wants to submit to the company. Tom's workbook has three worksheets. The Documentation sheet describes the workbook's purpose and content. The Yearly Sales sheet records the total sales of the X310 heart rate monitor for 2008 and 2009, including the total number of units sold per sales region (labeled R01 through R08) and the total revenue generated by those sales. The Monthly Sales sheet reports the number of X310 units sold in 2008 and 2009 by region and month as well as the corresponding increase in sales. You'll open the workbook and review its content.

To open the workbook:

▶ **1.** Open the **ExerComp** workbook located in the **Tutorial.02\Tutorial** folder included with your Data Files, and then save the workbook as **ExerComp Sales Report** in the same folder.

▶ **2.** In the Documentation sheet, enter your name in cell B4 and the current date in cell B5.

▶ **3.** Review the contents in the three worksheets.

In its current form, the data is difficult to read and interpret. Tom wants you to format the workbook contents to improve its readability and visual appeal. **Formatting** is the process of changing a workbook's appearance by defining the fonts, styles, colors, and decorative features. Formatting changes only the appearance of data—it does not affect the data itself.

InSight	**Formatting Workbooks Effectively**

A well-formatted workbook can be easier to read, establish a sense of professionalism, help draw attention to the points you want to make, and provide continuity between the worksheets. Too little formatting can make the data hard to understand, whereas too much formatting can overwhelm the data. Proper formatting is a balance between these two extremes. Always remember, the goal of formatting is not simply to make a "pretty workbook," but also to accentuate important trends and relationships in the data.

One goal of formatting is to maintain a consistent look within a workbook. Excel, along with all the Office 2007 programs, uses themes to do this. A **theme** is a collection of formatting that specifies the fonts, colors, and graphical effects used throughout the workbook. The Office theme is the default, although you can choose others or create your own. You can also use fonts and colors that are not part of the current theme.

As you work, **Live Preview** shows the effects of formatting options on the workbook's appearance before you apply them. This lets you see and evaluate different formats as you develop your workbook.

Formatting Text

Tom suggests that you first modify the title in the Documentation sheet. The appearance of text is determined by its **typeface**, which is the specific design used for the characters, including letters, numbers, punctuation marks, and symbols. Typefaces are organized into fonts; a **font** is a set of characters that employ the same typeface. Some commonly used fonts are Arial , Times New Roman , and Courier. **Serif fonts**, such as Times New Roman, have extra decorative strokes at the end of each character. **Sans serif fonts**, such as Arial, do not include these decorative strokes. Other fonts are purely decorative, such as a font used for specialized logos.

Fonts are organized into theme and non-theme fonts. A **theme font** is associated with a particular theme and used for headings and body text in the workbook. The Office theme uses the theme font Cambria for headings and the theme font Calibri for body text. When you don't want to associate a font with a particular design, you use a **non-theme font**. Text formatted with a non-theme font retains its appearance no matter what theme is used with the workbook.

Every font can be further formatted with a **font style**, such as *italic*, **bold**, or ***bold italic***, and special effects, such as underline, ~~strikethrough~~, and color to text. Finally, you can set the **font size** to increase or decrease the size of the text. Font sizes are measured in **points** where one point is approximately $1/72$ of an inch.

You'll format the company name displayed at the top of each worksheet to appear in large, bold letters using the default heading font from the Office theme. Tom wants the slogan "the Intelligent path to Fitness" displayed below the company name to appear in the heading font, but in smaller, italicized letters.

To format text in the Documentation sheet:

▶ 1. Click the **Documentation** sheet tab to make that worksheet active, and then click cell **A1** to make it active.

▶ 2. In the Font group on the Home tab, click the **Font arrow** to display a list of fonts available on your computer. The first two fonts are the theme fonts for headings and body text—Cambria and Calibri. See Figure 2-1.

Font list ◀ Figure 2-1

Trouble? If your screen displays more or less of the worksheet, your worksheet is at a different zoom level. If you want your worksheet zoomed to match the figures, click the Zoom In button on the status bar twice to increase the zoom magnification to 120%.

Tip

You can change the font size one point at a time. In the Font group on the Home tab, click the Increase Font Size or Decrease Font Size button.

3. Click **Cambria**. The company name in cell A1 changes to the Cambria font, the default headings font in the current theme.

4. In the Font group, click the **Font Size arrow** to display a list of font sizes, and then click **26**. The company name changes to 26 points.

5. In the Font group, click the **Bold** button **B**. The company name is boldfaced. Next, you'll format the company slogan.

6. Click cell **A2** to make it active. The slogan text is selected.

7. In the Font group, click the **Font arrow**, and then click **Cambria**. The slogan text changes to the Cambria font.

8. In the Font group, click the **Font Size arrow**, and then click **10**. The slogan text changes to 10 points.

9. In the Font group, click the **Italic** button **I**. The slogan is italicized.

10. Select the range **A4:A6**, click the **Bold** button **B** in the Font group, and then click cell **A7**. The column labels are bolded. See Figure 2-2.

Figure 2-2   **Formatted worksheet text**

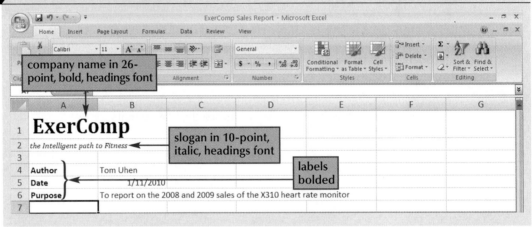

Working with Color

Color can transform a plain workbook filled with numbers and text into a powerful presentation that captures attention and adds visual emphasis to the points you want to make. By default, text is black and cells have no background fill color. You can add color to both the text and the cell background.

Colors are organized into two main categories. **Theme colors** are the 12 colors that belong to the workbook's theme. Four colors are designated for text and backgrounds, six colors are used for accents and highlights, and two colors are used for hyperlinks (followed and not followed links). These 12 colors are designed to work well together and to remain readable in all color combinations.

Ten **standard colors**—dark red, red, orange, yellow, light green, green, light blue, blue, dark blue, and purple—are always available regardless of the workbook's theme. You can also open an extended palette of 134 standard colors. In addition, you can create a **custom color** by specifying a mixture of red, blue, and green color values, making available 16.7 million custom colors—more colors than the human eye can distinguish. Some dialog boxes have an **automatic color** option that uses your Windows default text and background color values, usually black text on a white background.

Applying Font Color and Fill Color

Tom wants the labels in the Documentation sheet to stand out. You will change the ExerComp title and slogan to blue, and then you'll format the other labels in the worksheet with a blue background fill and a white font color.

To change the title and slogan font color and fill color:

▶ **1.** Select the range **A1:A2**.

▶ **2.** In the Font group on the Home tab, click the **Font Color button arrow** to display the available theme and standard colors. There are 10 theme colors (the two colors for hyperlinked text are not shown), and each theme color has five variations, or **accents**, in which a different tint or shading is applied to the theme color.

▶ **3.** Point to the **Blue** color (the eighth color) in the Standard Colors section. The color name appears in a ScreenTip. See Figure 2-3.

Font colors ◀ Figure 2-3

▶ **4.** Click the **Blue** color. The company name and slogan change to blue.

▶ **5.** Select the range **A4:A6**. You'll change both the fill and the font colors of these cells.

▶ **6.** In the Font group, click the **Fill Color button arrow** , and then click the **Blue** color in the Standard Colors section. The cell backgrounds change to blue.

▶ **7.** In the Font group, click the **Font Color button arrow** , and then click the **white** color (ScreenTip is White, Background1) in the Theme Colors section. The font color changes to white.

▶ **8.** Click cell **A7** to deselect the range. The white text on a blue background is visible. See Figure 2-4.

Figure 2-4 | Font colors and fill colors applied

Formatting Text Selections

The ExerComp logo usually appears in two colors—"Exer" in blue and "Comp" in red. Tom asks you to make this change to the text in cell A1. You'll need to format part of the cell content one way and the rest a different way. To do this, you first select the text you want to format in editing mode, and then apply the formatting to the selection. The **Mini toolbar** appears when you select text and contains buttons for commonly used text formats. You'll use the Mini toolbar to format "Comp" in a red font.

To format the "Comp" text selection:

▶ **1.** Double-click cell **A1** to select the cell and go into editing mode, and then select **Comp**. A transparent version of the Mini toolbar appears.

▶ **2.** Click the **Font Color button arrow** A ▾ on the Mini toolbar, and then click the **Red** color (the second color) in the Standard Colors section. The text color changes and the Mini toolbar remains open for additional formatting. See Figure 2-5.

Figure 2-5 | Mini toolbar used to format text

Trouble? If the Mini toolbar disappears before you can click the Font Color button arrow, you probably moved the pointer away from the Mini toolbar, pressed a key, or pressed a mouse button. Right-click the selected text to redisplay the Mini toolbar above a shortcut menu, immediately move your pointer to the Mini toolbar, and then repeat Step 2.

▶ **3.** Click cell **A7** to deselect the cell. The text "ExerComp" in cell A1 is blue and red.

Setting a Background Image

You can use a picture or image as the background for all the cells in a worksheet. An image can give the worksheet a textured appearance, like that of granite, wood, or fibered paper. The image is inserted until it fills the entire worksheet. The background image does not affect any cell's format or content. Any cells with a background color display the color on top, hiding that portion of the image. Background images do not print.

Tom has an image that resembles fibered paper that you will use as the background for the Documentation sheet.

To add a background image to the Documentation sheet:

▶ **1.** Click the **Page Layout** tab on the Ribbon. The page layout options appear on the Ribbon.

▶ **2.** In the Page Setup group, click the **Background** button. The Sheet Background dialog box opens.

▶ **3.** Navigate to the **Tutorial.02\Tutorial** folder included with your Data Files, click the **Background.jpg** image file, and then click the **Insert** button. The image file is added to the background of the Documentation sheet.

Next, you'll change the fill color of the cells with the author's name, the date, and the workbook's purpose to white to highlight them in the worksheet.

▶ **4.** Select the range **B4:B6**, and then click the **Home** tab on the Ribbon.

▶ **5.** In the Font group, click the **Fill Color button arrow** ☒, and then click the **white** color in the Theme Colors section.

▶ **6.** Increase the width of column B to **55** characters, and then click cell **A7** to deselect the range. See Figure 2-6.

Background image added to the Documentation sheet ◀ Figure 2-6

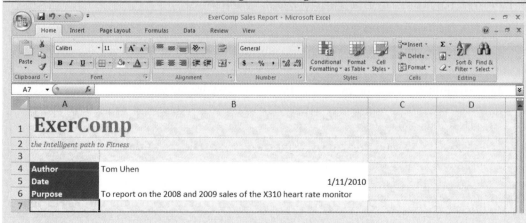

Color, used wisely, can enhance any workbook. Too much color can be just as bad as "not enough" color. An overuse of color can cause readers' eyes to wander around the workbook without focusing on a central point. As you format a workbook, keep in mind the following tips:

- Use colors from the same theme within a workbook to maintain a consistent look and feel across the worksheets. If the built-in themes do not fit your needs, you can create a custom theme.
- Use colors to differentiate types of cell content and to direct users where to enter data. For example, format a worksheet so formula results appear in cells without a fill color and users enter data in cells with a light gray fill color.
- Avoid garish color combinations that can annoy the reader and be difficult to read.
- Print on color and black-and-white printers to ensure that the output is readable in both versions.
- Understand your printer's limitations and features. Colors that look good on your monitor might not print well.
- Be sensitive to your audience. About 8% of all men and 0.5% of all women have some type of color blindness and might not be able to see the text with certain color combinations. Red-green color blindness is the most common color blindness, so avoid using red text on a green background or green text on a red background.

Formatting Data

The Yearly Sales worksheet contains the annual sales figures from 2008 and 2009 for the X310 heart rate monitor. The top of the worksheet displays the number of units sold in each sales region per year, and the bottom displays the sales revenue generated by region per year. You'll add formulas to calculate the total sales for each year as well as the difference and percentage difference in sales from one year to another.

To enter formulas in the Yearly Sales worksheet:

▶ 1. Click the **Yearly Sales** sheet tab. The Yearly Sales worksheet becomes active.

▶ 2. In cells B15 and B26, enter **Total**; in cells E6 and E17, enter **Increase**; in cells F6 and F17, enter **% Increase**; and then select cell **C15**.

▶ 3. In the Editing group on the Home tab, click the **Sum** button Σ, and then press the **Enter** key. The formula =SUM(C7:C14) is entered in the cell, adding the numbers in the range C7:C14.

▶ 4. Select cell **C15**, and then, in the Clipboard group, click the **Copy** button. The formula is copied to the Clipboard.

Next, you'll paste the formula into a nonadjacent range. Remember, to select a nonadjacent range, select the first cell or range, press and hold the Ctrl key as you select other cells or ranges, and then release the Ctrl key.

▶ 5. Select the range **D15;C26:D26**, and then, in the Clipboard group, click the **Paste** button. The formula is pasted into cells D15, C26, and D26, adding the values in each column.

▶ 6. Select cell **E7**, and then enter the formula **=D7–C7** to calculate the increase in sales from 2008 to 2009 for region R01.

▶ 7. Select cell **F7**, and then enter the formula **=E7/C7** to calculate the percentage increase from 2008 to 2009.

8. Select the range **E7:F7**, and then, in the Clipboard group, click the **Copy** button.

9. Select the range **E8:F15;E18:F26**, and then, in the Clipboard group, click the **Paste** button. The formulas are copied into the selected cells.

10. Click cell **A6** to deselect the range. See Figure 2-7.

Formulas added to the Yearly Sales sheet   **Figure 2-7**

	A	B	C	D	E	F	G
6	Units Sold	Region	2008 Sales	2009 Sales	Increase	% Increase	
7		R01	3605	3853	248	0.068793343	
8		R02	3966	3842	-124	-0.031265759	
9		R03	3760	4035	275	0.073138298	
10		R04	3777	4063	286	0.075721472	
11		R05	3974	3725	-249	-0.062657272	
12		R06	3656	3937	281	0.076859956	
13		R07	3554	3875	321	0.090320765	
14		R08	3844	3844	0	0	
15		Total	30136	31174	1038	0.034443855	
16							
17	Revenue	Region	2008 Sales	2009 Sales	Increase	% Increase	
18		R01	104364.75	115397.35	11032.6	0.105711938	
19		R02	114815.7	115067.9	252.2	0.002196564	
20			108852	120848.25	11996.25	0.110206978	
21			109344.15	121686.85	12342.7	0.112879381	
22			115047.3	111563.75	-3483.55	-0.030279285	
23		R06	105841.2	117913.15	12071.95	0.114057191	
24		R07	102888.3	116056.25	13167.95	0.127982968	
25		R08	111283.8	115127.8	3844	0.034542314	
26		Total	872437.2	933661.3	61224.1	0.070175939	

formulas calculate the sales and % increases

formulas calculate the totals of the data

Documentation | **Yearly Sales** | Monthly Sales

Ready   120%

The sales figures are hard to read, making them difficult to interpret and understand. By default, values appear in the **General number format**, which, for the most part, displays numbers exactly as you enter them. Calculated values show as many digits after the decimal point as will fit in the cell and the last displayed digit is rounded, as you can see with the percentage increase values in column F. Only the displayed number is rounded; the actual value stored in the cell is not. Calculated values too large to fit into the cell are displayed in scientific notation.

Formatting Numbers

The Number group on the Home tab has buttons for formatting the appearance of numbers. You can select a number format, apply accounting or other currency formats, change a number to a percentage, insert a comma as a thousands separator, and increase or decrease the number of digits displayed to the right of the decimal point.

You'll add a thousands separator to the sales values to make them easier to read and remove the digits shown to the right of the decimal point because the data values for units sold will always be whole numbers. You'll format the percentage difference values as percentages with two decimal places. Tom also wants you to format the revenue values in the range C18:E26 as currency by adding dollar signs. Because applying dollar signs to large columns of numbers often makes them unreadable, standard accounting practice displays currency symbols only in the first and last rows of the range.

To format the units sold, percentage differences, and revenue numbers:

1. Select the range **C7:E15;C18:E26**, and then, in the Number group on the Home tab, click the **Comma Style** button. The numbers include a thousands separator, but still display two digits to the right of the decimal point.

2. Select the range **C7:E15**, and then, in the Number group, click the **Decrease Decimal** button 🔽 twice. The two extra digits are removed.

3. Select the range **F7:F15;F18:F26**, and then, in the Number group, click the **Percent Style** button %. The values now include the percentage symbol.

4. In the Number group, click the **Increase Decimal** button 🔼 twice. Two digits are added to the right of the decimal point.

5. Select the range **C18:E18;C26:E26**, and then, in the Number group, click the **Accounting Number Format** button $. The first row and the Total row display the currency symbol.

6. Click cell **A6** to deselect the range. See Figure 2-8.

Figure 2-8 | **Worksheet after formatting numbers**

	A	B	C	D	E	F	G
6	Units Sold	Region	2008 Sales	2009 Sales	Increase	% Increase	
7		R01	3,605	3,853	248	6.88%	
8		R02	3,966	3,842	(124)	-3.13%	
		R03	3,760	4,035	275	7.31%	
		R04	3,777	4,063	286	7.57%	
		R05	3,974	3,725	(249)	-6.27%	
		R06	3,656	3,937	281	7.69%	
13		R07	3,554	3,875	321	9.03%	
14		R08	3,844	3,844	-	0.00%	
15		Total	30,136	31,174	1,038	3.44%	
16							
17	Revenue	Region	2008 Sales	2009 Sales	Increase	% Increase	
18		R01	$ 104,364.75	$ 115,397.35	$ 11,032.60	10.57%	
19		R02	114,815.70	115,067.90	252.20	0.22%	
		R03	108,852.00	120,848.25	11,996.25	11.02%	
		R04	109,344.15	121,686.85	12,342.70	11.29%	
		R05	115,047.30	111,563.75	(3,483.55)	-3.03%	
		R06	105,841.20	117,913.15	12,071.95	11.41%	
		R07	102,888.30	116,056.25	13,167.95	12.80%	
25		R08	111,283.80	115,127.80	3,844.00	3.45%	
26		Total	$ 872,437.20	$ 933,661.30	$ 61,224.10	7.02%	

units include commas and no decimal places

percentages include two decimal places and symbol

first and last rows display the currency symbol

revenues include commas and two decimal places

Documentation | **Yearly Sales** | Monthly Sales

Tom examines this reformatted data and notes that the company sold 1,038 more units in 2009 than in 2008—an increase of 3.44%, which increased revenue by $61,224.10, or 7.02%. This was not uniform across all sales regions. Total sales and revenue for Region R05, for example, decreased from 2008 to 2009.

Formatting Dates and Times

Although dates and times in Excel appear as text, they are actually numbers that measure the interval between the specified date and time and January 1, 1900 at 12:00 a.m. You can then calculate date and time intervals, and you can format a date or time value. For example, you can apply a date format that displays the day of the week for any date value stored in your worksheet.

The date in the Documentation sheet is an abbreviated format, *mm/dd/yyyy*. Tom wants you to use an extended format that includes the day of the week, the full month name, the day, and the year. This Long Date format is a built-in date format.

To format the date in the Long Date format:

▶ 1. Click the **Documentation** sheet tab to make that worksheet active, and then select cell **B5**.

▶ 2. In the Number group on the Home tab, click the **Number Format arrow** to open a list of built-in number formats.

▶ 3. Click **Long Date**. The date format changes to show the weekday name, month name, day, and year. See Figure 2-9.

Formatted date ◀ **Figure 2-9**

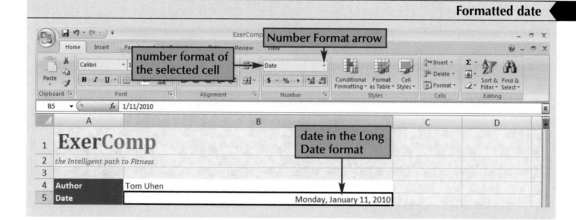

Formatting Dates for International Audiences | InSight

When your workbooks are intended for international audiences, be sure to use a date format that will be clear to everyone, such as November 10, 2010 or 10 November 2010. Many countries use a day/month/year format for dates rather than the month/day/year format commonly used in the United States. For example, the date 10/11/2010 is read as October 11, 2010 by people in the United States but as November 10, 2010 by people in most other countries.

Formatting Worksheet Cells

The date in the Documentation worksheet is formatted to display as text. Because all dates are actually numbers, they are right-aligned in the cell by default, regardless of their date format. Tom asks you to left-align the date to make it easier to read.

Aligning Cell Content

In addition to left and right alignments, you can change the vertical and horizontal alignments of cell content to make a worksheet more readable. You can also increase or decrease the space between the cell content and the cell border. In general, you should center column titles, left-align text, and right-align numbers to keep their decimal places lined up within the column. Figure 2-10 describes the alignment buttons located in the Alignment group on the Home tab.

Figure 2-10 ▶ **Alignment buttons**

Button	Description
☰	Aligns the cell content with the cell's top edge
☰	Vertically centers the cell content within the cell
☰	Aligns the cell content with the cell's bottom edge
☰	Aligns the cell content with the cell's left edge
☰	Horizontally centers the cell content within the cell
☰	Aligns the cell content with the cell's right edge
⯇☰	Decreases the size of the indentation used in the cell
☰⯈	Increases the size of the indentation used in the cell
✎▾	Rotates the cell content to an angle within the cell
☰	Forces the cell text to wrap within the cell borders
☰	Merges the selected cells into a single cell

You'll left-align the date in the Documentation worksheet and center the column titles in the Yearly Sales worksheet.

To left-align the date and center the column titles:

▶ 1. If necessary, select cell **B5**.

▶ 2. In the Alignment group on the Home tab, click the **Align Text Left** button ☰. The date shifts to the left edge of the cell.

▶ 3. Click the **Yearly Sales** sheet tab to make that worksheet active, and then select the range **C6:F6;C17:F17**.

▶ 4. In the Alignment group, click the **Center** button ☰. The column titles in columns C, D, E, and F are centered.

Indenting Cell Content

Sometimes, you want a cell's content moved a few spaces from the cell edge. This is particularly useful for entries that are considered subsections of a worksheet. For example, Tom recorded sales for eight regions and then added the totals. Each region can be considered a subsection, and Tom thinks it would look better if the region labels were indented a few spaces. You increase the indentation by roughly one character each time you click the Increase Indent button in the Alignment group on the Home tab. To decrease or remove an indentation, click the Decrease Indent button. You'll increase the indent for the region labels.

To indent the region labels:

▶ 1. Select the range **B7:B14;B18:B25**.

▶ 2. In the Alignment group on the Home tab, click the **Increase Indent** button ☰. Each region label indents one space.

▶ 3. Click cell **A6** to deselect the range. See Figure 2-11.

Centered and indented text ◄ **Figure 2-11**

You can make all text visible within a cell rather than extending the text into an adjacent empty cell or truncating it. Just click the Wrap Text button in the Alignment group on the Home tab. The row height increases as needed to wrap all the text within the cell.

Merging Cells

In the Yearly Sales worksheet, Tom wants the title "X310 Yearly Sales Analysis" in cell A4 centered over columns A through F. So far, you've aligned text only *within* a cell. One way to align text over several columns or rows is to **merge**, or combine, several cells into one cell. When you merge cells, only the content from the upper-left cell in the range is retained and the upper-left cell becomes the merged cell reference.

After you merge a range into a single cell, you can realign its content. The Merge button in the Alignment group on the Home tab includes a variety of merge options. Merge & Center merges the range into one cell and horizontally centers the content. Merge Across merges each of the rows in the selected range across the columns in the range. Merge Cells merges the range into a single cell, but does not horizontally center the cell content. Unmerge Cells reverses a merge, returning the merged cell back into a range of individual cells.

Tom wants you to merge and center the title in cell A4 across the range A4:F4.

To merge and center the range with the title:

▶ **1.** Select the range **A4:F4**.

▶ **2.** In the Alignment group on the Home tab, click the **Merge & Center** button 🔳. The range A4:F4 merges into one cell with a cell reference of A4 and the text is centered within the cell. See Figure 2-12.

| Figure 2-12 | Merged range with centered text |

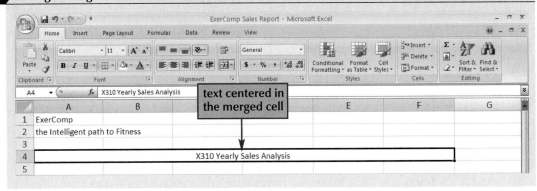

Rotating Cell Content

Text and numbers are oriented within a cell horizontally from left to right. To save space or to provide visual interest to a worksheet, you can rotate the cell contents so that they appear at any angle or orientation. These options are available on the Orientation button in the Alignment group on the Home tab.

Tom wants you to merge and center the ranges with the labels, and then rotate the labels in the merged cells A6 and A17 so they look better and take up less room.

To rotate the labels:

▶ **1.** Select the range **A6:A15**.

▶ **2.** In the Alignment group on the Home tab, click the **Merge & Center** button 🔳. The text from cell A6 is centered in the merged cell.

▶ **3.** In the Alignment group, click the **Orientation** button 📎▾, and then click **Rotate Text Up**. The cell text rotates 90 degrees counterclockwise.

▶ **4.** In the Alignment group, click the **Middle Align** button ☰. The rotated text vertically aligns within the merged cell.

▶ **5.** Select the range **A17:A26**, and then repeat Steps 2 through 4 to merge and center, rotate, and align the text.

▶ **6.** Reduce the width of column A to **5** characters. See Figure 2-13.

Merged and rotated cell text | **Figure 2-13**

	A	B	C	D	E	F	G	H
6		Region	2008 Sales	2009 Sales	Increase	% Increase		
7		R01	3,605	3,853	248	6.88%		
8		R02	3,966	3,842	(124)	-3.13%		
9		R03	3,760	4,035	275	7.31%		
10	Units Sold	R04	3,777	4,063	286	7.57%		
11		R05	3,974	3,725	(249)	-6.27%		
12		R06	3,656	3,937	281	7.69%		
13		R07	3,554	3,875	321	9.03%		
14		R08	3,844	3,844	-	0.00%		
15		Total	30,136	31,174	1,038	3.44%		
16								
17		Region	les	2009 Sales	Increase	% Increase		
18		R01	104,364.75 $	115,397.35 $	11,032.60	10.57%		
19		R02	114,815.70	115,067.90	252.20	0.22%		
20		R03	108,852.00	120,848.25	11,996.25	11.02%		
21	Revenue	R04	109,344.15	121,686.85	12,342.70	11.29%		
22		R05	115,047.30	111,563.75	(3,483.55)	-3.03%		
23		R06	105,841.20	117,913.15	12,071.95	11.41%		
24		R07	102,888.30	116,056.25	13,167.95	12.80%		
25		R08	111,283.80	115,127.80	3,844.00	3.45%		
26		Total	$ 872,437.20 $	933,661.30 $	61,224.10	7.02%		

rotated labels take up less space in the merged cells

Sheets: Documentation / Yearly Sales / Monthly Sales

Adding Cell Borders

When a worksheet is printed, the gridlines that surround the cells are not printed by default. Sometimes you will want to include such lines to enhance the readability of the rows and columns of data. One way to do this is by adding a line, or **border**, around a cell or range. You can add borders to the left, top, right, or bottom of a cell or range, around an entire cell, or around the outside edges of a range. You can also specify the thickness of and the number of lines in the border. To create a border, use the Border button located in the Font group on the Home tab.

Tom wants you to add borders to the column titles and Total rows. Standard accounting practice is to add a single top border and a double bottom border to the Total row to clearly identify a summary row from financial data.

To add cell borders to the column labels and Total rows:

1. Select the range **B6:F6;B17:F17**. You'll add a bottom border to these column labels.

2. In the Font group on the Home tab, click the **Border button arrow** , and then click **Bottom Border**. A bottom border is added to the selected cells.

3. Select the range **B15:F15;B26:F26**. You'll add top and bottom borders to these Total rows.

4. In the Font group, click the **Border button arrow** , and then click **Top and Double Bottom Border**. The Total rows both have a single top border and a double bottom border, which is standard accounting practice.

5. Click cell **A5** to deselect the range. See Figure 2-14.

| Figure 2-14 | Borders added to cells |

Working with the Format Cells Dialog Box

The buttons on the Home tab provide quick access to the most common formatting choices. For more options, you can use the Format Cells dialog box. For example, the numbers in cells E8 and E11 are displayed in parentheses to indicate that they are negative. Although parentheses are common in accounting to indicate negative currency values, Tom wants you to reformat the units sold numbers to display negative numbers with a minus symbol. You can do this in the Format Cells dialog box.

To open the Format Cells dialog box:

1. Select the range **C7:E15**.

2. In the Number group on the Home tab, click the **Dialog Box Launcher**. The Format Cells dialog box opens with the Number tab active.

The Format Cells dialog box has six tabs, each focusing on a different set of formatting options. You can apply the formats in this dialog box to selected worksheet cells. The six tabs are as follows:

- **Number**: Provides options for formatting the appearance of numbers, including dates and numbers treated as text (for example, telephone or Social Security numbers)
- **Alignment**: Provides options for how data is aligned within a cell
- **Font**: Provides options for selecting font types, sizes, styles, and other formatting attributes such as underlining and font colors
- **Border**: Provides options for adding cell borders
- **Fill**: Provides options for creating and applying background colors and patterns to cells
- **Protection**: Provides options for locking or hiding cells to prevent other users from modifying their contents

Although you've applied many of these formats from the Home tab, the Format Cells dialog box presents them in a different way and provides more options. You'll use the Number tab to change the number format for the selected cells. Remember, modifying the number format does not affect the value stored in the workbook.

To set the format for negative numbers of units:

▶ **1.** In the Category list on the left side of the Format Cells dialog box, click **Number**.

▶ **2.** Verify that **0** (zero) appears in the Decimal places box.

▶ **3.** Verify that the **Use 1000 Separator (,)** check box contains a check mark.

▶ **4.** In the Negative numbers list, verify that **−1,234** (the first option) is selected. See Figure 2-15.

Number tab in the Format Cells dialog box ◀ **Figure 2-15**

▶ **5.** Click the **OK** button. The Format Cells dialog box closes and the negative numbers in the range C7:E15 appear with minus symbols, a comma as the thousands separator, and no decimal places.

Tom wants the bottom border color used for the column titles changed from black to green. You'll use the Border tab in the Format Cells dialog box to make this change.

To set the border color for the column title cells:

▶ **1.** Select the range **B6:F6;B17:F17**.

▶ **2.** In the Font group on the Home tab, click the **Borders button arrow** , and then click **More Borders**. The Format Cells dialog box opens with the Border tab active.

In the Border tab, you can select a line style ranging from thick to thin, choose double to dotted lines, and place these lines anywhere around the cells in the selected range. Right now, you only want to set the border line color.

▶ **3.** In the Line group, click the **Color** arrow to display the color palette, and then click **Green** (the sixth color) in the Standard Colors section.

▶ **4.** Click the bottom border of the border preview. A green bottom border is added to the preview. See Figure 2-16.

Figure 2-16 ▶ **Border tab in the Format Cells dialog box**

▶ **5.** Click the **OK** button. The dialog box closes and the cells with column titles have a green bottom border.

Copying and Pasting Formats

You have not yet formatted the titles in cells A1 and A2 of the Yearly Sales worksheet to match the Documentation sheet. You could repeat the same steps to format these cells, but a quicker method is to copy the formats from the Documentation worksheet into the Yearly Sales worksheet.

Copying Formats with the Format Painter

The **Format Painter** copies the formatting from one cell or range to another cell or range, without duplicating any of the data. Using the Format Painter is a fast and efficient way of maintaining a consistent look and feel throughout a workbook.

You'll use the Format Painter to copy the cell formats from the range A1:A2 in the Documentation sheet into the same range in the Yearly Sales worksheet.

To copy and paste the format:

▶ 1. Click the **Documentation** sheet tab to make that worksheet active, and then select the range **A1:A2**.

▶ 2. In the Clipboard group on the Home tab, click the **Format Painter** button 🖌. The formats from the selected cells are copied to the Clipboard.

▶ 3. Click the **Yearly Sales** sheet tab to make that worksheet active, and then select the range **A1:A2**. The formatting from the Documentation sheet is removed from the Clipboard and applied to the selected cells except for the red color you applied to "Comp." Format Painter does not copy formatting applied to text selections.

▶ 4. Double-click cell **A1** to go into editing mode, and then select **Comp** in the text string.

▶ 5. Click the **Font Color button arrow** 🅰 ▾ on the Mini toolbar, and then click **Red** (the second color) in the Standard Colors section. The selected text changes to red.

▶ 6. Press the **Enter** key to exit editing mode.

▶ 7. Select the range **A1:A2** in the Yearly Sales worksheet, and then repeat Steps 2 through 6 to copy the formatting to the range A1:A2 in the Monthly Sales worksheet.

Tip

To paste a format to multiple selections, double-click the Format Painter button, select each cell or range to format, and then click the Format Painter button again to turn it off.

Copying Formats with the Paste Options Button

The Format Painter copies and pastes only formatting. When you copy and paste, you can also use the Paste Options button 📋, which lets you choose whether to paste the formatting from a copied range along with its contents. As shown in Figure 2-17, each time you paste, the Paste Options button appears in the lower-right corner of the pasted cell or range. When you click the Paste Options button, you can choose from a list of pasting options, such as pasting only the values or only the formatting.

Using the Paste Options button ◀ Figure 2-17

Copying Formats with Paste Special

The Paste Special command is another way to control what you paste from the Clipboard. To use Paste Special, select and copy a range, select the range where you want to paste the Clipboard contents, click the Paste button arrow in the Clipboard group on the Home tab, and then click Paste Special to open the dialog box shown in Figure 2-18. From the Paste Special dialog box, you can specify exactly what you want to paste.

| Figure 2-18 | Paste Special dialog box |

You can use the Transpose option in the Paste Special dialog box to paste a range of numbers cut from a row into a column. You can also use Paste Special to quickly modify all the values in a range. For example, you can copy the value 5 from a cell, select the range, open the Paste Special dialog box, click the Add option button in the Operation group, and then click the OK button. Excel adds 5 to every value in the selected range.

Applying Styles

A workbook often contains several cells that store the same type of data. For example, each worksheet might have a cell displaying the sheet title, or a range of financial data might have several cells containing summary totals. Using the same format on cells storing the same type of data gives your workbook a consistent look. You can do this using the Format Painter or by copying and pasting a format from one cell to another.

The Format Painter is effective, but it can also be time consuming if you have to copy the same format to many cells. Moreover, if you decide to modify the format, you must copy and paste the revised format all over again. Another way to ensure that cells displaying the same type of data use the same format is with styles. A **style** is a collection of formatting. For example, you can create a style to display sheet titles in a bold, white, 20-point Calibri font on a blue background. You can then apply that style to any sheet title in a workbook. If you later revise the style, the appearance of any cell formatted with that style is updated automatically. This saves you the time and effort of reformatting each cell individually.

Excel has a variety of built-in styles to format worksheet titles, column and row totals, and cells with emphasis. You used the built-in Currency and Percent styles when you formatted data in the Yearly Sales worksheet as currency and percentages. Some styles are connected to the workbook's current theme.

Applying Styles | Reference Window

- Select the cell or range to which you want to apply a style.
- In the Styles group on the Home tab, click the Cell Styles button.
- Point to each style in the Cell Styles gallery to see a Live Preview of that style on the selected cell or range.
- Click the style you want to apply to the selected cell or range.

Tom asks you to use some of the built-in styles to add more color and visual interest to the Yearly Sales worksheet.

To apply built-in styles to the Yearly Sales sheet:

▶ **1.** Click the **Yearly Sales** sheet tab to make that worksheet active, and then select the merged cell **A4**.

▶ **2.** In the Styles group on the Home tab, click the **Cell Styles** button. The Cell Styles gallery opens.

▶ **3.** Point to the **Heading 1** style in the Titles and Headings section. Live Preview shows cell A4 in a 15-point, bold font with a solid blue bottom border. See Figure 2-19.

Cell Styles gallery ◀ **Figure 2-19**

▶ **4.** Move the pointer over different styles in the Cell Styles gallery to preview cell A4 with each style, and then click the **Heading 1** style. The style is applied to cell A4.

▶ **5.** Select the range **B6:F6;B17:F17**, click the **Cell Styles** button, and then click the **Accent1** style in the Themed Cell Styles section. Each of the column headings is formatted.

▶ **6.** Select the range **E7:F15;E18:F26**, click the **Cell Styles** button, and then click the **20% – Accent1** style in the Themed Cell Styles section. The calculated values are formatted differently from the data.

▶ **7.** Click cell **F1** to deselect the range, and then zoom the worksheet to **90%**. See Figure 2-20.

Figure 2-20   **Formatted yearly sales data**

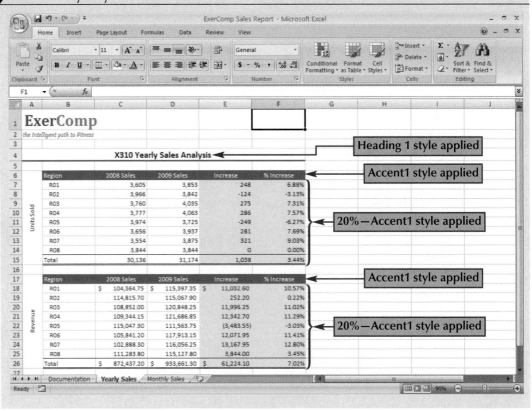

If the built-in styles don't meet your needs, you can modify an existing style or create a new one. To modify a style, right-click the style in the Cell Styles gallery, click Modify on the shortcut menu to open the Style dialog box, and then click the Format button to change the formatting for that style. Any cells formatted with that style are automatically updated. To create a new style, click New Cell Style in the Cell Styles gallery to open the Style dialog box, type a name in the Style name box, and then click the Format button to select the formatting for that style. The new cell style is added to the Cell Styles gallery.

Working with Themes

Most of the formatting you've applied so far is based on the workbook's current theme—the default Office theme. As you've seen, fonts, colors, and cell styles are organized in theme and non-theme categories. The appearance of these fonts, colors, and cell styles depends on the workbook's current theme. If you change the theme, the formatting of these elements also changes.

You'll change the workbook's theme to see its effect on the workbook's appearance.

To change the workbook's theme:

1. Click the **Page Layout** tab on the Ribbon, and then, in the Themes group, click the **Themes** button. The Themes gallery opens. Office—the current theme—is the default.

2. Point to each theme in the Themes gallery. Live Preview shows the impact of each theme on the appearance of the Yearly Sales worksheet.

▶ **3.** Click the **Aspect** theme. The Aspect theme is applied to the workbook. See Figure 2-21.

Yearly Sales data with the Aspect theme applied ◀ Figure 2-21

Changing the theme has made a significant difference in the worksheet's appearance. The most obvious changes are the fill colors and the fonts. Only elements directly tied to a theme change when you select a different theme. The cells you formatted with the Accent1 cell style changed because the Accent1 color is blue in the Office theme and orange in the Aspect theme. The Heading 1 style you used for the titles in cells A1 and A2 uses the Cambria typeface in the Office theme and the Verdana typeface in the Aspect theme. The Aspect theme also uses a different font for body text, which is why the rest of the text changed size and appearance.

The logo colors in cell A1 did not change because you used two standard colors, blue and red, which are not part of a theme. Changing the theme does not affect these colors.

Tom prefers the default Office theme, so you'll switch back to that theme and then save the workbook.

To select the Office theme and save the workbook:

▶ **1.** In the Themes group on the Page Layout tab, click the **Themes** button, and then click the **Office** theme.

▶ **2.** Save your changes to the workbook.

InSight	**Sharing Styles and Themes**

If you're part of a team creating files with Microsoft Office, you might want to use a common style and design theme for all your projects. The easiest way to do this is by saving the styles and themes as permanent files other members of your workgroup can use.

To copy a style from one workbook to another, open the workbook with the styles you want to copy, and then open the workbook in which you want to copy those styles. In the Styles group on the Home tab, click the Cell Styles button, and then click Merge Styles. The Merge Styles dialog box opens, listing the currently open workbooks. Select the workbook with the styles you want to copy, and then click the OK button to copy those styles into the current workbook. If you modify any styles, you must copy the styles to the other workbook; Excel does not update styles between workbooks.

You can save a workbook's theme as a file that can be used in other workbooks or Office files. Microsoft Excel, Word, and PowerPoint use the same file format for their theme files. To save a theme, in the Themes group on the Page Layout tab, click the Themes button, and then click Save Current Theme. The Save Current Theme dialog box opens. Select a save location (in a default Theme folder on your computer or another folder), type a descriptive name in the File name box, and then click the Save button. A Theme file saved in a default Theme folder appears in the Themes gallery, and any changes made to the theme are reflected in any Office file that uses that theme.

You've completed some formatting of Tom's workbook. In the process, you've formatted cells and ranges, applied built-in styles, and applied a new theme. In the next session, you'll work with table styles, conditional formatting, and page layout tools.

Review	**Session 2.1 Quick Check**

1. What is the difference between a serif font and a sans serif font?
2. What is the difference between a standard color and a theme color?
3. What is the General number format?
4. Why are dates right-aligned within a worksheet cell by default?
5. The range A1:C5 is merged into a single cell. What is the cell reference of this merged cell?
6. Where can you access all the formatting options for worksheet cells?
7. You want the range A1:A3 on all the worksheets in your workbook to be formatted the same way. Discuss two methods of applying the same format to different ranges.

Session 2.2

Formatting the Monthly Sales Worksheet

The Monthly Sales worksheet contains the sales results by month for the eight sales regions in 2008 and 2009. Tom's main goal for this data is to identify trends. He's more interested in the "big picture" than in specific numbers. He wants to know which sales regions are performing well, which are underperforming, and, in general, how the sales change throughout the year.

The top of the worksheet contains sales for 2008 and 2009. The bottom of the worksheet displays the increase in sales from 2008 to 2009 for each region and month. You need to calculate the monthly totals and do some basic formatting.

To calculate the monthly totals:

▶ **1.** If you took a break after the previous session, open the ExerComp Sales Report workbook located in the Tutorial.02\Tutorial folder included with your Data Files.

▶ **2.** Click the **Monthly Sales** sheet tab to make the worksheet active, and then, in cells B19, B34, B49, K6, K21, and K36, enter **Total**.

▶ **3.** Select the range **K7:K18;K22:K33;K37:K48**, and then click the **Home** tab on the Ribbon.

▶ **4.** In the Editing group, click the **Sum** button Σ to add the total of each row.

▶ **5.** Select the range **C19:K19;C34:K34;C49:K49**, and then, in the Editing group, click the **Sum** button Σ to add the total of each column.

Next, you'll format the row and column titles.

To format the titles:

▶ **1.** Select the range **A4:K4**, and then, in the Alignment group on the Home tab, click the **Merge & Center** button. The title is centered in the merged cell.

▶ **2.** In the Styles group, click the **Cell Styles** button, and then click the **Heading 1** style. The Heading 1 style is applied to the title.

▶ **3.** Select the range **A6:A19;A21:A34;A36:A49**, and then, in the Alignment group, click the **Merge & Center** button. The labels are centered in the merged cells.

▶ **4.** In the Alignment group, click the **Orientation** button, and then click **Rotate Text Up**. The text in the three cells rotates 90 degrees.

▶ **5.** In the Alignment group, click the **Middle Align** button. The text is centered both horizontally and vertically in the cells.

▶ **6.** Reduce the width of column A to **5** characters.

▶ **7.** Select the range **C7:K19;C22:K34;C37:K49**, and then, in the Number group, click the **Dialog Box Launcher**. The Format Cells dialog box opens with the Number tab displayed.

▶ **8.** Click **Number** in the Category list, type **0** (a zero) in the Decimal places box, click the **Use 1000 Separator (,)** check box to insert a check mark, verify that the **−1,234** option is selected, and then click the **OK** button. The numbers display a thousands separator and use a minus symbol for negatives.

▶ **9.** Click cell **A1** to deselect the cells. Figure 2-22 shows the formatted Monthly Sales worksheet for the first range. The other ranges are formatted similarly.

| Figure 2-22 | Monthly Sales worksheet with formulas and formatting |

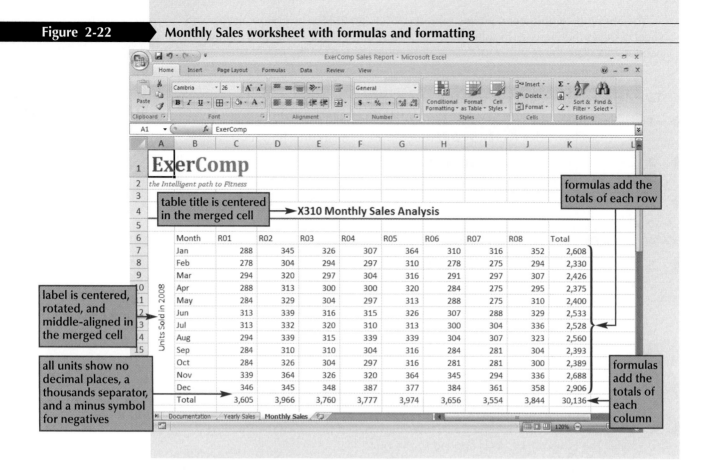

Working with Table Styles

You can treat a range of data as a distinct object in a worksheet known as an **Excel table**. After you identify a range as an Excel table, you can apply a **table style** that formats the entire table as a single unit. Excel tables can include some common elements, such as a header row that contains titles for the different columns in the table and a total row that contains formulas summarizing the values in the table's data. A table style specifies formats for each of these elements, such as font color, fill color, and so forth. Formatting an entire table with a table style is more efficient than formatting individual cells in the range.

| Reference Window \| | **Applying a Table Style to an Existing Table** |

- Select the range to which you want to apply the table style.
- In the Styles group on the Home tab, click the Format as Table button.
- Click a table style in the Table Style gallery.

A table style will update the table's formatting to reflect changes you make to the table, such as adding or deleting table rows or columns. For example, many tables display alternate rows with different fill colors. This effect, known as **banded rows**, makes the text easier to read, especially in large tables with many rows. You could create the banded rows effect by applying a cell style with a background fill to every other row in the table, but then, if you add or delete a row from the table, the banded rows effect might be lost. A table style, on the other hand, applies alternating row colors to the entire Excel table and adjusts the banded rows effect as needed if you add or delete rows. This is because a table style treats the table as a single object rather than a collection of cells. Figure 2-23 shows the banded rows effect applied both manually and with a table style.

Banded rows effect applied manually and with a table style ◄ **Figure 2-23**

fill color is pink

fill color is changed to white, retaining the banded rows effect

fill color remains pink, losing the banded rows effect

original table with banded rows

table formatted with a table style retains banded rows after rows are deleted

table formatted manually loses banded rows after rows are deleted

Tom wants you to format the 2008, 2009, and sales increase data in the Monthly Sales worksheet as Excel tables. First, you'll apply a table style to the units sold in 2008 data.

To apply a table style to the units sold in 2008 data:

▶ 1. Select the range **B6:K19**.

▶ 2. In the Styles group on the Home tab, click the **Format as Table** button, and then click **Table Style Medium 2** (the second style in the first row in the Medium section). The Format as Table dialog box opens, confirming the range you selected for the table and whether the table includes header rows.

▶ 3. Verify that the range is **=$B$6:$K$19**, verify that the **My table has headers** check box contains a check mark, and then click the **OK** button. The table style is applied.

▶ 4. Click cell **A5** to deselect the range. See Figure 2-24.

Figure 2-24 **Data formatted with a table style**

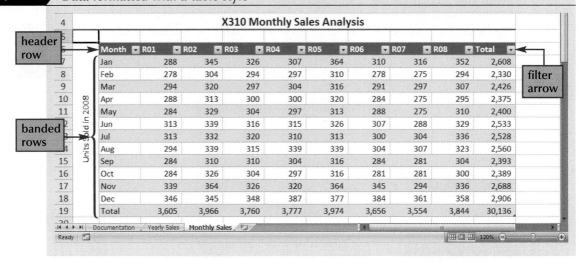

The table style treated the range as a single unit and modified its overall appearance. In this case, Table Style Medium 2 formatted the range so the header row appears in a white font on a blue fill and the remaining rows are formatted as banded rows.

Applying a table style also marks the range as a table, making available tools designed for analyzing tabular data, such as the ability to sort data, transfer data to and from an external file, and filter the data to show only those rows that match specified criteria. The filter arrows next to the column titles in the header row are used for filtering and sorting the table. Tom doesn't want to filter or sort the data right now; he asks you to remove the arrows so he can focus on the table data.

To remove the filter arrows from the table:

▶ **1.** Click cell **B6** to make the table active, and then click the **Data** tab on the Ribbon.

▶ **2.** In the Sort & Filter group, click the **Filter** button. The filter arrows disappear from the header row.

Selecting Table Style Options

After you apply a table style, you can choose which table elements you want included in the style. Table styles have six elements that can be turned on or off: (1) Header Row, which formats the first row of the table; (2) Total Row, which inserts a new row at the bottom of the table that adds the column values; (3) First Column, which formats the first column of the table; (4) Last Column, which formats the last column of the table; (5) Banded Rows, which formats alternating rows in different colors; and (6) Banded Columns, which formats alternating columns in different colors. For example, if you turn on the Header Row option, you can specify a format for the table's first row, which usually contains text that describes the contents of each table column. If you insert a new row at the top of the table, the new row becomes the header row and is formatted with the table style.

In the table style you just used, only the Header Row and Banded Rows options are turned on. Although the other elements are still part of the table structure, the current style does not format them. Tom wants you to format the table's last column and the header row and remove the banded rows effect.

To select the table style options:

▶ **1.** If necessary, click cell **B6** to make the table active.

▶ **2.** Click the **Design** tab on the Ribbon. The table design options appear on the Ribbon.

▶ **3.** In the Table Style Options group, click the **Last Column** check box to insert a check mark. The last column is formatted.

▶ **4.** In the Table Style Options group, click the **Banded Rows** check box to remove the check mark. The banded rows are removed from the table.

Only the Header Row and Last Column elements appear in the table. You'll use a built-in table style to format them.

▶ **5.** In the Table Styles group, click the **More** button to open the Table Styles gallery, and then, in the Medium section, click **Table Style Medium 20** (the third table style in the sixth column). The table styles in the gallery show the formatting applied to the current table elements. See Figure 2-25.

Tip

To select a table style option, you can click in the table to make it active. You do not need to select the entire table.

Revised table style ◀ **Figure 2-25**

A table style might not format a table exactly the way you want. For example, Tom wants the column titles in the header row to be centered and the Total row to have a single top border and a double bottom border. Because the table style you used does not include either of these formats, you'll add these formats to the table cells. You can use cell styles and the formatting tools you've used with individual cells and ranges to format Excel tables.

To format the header row and the Total row:

▶ 1. Select the range **C6:K6**, click the **Home** tab on the Ribbon, and then, in the Alignment group, click the **Center** button ≣. The column titles are centered.

▶ 2. Select the range **B19:K19**.

▶ 3. In the Styles group, click the **Cell Styles** button, and then, in the Titles and Headings section, click **Total** (the sixth cell style).

▶ 4. Click cell **A5** to deselect the range. The Total row is formatted in bold with a single top border and a double bottom border.

Tom likes the formatting of the first table, and wants you to format the other two tables similarly. You cannot use the Format Painter to copy table formats, and you must format each range as a table separately.

To format the other two tables:

▶ 1. Select the range **B21:K34**.

▶ 2. In the Styles group on the Home tab, click the **Format as Table** button, click **Table Style Medium 6** (the sixth table style in the first row of the Medium section), and then click the **OK** button in the Format as Table dialog box.

▶ 3. Click the **Data** tab on the Ribbon, and then, in the Sort & Filter group, click the **Filter** button to turn off the filter arrows.

▶ 4. Click the **Design** tab on the Ribbon, and then, in the Table Style Options group, click the **Banded Rows** check box to remove the check mark and click the **Last Column** check box to insert a check mark.

▶ 5. In the Table Styles group, click the **More** button, and then click **Table Style Medium 20** (the sixth table style in the third row of the Medium section).

▶ 6. Select the range **C21:K21**, click the **Home** tab on the Ribbon, and then, in the Alignment group, click the **Center** button ≣.

▶ 7. Select the range **B34:K34**. You'll apply the Total cell style to this range.

▶ 8. In the Styles group, click the **Cell Styles** button, and then click **Total** (the sixth cell style in the Titles and Headings section).

▶ 9. Select the range **B36:K49** and repeat Steps 2 through 5, select the range **C36:K36** and repeat Step 6, and then select the range **B49:K49** and repeat Step 8.

Introducing Conditional Formats

So far, you have used formatting to make the workbook more readable or visually interesting. Formatting can also help you analyze data by highlighting significant numbers or trends in the data. Tom wants the sales report to highlight sales regions that have performed particularly well or done poorly in the past two years. Tom also wants to show how sales of the X310 heart rate monitor changed during the year. This information can help him plan inventory for the next year as well as project future sales and revenue.

To prepare this kind of report, you can use conditional formatting. A **conditional format** applies formatting only when a cell's value meets a specified condition. For example, a conditional format can make negative numbers red and positive numbers black. Conditional formats are dynamic, so a cell's appearance will change to reflect its current value.

Excel has four conditional formats—data bars, highlighting, color scales, and icon sets. This tutorial looks at data bars and cell highlighting.

Applying Conditional Formats (Data Bars and Highlights) | Reference Window

- Select the range or ranges to which you want to add data bars.
- In the Styles group on the Home tab, click the Conditional Formatting button, point to Data Bars, and then click a data bar color.

or

- Select the range in which you want to highlight cells that match a specified rule.
- In the Styles group, click the Conditional Formatting button, point to Highlight Cells Rules or Top/Bottom Rules, and then click the appropriate rule.
- Select the appropriate options in the dialog box, and then click the OK button.

Adding Data Bars

A **data bar** is a horizontal bar added to the background of a cell to provide a visual indicator of the cell's value. Larger values are associated with longer data bars; smaller values are associated with shorter data bars. Data bars will help Tom see how the 2008 and 2009 sales totals vary throughout the year.

To format the 2008 monthly sales with data bars:

▶ **1.** Select the range **K7:K18**.

▶ **2.** In the Styles group on the Home tab, click the **Conditional Formatting** button, point to **Data Bars** to open the Data Bars gallery, and then click **Purple Data Bar** (the third data bar in the second row of the Data Bars gallery). Data bars appear for the 2008 monthly sales.

▶ **3.** Click cell **A3** to deselect the range. See Figure 2-26.

Data bars added to the 2008 monthly sales ◀ **Figure 2-26**

	Month	R01	R02	R03	R04	R05	R06	R07	R08	Total
7	Jan	288	345	326	307	364	310	316	352	2,608
8	Feb	278	304	294	297	310	278	275	294	2,330
9	Mar	294	320	297	304	316	291	297	307	2,426
10	Apr	288	313	300	300	320	284	275	295	2,375
11	May	284	329	304	297	313	288	275	310	2,400
12	Jun	313	339	316	315	326	307	288	329	2,533
13	Jul	313	332	320	310	313	300	304	336	2,528
14	Aug	294	339	315	339	339	304	307	323	2,560
15	Sep	284	310	310	304	316	284	281	304	2,393
16	Oct	284	326	304	297	316	281	281	300	2,389
17	Nov	339	364	326	320	364	345	294	336	2,688
18	Dec	346	345	348	387	377	384	361	358	2,906
19	Total	3,605	3,966	3,760	3,777	3,974	3,656	3,554	3,844	30,136

(Units Sold in 2008)

	Month	R01	R02	R03	R04	R05	R06	R07
22	Jan	352	364	345	352	336	361	
23	Feb	297	326	310	313	288	300	

data bar length is based on the cell value

Documentation / Yearly Sales / **Monthly Sales**

Ready   120%

The data bars highlight several important facts that might not be immediately apparent from viewing the cell values. First, the highest sales occurred during the months of November, December, and January—a reflection of heavy shopping during the holiday season. Second, an increase in sales occurred during the summer months. Again, this is expected because customers are more physically active during those months and likely to purchase a heart rate monitor. Third, the periods of lowest sales occurred in the spring and fall. To find out if all of the sales regions reflect this seasonal trend, you'll add data bars to the individual sales region figures.

To add data bars for all sales regions:

▶ **1.** Select the range **C7:J18**.

▶ **2.** In the Styles group on the Home tab, click the **Conditional Formatting** button, point to **Data Bars**, and then click **Light Blue Data Bar** (the second data bar in the second row of the Data Bars gallery). Monthly data bars appear for all the sales regions in 2008.

▶ **3.** Click cell **A3** to deselect the range. See Figure 2-27.

Figure 2-27 ▶ **Data bars added to the regional monthly sales data**

January sales for the R01 region are lower than expected

Month	R01	R02	R03	R04	R05	R06	R07	R08	Total
Jan	288	345	326	307	364	310	316	352	2,608
Feb	278	304	294	297	310	278	275	294	2,330
Mar	294	320	297	304	316	291	297	307	2,426
Apr	288	313	300	300	320	284	275	295	2,375
May	284	329	304	297	313	288	275	310	2,400
Jun	313	339	316	315	326	307	288	329	2,533
Jul	313	332	320	310	313	300	304	336	2,528
Aug	294	339	315	339	339	304	307	323	2,560
Sep	284	310	310	304	316	284	281	304	2,393
Oct	284	326	304	297	316	281	281	300	2,389
Nov	339	364	326	320	364	345	294	336	2,688
Dec	346	345	348	387	377	384	361	358	2,906
Total	3,605	3,966	3,760	3,777	3,974	3,656	3,554	3,844	30,136

(Units Sold in 2008)

Month	R01	R02	R03	R04	R05	R06	R07	R08	Total
Jan	352	364	345	352	336	361	325	342	2,777
Feb	297	326	310	313	288	300	297	300	2,431

Documentation / Yearly Sales / Monthly Sales

Ready | | 120%

For the most part, the seasonal trend is reflected in all the sales regions, with some exceptions. For example, the R01 region had lower-than-expected sales during January 2008. Tom discovers that a distribution problem prevented several stores in the R01 region from receiving its stock of ExerComp heart rate monitors until near the end of January, causing the decreased sales totals. Data bars highlight this important piece of information.

Data bar lengths depend on the values in the selected range. The largest value in the range has the longest data bar; the smallest value has the shortest data bar. For example, in the Total column, the shortest data bar represents the February total of 2,330 and the longest data bar represents the December total of 2,906. You should use different colored data bars to distinguish data bars for different ranges. For example, you used blue data bars for the regional sales and purple data bars for the totals.

Because data bar lengths are based on the values in the range, changing the value of one cell in the range can affect the size of all the other cells' data bars. You'll change the units sold value in cell C7 and see how this affects the data bars.

To see the effect on data bars of changing a units sold value:

▶ **1.** In cell C7, enter **588**. The lengths of all the data bars in the 2008 sales table change to reflect this increased value.

▶ **2.** On the Quick Access Toolbar, click the **Undo** button 🔄. The value in cell C7 returns to 288, its original value.

Clearing a Conditional Format

Tom wants you to add data bars to the 2009 sales table. You can base the data bars on the values in only the 2009 sales table, or you can base them on the values in both the 2008 and 2009 sales tables. Both approaches have advantages. Basing the data bars on only the 2009 sales allows you to focus on that data and see more detail on the seasonal and regional trends within that year. However, basing the data bars on sales results from both years makes it easier to compare sales trends from one year to another. Tom wants you to base the length of the data bars on the values from both years. First, you need to remove the data bars you created for the 2008 sales table. Then, you can add a new set of data bars based on a different selection of cells.

To clear the data bars from the 2008 sales table:

▶ **1.** If necessary, click cell **C7** to select it and make the table active.

▶ **2.** In the Styles group on the Home tab, click the **Conditional Formatting** button, point to **Clear Rules**, and then click **Clear Rules from This Table**. Both sets of data bars are removed from the 2008 sales table.

Next, you'll add data bars for the sales data in both the 2008 and 2009 sales tables.

To add data bars to both the 2008 and 2009 sales tables:

▶ **1.** Select the range **K7:K18;K22:K33**. This selects the 2008 and 2009 monthly sales totals.

▶ **2.** In the Styles group on the Home tab, click the **Conditional Formatting** button, point to **Data Bars**, and then click **Purple Data Bar** (the third data bar in the second row of the Data Bars gallery).

▶ **3.** Select the range **C7:J18;C22:J33**. This selects the 2008 and 2009 monthly sales for each region.

▶ **4.** In the Styles group, click the **Conditional Formatting** button, point to **Data Bars**, and then click **Light Blue Data Bar** (the second data bar in the second row of the Data Bars gallery).

▶ **5.** Click cell **A20** to deselect the range. See Figure 2-28.

> **Tip**
>
> To remove all conditional formatting from a worksheet, click Clear Rules from Entire Sheet. To remove it from the selected range, click Clear Rules from Selected Cells.

Figure 2-28 | **Data bars added to the 2008 and 2009 sales tables**

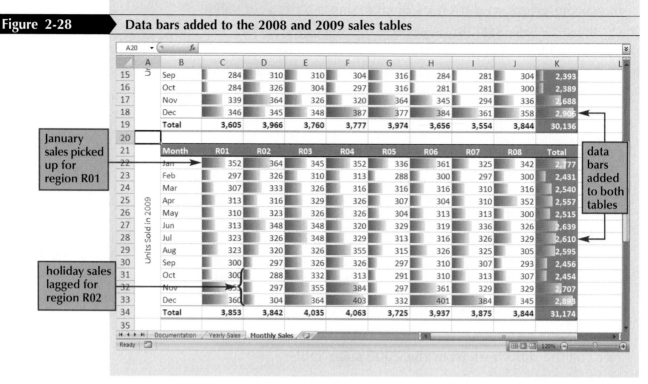

Tom sees some of the same seasonal trends in 2009 as he saw for 2008. He notes that sales in the R01 region did not lag as they did in 2008, but sales in the R02 region were lower than expected during the holiday season. Other than that, it's hard to compare the regional and monthly sales to determine any trends from 2008 to 2009. He knows that, overall, the number of heart rate monitors sold increased in 2009, but he doesn't know if this is true for all regions and for all months. Tom wants to highlight those sales regions and months in which sales increased from 2008 to 2009.

Highlighting Cells

The third table shows the increase in sales from 2008 to 2009, which is the data that Tom wants to analyze. Because Tom wants to highlight those regions and months in 2008 in which the sales increased, you'll highlight only those cells that contain positive values. Highlighting cells based on their values is another type of conditional format. Figure 2-29 describes some of the ways that cells can be highlighted.

Figure 2-29 | **Highlighting rules**

Rule	Highlights
Greater Than	Cells that are greater than a specified number
Less Than	Cells that are less than a specified number
Between	Cells that are between two specified numbers
Equal To	Cells that are equal to a specified number
Text That Contains	Cells that contain specified text
A Date Occurring	Cells that contain a specified date
Duplicate Values	Cells that contain duplicate or unique values

Tom wants you to highlight all the positive numbers in the third table to show those months and sales regions that increased sales from 2008 to 2009.

To highlight the positive sales numbers:

▶ **1.** Select the range **C37:J48**. This selects the difference in sales by region and month for 2008 and 2009.

▶ **2.** In the Styles group on the Home tab, click the **Conditional Formatting** button, point to **Highlight Cells Rules**, and then click **Greater Than**. The Greater Than dialog box opens. You want to highlight positive sales numbers, which are numbers greater than zero.

▶ **3.** Type **0** (a zero) in the Format cells that are GREATER THAN box, click the **with** arrow, and then click **Green Fill with Dark Green Text**.

▶ **4.** Click the **OK** button to apply the highlight rule.

▶ **5.** Click cell **A35** to deselect the range. Cells with positive numbers are highlighted in green. See Figure 2-30.

Positive cells highlighted ◀ Figure 2-30

	Month	R01	R02	R03	R04	R05	R06	R07	R08	Total
37	Jan	64	19	19	45	-28	51	9	-10	169
38	Feb	19	22	16	16	-22	22	22	6	101
39	Mar	13	13	29	12	0	25	13	9	114
40	Apr	25	3	29	26	-13	20	35	57	182
41	May	26	-6	22	29	-9	25	38	-10	115
42	Jun	0	9	32	5	3	12	48	-3	106
43	Jul	10	-6	28	19	0	16	22	-7	82
44	Aug	29	-19	11	16	-24	22	18	-18	35
45	Sep	16	-13	16	22	-19	26	26	-11	63
46	Oct	16	-38	28	16	-25	29	32	7	65
47	Nov	16	-67	29	64	-67	16	35	-7	19
48	Dec	14	-41	16	16	-45	17	23	-13	-13
49	Total	248	-124	275	286	-249	281	321	0	1,038

(Column at left, rows 37–49, labeled "Net Increase from 2008 to 2009")

green cells indicate an increase in sales from 2008 to 2009

Documentation / Yearly Sales / Monthly Sales

Ready   120%

From the highlighting, you can tell that most regions and months had increased sales in 2009. Most of the declines occurred in regions R02, R05, and R08. Tom wonders if some months or regions had particularly strong sales increases. You'll remove the current highlighting, and then highlight the top 10% in sales increases.

To highlight the top 10 percent in sales increases:

▶ **1.** Select the range **C37:J48**.

▶ **2.** In the Styles group on the Home tab, click the **Conditional Formatting** button, point to **Clear Rules**, and then click **Clear Rules from Selected Cells**. The current highlighting is removed.

▶ **3.** In the Styles group, click the **Conditional Formatting** button, point to **Top/Bottom Rules**, and then click **Top 10 %**. The Top 10% dialog box opens.

▶ **4.** Verify that **10** is entered in the % box, click the **with** arrow, and then click **Green Fill with Dark Green Text**.

▶ **5.** Click the **OK** button. Cells whose sales increases for 2008 and 2009 were in the top 10% are highlighted in green.

▶ **6.** Click cell **A35** to deselect the range. See Figure 2-31.

Figure 2-31 ▶ **Top 10% sales increases highlighted**

green cells indicate sales increases that were in the top 10%

	Month	R01	R02	R03	R04	R05	R06	R07	R08	Total
37	Jan	64	19	19	45	-28	51	9	-10	169
38	Feb	19	22	16	16	-22	22	22	6	101
39	Mar	13	13	29	12	0	25	13	9	114
40	Apr	25	3	29	26	-13	20	35	57	182
41	May	26	-6	22	29	-9	25	38	-10	115
42	Jun	0	9	32	5	3	12	48	-3	106
43	Jul	10	-6	28	19	0	16	22	-7	82
44	Aug	29	-19	11	16	-24	22	18	-18	35
45	Sep	16	-13	16	22	-19	26	26	-11	63
46	Oct	16	-38	28	16	-25	29	32	7	65
47	Nov	16	-67	29	64	-67	16	35	-7	19
48	Dec	14	-41	16	16	-45	17	23	-13	-13
49	**Total**	248	-124	275	286	-249	281	321	0	1,038

(Net Increase from 2008 to 2009)

Documentation | Yearly Sales | **Monthly Sales**

Ready — 120%

The results provide Tom with some interesting information. For example, region R08, which underperformed for most of the year, had one of the largest sales increases during April (cell J40). In fact, the increase in sales during that one month compensated for the sales declines in other months, so that by the end of the year, region R08 showed no overall decline in sales. Also, region R01 had a large increase in sales during January 2009, indicating that this region fixed the distribution problems that occurred in 2008. Finally, of the nine cells highlighted in the table, four of them come from region R07, three of those occurring during the usually slow spring months.

Tom wonders what insights he could gain from highlighting the bottom 10% of the table—the regions and months that showed the lowest sales increases in 2009.

To highlight the bottom 10 percent in sales increases:

1. Select the range **C37:J48**.

2. In the Styles group on the Home tab, click the **Conditional Formatting** button, point to **Top/Bottom Rules**, and then click **Bottom 10 %**. The Bottom 10% dialog box opens.

3. Verify that **10** is entered in the % box and **Light Red Fill with Dark Red Text** is selected in the with box, and then click the **OK** button. Red cells highlight the regions and months that placed in the bottom 10% for sales increases from 2008 to 2009.

4. Click cell **A35** to deselect the range. See Figure 2-32.

	Month	R01	R02	R03	R04	R05	R06	R07	R08	Total
37	Jan	64	19	19	45	-28	51	9	-10	169
38	Feb	19	22	16	16	-22	22	22	6	101
39	Mar	13	13	29	12	0	25	13	9	114
40	Apr	25	3	29	26	-13	20	35	57	182
41	May	26	-6	22	29	-9	25	38	-10	115
42	Jun	0	9	32	5	3	12	48	-3	106
43	Jul	10	-6	28	19	0	16	22	-7	82
44	Aug	29	-19	11	16	-24	22	18	-18	35
45	Sep	16	-13	16	22	-19	26	26	-11	63
46	Oct	16	-38	28	16	-25	29	32	7	65
47	Nov	16	-67	29	64	-67	16	35	-7	19
48	Dec	14	-41	16	16	-45	17	23	-13	-13
49	Total	248	-124	275	286	-249	281	321	0	1,038

(Net increase from 2008 to 2009)

red cells indicate sales increases were in the bottom 10%

Documentation / Yearly Sales / Monthly Sales

Tom immediately sees that the bottom 10% come from only regions R02 and R05, and that six of the nine cells highlighted occurred in the most recent months: October, November, and December. Conditional formatting has helped Tom isolate and highlight potential problem areas, which he can investigate further.

When you use conditional formatting to highlight cells in a worksheet, you should always include a **legend**, which is a key that shows each color used in the worksheet and what it means, so others know why certain cells are highlighted. Tom asks you to add a legend to the Monthly Sales worksheet.

To create a conditional formatting legend:

1. In cell D51, enter **light red**, and then click cell **D51** to select it. You'll use a highlight rule to fill this cell with the light red color used for the bottom 10% sales increases.

2. In the Styles group on the Home tab, click the **Conditional Formatting** button, point to **Highlight Cells Rules**, and then click **Text that Contains**. The Text That Contains dialog box opens.

3. Verify that **light red** appears in the Format cells that contain the text box, select **Light Red Fill with Dark Red Text** in the with box, and then click the **OK** button. Cell D51 is filled with the same light red fill color used for the bottom 10% values.

4. In cell D52, enter **light green**, and then click cell **D52** to select it. You'll use a highlight rule to fill this cell with the green color used for the top 10% sales increases.

5. In the Styles group on the Home tab, click the **Conditional Formatting** button, point to **Hightlight Cells Rules**, and then click **Text that Contains**. The Text That Contains dialog box opens.

6. Verify that **light green** appears in the Format cells that contain the text box, select **Green Fill with Dark Green Text** in the with box, and then click the **OK** button. Cell D52 is filled with the same light green fill color used for the top 10% values.

7. In cell E51, enter **Bottom 10% in terms of sales increase**, and then, in cell E52, enter **Top 10% in terms of sales increase**.

▶ **8.** Select the range **E51:E52**. You'll format these cells with a cell style to distinguish them from the rest of the text in the worksheet.

▶ **9.** In the Styles group, click the **Cell Styles** button, and then, in the Data and Model group, click **Explanatory** (the third cell style in the first row).

▶ **10.** Click cell **A35** to deselect the range. See Figure 2-33.

| Figure 2-33 | | Cell highlighting legend |

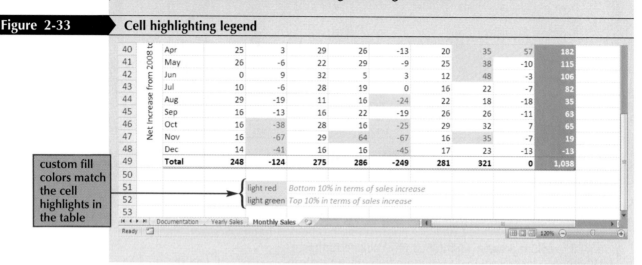

custom fill colors match the cell highlights in the table

40		Apr	25	3	29	26	-13	20	35	57	182
41		May	26	-6	22	29	-9	25	38	-10	115
42		Jun	0	9	32	5	3	12	48	-3	106
43		Jul	10	-6	28	19	0	16	22	-7	82
44		Aug	29	-19	11	16	-24	22	18	-18	35
45		Sep	16	-13	16	22	-19	26	26	-11	63
46		Oct	16	-38	28	16	-25	29	32	7	65
47		Nov	16	-67	29	64	-67	16	35	-7	19
48		Dec	14	-41	16	16	-45	17	23	-13	-13
49		**Total**	**248**	**-124**	**275**	**286**	**-249**	**281**	**321**	**0**	**1,038**
50											
51		light red	Bottom 10% in terms of sales increase								
52		light green	Top 10% in terms of sales increase								
53											

Net Increase from 2008 to

Documentation | Yearly Sales | **Monthly Sales**

Ready   120%

The conditional formatting in the Monthly Sales worksheet helps Tom understand how sales of the X310 heart rate monitor changed over the past two years and helps him focus on particular sales regions for additional analysis.

| InSight | | **Using Conditional Formatting Effectively** |

Conditional formatting is an excellent way to point out trends and highlight key data values, but it should be used judiciously. An overuse of conditional formatting can sometimes obscure the very data values you want to emphasize. Keep in mind the following tips:

- Document the conditional formats you use. If a bold, green font means that a sales number is in the top 10% of all sales, include that information in a legend in the worksheet.
- Don't clutter data with too much highlighting. Limit highlight rules to one or two per data set. Highlights are designed to draw attention to points of interest. If you use too many, you'll end up highlighting everything—and, therefore, nothing.
- Use color sparingly in worksheets with highlights. It's difficult to tell a highlight color from a regular fill color, especially when fill colors are used in every cell.
- Consider alternatives to conditional formats. If you want to highlight the top 10 sales regions, it might be more effective to simply sort the data with the best-selling regions at the top of the list.
- Don't let data bars overwhelm cell text. Use data bars when you're more interested in the "big picture" rather than specific cell values. If you want to show both, use a chart.

Hiding Worksheet Data

The Monthly Sales worksheet contains too much data to fit into the worksheet window without drastically reducing the zoom level. This would make the contents too small to read easily. Another way to view a large worksheet is by selectively hiding rows or columns (or even entire worksheets in a workbook). Hiding rows, columns, and worksheets is an excellent way to conceal extraneous or distracting information; but you should never hide data that is crucial to understanding a workbook.

Tom wants to view only the third table, which shows the difference in sales between 2008 and 2009, but not the other tables. You'll hide the rows that contain the first two tables and then unhide those rows after Tom has looked at the third table.

To hide and unhide worksheet rows:

▶ **1.** Select row **6** through row **35** in the Monthly Sales worksheet.

▶ **2.** In the Cells group on the Home tab, click the **Format** button, point to **Hide & Unhide**, and then click **Hide Rows**. Rows 6 to 35 are hidden, and the row numbers in the worksheet jump from row 5 to row 36. The data in the third table hasn't changed even though its formulas use data from the hidden tables.

▶ **3.** Select row **5** and row **36**, which are the rows before and after the hidden rows.

▶ **4.** In the Cells group, click the **Format** button, point to **Hide & Unhide**, and then click **Unhide Rows**. The hidden rows 6 through 35 reappear.

Formatting the Worksheet for Printing

Tom wants you to print this analysis of the monthly sales figures. In preparing the worksheet for the printer, you can select the position of the report on the page, the orientation of the page, and whether the page will include headers or footers. First, you'll look at the Monthly Sales worksheet in Page Layout view to see how it would currently print.

To view the Monthly Sales worksheet in Page Layout view:

▶ **1.** Click the **Page Layout** button 🔲 on the status bar. The worksheet switches to Page Layout view.

▶ **2.** Zoom the worksheet to **60%** to view more of the page layout. See Figure 2-34.

Page Layout view of the Monthly Sales worksheet ◀ **Figure 2-34**

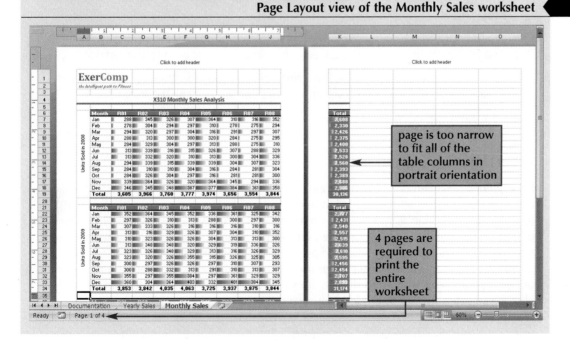

In the worksheet's current orientation, its contents do not fit on a single page and the tables break across pages. You'll change the orientation from portrait to landscape so that the page is wide enough to fit all the table columns on one page.

To change the page orientation to landscape:

▶ **1.** Click the **Page Layout** tab on the Ribbon.

▶ **2.** In the Page Setup group, click the **Orientation** button, and then click **Landscape**. The page orientation changes to landscape, making each page wide enough to display all of the columns of each table.

Defining the Print Area

By default, all parts of the active worksheet containing text, formulas, or values are printed. You can also select the cells you want to print, and then define them as a **print area**. A print area can cover an adjacent or nonadjacent range.

For his report, Tom wants to print only the first table. You'll set the print area to cover only those cells. It's generally easier to work with the print area in Page Break Preview.

To switch to Page Break Preview and define the print area:

▶ **1.** Click the **Page Break Preview** button 🖳 on the status bar, and then zoom the worksheet to **70%**.

Trouble? If the Welcome to Page Break Preview dialog box opens, click the OK button.

▶ **2.** Select the range **A1:K19**, which is the range of the first table.

▶ **3.** In the Page Setup group on the Page Layout tab, click the **Print Area** button, and then click **Set Print Area**. The print area changes to cover only the range A1:K19. The rest of the worksheet content is shaded to indicate that it will not be part of the printout.

Tom decides that he wants you to print all the content in the worksheet, so you'll clear the print area you just defined, resetting the print area to the default.

▶ **4.** In the Page Setup group, click the **Print Area** button, and then click **Clear Print Area**. The print area again covers the entire contents of the worksheet.

Inserting Page Breaks

Large worksheets often do not fit onto one page unless you scale the printout to fit, but that usually results in text that is too small to read comfortably. When a printout extends to multiple pages, Excel prints as much as fits on a page and then inserts a **page break** to continue printing the remaining worksheet content on the next page. This can result in page breaks that split worksheet content in awkward places, such as within a table.

Instead, you can insert **manual page breaks** that specify exactly where the page breaks occur. A page break is inserted directly above and to the left of a selected cell, directly above a selected row, or to the left of a selected column.

Setting and Removing Page Breaks | Reference Window

To set a page break:

- Select the first cell below the row where you want to insert a page break.
- In the Page Setup group on the Page Layout tab, click the Breaks button, and then click Insert Page Break.

To remove a page break:

- Select any cell below or to the right of the page break you want to remove.
- In the Page Setup group on the Page Layout tab, click the Breaks button, and then click Remove Page Break (or click Reset All Page Breaks to remove all the page breaks from the worksheet).

Tom wants the three tables in the Monthly Sales worksheet to print on separate pages. You'll insert page breaks to accomplish this.

To insert page breaks between the tables:

1. Click cell **A20**.

2. In the Page Setup group on the Page Layout tab, click the **Breaks** button, and then click **Insert Page Break**. A page break separates row 19 from row 20.

3. Click cell **A35**, and then repeat Step 2 to insert a second page break that splits the second table from the third. The printout is now three pages. See Figure 2-35.

Worksheet in Page Break Preview ◀ Figure 2-35

Tip

In Page Break Preview, a dashed blue line indicates an automatic page break and a solid blue line indicates a manual page break.

4. Click the **Page Layout** button 📄 on the status bar, and then verify that each table appears on a separate page.

Adding Print Titles

The company name, the slogan, and the worksheet title all appear on the first page of the printout, but do not appear on the other two pages. This is because the range that includes that text is limited to the first page of the printout. It's a good practice to include the company name, logo, and worksheet title on each page of a printout in case a page becomes separated from the other pages. You can repeat information, such as the company name, by specifying which rows or columns in the worksheet act as **print titles**, information that prints on each page.

Tom wants the first four rows of the Monthly Sales worksheet printed on each page.

To define the print titles for the pages:

1. In the Page Setup group on the Page Layout tab, click the **Print Titles** button. The Page Setup dialog box opens with the Sheet tab displayed.

2. Click the **Rows to repeat at top** box, move your pointer over the worksheet, and then select the range **A1:A4**. A flashing border appears around the first four rows of the worksheet as a visual indicator that the contents of the first four rows will be repeated on each page of the printout. The cell reference $1:$4 appears in the Rows to repeat at top box.

3. Click the **OK** button.

4. Click the **Page Layout** button on the status bar, and then scroll through the second and third pages of the printout in Page Layout view to verify that the company name, slogan, and worksheet title appear on each page. See Figure 2-36.

Figure 2-36 | **Second page of the printout**

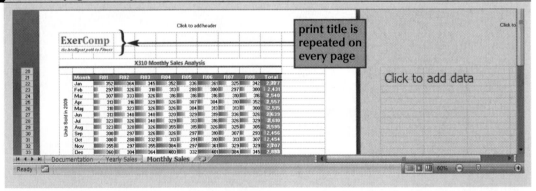

The Sheet tab in the Page Setup dialog box provides other print options, such as printing the gridlines or row and column headings. You can also print the worksheet in black and white or in draft quality. For a multiple page printout, you can specify whether the pages are ordered by first going down the worksheet and then across or across first and then down.

Adding Headers and Footers

Another way to repeat information on each page of a printout is with headers and footers. A **header** is the text printed in the top margin of each page. A **footer** is the text printed in the bottom margin of each page. A **margin** is the space between the page content and the edges of the page. Headers and footers can be used to add information to the printed page that is not found in the worksheet cells, such as the workbook's author, the date the page was printed, or the workbook filename. If the printout covers multiple pages, you can add a footer that displays the page number and the total number of pages in the printout to help ensure you and others have the entire printout.

The header and footer have three sections: a left section, a center section, and a right section. Within each section, you type the text you want to appear or insert elements such as the worksheet name or current date and time. These header and footer elements are dynamic; if you rename the worksheet, for example, the name is automatically updated in the header or footer.

Tom wants his printouts to display the workbook's filename in the header's left section and the current date in the header's right section. He wants the center footer to display the page number and the total number of pages in the printout, and the right footer to display your name as the workbook's author.

To insert the header and footer text:

▶ **1.** Zoom the worksheet to **90%** in Page Layout view.

▶ **2.** Scroll to the top of the worksheet, and then click the left section of the header directly above cell A1. The Header & Footer Tools contextual tab appears on the Ribbon.

▶ **3.** Type **Filename:** in the left section of the header, press the **spacebar**, and then, in the Header & Footer Elements group on the Header & Footer Tools Design tab, click the **File Name** button. The code &[File], which displays the filename of the current workbook, is added into the left section of the header.

▶ **4.** Press the **Tab** key twice to move to the right section of the header, and then, in the Header & Footer Elements group, click the **Current Date** button. The code &[Date] is added into the right section of the header. See Figure 2-37.

Page header ◀ **Figure 2-37**

▶ **5.** In the Navigation group, click the **Go to Footer** button. The right section of the footer is selected.

▶ **6.** Click the center section of the footer, type **Page**, press the **spacebar**, and then, in the Header & Footer Elements group, click the **Page Number** button.

▶ **7.** Press the **spacebar**, type **of**, press the **spacebar**, and then, in the Header & Footer Elements group, click the **Number of Pages** button. The text, "Page &[Page] of &[Pages]" appears in the center section of the footer.

▶ **8.** Press the **Tab** key to move to the right section of the footer, type **Prepared by:**, press the **spacebar**, and then type your name. See Figure 2-38.

Figure 2-38   Page footer

> **9.** Click cell **A1**, and then scroll through the other two pages of the worksheet to verify that the same header appears for each page and the center section of the footer displays the correct page number and total number of pages.

Adjusting Margins

Tom wants you to try different margins to see the effect on the Monthly Sales worksheet and how it will print. You can use the preset Normal margins, Wide margins, or Narrow margins. Or, you can enter custom settings for each margin in the Page Setup dialog box.

To adjust the worksheet's margins:

> **1.** In the Page Setup group on the Page Layout tab, click the **Margins** button. The Margins menu opens. The default margin setting, Normal, is selected.

> **2.** Click **Custom Margins**. The Page Setup dialog box opens, and the Margins tab is active. You can enter the exact margin setting you want in each box. The preview image changes to show the new margins.

> **3.** Select the text in the Top box, type **2** (you do not need to type the inches symbol), press the **Tab** key to select the text in the Bottom box, and then type **3**.

> **4.** Press the **Tab** key to select the text in the Left box, type **1**, press the **Tab** key to select the text in the Right box, and then type **1**. The preview image shows the new margins.

> **5.** Click the **OK** button. The worksheet reflects the new margins.
>
> Tom prefers the default margin settings, so you'll return the margins to their original settings.

> **6.** In the Page Setup group on the Page Layout tab, click the **Margins** button, and then click **Normal**. The margins change back to their default settings.

> Tip
>
> The settings most recently selected in the Page Setup dialog box appear as the Last Custom Setting option in the Margins menu.

     The worksheet is formatted for printing. Tom asks you to save and print the Monthly Sales worksheet.

To save the workbook and print the worksheet:

> **1.** Click the **Normal** button ⊞ on the status bar to return the Monthly Sales worksheet to Normal view.

> **2.** Save your changes to the workbook.

3. Print the contents of the Monthly Sales worksheet, and then close the workbook. Each table is printed on a separate page and the headers and footers display the filename, current date, page number and total number of pages, and your name.

Tom will analyze the finished report, and distribute it during the upcoming sales meeting.

Session 2.2 Quick Check | Review

1. What is a table style?
2. What are the six table style options you can turn on and off?
3. What is conditional formatting?
4. How is the length of a data bar determined by default?
5. How would you highlight the top five values in the range A1:C20?
6. What are print titles?
7. How do you insert a page break into your worksheet?

Tutorial Summary | Review

In this tutorial, you used formatting tools to create visually appealing and informative workbooks. You formatted text, backgrounds, borders, numbers, and dates, and copied formats from one range into another. You applied built-in styles and themes to the workbook. Next, you looked at how formatting can be helpful for analyzing and interpreting data. You applied a table style to format an Excel table. Then, you used two types of conditional formatting—data bars and highlighting rules—to better understand the data entered into the workbook. Finally, you formatted the worksheet for printing by setting page breaks and page titles, and inserting headers and footers.

Key Terms

accent	Format Painter	points
automatic color	formatting	print area
banded rows	General number format	print title
border	header	sans serif font
conditional format	legend	serif font
custom color	Live Preview	standard color
data bar	manual page break	style
Excel table	margin	table style
font	merge	theme
font size	Mini toolbar	theme color
font style	non-theme font	theme font
footer	page break	typeface

| **Review Assignments**

Practice the skills you learned in the tutorial using the same case scenario.

Data Files needed for the Review Assignments: X410.xlsx, Paper.jpg

ExerComp introduced another heart rate monitor, the X410, two years ago. Tom wants you to format a workbook that compares the sales of the X310 and X410 models during that time. The workbook has a Documentation sheet, a Model Comparison sheet comparing the total units sold for each model in the eight sales regions, and a Monthly Sales sheet reporting the number of units sold per month.

In the Model Comparison sheet, Tom wants you to highlight the sales regions that showed the greatest sales increases from 2008 to 2009. Figure 2-39 shows a preview of the formatted Model Comparison sheet.

Figure 2-39

	Region	Units Sold (2008)	Units Sold (2009)	Increase	% Increase
			highest	Highest increase in units sold	
			highest	Highest % increase in units sold	
X310	R01	3,605	3,853	248	6.88%
	R02	3,966	3,842	-124	-3.13%
	R03	3,760	4,035	275	7.31%
	R04	3,777	4,063	286	7.57%
	R05	3,974	3,725	-249	-6.27%
	R06	3,656	3,937	281	7.69%
	R07	3,554	3,875	321	9.03%
	R08	3,844	3,844	0	0.00%
	Total	30,136	31,174	1,038	3.44%
X410	R01	2,488	4,156	1,668	67.04%
	R02	2,531	4,293	1,762	69.62%
	R03	2,231	4,292	2,061	92.38%
	R04	2,613	4,851	2,238	85.65%
	R05	2,512	4,308	1,796	71.50%
	R06	2,824	4,689	1,865	66.04%
	R07	2,355	4,529	2,174	92.31%
	R08	2,412	4,140	1,728	71.64%
	Total	19,966	35,258	15,292	76.59%

ExerComp — the Intelligent path to Fitness

In the Monthly Sales sheet, Tom wants you to include data bars that show the monthly sales totals for both models during 2008 and 2009. Figure 2-40 shows a preview of the completed Monthly Sales sheet.

Figure 2-40

ExerComp
the Intelligent path to Fitness

2008 Sales (Units Sold)

Month	X310	X410	All Models
Jan	2,608	-	2,608
Feb	2,330	-	2,330
Mar	2,426	25	2,451
Apr	2,375	75	2,450
May	2,400	1,500	3,900
Jun	2,533	1,750	4,283
Jul	2,528	2,135	4,663
Aug	2,560	2,620	5,180
Sep	2,393	2,714	5,107
Oct	2,389	2,689	5,078
Nov	2,688	3,144	5,832
Dec	2,906	3,314	6,220
Total	30,136	19,966	50,102

2009 Sales (Units Sold)

Month	X310	X410	All Models
Jan	2,777	3,223	6,000
Feb	2,431	2,612	5,043
Mar	2,540	2,714	5,254
Apr	2,557	2,877	5,434
May	2,515	2,749	5,264
Jun	2,639	2,955	5,594
Jul	2,610	2,839	5,449
Aug	2,595	2,875	5,470
Sep	2,456	2,823	5,279
Oct	2,454	2,791	5,245
Nov	2,707	3,278	5,985
Dec	2,893	3,522	6,415
Total	31,174	35,258	66,432

Complete the following. (*Note:* Text you need to enter is shown in bold for ease of reference only; do not bold the text unless otherwise instructed.)

1. Open the **X410** workbook located in the Tutorial.02\Review folder included with your Data Files, and then save the workbook as **X410 Sales Comparison** in the same folder. In the Documentation sheet, enter your name in cell B4 and the current date in cell B5 in the format *mm/dd/yyyy*.

2. In the Documentation sheet, set the font color of cells A1 and A2 to blue, format the text in cell A1 in a 26-point Times New Roman font, and then format the text in cell A2 in a 10-point italicized Times New Roman font. In cell A1, change the font color of the text string "Comp" to red.

3. In the range A4:A6, set the font color to white and set the fill color to blue. In the range B4:B6, set the fill color to white. In the range A4:B6, add border lines around all of the cells.

4. In cell B5, display the date with the Long Date format and left-aligned within the cell.

5. In the Documentation sheet, insert a background image, using the **Paper.jpg** image file located in the Tutorial.02\Review folder included with your Data Files.

6. Use the Format Painter to copy the format from the range A1:A2 in the Documentation sheet to the range A1:A2 in the other two sheets. In cell A1, change the font color of the text string "Comp" to red.

7. In the Model Comparison sheet, merge and center the range A6:A15, center the text vertically, and then rotate the text to a vertical orientation. (*Hint:* In the Alignment group on the Home tab, click the Orientation button, and then click Vertical Text.) Center the text in the range C6:F6, and then indent the region labels in the range B7:B14 one character.

8. In the range C7:E15, format the numbers in a Number format using a thousands separator, no decimal places, and negative numbers displayed with a minus symbol. In the range F7:F15, format the numbers in a Percentage format with two decimal places.

9. Apply the Accent1 cell style to the range B6:F6. Apply the Accent1 cell style to the merged cell A6, and then increase that cell's font size to 18 points and bold. Apply the Total cell style to the range B15:F15.

10. In the range E7:E14, apply a conditional format that adds a Top/Bottom Rule to display the highest number in the range in dark green text with a green fill. In the range F7:F14, apply a conditional format that adds a Top/Bottom Rule to display the highest number in the range in dark red text with a light red fill.

11. Use the Format Painter to copy all of the formats from the range A6:F15 to the range A17:F26.

12. In cell D3, enter **highest**, and then apply a conditional format to cell D3 that adds a Highlight Cells Rule to format the cell that contains the text "highest" with Green Fill with Dark Green Text. In cell D4, enter **highest**, and then apply a conditional format to cell D3 that adds a Highlight Cells Rule to format the cell that contains the text "highest" with Light Red Fill with Dark Red Text.

13. In cell E3, enter **Highest increase in units sold**. In cell E4, enter **Highest % increase in units sold**. Format both cells with the Explanatory Text cell style.

14. In the Monthly Sales sheet, merge and center the range A4:D4, merge and center the range F4:I4, and then apply the Heading 1 style to both merged cells. In the range B5:D5;G5:I5, center the text.

15. In the range B6:D18;G6:I18, format the numbers to show a thousands separator (,) with no decimal places to the right of the decimal point.

16. Select the range A5:D18, and then apply Table Style Light 8 (the first table style in the second row of the Light section in the Table Styles gallery). Turn off the filter arrows, and then turn on only the header row, first column, and last column table style options. In the range A18:D18, apply the Total cell style.

17. Select the range F5:I18, and then repeat Step 16, applying the Total cell style to the range F18:I18.

18. In the range D6:D17, add green data bars. In the range I6:I17, add purple data bars.

19. For the Model Comparison and Monthly Sales worksheets, set the page orientations to landscape, display your name in the center section of the header, display the sheet name in the left section of the footer, display the workbook filename in the center section of the footer, and then display the current date in the right section of the footer.

20. Save and close your workbook. Submit the finished workbook to your instructor, either in printed or electronic form, as requested.

Apply | **Case Problem 1**

Use the skills you learned to create a sales report for a winter clothing company.

Data File needed for this Case Problem: Frosti.xlsx

FrostiWear Linda Young is a sales manager for FrostiWear, a successful new store based in Hillsboro, Oregon. She's tracking the sales figures for FrostiWear's line of gloves. She created a workbook that contains the sales figures from the past year for three glove models. She wants you to help format the sales report. Figure 2-41 shows a preview of the formatted report.

Figure 2-41

	Month	Region 1	Region 2	Region 3	Region 4	Region 5	Total	
								FrostiWear
								2009 Sales Report

FrostiWear

2009 Sales Report

	Month	Region 1	Region 2	Region 3	Region 4	Region 5	Total	
PolyFleece Mitts	Jan	1,150	1,690	930	2,850	1,210		7,830
	Feb	1,100	2,200	680	2,340	1,100		7,420
	Mar	1,070	1,290	960	2,740	1,180		7,240
	Apr	780	1,520	720	2,170	1,180		6,370
	May	1,070	1,370	700	1,940	1,210		6,290
	Jun	670	1,300	780	3,430	1,170		7,350
	Jul	1,390	1,590	1,240	2,230	1,430		7,880
	Aug	1,310	1,730	610	2,560	980		7,170
	Sep	1,100	1,820	370	3,040	1,100		7,430
	Oct	1,350	2,010	750	2,430	1,230		7,770
	Nov	680	1,620	780	3,210	1,230		7,520
	Dec	1,120	1,170	670	1,920	1,310		6,190
	Total	12,790	19,310	9,190	30,860	14,310		86,460
	Month	Region 1	Region 2	Region 3	Region 4	Region 5	Total	
ArcticBlast Gloves	Jan	790	1,160	620	2,590	760		5,920
	Feb	1,010	1,170	610	1,950	1,010		5,750
	Mar	710	1,270	600	2,050	930		5,560
	Apr	890	1,190	750	2,030	980		5,840
	May	990	1,340	660	2,670	1,040		6,700
	Jun	990	1,280	620	2,330	800		6,020
	Jul	780	1,180	690	2,260	920		5,830
	Aug	800	1,220	560	2,460	900		5,940
	Sep	810	1,150	670	2,500	970		6,100
	Oct	760	1,070	630	2,350	1,040		5,850
	Nov	770	1,140	630	2,540	1,080		6,160
	Dec	850	1,370	590	2,490	1,060		6,360
	Total	10,150	14,540	7,630	28,220	11,490		72,030
	Month	Region 1	Region 2	Region 3	Region 4	Region 5	Total	
Glomitts	Jan	340	780	280	1,670	600		3,670
	Feb	460	810	280	1,770	480		3,800
	Mar	410	820	310	1,490	460		3,490
	Apr	490	890	330	1,610	650		3,970
	May	470	960	290	1,580	540		3,840
	Jun	480	740	340	1,780	640		3,980
	Jul	470	760	320	1,500	640		3,690
	Aug	490	690	340	1,610	600		3,730
	Sep	420	780	340	1,660	680		3,880
	Oct	460	820	350	1,800	660		4,090
	Nov	550	830	440	1,250	590		3,660
	Dec	400	790	220	1,620	540		3,570
	Total	5,440	9,670	3,840	19,340	7,080		45,370

Complete the following. (*Note:* Text you need to enter is shown in bold for ease of reference only; do not bold the text unless otherwise instructed.)

1. Open the **Frosti** workbook located in the Tutorial.02\Case1 folder included with your Data Files, and then save the workbook as **FrostiWear Sales Report** in the same folder.

2. In the Documentation sheet, enter your name in cell B3 and the date in cell B4. Set the background color for all the cells in the worksheet to standard blue, and then set the background color for the range B3:B5 to white. Add a border line around each cell in the range B3:B5.

3. Change the font of cell A1 to the Headings font of the current theme, change the font size to 36 points, change the font color to white, and then bold the text. Change the font size of the range A3:A5 to 16 points, change the font color to white, and then bold the text.

4. In the Glove Sales worksheet, merge and center the range A1:H1, apply the Title cell style, and then increase the font size to 26 points. Merge and center the range A2:H2, apply the Heading 4 cell style, and then increase the font size to 16 points.

5. Merge and center the range A3:A16, set the alignment to Middle Align, rotate the text 90° counterclockwise, apply the Accent1 cell style, increase the font size to 18 points, and then bold the text.

6. Use the Format Painter to copy the format of merged cell A3 into the range A18:A31;A33:A46.

7. Center the text in the range C3:H3. Format the range C4:H16 to include thousands separators (,) and no decimal places. Use the Format Painter to copy the formats in the range C3:H16 to the range C18:H31;C33:H46.

8. In the range B3:H16, apply the Table Style Medium 2 table style. Turn off the filter arrows, and then display the header row, first column, last column, and banded rows. In the range B16:H16, change the fill color of the Total row to standard yellow. In the range H4:H15, change the fill color of the Total column to white.

9. Repeat Step 8 for the other two tables in the worksheet.

10. Increase the width of column H to 25 characters.

11. Add blue data bars to the range H4:H15. Also add blue data bars to the ranges H19:H30 and H34:H45.

12. In the Glove Sales worksheet, set the page orientation to landscape, insert manual page breaks at cells A18 and A33, and then repeat the first two rows of the worksheet on every printed page.

13. Display your name in the center header, display the filename in the left footer, display **Page** *page number* **of** *number of pages* in the center footer, and then display the current date in the right footer.

14. Save and close your workbook. Submit the finished workbook to your instructor, either in printed or electronic form, as requested.

| Create | Case Problem 2 |

Create and format a worksheet as a packing slip for GrillRite Grills.

Data File needed for this Case Problem: GrillRite.xlsx

GrillRite Grills Brian Simpko is a shipping manager at GrillRite Grills in Hammond, Indiana. He uses an Excel workbook to provide shipping and order information for customer orders and deliveries. He asks you to help create and format a worksheet that he can use to enter information for packing slips. Figure 2-42 shows the worksheet you'll create for Brian.

Figure 2-42

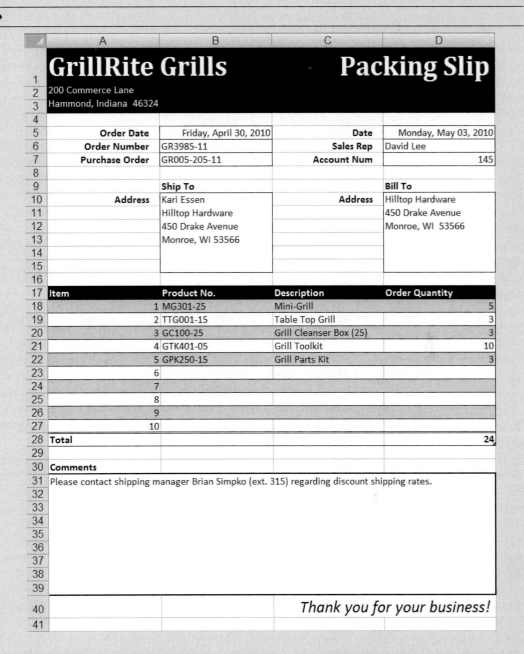

	A	B	C	D
1	**GrillRite Grills**		**Packing Slip**	
2	200 Commerce Lane			
3	Hammond, Indiana 46324			
4				
5	Order Date	Friday, April 30, 2010	Date	Monday, May 03, 2010
6	Order Number	GR3985-11	Sales Rep	David Lee
7	Purchase Order	GR005-205-11	Account Num	145
8				
9		Ship To		Bill To
10	Address	Kari Essen	Address	Hilltop Hardware
11		Hilltop Hardware		450 Drake Avenue
12		450 Drake Avenue		Monroe, WI 53566
13		Monroe, WI 53566		
14				
15				
16				
17	Item	Product No.	Description	Order Quantity
18	1	MG301-25	Mini-Grill	5
19	2	TTG001-15	Table Top Grill	3
20	3	GC100-25	Grill Cleanser Box (25)	3
21	4	GTK401-05	Grill Toolkit	10
22	5	GPK250-15	Grill Parts Kit	3
23	6			
24	7			
25	8			
26	9			
27	10			
28	Total			24
29				
30	Comments			
31	Please contact shipping manager Brian Simpko (ext. 315) regarding discount shipping rates.			
32				
33				
34				
35				
36				
37				
38				
39				
40			*Thank you for your business!*	
41				

Complete the following. (*Note:* Text you need to enter is shown in bold for ease of reference only; do not bold the text unless otherwise instructed.)

1. Open the **GrillRite** workbook located in the Tutorial.02\Case2 folder included with your Data Files, and then save the workbook as **GrillRite Grills Packing Slip** in the same folder. In the Documentation sheet, enter your name in cell B3 and the date in cell B4.

2. Insert a new worksheet at the end of the document named **Packing Slip**.

3. In the Packing Slip worksheet, select all of the cells in the worksheet. (*Hint:* Click the Select All button at the intersection of the row and column headings.) Change the font to the Body font of the current theme. For the range A1:D3, set the fill color to black and the font color to white.

4. Set the width of columns A through D to 20 characters. Set the height of the first row to 36.

5. Merge the range A1:B3, merge the range C1:D3, and then left- and top-align both merged cells.

6. In cell A1, enter the following three lines of text, and then format the first line in a 26-point bold font using the Headings font of the current theme:
   GrillRite Grills
   200 Commerce Lane
   Hammond, Indiana 46324

7. In cell C1, enter **Packing Slip**, format the text in a 26-point bold font using the Headings font of the current theme, and then right-align the text.

8. In the range A5:A7, enter the following three lines of text in a bold font, and then right-align the text and indent the text one character:
   Order Date
   Order Number
   Purchase Order

9. Format cell B5 in the Long Date format. Insert border lines around each of the cells in the range B5:B7.

10. In the range C5:C7, enter the following three lines of text, and then use the Format Painter to copy the formats from the range A5:B7 to the range C5:D7:
    Date
    Sales Rep
    Account Num

11. In cell B9, enter **Ship To** and in cell D9, enter **Bill To** and then format both in a bold font.

12. In cell A10, enter **Address** in a bold font, right-align the text, and then indent it one character.

13. Merge the cells in the range B10:B15, left- and top-align the cell contents, and then insert a border around the merged cell.

14. In cell C10, enter **Address**. Copy the format from the range A10:B15 into the range C10:D15.

15. Enter the following data into the worksheet:

Cell	Data
A17	**Item**
B17	**Product No.**
C17	**Description**
D17	**Order Quantity**
A18:A27	*the numbers from 1 to 10*

⊕ EXPLORE

16. For the range A17:D27, apply Table Style Medium 1, turn off the filter arrows, and display the header row, total row, and banded rows. In cell D28, select the SUM function from the list.

17. In cell A30, enter **Comments** in a bold font.

18. Merge the range A31:D39, left- and top-align the cell contents, and then add a thick box border around the merged cell.

19. In cell D40, enter **Thank you for your business!** in an italic, 16-point font, and then right-align the cell contents.

20. Enter the packing slip data shown in Figure 2-42.

21. Make sure the worksheet's page orientation is set to portrait, and then add a footer that displays your name in the left section, the filename in the center section, and the current date in the right section.

22. Save and close your workbook. Submit the finished workbook to your instructor, either in printed or electronic form, as requested.

Challenge | Case Problem 3

Explore how to use different Excel formatting features to create an election report.

Data File needed for this Case Problem: Iowa.xlsx

Lewis Reports Kay Lewis is a political columnist, commentator, and blogger. Her Web site, *Lewis Reports*, contains historical information on campaigns and elections. Recently, Kay compiled state-by-state and county-by-county voting totals for the past 15 presidential elections. She wants this information in an Excel workbook so she can analyze voting preferences and trends. Kay has created a workbook that contains the election results from the 2004 presidential election in Iowa. She asks you to format the workbook. She wants formats that quickly show which candidates won at the state and county levels as well as the margin of victory. Counties that went heavily Democratic or Republican should have formats that reflect this fact. Figure 2-43 shows a preview of the worksheet you'll format for Kay.

Figure 2-43

	A	B	C	D	E	F
1	**2004 Presidential Election**					
2						
3	**Iowa Vote Totals**					
4	State	Counties	Candidate	Votes		%
5	Iowa	99	George W. Bush (Rep)	746,600		50.46%
6			John F. Kerry (Dem)	733,102		49.54%
7			Total	1,479,702		
8						
9	**County-by-County Totals**					
10	County	Precincts	Candidate	Votes		%
11	Adair	10	Bush	2,393		56.63%
12			Kerry	1,833		43.37%
13			Total	4,226		
14	Adams	12	Bush	1,313		57.44%
15			Kerry	973		42.56%
16			Total	2,286		
17	Allamakee	23	Bush	3,523		50.62%
18			Kerry	3,437		49.38%
19			Total	6,960		

Complete the following. (*Note:* Text you need to enter is shown in bold for ease of reference only; do not bold the text unless otherwise instructed.)

1. Open the **Iowa** workbook located in the Tutorial.02\Case3 folder included with your Data Files, and then save the workbook as **Iowa Election Results** in the same folder. In the Documentation sheet, enter your name in cell B3 and the date in cell B4.

2. In the Iowa worksheet, apply the Title style to cell A1, and then apply the Heading 1 style to cells A3 and A9.

3. Apply the Accent3 style to the range A4:F4, and then center the heading text in cells D4:F4.

4. In the range D5:D7, format the numbers with a thousands separator (,) and no decimal places. In the range F5:F7, format the numbers as percentages with two decimal places.

5. Merge the range A5:A7, and then left- and top-align the cell contents. Merge the range B5:B7, and then right- and top-align the cell contents. Merge the range E5:E7.

6. Add border lines around each cell in the range A4:F7.

7. Format the range C5:D5 as white text on a standard red background. Format the range C6:D6 as white text on a standard light blue background.

8. Copy the format in the range A4:F7 to the range A10:F13.

⊕ EXPLORE
9. Add a double bottom border to the range A11:F13, and then copy the format in the range A11:F13 to the larger range A14:F307. Excel repeats the format until it fills up the larger range.

⊕ EXPLORE
10. Select the range E5;E11:E307, which shows the difference in votes between the Republican and Democratic candidates. Create a highlight rule to format cells with values greater than zero (indicating a Republican winner) in red text on a red background (thus, obscuring the text). (*Hint:* In the Greater Than dialog box, click Custom Format in the with list to open the Format Cells dialog box, and then use the Font tab and the Fill tab to select the colors.) Create a second highlight rule to format cells with values less than zero (indicating a Democratic winner) in light blue text on a light blue background. Reduce the width of column E to 3 characters.

11. Select the range F5:F7;F11:F307, which shows the vote percentages for each candidate. Apply green data bars, left-align the cells, and then increase the width of column F to 23 characters.

12. Verify the conditional formatting by entering different totals in column D and checking that the highlights and data bars are changed accurately. Restore the original values to the worksheet.

13. For the Iowa worksheet, make sure the page orientation is set to portrait, and then scale the page so that the width of the printout is one page and the height is automatic. (*Hint:* Use the buttons in the Scale To Fit group on the Page Layout tab.)

⊕ EXPLORE
14. Format the printout of the Iowa worksheet to repeat the first 10 rows of the worksheet on every page of the printout. Insert manual page breaks into the rest of the table to keep each county's vote from splitting between two pages.

15. Display your name in the center section of the header, and then display the filename in the left section of the footer, **Page** *page number* **of** *number of pages* in the center section of the footer, and the current date in the right section of the footer.

16. Save and close your workbook. Submit the finished workbook to your instructor, either in printed or electronic form, as requested.

Create	**Case Problem 4**

Use your creativity to format a meal-planning worksheet that highlights foods with high calorie counts and fat contents.

Data File needed for this Case Problem: Life.xlsx

Life Managers   Kate Dee is a dietician at *Life Managers*, a company in Kleinville, Michigan, that specializes in personal improvement, particularly in areas of health and fitness. Kate wants to create a meal-planning workbook for her clients who want to lose weight and improve their health. One goal of meal planning is to decrease the percentage of fat in the diet. Kate thinks it would be helpful to highlight foods that have a high percentage of fat as well as list their total fat calories. She already created an Excel workbook that contains a few sample food items and lists the number of calories and grams of fat in each item. She wants you to format this workbook.

Complete the following:

1. Open the **Life** workbook located in the Tutorial.02\Case4 folder included with your Data Files, and then save the workbook as **Life Managers Nutrition Table** in the same folder. In the Documentation sheet, enter your name in cell B3 and the date in cell B4.

2. Fat contains nine calories per gram. In the Meal Planner worksheet, add a column that calculates the calories from fat for each food item. The percentage of fat is calculated by dividing the calories from fat by the total number of calories. Enter this calculated value to the table for each food item.

3. Display all calories and grams of fat values with one decimal place. Display the fat percentages as percentages with one decimal place.

4. Design the rest of the Meal Planner worksheet as you'd like, but be sure to include at least one example of each of the following design elements:
   - A range merged into a single cell
   - Text centered and rotated within a cell
   - Cell styles applied to one or more elements
   - Border line styles applied to one or more elements

5. The FDA recommends for good health that the fat percentage should not exceed 30% of the total calories. Apply a rule to the fat percentages to highlight those food items that exceed the FDA recommendations. Include a legend to document the highlighting color you used.

6. Add data bars to the display of calories from fat values to graphically show the relative amounts of fat calories for different food items.

7. Add descriptive headers and footers to the printed document. Also insert page breaks and print titles to ensure that the printout is easily read and interpreted.

8. Save and close your workbook. Submit the finished workbook to your instructor, either in printed or electronic form, as requested.

Research | **Internet Assignments**

Use the Internet to find and work with data related to the topics presented in this tutorial.

The purpose of the Internet Assignments is to challenge you to find information on the Internet that you can use to work effectively with this software. The actual assignments are updated and maintained on the Course Technology Web site. Log on to the Internet and use your Web browser to go to the Student Online Companion for New Perspectives Office 2007 at **www.course.com/np/office2007**. Then navigate to the Internet Assignments for this tutorial.

Assess | **SAM Assessment and Training**

If you have a SAM user profile, you may have access to hands-on instruction, practice, and assessment of the skills covered in this tutorial. Log in to your SAM account (**http://sam2007.course.com**) to launch any assigned training activities or exams that relate to the skills covered in this tutorial.

Review | **Quick Check Answers**

Session 2.1

1. Serif fonts have extra decorative strokes at the end of each character. Sans serif fonts do not include these decorative strokes.

2. Theme colors are the colors that belong to a workbook's basic design, giving the elements in the workbook a uniform appearance. A standard color is always available to every workbook regardless of which themes might be in use.

3. the default Excel number format that displays numbers just as they're entered

4. Dates are formatted numeric values and, as such, are right-aligned in cells.

5. A1

6. Open the Format Cells dialog box.

7. You can use the Format Painter to copy and paste the format from one range into another, or you can define a style for the different ranges.

Session 2.2

1. A style applied to a table allows you to turn on table style options.

2. header row, total row, first column, last column, banded rows, and banded columns

3. A conditional format depends on the cell's value.

4. by the cell's value relative to other cells in the range for which the data bars have been defined

5. Select the range A1:C20, click the Conditional Formatting button in the Styles group on the Home tab, point to Top/Bottom Rules, and then click Top 10%. In the dialog box, enter 5 for the top items to show, and then click the OK button.

6. titles taken from worksheet rows or columns that are repeated on every page of the printed sheet

7. Select the first cell below the row at which you want to insert the page break, click the Breaks button in the Page Setup group on the Page Layout tab, and then click Insert Break.

Ending Data Files

Tutorial.02 →

Tutorial
ExerComp Sales
Report.xlsx

Review
X410 Sales
Comparison.xlsx

Case1
FrostiWear
Sales Report.xlsx

Case2
GrillRite Grills
Packing Slip.xlsx

Case3
Iowa Election
Results.xlsx

Case4
Life Managers
Nutrition Table.xlsx

Objectives

Session 3.1
- Copy formulas
- Build formulas containing relative, absolute, and mixed references
- Review function syntax
- Insert a function with the Insert Function dialog box
- Search for a function
- Type a function directly in a cell

Session 3.2
- Use AutoFill to fill in a formula and complete a series
- Enter the IF logical function
- Insert the date with the TODAY function
- Calculate monthly mortgage payments with the PMT financial function

Working with Formulas and Functions

Developing a Budget

Case | Drake Family Budget

Diane and Glenn Drake, newly married, are trying to balance career, school, and family life. Diane works full-time as a legal assistant, and Glenn is in a graduate program at a nearby university where he recently was hired as a lab assistant. In the summer, he does other work that brings additional income to the family. The couple just moved into a new apartment. Although Glenn and Diane's salaries have grown in the past years, the couple seems to have less cash on hand. This financial shortage has prompted them to take a closer look at their finances and figure out how to best manage them.

Diane has set up an Excel workbook and entered the take-home pay from their two jobs. She has identified and entered expenses the family pays on a monthly basis, such as the rent and grocery bill, as well as other expenses that occur only a few times a year, such as Glenn's tuition and vacations. She wants to calculate how much money they are bringing in and how much money they are spending. She also wants to come up with a savings plan for the down payment on a house they hope to buy in a few years.

You'll help Diane complete the workbook. Diane wants you to enter formulas to perform the calculations she needs to get a better overall picture of the family's finances, which, in turn, should help the couple manage their money more effectively.

Starting Data Files

Tutorial.03 →	Tutorial	Review	Case1	Case2	Case3	Case4
	Drake.xlsx	Timov.xlsx	Chemistry.xlsx	Wizard.xlsx	Loan.xlsx	V6.xlsx

Session 3.1

Understanding Cell References When Copying Formulas

Diane has already done a lot of the work on her family budget. She used data from the past year to estimate the couple's monthly expenses for the upcoming year and she knows their monthly take-home pay. She already entered this data into an Excel workbook. You'll open this workbook now.

To open Diane's workbook:

▶ **1.** Open the **Drake** workbook located in the **Tutorial.03\Tutorial** folder included with your Data Files, and then save the workbook as **Drake Family Budget** in the same folder.

▶ **2.** In the Documentation sheet, enter your name in cell B3 and the date in cell B4.

▶ **3.** Review the contents of the **2010 Proposed Budget** worksheet.

Diane organized the worksheet so the top displays the values that she'll use throughout her budget, such as the family's monthly take-home pay. One of the advantages of placing these values in their own cells in one location is that you can reference them in formulas throughout the worksheets. Then, rather than changing the same value in several locations, you can change it once and any formulas based on that cell are automatically updated to reflect the new value. The top of the worksheet will also include some summary calculations, such as the total take-home pay and expenses for the upcoming year as well as what Diane can expect to earn and spend on average each month. Below that section is a grid in which Diane wants to record how the family's take-home pay and expenses change month by month.

Diane points out a few things about her data. First, she has two possible values for the couple's take-home pay: one for months during the school year and one for months during the summer. Because Glenn works only part-time during the school year as a lab assistant, he earns less during that time than during the summer months. On the other hand, Diane earns the same amount throughout the year. The couple's expenses also vary throughout the year. January and August are particularly expensive months because Glenn has to pay for tuition and books for the upcoming semester. The couple is planning a trip next summer for a family reunion and expenses always seem to add up during the holiday season. With all of these factors in mind, Diane wants to make sure that they will not be caught short in any month. Glenn and Diane hope to purchase a house in about three years, so they need to follow a well-planned budget.

In the range D19:O20, Diane reserved space for entering the couple's monthly take-home pay. You'll enter their projected take-home pay for January through May, using the values at the top of the worksheet.

To insert the monthly take-home pay for January through May:

▶ **1.** Click cell **D19**, type **=E5**, and then press the **Enter** key. The value 2,000, Diane's take-home pay for January, appears in cell D19.

▶ **2.** In cell D20, enter the formula **=E6**. The value 950, Glenn's take-home pay for January, appears in cell D20.

3. In cell D21, enter the formula **=D19+D20**. This formula calculates the total take-home pay for the couple in the month of January.

The couple will have the same take-home pay for the next four months as they did in January, so you can copy the formulas from January into February through May.

4. Select the range **D19:D21**, and then, in the Clipboard group on the Home tab, click the **Copy** button.

5. Select the range **E19:H21**, and then, in the Clipboard group, click the **Paste** button. Figure 3-1 shows the couple's take-home pay for January through May.

Tip

You can also use the SUM function to calculate the total take-home pay by clicking the Sum button in the Editing group on the Home tab.

| | Take-home pay values copied through May | Figure 3-1 |

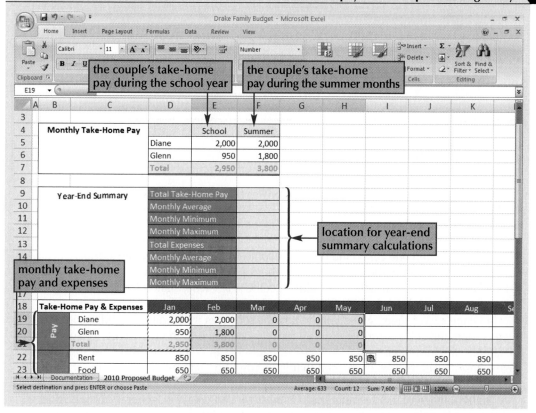

Notice that the formulas you copied and pasted from January resulted in incorrect values for February, March, April, and May. Diane's take-home pay of $2,000 is correct for January and February, but incorrectly changed to 0 for March, April, and May. Likewise, Glenn's take-home pay of $950 is correct for January, but incorrectly changed to $1,800 for February and 0 for March, April, and May. You need to investigate why you didn't get the results you expected. You'll examine how formulas change when copied to new locations in the workbook.

Using Relative References

When you enter a formula into a cell, Excel interprets cell references in the formula in relation to the cell's location. For example, the formula =A1 entered into cell A3 tells Excel to insert the value from the cell two rows above cell A3. When you copy the formula into other cells, Excel applies the same interpretation to the formula's new location, always displaying the value from the cell two rows above. Such cell references are called **relative references** because they are always interpreted in relation, or relative, to the location of the cell containing the formula. Figure 3-2 illustrates how a relative reference in a formula changes when the formula is copied to another range.

Figure 3-2 — Formula using a relative reference

original formula with a relative reference

	A	B	C	D
1	10	20	30	
2				
3	=A1			
4				
5				

formula copied to a new range (column and row references shift based on cell location)

	A	B	C	D
1	10	20	30	
2				
3	=A1	=B1	=C1	
4				
5				

formula results

	A	B	C	D
1	10	20	30	
2				
3	10	20	30	
4				
5				

In this figure, the formula =A1 entered in cell A3 produced the result of 10, which is the value in cell A1. After the formula in cell A3 was copied to cell B3, the copied formula changed to =B1 and produced the result of 20, which is the value in cell B1. As you can see, when the formula was copied one cell to the right, the relative reference in the original formula (A1) adjusted one cell to the right to become B1. Similarly, when the formula in cell A3 was copied two cells to the right to cell C3, the copied formula changed to =C1 and produced the result of 30, which is the value in cell C1. In each instance, the formula references the cell two rows above the cell that contains the formula.

In Diane's worksheet, when you copied the formulas in the range D19:D21 into a new range, the cell references in those formulas adjusted to their new cell location. For example, the formula in cell E19 is =F5, the formula in cell F19 is =G5, and so forth. In each case, Excel references the cell that is 14 rows up and one column to the right of the current location.

The advantage of relative references is that you can create a "general" formula that you can use again and again in your worksheet. Relative references free you from having to rewrite a formula each time you copy it to a new location. For example, you can write a formula to add the values in a column of data, and then copy that formula to other columns to quickly add their values. You used this technique in the previous set of steps to calculate the couple's total take-home pay for each of the months from January to May.

Using Absolute References

Sometimes, you want references that are fixed on specific cells in the worksheet. This usually occurs when the referenced cell contains a value that needs to be repeated in different formulas throughout the workbook. In Diane's worksheet, any formulas involving take-home pay should be fixed on those cells that contain those values, which are the range E5:E6 for the school months and the range F5:F6 for the summer months.

References that are fixed are called **absolute references**. In Excel, absolute references are marked with a $ (dollar sign) before each column and row designation. For example, B8 is a relative reference to cell B8, whereas $B$8 is an absolute reference to cell B8. When you copy a formula that contains an absolute reference to a new location, the reference does not change. Figure 3-3 shows an example of how copying a formula with an absolute reference does not change the cell reference.

Formula using an absolute reference Figure 3-3

original formula
with an absolute
reference

	A	B	C	D
1	10	20	30	
2				
3	=$A$1			
4				
5				

formula copied
into a new range
(column and row
references fixed
regardless of
cell location)

	A	B	C	D
1	10	20	30	
2				
3	=$A$1	=$A$1	=$A$1	
4				
5				

formula results

	A	B	C	D
1	10	20	30	
2				
3	10	10	10	
4				
5				

In this figure, the formula =$A$1 entered in cell A3 produced the result of 10, which is the value in cell A1. After the formula in cell A3 was copied to cell B3, the copied formula remained unchanged and produced the result of 10, which is the value in cell A1. As you can see, when the formula was copied one cell to the right, the absolute reference in the original formula (A1) did not change. Similarly, when the formula in cell A3 was copied two cells to the right to cell C3, the copied formula and the results did not change. In each instance, the formula references the cell A1.

You'll see how absolute references work when you fix the formulas in cells D19 and D20, and then recopy the formulas.

To use absolute references in the take-home pay formulas:

▶ 1. In cell D19, enter **=$E$5**. This formula contains an absolute reference to cell E5, which contains Diane's take-home pay during the school months.

▶ 2. In cell D20, enter **=$E$6**. This formula contains an absolute reference to cell E6, which contains Glenn's take-home pay during the school months.

▶ 3. Copy the corrected formulas in the range **D19:D20**, and then paste them in the range **E19:H20**. As shown in Figure 3-4, the months of February through May now correctly show the take-home pay values that Diane has specified for the school months.

| Figure 3-4 | Results of formulas with absolute references |

> **4.** Click each cell in the range E19:H20 to verify that the formulas =$E$5 and =$E$6 were copied into the appropriate cells.

| **Understanding Relative and Absolute References**

Part of writing effective formulas is knowing when to use relative and absolute references. Use relative references when you want to repeat the same formula with different cells. For example, in a customer order worksheet, you might need to calculate the cost of an item multiplied by the quantity being purchased. To repeat this formula for all of the items in an order, you would use relative references for the item cost and item quantity. Use absolute references when you want different formulas to refer to the same cell. For example, in a customer order worksheet, you might need to apply the same sales tax percentage to each order. You could store the sales tax percentage in a worksheet cell, and then use an absolute reference to that cell in the formula that multiples the order total with the sales tax percentage.

Using Mixed References

A formula can also contain mixed references. A **mixed reference** contains both relative and absolute references. For example, a mixed reference for cell A2 can be either $A2 or A$2. In the mixed reference $A2, the column reference is fixed on column A and the reference to row 2 is relative. In the mixed reference A$2, the column reference is relative and the row reference is fixed. In other words, a mixed reference "locks" one part of the cell reference while the other part can change. When you copy and paste a formula with a mixed reference to a new location, the absolute portion of the cell reference remains fixed and the relative portion shifts. For example, the mixed reference in the formula =$A2 in cell B2 becomes =$A3 when copied to cell B3, and the mixed reference in the formula =B$1 in cell B2 becomes =C$1 when copied to cell C2.

Figure 3-5 shows an example of using a formula with a mixed reference in which the column is relative and the row is fixed. When you copy and paste the formula from cell A3 into cells A4 and A5, the row reference remains fixed on row 1. In this instance, the column reference, which is relative, doesn't change either, because the formula was copied to the same column. However, when you copy the formula to other columns, the column reference, which is relative, shifts to reflect the new column location. The row reference remains fixed on row 1 and doesn't change no matter where you copy the formula.

Formulas using mixed references ◀ **Figure 3-5**

original formula
with a mixed
reference

	A	B	C	D
1	10	20	30	
2				
3	=A$1			
4				
5				

formula copied
to a new range
(row reference
fixed on row 1,
column reference
shifts based on
the cell location)

	A	B	C	D
1	10	20	30	
2				
3	=A$1	=B$1	=C$1	
4	=A$1	=B$1	=C$1	
5	=A$1	=B$1	=C$1	

formula results

	A	B	C	D
1	10	20	30	
2				
3	10	20	30	
4	10	20	30	
5	10	20	30	

As you develop formulas, you might want to switch a cell reference from relative to absolute or mixed. Rather than retyping the formula, you can switch the reference in editing mode by selecting the cell reference and pressing the **F4 key**. As you press the function key, Excel cycles through the different reference types, starting by changing a relative reference to an absolute reference, then to a mixed reference with the row absolute, then to a mixed reference with the column absolute, and then finally back to a relative reference.

Entering Relative, Absolute, and Mixed References | Reference Window

- To enter a relative reference, type the cell reference as it appears in the worksheet. For example, enter B2 for cell B2.
- To enter an absolute reference, type $ (a dollar sign) before both the row and column references. For example, enter $B$2.
- To enter a mixed reference, type $ before either the row or column reference. For example, enter $B2 or B$2.

or

- Select the cell reference you want to change.
- Press the F4 key to cycle the reference from relative to absolute to mixed and then back to relative.

You'll use the F4 key to cycle through the different types of references as you enter the remaining formulas with the take-home pay for the summer months.

To insert the remaining take-home pay formulas:

▶ **1.** Click cell **I19**, type **=**, and then click cell **F5**. The formula =F5 appears in the cell, which remains in editing mode. This formula enters Diane's summer take-home pay for June.

▶ **2.** Select the cell reference **F5** in the formula, and then press the **F4** key. The formula changes to =$F$5, which is an absolute reference.

▶ **3.** Press the **F4** key again. The formula changes to =F$5, which is a mixed reference with a relative column reference and an absolute row reference.

▶ **4.** Press the **F4** key again to change to formula to =$F5, which is a mixed cell reference with an absolute column reference and a relative row reference.

▶ **5.** Press the **F4** key again to return to the formula to =F5, which is a relative reference.

▶ **6.** Press the **F4** key one more time to change the formula back to =$F$5, and then press the **Enter** key to exit editing mode. You want an absolute reference to cell F5 so that the formula always references Diane's summer take-home pay.

▶ **7.** In cell I20, enter the formula **=$F$6**. This formula uses an absolute reference to enter Glenn's summer take-home pay for June, and won't change when copied to the rest of the months.

▶ **8.** In cell I21, enter the formula **=I19+I20**. This formula adds Diane and Glenn's take-home pay for June.

▶ **9.** Copy the range **I19:I21**, and then paste the copied formulas into the range **J19:K21**. The summer take-home pay values appear for the months of June through August.

You'll complete the take-home pay values for the remaining school months.

▶ **10.** Copy the range **D19:D21**, and then paste it into the range **L19:O21**. The take-home pay for the couple is entered for all twelve months of the year.

Now that you've calculated the monthly take-home pay and expenses for Diane and Glenn, you'll summarize these for the entire year. Diane wants to compare the couple's annual take-home pay to their annual expenses. She also wants to know the average take-home pay and average expenses for a typical month.

Working with Functions

The month-by-month data is too large to see in the workbook window unless you reduce the zoom level, but then the resulting text would be too small to read. Rather than adding another column to this large collection of data, Diane wants to summarize the data at the top of the worksheet. You'll use Excel functions to do these summary calculations.

Summarizing Data | InSight

Statisticians, scientists, and economists often want to reduce a large sample of data into a few easy-to-use statistics. How do they best summarize the data? The most common approach is to average the sample data. You can calculate the average in Excel with the AVERAGE function. However, this is not always the best choice. Averages are susceptible to extremely large or small data values. Imagine calculating the average price of houses on a block that has one mansion and several small homes. The average value is heavily affected by the mansion. When the data includes a few extremely large or extremely small values, it might be best to use the **median**, or middle, value from the sample. You can calculate the median in Excel with the MEDIAN function.

Another approach is to calculate the most common value in the data, otherwise known as the **mode**. The mode is most often used with data that has only a few possible values, such as the number of bedrooms in a house. The most common number of bedrooms per house might provide more relevant information than the average number of bedrooms. You can calculate the mode in Excel using the MODE function.

Understanding Function Syntax

Recall from Tutorial 1 that a function is a named operation that returns a value. Every function has to follow a set of rules, or **syntax**, which specifies how the function should be written. The general syntax of all functions is as follows:

FUNCTION(argument1, argument2, ...)

In this syntax, *FUNCTION* is the name of the function and *argument1*, *argument2*, and so forth are **arguments**, which are the numbers, text, or cell references used by the function to return a value. Arguments are always separated by a comma.

Not all functions have arguments, and some functions have **optional arguments**, which are not required for the function to return a value, but can be included to provide more control over the returned value. If an optional argument is not included, Excel assumes a default value for it. These tutorials show optional arguments within square brackets along with the argument's default value, as follows:

Tip
Optional arguments are always placed last in the argument list.

FUNCTION(argument1, [argument2=value2, ...])

In this function, *argument2* is an optional argument and *value2* is the default value used for this argument. As you learn more about individual functions, you will learn which arguments are required and which are optional, and the default values used for optional arguments.

There are hundreds of Excel functions, which are organized into 11 categories. Figure 3-6 describes these different categories.

Figure 3-6 **Categories of Excel functions**

Category	Contains functions that
Cube	Retrieve data from multidimensional databases involving online analytical processing or OLAP
Database	Retrieve and analyze data stored in databases
Date & Time	Analyze or create date and time values and time intervals
Engineering	Analyze engineering problems
Financial	Have financial applications
Information	Return information about the format, location, or contents of worksheet cells
Logical	Return logical (true-false) values
Lookup & Reference	Look up and return data matching a set of specified conditions from a range
Math & Trig	Have math and trigonometry applications
Statistical	Provide statistical analyses of a set of data
Text	Return text values or evaluate text

You can learn about each function using the Help system. Figure 3-7 describes some of the more common Math, Trig, and Statistical functions that you might often use in your workbooks.

Figure 3-7 **Math, Trig, and Statistical functions**

Function	Category	Description
AVERAGE(number1 [, number2, number3, ...])	Statistical	Calculates the average of a collection of numbers, where number1, number2, and so forth are either numbers or cell references. Only number1 is required. For more than one cell reference or to enter numbers directly into the function, use the optional arguments number2, number3, and so forth.
COUNT(value1 [, value2, value3, ...])	Statistical	Counts how many cells in a range contain numbers, where value1, value2, and so forth are text, numbers, or cell references. Only value1 is required. For more than one cell reference or to enter numbers directly into the function, use the optional arguments value2, value3, and so forth.
COUNTA(value1 [, value2, value3, ...])	Statistical	Counts how many cells are not empty in ranges value1, value2, and so forth, or how many numbers are listed within value1, value2, and so forth.
INT(number)	Math & Trig	Displays the integer portion of a number, number.
MAX(number1 [, number2, number3, ...])	Statistical	Calculates the maximum value of a collection of numbers, where number1, number2, and so forth are either numbers or cell references.
MEDIAN(number1 [, number2, number3, ...])	Statistical	Calculates the median, or middle, value of a collection of numbers, where number1, number2, and so forth are either numbers or cell references.
MIN(number1 [, number2, number3, ...])	Statistical	Calculates the minimum value of a collection of numbers, where number1, number2, and so forth are either numbers or cell references.
RAND()	Math & Trig	Returns a random number between 0 and 1.
ROUND(number, num_digits)	Math & Trig	Rounds a number to a specified number of digits, where number is the number you want to round and num_digits specifies how many digits to which you want to round the number.
SUM(number1 [, number2, number3, ...])	Math & Trig	Adds a collection of numbers, where number1, number2, and so forth are either numbers or cell references.

For example, the AVERAGE function calculates the average value from a collection of numbers. The syntax of the AVERAGE function is as follows:

```
AVERAGE(number1, [number2, number3, ...])
```

In this function, *number1*, *number2*, *number3*, and so forth are either numbers or cell references to numbers. For example, the following function calculates the average of 1, 2, 5, and 8:

```
AVERAGE(1, 2, 5, 8)
```

This function returns the value 4. However, you usually reference values entered in the worksheet. So, if the range A1:A4 contains the values 1, 2, 5, and 8, the following function also returns a value of 4:

```
AVERAGE(A1:A4)
```

Functions can be incorporated as part of larger formulas. For example, consider the following formula:

```
=MAX(A1:A100)/100
```

This formula returns the maximum value from the range A1:A100, and then divides that value by 100. Functions can also be placed inside another function, or **nested**. If a formula contains several functions, Excel starts with the innermost function and then moves outward. For example, the following formula first calculates the average of the values in the range A1:A100 using the AVERAGE function, and then extracts the integer portion of that value using the INT function.

```
=INT(AVERAGE(A1:A100))
```

One challenge of nesting functions is to make sure that you include all of the parentheses. You can check this by counting the number of left parentheses, and making sure that number matches the number of right parentheses. If the numbers don't match, Excel will not accept the formula and offers a suggestion for rewriting the formula so the left and right parentheses do match.

Inserting a Function

Functions are organized in the Function Library group in the Formulas tab on the Ribbon. In the Function Library, you can select a function from a function category or you can open the Insert Function dialog box to search for a particular function.

Inserting a Function | Reference Window

- Click the Formulas tab on the Ribbon.
- To insert a function from a specific category, click the appropriate category button in the Function Library group. To search for a function, click the Insert Function button in the Function Library group, enter a description of the function, and then click the Go button.
- Select the appropriate function from the list of functions.
- Enter the argument values in the Function Arguments dialog box, and then click the OK button.

You'll use the SUM function to add the total take-home pay for the entire year in Diane's proposed budget.

To insert the SUM function:

▶ **1.** Click cell **F9** to select it.

▶ **2.** Click the **Formulas** tab on the Ribbon.

▶ **3.** In the Function Library group on the Formulas tab, click the **Math & Trig** button. A list displays all of the math and trigonometry functions arranged in alphabetical order.

▶ **4.** Scroll down the list, and then click **SUM**. The Function Arguments dialog box opens.

The Function Arguments dialog box lists all of the arguments associated with the SUM function. Required arguments are in bold type; optional arguments are in normal type. Excel tries to "anticipate" the values for the different arguments based on the location of the cell containing the formula and the data contained in other cells of the worksheet. In this case, the range reference F5:F8, which is the range that contains the couple's take-home pay for the summer months and is the range of numbers closest to the cell in which you are entering the SUM function, already appears for the first argument. Because you want to calculate the total take-home pay for the year, you'll replace this range reference with the reference D21:O21.

To enter the argument for the SUM function:

▶ **1.** Click in the worksheet, and then select the range **D21:O21**. The range reference appears as the value of the Number1 argument. See Figure 3-8.

Figure 3-8 **Function Arguments dialog box**

Tip

You can click the Collapse Dialog Box button to shrink the Function Arguments dialog box to see more of the worksheet, select the range, and then click the Expand Dialog Box button to restore the dialog box.

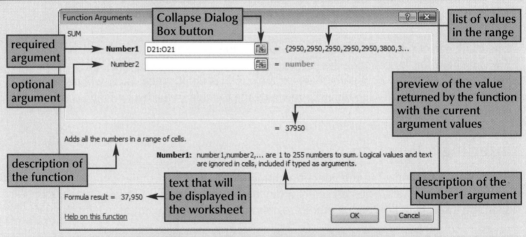

▶ **2.** Click the **OK** button. The formula =SUM(D21:O21) is inserted into cell F9, which displays the value 37,950. This represents the total take-home pay for the year from both Diane and Glenn.

Diane also wants to know how this value compares to the total expenses for the year.

▶ **3.** Click cell **F13**. This is where you want to enter the second SUM function.

▶ **4.** In the Function Library group on the Formulas tab, click the **Math & Trig** button, and then click **SUM**. The Function Arguments dialog box opens. You'll enter the monthly expenses stored in the range D32:O32 for the argument.

> **5.** Select the range **D32:O32** in the worksheet, and then click the **OK** button in the Function Arguments dialog box. The formula =SUM(D32:O32) is inserted in cell F13, which displays the value 35,840. This represents the total projected expenses for the upcoming year. See Figure 3-9.

SUM functions entered ◄ **Figure 3-9**

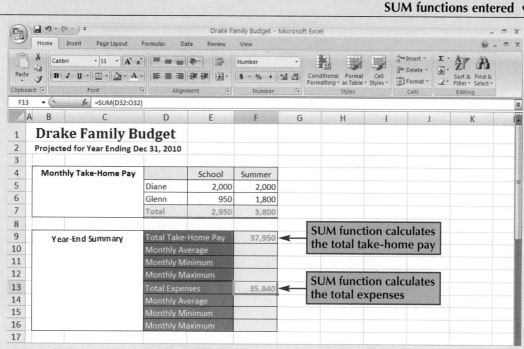

Diane projects that she and Glenn will earn roughly $2,000 more than they will spend throughout the year. It's easier for Diane to plan her budget if she knows how much, on average, the couple takes home and spends each month. You can use the AVERAGE function to do this calculation using the same method you used for the SUM function; but what if you weren't sure of the function's name or its function category? You can use the Insert Function dialog box. The **Insert Function dialog box** organizes all of the functions by category and allows you to search for functions that perform particular calculations.

To insert the AVERAGE function to calculate the average take-home pay:

> **1.** Click cell **F10**.

> **2.** In the Function Library group on the Formulas tab, click the **Insert Function** button. The Insert Function dialog box opens.

> **3.** Type **Calculate an average value** in the Search for a function box, and then click the **Go** button. Functions for calculating an average appear in the Select a function box. See Figure 3-10.

Figure 3-10	Insert Function dialog box

description of function

list of functions that match the search description

syntax and description of the selected function

4. Verify that **AVERAGE** is selected in the Select a function box, and then click the **OK** button. The Function Arguments dialog box opens with the arguments for the AVERAGE function. As before, a range reference for cells directly above this cell already appears for the Number1 argument.

5. Select the range reference in the Number1 argument box, and then select the range **D21:O21** in the worksheet.

6. Click the **OK** button. The dialog box closes, and the formula =AVERAGE(D21:O21) is entered in cell F10, displaying the value 3,163, the average take-home pay.

Although the exact average take-home pay is 3,162.50, you see the value 3,163 in the cell because Diane formatted the worksheet to display currency values to the nearest dollar.

How does the couple's average take-home pay compare to their average expenses? To find out, you'll use the AVERAGE function again. Because the function has already been used in your workbook, you can select it from a list of recently used functions.

To calculate the average monthly expenses:

1. Click cell **F14**, and then click the **Insert Function** button f_x on the formula bar. The Insert Function dialog box opens.

2. If necessary, click the **Or select a category** arrow, and then click **Most Recently Used**. The most recently used functions, sorted in order of recent use, appear in the Select a function box. The AVERAGE function is at the top followed by the SUM function.

3. Verify that **AVERAGE** is selected in the Select a function box, and then click the **OK** button.

4. Select the range **D32:O32** to insert the range reference D32:O32 in the Number1 box.

5. Click the **OK** button. The formula =AVERAGE(D32:O32) is inserted into cell F14, displaying the value 2,987. This represents the average expenses per month under Diane's budget. See Figure 3-11.

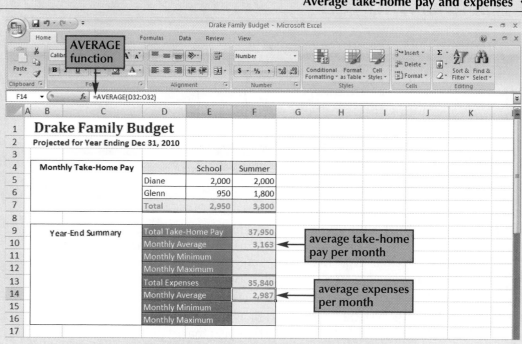

Average take-home pay and expenses | **Figure 3-11**

From the two averages, Diane sees that the couple will bring in about $200 more than they spend each month. That is not much, so Diane wants to know how much variation is in the budget. What is the most money she could expect to take home during a single month in the upcoming year? What is the least? And what are the largest and smallest values for the monthly expenses? You'll use the MAX and MIN functions to calculate those values.

Typing a Function

After you become more familiar with functions, it is often faster to type the functions directly in cells rather than using the Insert Function dialog box or the Function Library. As you begin to type a function name within a formula, a list of functions that begin with the letters you typed appears. For example, when you type *S*, the list shows all of the functions starting with the letter *S*; when you type *SU,* the list shows only those functions starting with the letters *SU,* and so forth. This helps to ensure that you're entering a legitimate Excel function name.

You'll type the formulas to calculate the minimum monthly take-home pay and expenses under Diane's proposed budget.

To calculate the minimum values for monthly take-home pay and expenses:

1. Click cell **F11**. This is the cell in which you want to enter the minimum take-home pay.

2. Type **=M**. As you type a formula, a list with function names starting with *M* opens.

3. Type **I**. The list shows only those functions starting with *MI*. See Figure 3-12. As soon as the function you want appears in the list, you can double-click its name to enter it in the cell without typing the rest of its name.

Figure 3-12 **Typing a function**

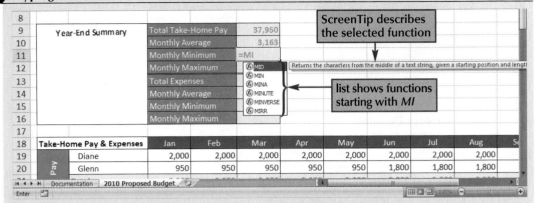

4. Double-click **MIN** in the list box. The MIN function with its opening parenthesis is inserted into cell F11 and a ScreenTip shows the syntax for the function. At this point, you can either type in the range reference or select the range with your mouse. To avoid typing errors, it's often better to use your mouse to enter range references.

5. Select the range **D21:O21**, type **)**, and then press the **Enter** key. The formula =MIN(D21:O21) is inserted in cell F11, displaying the value 2,950. This is the minimum amount that Diane expects the couple to bring home in a single month for the upcoming year.

Next, you'll calculate the minimum monthly expense projected for the year.

6. Click cell **F15**, and then follow Steps 2 through 5 to enter the formula **=MIN(D32:O32)** in cell F15. The cell displays the value 2,265, which is the least amount that Diane expects to spend in a single month in the upcoming year.

The final piece of the year-end summary is the maximum monthly value for both take-home pay and expenses. Maximum values are calculated using the MAX function.

To calculate the maximum values for monthly take-home pay and expenses:

1. Click cell **F12**, and then enter the formula **=MAX(D21:O21)**. The value 3,800 appears in cell F12, indicating that the maximum take-home pay the couple can expect in a single month is $3,800.

Trouble? If #NAME? appears in the cell, you probably mistyped the function name. Edit the formula to correct the misspelling.

2. Click cell **F16**, and then enter the formula **=MAX(D32:O32)**. The value 5,170 appears in cell F16, indicating that the maximum expenses for a single month are projected to be $5,170. See Figure 3-13.

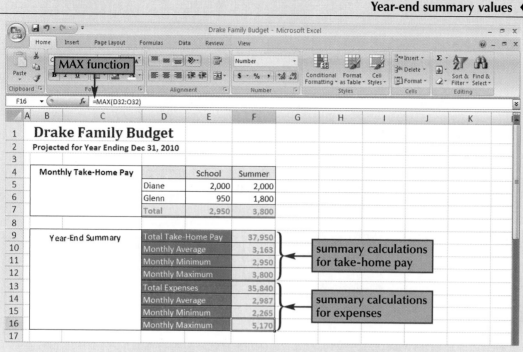

Year-end summary values | **Figure 3-13**

Based on the year-end summary, Diane and Glenn's monthly take-home pay will range from a minimum of $2,950 to a maximum of $3,800 with an average of about $3,163. Monthly expenses, on the other hand, range from a minimum of $2,265 to a maximum of $5,170 with an average of $2,987. Clearly, the Drake family budget does not have a lot of wiggle room.

Diane has just been promoted at work. Her take-home pay will increase from $2,000 per month to $2,500 per month. She wants to know how this affects the year-end summary.

To modify Diane's estimates of her take-home pay:

▶ **1.** In cell E5, enter the value **2500**.

▶ **2.** In cell F5, enter the value **2500**. Figure 3-14 shows the updated calculations for the couple's take-home pay for the entire year as well as the monthly average, minimum, and maximum values.

| Figure 3-14 | Revised salary values |

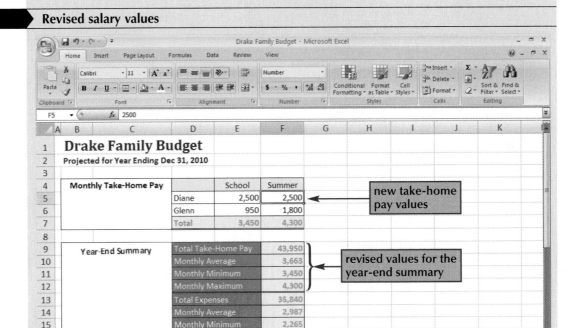

With Diane's new position, the couple's annual take-home pay increases from $37,950 to $43,950 and the monthly average increases from $3,163 to $3,663. The couple's take-home pay should exceed their expenses by an average of $700 per month. The monthly take-home pay now ranges from a minimum of $3,450 up to a maximum of $4,300. The raise has brightened the couple's financial picture quite a bit.

Diane now has a better picture of the family's finances for the upcoming year, and she's more confident about how to manage the couple's budget. She and Glenn hope to save enough for a down payment on a house in a few years. With the promotion, this seems like a real possibility. In the next session, you'll help Diane explore the couple's options in planning for a purchase of a house.

Review | Session 3.1 Quick Check

1. What is the absolute cell reference for cell B21? What are the two mixed references?
2. Cell B10 contains the formula =B1+B2. What formula is entered if this formula is copied and pasted into cell C20?
3. Cell B10 contains the formula =$B1+B$2. What formula is entered if this formula is copied and pasted into cell C20?
4. Cell B10 contains the formula =AVERAGE($A1:$A5). What formula is entered if this formula is copied and pasted into cell C20?
5. What are optional arguments? What happens if you do not include an optional argument in a function?
6. What formula should you enter to add the numbers in the range B1:B10?
7. The range of a set of values is defined as the maximum value minus the minimum value. What formula would you enter to calculate the range of the values in B1:B10?
8. What formula would you enter to calculate the ratio of the maximum value in the range B1:B10 to the minimum value?

Session 3.2

Working with AutoFill

Diane and Glenn hope to purchase a home in the next three years. Currently, the couple has $4,000 in their savings account, and they plan to start putting money into a home savings account. Diane wants to see what impact her proposed budget will have on their savings. To do that, you'll enter the current account information at the top of the worksheet. You'll include the current savings balance and the expected balance at the end of the next year under Diane's proposed budget.

To produce the results Diane wants, you will use a feature known as **AutoFill**, which copies content and formats from a cell or range into an adjacent cell or range. You'll begin by copying the formatting from the Monthly Take-Home Pay section to the range where you'll enter this new Savings section.

To format the range and insert data about the couple's savings account:

▶ 1. If you took a break after the previous session, make sure the Drake Family Budget workbook is open and the 2010 Proposed Budget worksheet is active.

▶ 2. Select the range **B4:F7**, and then, in the Clipboard group on the Home tab, click the **Format Painter** button to copy the formatting for the new section.

▶ 3. Select the range **H4:L7** to paste the selected format to this range.

▶ 4. Referring to Figure 3-15, enter the labels and data shown in the range H4:L7. In cell K7, enter a formula to add the values in the range K5:K6. In cell L7, enter a formula to add the values in the range L5:L6.

Initial savings data ◀ Figure 3-15

Diane wants to learn how much the couple could save each month. To find out, you must first determine the couple's monthly net cash flow, which is equal to their take-home pay minus their expenses. You'll start by formatting the cells where you'll enter this data and calculating the net cash flow during the month of January.

To format the range and calculate the net cash flow for January:

▶ 1. Click cell **B18**, and then, in the Clipboard group on the Home tab, click the **Format Painter** button.

▶ 2. Select the range **B33:C33**. The formatting from cell B18 is pasted into the range, merging the two cells.

▶ **3.** In cell B33, type **Net Cash Flow**, and then right-align the contents of the cell.

▶ **4.** In cell D33, enter the formula **=D21–D32**. This formula subtracts total expenses from total take-home pay for the month of January. The value –1,590 is displayed, indicating a projected shortfall of $1,590 for the month of January. Next, you'll format cell D33 to distinguish net cash flow amount from the other values.

▶ **5.** Click cell **D33**.

▶ **6.** In the Styles group, click the **Cell Styles** button, and then click the **60% – Accent6** style. See Figure 3-16.

Figure 3-16 ▶ **January net cash flow**

		Jan	Feb	Mar	Apr	May	Jun	Jul	Aug	S
18	**Take-Home Pay & Expenses**	Jan	Feb	Mar	Apr	May	Jun	Jul	Aug	
19	Diane	2,500	2,500	2,500	2,500	2,500	2,500	2,500	2,500	
20	Glenn	950	950	950	950	950	1,800	1,800	1,800	
21	Total	3,450	3,450	3,450	3,450	3,450	4,300	4,300	4,300	
22	Rent	850	850	850	850	850	850	850	850	
23	Food	650	650	650	650	650	650	650	650	
24	Utilities	225	210	175	165	120	135	145	145	
25	Phone	75	75	75	75	75	75	75	75	
26	Car Payments	175	175	175	175	175	175	175	175	
27	Insurance	125	125	125	125	125	125	125	125	
28	Tuition	1,900	0	0	0	0	900	0	1,900	
29	Books	700	0	0	0	0	300	0	700	
30	Travel	190	120	150	450	120	180	720	400	
31	Miscellaneous	150	150	150	150	150	150	150	150	
32	Total	5,040	2,355	2,350	2,640	2,265	3,540	2,890	5,170	
33	Net Cash Flow	-1,590								
34										
35	**Monthly Savings**									
36	Starting Balance									

January shows a negative net cash flow

Documentation | 2010 Proposed Budget

Ready | 120%

AutoFilling a Formula

You could copy and paste the formula and format from cell D33 into the rest of the row to calculate the net cash flow for the other months, as you've done before, but AutoFill is faster. The small black square in the lower-right corner of a selected cell or range is called the **fill handle**. When you drag the fill handle over an adjacent range, Excel copies the formulas and formats from the original cell into the adjacent range. This process is more efficient than the two-step process of copying and pasting.

Reference Window | **Copying Formulas and Formats with AutoFill**

- Select the cell or range that contains the formula or formulas you want to copy.
- Drag the fill handle in the direction you want to copy the formula(s) and then release the mouse button.
- To copy only the formats or only the formulas, click the AutoFill Options button and select the appropriate option.

or

- Select the cell or range that contains the formula or formulas you want to copy.
- In the Editing group on the Home tab, click the Fill button.
- Select the appropriate fill direction and fill type (or click Series, enter the desired fill series options, and then click the OK button).

You'll use AutoFill to fill in the cash flow values for the remaining months of the year.

To copy the formulas and formats using AutoFill:

▶ **1.** Click cell **D33**, if necessary. The fill handle appears in the lower-right corner of the cell.

▶ **2.** Position the pointer over the fill handle until the pointer changes to **+**.

▶ **3.** Drag the fill handle over the range **E33:O33**. A solid outline appears around the selected range as you move the pointer.

▶ **4.** Release the mouse button. The selected range is filled in with the formula and format from cell D33, and the AutoFill Options button appears in the lower-right corner of the selected cells. See Figure 3-17.

Tip

With AutoFill, it's easy to copy formulas into the wrong range; if that happens, click the Undo button and try again.

Formulas and formats copied with AutoFill ◄ Figure 3-17

	Mar	Apr	May	Jun	Jul	Aug	Sep	Oct	Nov	Dec	
18	Mar	Apr	May	Jun	Jul	Aug	Sep	Oct	Nov	Dec	
19	2,500	2,500	2,500	2,500	2,500	2,500	2,500	2,500	2,500	2,500	
20	950	950	950	1,800	1,800	1,800	950	950	950	950	
21	3,450	3,450	3,450	4,300	4,300	4,300	3,450	3,450	3,450	3,450	
22	850	850	850	850	850	850	850	850	850	850	
23	650	650	650	650	650	650	650	650	650	650	
24	175	165	120	135	145	145	140	140	170	210	
25	75	75	75	75	75	75	75	75	75	75	
26	175	175	175	175	175	175	175	175	175	175	
27	125	125	125	125	125	125	125	125	125	125	
28	0	0	0	900	0	1,900	0	0	0	0	
29	0	0	0	300	0	700	0	0	0	0	
30	150	450	120	180	720	400	130	150	250	300	**AutoFill**
31	150	150	150	150	150	150	150	150	150	150	**Options**
32	2,350	2,640	2,265	3,540	2,890	5,170	2,295	2,315	2,445	2,535	**button**
33	1,100	810	1,185	760	1,410	-870	1,155	1,135	1,005	915	
34											
35											
36											

formula and formats copied to the selected range

fill handle

Ready Average: 676 Count: 12 Sum: 8,110 120%

▶ **5.** Review the monthly net cash flows to confirm that AutoFill correctly copied the formula into the selected range.

These calculations provide Diane with a better picture of how the couple's net cash flow varies from month to month. Only in January and August do the couple's expenses exceed their take-home pay. In most months, their take-home pay exceeds expenses by at least $1,000, and in July, it exceeds expenses by $1,410.

Using the AutoFill Options Button

By default, AutoFill copies both the formulas and the formats of the original range to the selected range. However, sometimes you might want to copy only the formulas or only the formatting. You can specify what is copied by using the AutoFill Options button that appears after you release the mouse button. As shown in Figure 3-18, clicking this button provides a list of AutoFill options. The Copy Cells option, which is the default, copies both the formulas and the formatting. The Fill Formatting Only option copies the formatting into the selected cells but not any formulas. The Fill Without Formatting option copies the formulas but not the formatting.

AutoFill options ◄ Figure 3-18

copies the cells, filling in both formats and formulas

copies only the formats ▶ Fill Formatting Only

○ Copy Cells

○ Fill Without Formatting ◄ copies only the formulas

Filling a Series

AutoFill can also be used to create a series of numbers, dates, or text based on a pattern. To create a series of numbers, you enter the initial values in the series in a selected range and then use AutoFill to complete the series. Figure 3-19 shows how AutoFill can be used to insert the numbers from 1 to 10 in a selected range. You enter the first few numbers in the range A1:A3 to establish the pattern for AutoFill to use. Then, you select the range and drag the fill handle over the cells where you want the pattern continued. In Figure 3-19, the fill handle is dragged over the range A4:A10 and the rest of the series is filled in.

| Figure 3-19 | AutoFill extends a numeric sequence |

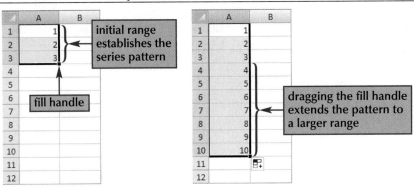

AutoFill can fill in a wide variety of series, including dates and times and text. Figure 3-20 shows examples of some series that AutoFill can generate. In each case, you must provide enough information for AutoFill to identify the pattern. AutoFill can recognize some patterns from only a single value, such as Jan or January to create a series of month abbreviations or names, or Mon or Monday to create a series of the days of the week.

| Figure 3-20 | AutoFill applied to different series |

Type	Initial Entry	Extended Series
Values	1, 2, 3	4, 5, 6, ...
	2, 4, 6	8, 10, 12, ...
Dates and Times	Jan	Feb, Mar, Apr, ...
	January	February, March, April, ...
	15-Jan, 15-Feb	15-Mar, 15-Apr, 15-May, ...
	12/30/2010	12/31/2010, 1/1/2011, 1/2/2011, ...
	12/31/2010, 1/31/2011	2/28/2011, 3/31/2011, 4/30/2011, ...
	Mon	Tue, Wed, Thu, ...
	Monday	Tuesday, Wednesday, Thursday, ...
	11:00AM	12:00PM, 1:00PM, 2:00PM, ...
Patterned Text	1st period	2nd period, 3rd period, 4th period, ...
	Region 1	Region 2, Region 3, Region 4, ...
	Quarter 3	Quarter 4, Quarter 1, Quarter 2, ...
	Qtr3	Qtr4, Qtr1, Qtr2, ...

For more complex patterns, you can use the Series dialog box. Enter the first value of the series in a worksheet cell, select the entire range that will contain the series, click the Fill button in the Editing group on the Home tab, and then click Series. The Series dialog box opens. You then choose how a series grows, set how fast the series grows and its stopping value, and decide whether to use existing values in the selected range as the basis for the series trend.

Creating a Series with AutoFill
|Reference Window

- Enter the first few values of the series into a range.
- Select the range, and then drag the fill handle of the selected range over the cells you want to fill.

or

- Enter the first few values of the series into a range.
- Select the entire range into which you want to extend the series.
- In the Editing group on the Home tab, click the Fill button, and then click Down, Right, Up, Left, Series, or Justify to set the direction you want to extend the series.

Diane wants to see how the monthly balances in her savings account are affected by the couple's changing expenses and take-home pay. She wants to make sure that the balance doesn't drop too low after months with particularly high expenses—such as January and August when Glenn's tuition payments are due. You'll add data to the worksheet to display the monthly savings balance. Diane already entered titles for the couple's different savings accounts. You'll use AutoFill to enter the month titles.

To use AutoFill to enter a series of months:

▶ **1.** In cell D35, enter **Jan**. This is the first value in the series. Because Jan is a common abbreviation for January, Excel recognizes it as a month and you don't need to type Feb for the next month in the series.

▶ **2.** Click cell **D35**, center the text, format it using the **Accent1** cell style, and then add a single border around the cell. This is the formatting you want to use for all the month abbreviations.

▶ **3.** Position the pointer over the fill handle in cell D35 until the pointer changes to **+**.

▶ **4.** Drag the fill handle over the range **E35:O35**. As you drag the fill handle, Screen-Tips show the month abbreviations. When you release the mouse button, AutoFill enters the remaining three-letter abbreviations for each month of the year with the formatting you applied to cell D35. See Figure 3-21.

Formatted month titles ◀ Figure 3-21

Next, you'll enter formulas to calculate the changing balance in the couple's main savings account and their home savings account. The main savings account balance is determined by four factors: the initial balance, the amount of money they deposit, the amount of money they withdraw, and the amount of money they transfer into their home savings account. The amount Diane and Glenn deposit will always equal their take-home pay, and the amount they withdraw will always equal their expenses. For now, you'll assume that the couple won't transfer any money from their main savings account into their home savings account.

To calculate the initial balances in the savings accounts:

▶ 1. In cell D36, enter the formula **=$K$5**. The formula uses an absolute reference to set the starting balance in the main savings account (cell D36) equal to the starting balance for the year (cell K5), which is already entered at the top of the worksheet. The absolute reference ensures that the copied formula always refers to the correct cell.

▶ 2. In cell D37, enter **=D21** to retrieve the couple's take-home pay for January.

▶ 3. In cell D38, enter **=D32** to retrieve the January expenses. You'll leave cell D39 blank because, at this point, you won't assume that any money will be transferred from the main savings account to the home savings account.

▶ 4. In cell D40, enter **=D36+D37−D38−D39**. This formula calculates the ending balance for the main savings account, which is equal to the starting balance plus any deposits minus the withdrawals and transfers. Cell D40 displays the value 2,410, representing the balance in the main savings account at the end of January.

▶ 5. In cell D41, enter the formula **=$K$6**. The formula sets the starting balance for the home savings account equal to the starting balance for the year. Again, you used an absolute reference to ensure that the formula won't change when copied.

▶ 6. In cell D42, enter the formula **=D39**. Any deposits in the home savings account will be the result of transfers from the main savings account.

▶ 7. In cell D43, enter the formula **=D41+D42**. The ending balance in the home savings account will be equal to the starting balance plus any deposits.

▶ 8. In cell D44, enter the formula **=D40+D43**. The total savings is equal to the amount in both accounts at the end of the month.

▶ 9. Add borders around the cells in the range D36:D43.

▶ 10. Use the Format Painter to copy the formats from cell D32 into cells D40 and D43, and then use the Format Painter to copy the formats from cell D33 into cell D44. See Figure 3-22.

Figure 3-22 ▶ Formatted savings account values for January

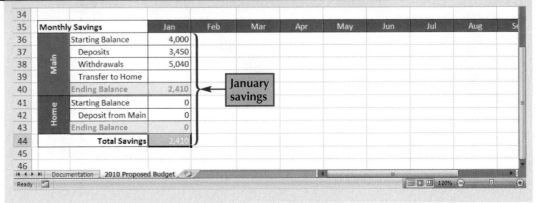

At this point, the couple's projected savings at the end of January will be $2,410, which is $1,590 less than their starting balance of $4,000 at the beginning of the year. The savings formulas for the remaining months are the same as for January except that their starting balances are based on the ending balance of the previous month.

To calculate the remaining balances in the savings accounts:

▶ 1. Copy the range **D36:D44**, and then paste it into the range **E36:E44**.

▶ 2. Change the formula in cell E36 to **=D40** so that the February starting balance for the main savings account equals the January ending balance.

▶ 3. Change the formula in cell E41 to **=D43** so that the starting February balance in the home savings account is equal to the ending January balance.

Next, you'll use AutoFill to copy the February formulas into the remaining months of the year.

▶ 4. Select the range **E36:E44**, and then drag the fill handle over the range **F36:O44**. All of the formulas and formatting for the rest of the year are filled in. See Figure 3-23.

Savings values for the remaining months ◀ **Figure 3-23**

Diane wants to see the ending balances for the two savings accounts without scrolling, so you'll add the ending balances at the top of the worksheet.

▶ 5. In cell L5, enter the formula **=$O$40**. You used an absolute reference so that the formula won't change if you later copy it to another cell. The ending balance of the main savings account in December—12,110—appears in cell L5.

▶ 6. In cell L6, enter the formula **=$O$43**. Again, you used an absolute reference to ensure the formula won't change if you later copy it to another cell. The ending balance of the home savings account in December—0—appears in cell L6.

Developing a Savings Plan

Under her current budget projections, Diane expects to have $12,110 in the main savings account at the end of the next year but nothing in the home savings account. Diane wants to transfer some money into the home savings account each month. Because the home savings account is used for longer-term savings, Diane cannot withdraw money from it without penalty. So, she wants to make sure the main savings account always has enough money to meet monthly expenses and any unexpected bills without relying on money from the home savings account.

Diane needs to balance two things in her savings plan: a desire to keep a reasonable amount in the main savings account and the desire to save enough for a future down payment on a home mortgage. To achieve this balance, she needs to determine her overall savings goal and how soon she and Glenn want to meet that goal.

To help Diane determine an overall savings goal, you'll create a new worksheet with calculations for different savings plans. Diane wants to know how much money the couple can save if they put $500 to $1,000 into the home savings account each month for the next three years. You'll create a worksheet that shows the total amount saved in one, two, and three years from deposits starting at $500 that increase in $100 increments through $1,000.

To create the savings plan:

▶ 1. Insert a new worksheet named **Home Savings Plan** at the end of the workbook.

▶ 2. In cell A1, enter **Home Savings Projections**, and then format the title using the **Title** cell style.

▶ 3. Merge and center the range **B3:G3**, enter **Savings Deposit per Month** in the merged cell, and then format the merged cell using the **Heading 2** cell style.

▶ 4. In cell A4, enter **Months**, format the cell in bold.

▶ 5. In cell B4, enter **500**; in cell C4, enter **600**; select the range **B4:C4**; and then drag the fill handle to cell **G4**. The values entered in the series—500, 600, 700, 800, 900, and 1,000—are the different amounts the couple might transfer into their home savings account each month.

▶ 6. In the range A5:A7, enter the values **12, 24**, and **36**. These monthly values are equal to one year, two years, and three years, respectively. You entered the years in months because Diane and Glenn plan to deposit money into their home savings account each month. So, they would make 12 deposits in one year, they would make 24 deposits in two years, and they would make 36 deposits in three years.

▶ 7. Format the range B4:G4;A5:A7 with the **Input** cell style.

Next, you'll use mixed cell references to calculate the amount of money saved under each plan. The amount saved is equal to the number of months of savings multiplied by the deposit per month.

▶ 8. In cell **B5**, enter **=$A5*B$4**. This formula uses mixed references to calculate the amount of savings generated by saving $500 per month for 12 months. The first mixed reference in the formula, $A5, has a fixed column reference and a relative row reference. When you copy the formula across row 5, the reference to cell A5 remains unchanged. When you copy the formula down column B, the reference to cell A5 changes to cell A6 in row 6 and cell A7 in row 7, which references the correct number of months of savings in the formula. The second mixed cell reference, B$4, has a relative column reference and a fixed row reference. When you copy the formula down column B, the reference to cell B4 remains unchanged. When you copy the formula across row 5, the reference to cell B4 changes to cell C4 in column C, cell D4 in column D, and so forth, which references the correct deposit per month in the formula.

▶ 9. Copy cell **B5** and paste the formula into the range **B5:G7**. The formula results show the projected savings based on different combinations of monthly deposits and lengths of time. Notice that the mixed references in each cell always reference a monthly deposit value from the range B4:G4 and a time length from the range A5:A7. The mixed references enable you to copy and paste the correct formulas quickly.

▶ 10. Format the values in the range B5:G7 using a thousands separator with no digits to the right of the decimal point, and add a single border around each cell in the range. Figure 3-24 shows the completed and formatted values.

Savings from monthly deposits | Figure 3-24

The data shows how increasing the amount that Diane and Glenn save toward their home each month quickly adds up. For example, if they save $800 per month, at the end of three years (36 months), they would have saved $28,800. This is just a little less than the $30,000 they want to save for the down payment. Diane asks you to enter in the budget projections the transfer of $800 from the main savings account to the home savings account each month.

To enter and format the home savings plan section:

▶ 1. Switch to the **2010 Proposed Budget** worksheet.

▶ 2. In cell H9, enter **Home Savings Plan**, and then format the cell in bold.

▶ 3. In cell H10, enter **Monthly Transfer to Home Acct**, and then, in cell K10, enter **800**.

▶ 4. Merge the range **H10:J10**, left-align the merged cell, and then format the cell using the **20% – Accent6** cell style.

▶ 5. Add a border around cell H10 and cell K10. See Figure 3-25.

Formatted savings plan | Figure 3-25

amount to deposit in the home savings account each month

Next, you'll apply this $800 per month deposit value to the monthly transfer of funds from the main savings account to the home savings account.

To project the new savings account balances:

▶ 1. In cell D39, enter the formula **=$K$10**. You used an absolute value in this formula because the amount to transfer to the home savings account each month is always in cell K10 and you don't want the cell reference to change when you copy the formula to the rest of the months. The value 800 is displayed in the cell, indicating that for the month of January, $800 will be transferred from the couple's main savings account into the home savings account. The ending balance of the home savings account is now $800.

▶ 2. Copy cell **D39** and paste it into the range **E39:O39**. The value 800 is pasted into the rest of the row, indicating that each month the couple will transfer $800 into the home savings account. See Figure 3-26.

Figure 3-26	Monthly savings balance

		Jan	Feb	Mar	Apr	May	Jun	Jul	Aug	Se
Monthly Savings										
Main	Starting Balance	4,000	1,610	1,905	2,205	2,215	2,600	2,560	3,170	
	Deposits	3,450	3,450	3,450	3,450	3,450	4,300	4,300	4,300	
	Withdrawals	5,040	2,355	2,350	2,640	2,265	3,540	2,890	5,170	
	Transfer to Home	800	800	800	800	800	800	800	800	
	Ending Balance	1,610	1,905	2,205	2,215	2,600	2,560	3,170	1,500	
Home	Starting Balance	0	800	1,600	2,400	3,200	4,000	4,800	5,600	
	Deposit from Main	800	800	800	800	800	800	800	800	
	Ending Balance	800	1,600	2,400	3,200	4,000	4,800	5,600	6,400	
Total Savings		2,410	3,505	4,605	5,415	6,600	7,360	8,770	7,900	

amount transferred to the home savings account each month

balance in the home savings account

▶ 3. Examine the monthly balance in both the main savings account and the home savings account under Diane's proposed savings plan. Notice that the ending balance in the main savings account falls below $2,000 some months.

▶ 4. Scroll to the top of the worksheet and verify that the value displayed in cell L5 is 2,510 and the value displayed in cell L6 is 9,600.

Under this savings plan, Diane and Glenn will have deposited $9,600 into the home savings account by the end of the year and the balance in their main savings account will be down to $2,510. Although Diane is pleased that $9,600 will be moved into the home savings account in the next year, she's concerned about the amount of money left in the main savings account. Even more troubling are the month-to-month balances in that account. For example, the balance in the main savings account will be $1,500 at the end of August and will remain below $2,000 for several months of the year. Recall that Diane does not want to have a savings plan that will leave the couple with insufficient funds in the main savings account to handle unforeseen expenses.

Part of the problem is that the couple's net cash flow is negative during several months of the year. If they continue to transfer $800 into the home savings account during those months, the main savings account might fall below an acceptable level. Diane wants to modify her savings plan so that money is not transferred into the home savings account during months of negative cash flow. You need a formula that can "choose" whether to transfer the funds. You can build this kind of decision-making capability into a formula through the use of a logical function.

Working with Logical Functions

A **logical function** is a function that works with values that are either true or false. If it seems strange to think of a value as being true or false, consider a statement such as "Today is Monday." If today is Monday, that statement is true or has a true value. If today isn't Monday, the statement has a value of false. In Excel, you usually will not work with statements regarding days of the week (unless you're creating a calendar application), but instead you'll examine statements such as "Is cell A5 equal to 3?" or "Is cell B10 greater than cell C10?"

Using the IF Function

You can use the IF function to evaluate a statement such as "Is cell A5 equal to 3?" The **IF function** is a logical function that returns one value if the statement is true and returns a different value if the statement is false. The syntax of the IF function is as follows:

```
IF(logical_test, value_if_true, [value_if_false])
```

In this function, *logical_test* is a statement that is either true or false, *value_if_true* is the value returned by the IF function if the statement is true, and *value_if_false* is the value returned by the function if the statement is false. Although the *value_if_false* argument is optional, you should usually include this argument so that the IF function covers both possibilities.

The statement in the *logical_test* argument of the IF function always includes a comparison operator. A **comparison operator** is a symbol that indicates the relationship between two values. Figure 3-27 describes the different comparison operators. The most common comparison operator is the equal sign.

Comparison operators ◄ **Figure 3-27**

Operator	Statement	Tests whether
=	A1 = B1	the value in cell A1 *is equal to* the value in cell B1
>	A1 > B1	the value in cell A1 *is greater than* the value in cell B1
<	A1 < B1	the value in cell A1 *is less than* the value in cell B1
>=	A1 >= B1	the value in cell A1 *is greater than or equal to* the value in cell B1
<=	A1 <= B1	the value in cell A1 *is less than or equal to* the value in cell B1
<>	A1 <> B1	the value in cell A1 *is not equal to* the value in cell B1

For example, you might want a formula that compares the values in cells A1 and B1. If they're equal, you want to return a value of 100; if they're not equal, you want to return a value of 50. The IF function to perform this test is as follows:

```
=IF(A1=B1, 100, 50)
```

In many cases, however, you will not use values directly in the IF function. The following formula uses cell references, returning the value of cell C1 if A1 equals B1; otherwise, it returns the value of cell C2.

```
=IF(A1=B1, C1, C2)
```

The IF function also works with text. For example, consider the following formula:

```
=IF(A1="YES", "DONE", "RESTART")
```

This formula tests whether the value of cell A1 is equal to YES. If it is, the formula returns the text DONE; otherwise, it returns the text RESTART. Also, you can nest other functions inside an IF statement. Consider the following formula:

```
=IF(A1="MAXIMUM", MAX(B1:B10), MIN(B1:B10))
```

This function first tests whether cell A1 contains the text MAXIMUM. If it does, the formula uses the MAX function to return the maximum of the values in the range B1:B10. If it doesn't, the formula uses the MIN function to return the minimum of the values in that range.

Diane wants the IF function to test whether the net cash flow for the current month is greater than zero. If it is, the couple has increased their savings and she wants to transfer some of it into the home savings account. On the other hand, if the net cash flow is negative, the couple has not saved any money and Diane doesn't want to transfer any funds to the home savings account. For the month of January, the formula to determine how much money is transferred is as follows:

```
=IF(D33>0, $K$10, 0)
```

Recall that cell D33 contains the net cash flow for the month of January and cell K10 contains the amount of money that Diane wants to transfer when she can. So, this function tests whether the net cash flow for the month of January (cell D33) is positive (greater than zero). If it is, the formula returns $800 (the value in cell K10) as the amount to transfer from the main savings account into the home savings account; otherwise, it returns 0 and no money will be transferred that month. You'll delete the formula currently in cell D39, and then insert this function.

To insert the IF function:

▶ 1. Right-click cell **D39**, and then click **Clear Contents** on the shortcut menu. The cell's contents are erased.

▶ 2. In the Function Library group on the Formulas tab, click the **Logical** button, and then click **IF** in the list of logical functions. The Function Arguments dialog box opens.

▶ 3. Enter **D33>0** in the Logical_test argument box. This tests whether the net cash flow for January is positive (greater than zero).

▶ 4. Enter **$K$10** in the Value_if_true argument box. If the value in cell D33 is greater than zero (the net cash flow for the month is positive), then the formula returns the value in cell K10, which is the amount of money to transfer from the main savings account into the home savings account. You used an absolute reference because you don't want the cell reference to change when you copy the formula to the other months.

▶ 5. Enter the value **0** in the Value_if_false argument box. If the value in cell D33 is less than zero (the net cash flow for the month is negative), the formula returns the value 0 and no money will be transferred from the main savings account into the home savings account that month. See Figure 3-28.

Function arguments for the IF function | Figure 3-28

6. Click the **OK** button. A value of 0 is displayed in cell D39. Because the net cash flow for January is –1,590, no money will be transferred from the main savings account into the home savings account. You'll copy this formula into the remaining months of Diane's proposed budget.

7. Click cell **D39**, and then drag the fill handle over the range **E39:O39**. The remaining values are filled in, as shown in Figure 3-29. Examine the monthly balance in both savings accounts.

Amount to transfer to the home savings account each month | Figure 3-29

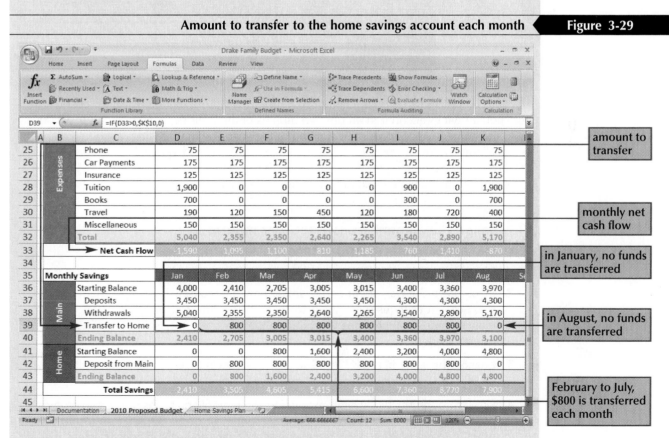

The monthly ending balance in the main savings account remains above $3,000 for most of the year, and $800 is transferred from the main savings account into the home savings account in ten months of the year. Diane wants you to document what the formula results are showing. You'll enter text that clarifies when funds are transferred between accounts in the Home Savings Plan section.

▶ **8.** Double-click cell **H10** to enter editing mode, type an asterisk (*****) at the end of the text in the cell, and then press the **Enter** key.

▶ **9.** In cell H11, enter ***Only during months of positive cash flow**, and then format cell H11 using the **Explanatory** cell style. See Figure 3-30.

Figure 3-30	Results of the revised savings plan

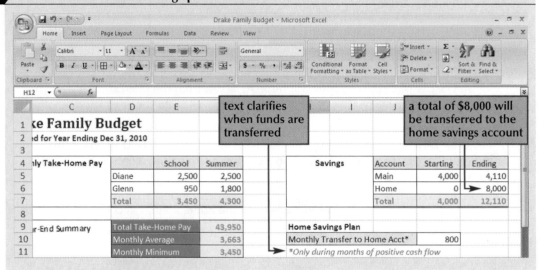

Based on this savings plan, Diane can transfer $800 from the main savings account to the home savings account in all but two months of the year, depositing a total of $8,000 into the home savings account by the end of the year. The main savings account balance stays above $3,000 for most of the year. Diane feels this is adequate, but wants to explore what would happen if she increases the monthly transfer from $800 to $1,000. How would that affect the monthly balance of the main savings account?

To change the amount transferred per month:

▶ **1.** Change the value in cell K10 to **1000**. The total in the home savings account at the end of the year increases to $10,000.

▶ **2.** Scroll down the worksheet and examine how the monthly balance in the main savings account changes throughout the year. Under this scenario, the balance in the main savings account drops to $1,900 in the month of August. This is a little too low for Diane.

▶ **3.** Change the value in cell K10 to **900**. With this savings plan, the couple will save $9,000 toward the purchase of a home.

▶ **4.** Scroll through the worksheet, examining the monthly balances of the two savings accounts. The balance in their savings account stays above $2,500 for most of the year. This seems like a good compromise to Diane, and she decides to adopt it as a model budget for the upcoming year.

Working with Date Functions

Diane's budget is just the start of her financial planning. To be effective, budgets need to be monitored and updated as conditions change. In the upcoming year, Diane plans to use this workbook to enter the actual salaries, expenses, and savings. This will enable her to track how well her projected values match the actual values. Because Diane will be updating the workbook throughout the year, she wants the worksheet to always display the current date so she can tell how far she is into her budget projections. You can accomplish this using a **date function**. Seven of the date functions supported by Excel are described in Figure 3-31. You can use these functions to help with scheduling or to determine on what days of the week certain dates occur.

Date functions ◄ Figure 3-31

Function	Description
DATE(*year, month, day*)	Creates a date value for the date represented by the *year, month,* and *day* arguments
DAY(*date*)	Extracts the day of the month from the *date* value
MONTH(*date*)	Extracts the month number from the *date* value where 1=January, 2=February, and so forth
YEAR(*date*)	Extracts the year number from the *date* value
WEEKDAY(*date, [return_type]*)	Calculates the day of the week from the *date* value, where 1=Sunday, 2=Monday, and so forth; to choose a different numbering scheme, set the optional *return_type* value to "1" (1=Sunday, 2=Monday, ...), "2" (1=Monday, 2=Tuesday, ...), or "3" (0=Monday, 1=Tuesday, ...)
NOW( )	Displays the current date and time
TODAY( )	Displays the current date

Perhaps the most commonly used date function is the TODAY function, which returns the current date. The syntax of the TODAY function is as follows:

```
=TODAY()
```

The TODAY function doesn't have any arguments. Neither does the NOW function, which returns both the current date and current time. The values returned by the TODAY and NOW functions are updated automatically whenever you reopen the workbook or enter a new calculation. If you don't want the date and time to change, you must enter the date and time value directly in the cell.

Diane wants the 2010 Proposed Budget workbook to display the current date.

To enter the TODAY function to display the current date:

▶ 1. In cell J1, enter **Current Date**.

▶ 2. Merge cells **J1** and **K1**, right-align the merged cell, and then apply the **20% – Accent6** cell style.

▶ 3. Click cell **L1**. You'll enter the TODAY function in this cell.

▶ 4. In the Function Library group on the Formulas tab, click the **Date & Time** button, and then click **TODAY** in the date functions list. The Function Arguments dialog box opens, but there are no arguments for the TODAY function.

> **5.** Click the **OK** button. The Function Arguments dialog box closes, and the current date appears in cell L1. See Figure 3-32.

Figure 3-32 ▶ **TODAY function displays the current date**

Working with Financial Functions

Diane wants to estimate how much monthly mortgage payments for a house might be. You can use the **PMT function** to calculate the payments for any type of loan.

The PMT function is one of many **financial functions** in Excel that calculate values from loans and investments. Figure 3-33 describes this and some of the other financial functions often used to develop budgets. These financial functions are the same as those widely used in business and accounting to perform various financial calculations, such as depreciation of an asset, the amount of interest paid on an investment, and the present value of an investment.

Figure 3-33 ▶ **Financial functions for loans and investments**

Function	Description
FV(rate, nper, pmt, [pv=0] [,type=0])	Returns the future value of an investment, where *rate* is the interest rate per period, *nper* is the total number of periods, *pmt* is the payment in each period, *pv* is the present value of the investment, and *type* indicates whether payments should be made at the end of the period (0) or the beginning of the period (1)
PMT(rate, nper, pv, [fv=0] [,type=0])	Calculates the payments required each period on a loan or investment
IPMT(rate, per, nper, pv, [fv=0] [,type=0])	Calculates the amount of a loan payment devoted to paying the loan interest, where *per* is the number of the payment period
PPMT(rate, per, nper, pv, [fv=0] [,type=0])	Calculates the amount of a loan payment devoted to paying off the principal of a loan, where *per* is the number of the payment period
PV(rate, nper, pmt, [fv=0] [,type=0])	Calculates the present value of a loan or investment based on periodic, constant payments
NPER(rate, pmt, pv, [fv=0] [,type=0])	Calculates the number of periods required to pay off a loan or investment
RATE(nper, pmt, pv, [fv=0] [,type=0])	Calculates the interest rate of a loan or investment based on periodic, constant payments

For expensive items, such as cars and houses, people often borrow money from a bank to make the purchase. Every loan has two main components: the principal and the interest. **Principal** is the amount of money being loaned, and **interest** is the amount charged for lending the money. You can think of interest as a kind of "user fee" because the borrower is paying for the right to use the lender's money for a period of time. The more money borrowed and the longer time for which it's borrowed, the higher the user fee. A few years ago, Diane and Glenn borrowed money to buy a second car and are still repaying the principal and interest on that loan.

Interest is calculated either as simple interest or as compound interest. In **simple interest**, the interest paid is equal to a percentage of principal for each period that the money has been lent. For example, if Diane and Glenn deposit $1,000 in an account that pays simple interest at a rate of 5% per year, they'll receive $50 in interest each year that the money is deposited. More often, interest is calculated as **compound interest** in which the interest paid is calculated on the principal and any previous interest payments that have been added to that principal. For example, the interest payment for a $1,000 deposit at a 5% interest that is compounded every year is $50. If the interest is left in the account, the interest payment for the second year is calculated on $1,050 (the original principal plus the previous year's interest), resulting in an interest payment for the second year of $52.50. With compound interest, the borrower always pays more money to the lender the following year. Most banks and financial institutions use compound interest in their financial transactions.

Using Functions to Manage Personal Finances | InSight

Excel has many financial functions you can use to manage your personal finances. The following list can help you determine which function to use for the most common personal finance problems:

- To determine how much an investment will be worth after a series of monthly payments at some future time, use the FV (future value) function.
- To determine how much you have to spend each month to repay a loan or mortgage within a set period of time, use the PMT (payment) function.
- To determine how much of your monthly loan payment is used to pay the interest, use the IPMT (interest payment) function.
- To determine how much of your monthly loan payment is used for repaying the principal, use the PPMT (principal payment) function.
- To determine the largest loan or mortgage you can afford at present, given a set monthly payment, use the PV (present value) function.
- To determine how long it will take to pay off a loan with constant monthly payments, use the NPER (number of periods) function.

In each case, you usually need to enter the annual interest rate divided by the number of times the interest is compounded during the year. If interest is compounded monthly, divide the annual interest rate by 12; if interest is compounded quarterly, divide the annual rate by 4. You must also convert the length of the loan or investment to the number of interest payments per year. If you will make payments monthly, multiply the number of years of the loan or investment by 12.

Using the PMT Function to Determine a Monthly Loan Payment

You'll use the PMT function to calculate the potential monthly loan payment for Diane and Glenn. For loan or investment calculations, you need to know the following information:

- The annual interest rate
- The payment period, or how often payments are due and interest is compounded (usually monthly for mortgages)

- The length of the loan in terms of the number of payment periods
- The amount being borrowed or invested

In Diane and Glenn's neighborhood, starter homes are selling for about $200,000. If Diane and Glenn can keep to their savings plan, they will have saved $9,000 by the end of the year (as shown in cell L6 in the Proposed Budget 2010 worksheet). If they save this same amount for the next three years, they will have at least $27,000 in their home savings account to put toward the down payment. Based on this, Diane estimates that she and Glenn will need a home loan of about $170,000. To calculate how much it would cost to repay such a loan, you can use the PMT (payment) function. The PMT function has the following syntax:

```
PMT(rate, nper, pv, [fv=0] [type=0])
```

In this function, *rate* is the interest rate for each payment period, *nper* is the total number of payment periods required to pay off the loan, and *pv* is the present value of the loan or the amount that needs to be borrowed. For Diane and Glenn, the present value of the loan is $170,000.

The PMT function has two optional arguments: *fv* and *type*. The *fv* argument is the future value of the loan. Because the intent with most loans is to pay them off completely, the future value is equal to 0 by default. The *type* argument specifies when the interest is charged on the loan, either at the end of the period (*type=0*), which is the default, or at the beginning of the period (*type=1*).

For most loans, the payment period is one month. This means that Diane and Glenn must make a payment on the loan every month, and interest on the loan is compounded every month. The annual interest rate on home loans in Diane and Glenn's area is 6.5%. To determine the interest rate per month, you divide the annual interest rate by 12. For Diane and Glenn, the interest rate each month or payment period is 6.5% divided by 12, or about 0.541% per month.

Diane and Glenn want to pay off their home loan in 20 years, which is a payment period of 240 months (20 years multiplied by 12 payment periods each year). Putting all of this information together, you can calculate the monthly payment for the couple's home loan with the following formula:

```
=PMT(0.065/12, 20*12, 170000)
```

This formula returns a value of –$1,267.47. The value is negative because the payment is considered an expense, or a negative cash flow. If you want to display this value as a positive number in a worksheet, enter a minus symbol directly before the PMT function as follows:

```
=-PMT(0.065/12, 20*12, 170000)
```

Based on these calculations, Diane and Glenn would have to pay the bank $1,267.47 every month for 20 years before the loan and the interest are completely paid. Right now, the couple is spending about $850 per month on rent. So this home loan is a significant increase over their current expenses. Diane asks you to calculate the monthly payment for a home loan of $160,000. You'll make that calculation in another worksheet.

To set up the monthly loan payment calculation:

▶ 1. Insert a new worksheet named **Loan Analysis** at the end of the workbook.

▶ 2. In cell A1, enter **Home Loan**, format cell A1 using the **Title** cell style, and then increase the width of column A to **25** characters.

▶ 3. In the range A3:A9;B3:B8, enter the labels and components of the home loan shown in Figure 3-34. In cell B5, enter **=B3/B4** to calculate the interest rate per period by dividing the annual interest rate by the number of payments per year. In cell B7, enter **=B4*B6** to calculate the number of loan payments per year by multiplying the number of payments per year (12) by the number of years of the loan (20).

Loan Analysis worksheet ◄ **Figure 3-34**

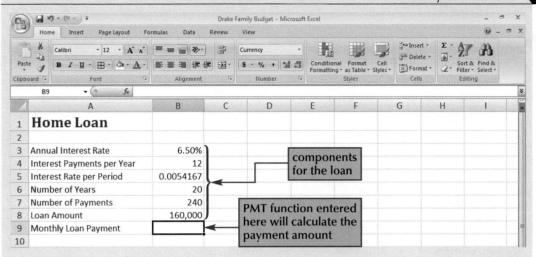

Next, you'll enter the PMT function to calculate the monthly payment for the $160,000 home loan.

To enter the PMT function to calculate the monthly payment:

▶ **1.** Apply the **Calculation** cell style to cell B9 to distingish the monthly loan payment amount from the loan components.

▶ **2.** In the Function Library group on the Formulas tab, click the **Financial** button, and then click **PMT** in the list of financial functions. The Function Arguments dialog box opens.

▶ **3.** For the Rate argument, enter the cell reference **B5**, which is the cell with the interest rate per payment period.

▶ **4.** For the Nper argument, enter the cell reference **B7**, which is the cell with the total number of payments.

▶ **5.** For the Pv argument enter the cell reference **B8**, which is the cell with the present value of the loan. See Figure 3-35.

Function Arguments dialog box for the PMT function ◄ **Figure 3-35**

▶ **6.** Click the **OK** button. The value $1,192.92 is displayed in parentheses in cell B9 to indicate a negative currency value.

▶ **7.** Double-click cell **B9**, type **–** (minus symbol) between = and PMT, and then press the **Enter** key. The value $1,192.92 is displayed as a positive currency value. See Figure 3-36.

Figure 3-36 **Monthly payment for a $160,000 loan**

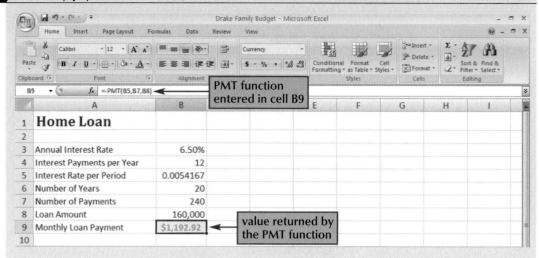

Diane and Glenn would have to pay about $1,193 per month for 20 years to repay a $160,000 loan at 6.5% interest. Diane is interested in other loan possibilities. Because you already set up the worksheet, you can quickly try other scenarios without having to reenter any formulas. Diane wonders whether extending the length of the loan would reduce the monthly payment by a sizeable margin. She asks you to calculate the monthly payment for a 30-year loan.

To calculate other loan options:

▶ **1.** In cell B6, change the value to **30**. The amount of the monthly payment drops to $1,011.31, which is $180 less per month. Next, Diane wants to see the monthly payments for a $150,000 loan with these same conditions.

▶ **2.** In cell B8, change the value to **150,000**. For this smaller home loan, the monthly payment drops even further to $948.10 per month. This is only about $100 more than the couple is currently paying in rent.

▶ **3.** Save your changes to the workbook, and then close it.

You've completed your work on Diane and Glenn's budget. Based on your analysis, Diane has learned several important things. She's discovered that the projected budget allows the couple to transfer enough money to the home savings account to make a down payment on a home in about three years. The savings plan seems reasonable to Diane and leaves enough funds in the main savings account to cover their monthly expenses. Finally, by analyzing some of the possible loan options they might encounter when they buy a home, Diane realizes that the monthly mortgage payments will not be substantially more than what they are currently paying in rent. So, not only will Diane and Glenn be able to save enough to make the initial down payment, their monthly income should also cover the monthly payments. Of course, all budgets must be revised periodically to meet changing expenses and income. However, your work has given Diane and Glenn enough information to make informed choices about their immediate financial future.

Session 3.2 Quick Check | Review

1. How do you use AutoFill to copy a set of cell values, but not the formatting?
2. The first three selected values in a series are 3, 6, and 9. What are the next three values that will be inserted using AutoFill?
3. Cell A5 contains the text Mon. If you select the cell and drag the fill handle over the range A6:A8, what text will be entered into those cells?
4. If cell A3 is greater than cell A4, you want to display the text "OK"; otherwise, you want to display the text string "RETRY". What formula accomplishes this?
5. What formula do you use to display the current date?
6. What formula do you use to display the current date and time?
7. You want to take out a loan for $130,000. The interest on the loan is 5% compounded monthly. You intend to pay back the loan in 20 years. What formula do you enter to calculate the monthly payment required to pay off the loan under those conditions?
8. What financial function do you use to determine how payment periods are required to pay off a loan?

Tutorial Summary | Review

In this tutorial, you learned how to work with Excel functions and formulas. First, you learned about relative, absolute, and mixed cell references and under what conditions you would use each. Then, you looked at function syntax, entered a function using the Insert Function dialog box, and then you entered a function directly into the worksheet to calculate sums, counts, averages, maximums, and minimums. You also searched for a function that matched search criteria. Next, you used AutoFill to quickly copy formulas and formatting and to extend a series of numbers, text, or dates. Then, you used logical functions to return different values based on conditions in the worksheet, and then you entered a date function. Finally, you examined financial functions and used the PMT function to calculate the monthly payments to repay a loan within a set interval of time.

Key Terms

absolute reference	financial function	nested
argument	IF function	optional argument
AutoFill	Insert Function dialog box	PMT function
comparison operator	interest	principal
compound interest	logical function	relative reference
date function	median	simple interest
F4 key	mixed reference	syntax
fill handle	mode	

| Practice | | Review Assignments |

Practice the skills you learned in the tutorial using the same case scenario.

Data File needed for the Review Assignments: Timov.xlsx

Diane and Glenn appreciate the work you did on their budget. Their friends, Sergei and Ava Timov, ask you to create a similar workbook for their family budget. The Timovs want to purchase a new home. They are considering two houses with different mortgages. They want the budget worksheet you create to display the impact of monthly mortgage payments on the couple's cash flow. The couple has already designed the workbook and entered estimates of their take-home pay and expenses for the upcoming year. They want you to set up the formulas.

Complete the following:

1. Open the **Timov** workbook located in the Tutorial.03\Review folder included with your Data Files, and then save the workbook as **Timov Family Budget** in the same folder.
2. In the Documentation sheet, enter your name in cell B3 and the date in cell B4.
3. In the Family Budget worksheet, in the range C17:N17, use AutoFill to enter the month names **January** through **December**.
4. In the range C20:N20, calculate the family's take-home pay. In the range C26:N26, calculate the monthly expenses. In the range C27:N27, calculate the monthly net cash flow (equal to the monthly take-home pay minus the expenses).
5. In cell C6, enter a formula to calculate the sum of Sergei's monthly salary for the entire year. In cell D6, calculate Sergei's average take-home pay each month. In cell E6, calculate Sergei's maximum monthly take-home pay. In cell F6, calculate Sergei's minimum monthly take-home pay.
6. Select the range C6:F6, and then use AutoFill to copy the formula in the C6:F6 range into the C7:F15 range. Use the AutoFill Options button to copy only the formulas into the selected range and not both the formulas and formats. (*Hint:* Because you haven't yet entered any mortgage payment values, cell D13 will show the value #DIV/0!, indicating that Excel cannot calculate the average mortgage payment. You'll correct that problem shortly.)
7. In the range J5:J12, enter the following loan and loan conditions of the first mortgage:
   • The loan amount (or value of the principal) is **$315,000**.
   • The annual interest rate is **6.7%**.
   • The interest rate is compounded **12** times a year (or monthly).
   • The mortgage will last **30** years.
   The monthly rate is equal to the annual interest rate divided by how often the interest rate is compounded. The number of payments is equal to the number of years the mortgage will last multiplied by 12.
8. In cell J11, enter the PMT function to calculate the monthly payment required to repay this loan. The *rate* argument is equal to the monthly rate, the *nper* argument is equal to the number of payments, and the *pv* argument is equal to the value of the principal.
9. In cell J11, enter a minus symbol between = and PMT to make the value positive.
10. In the range N5:N12, enter the following loan and loan conditions of the second mortgage:
    • The loan amount (or value of the principal) is **$218,000**.
    • The annual interest rate is **6.7%**.
    • The interest rate is compounded **12** times a year (or monthly).
    • The mortgage will last **20** years.

11. In cell N11, enter the PMT function to calculate the monthly payment needed to pay off this loan, and then make the PMT value positive.

12. Sergei and Ava want to be able to view their monthly cash flow under both mortgage possibilities. The mortgage being applied to the budget will be determined by whether 1 or 2 is entered into cell C3. To switch from one mortgage to another, do the following:

    - In cell C25, enter an IF function that tests whether cell C3 equals 1. If it does, display the value from cell J11; otherwise, display the value from cell N11. Use absolute cell references in the formula.
    - Use AutoFill to copy the formula in cell C25 into the range D25:N25.
    - Verify that the values in the range C25:N25 match the monthly payment for the first mortgage condition.

13. In cell C3, edit the value from 1 to **2**. Verify that the monthly payment for the second mortgage appears in the range C25:N25.

14. Sergei and Ava want to maintain an average net cash flow of at least $1,000 per month. Under which mortgage is this achieved?

15. Save and close the workbook, and then submit the finished workbook to your instructor, either in printed or electronic form, as requested.

| Apply | **Case Problem 1** |

Use the skills you learned to create a grading sheet for a chemistry course.

Data File needed for this Case Problem: Chemistry.xlsx

Chemistry 303   Karen Raul is a professor of chemistry at a community college in Shawnee, Kansas. She has started using Excel to calculate the final grade for students in her Chemistry 303 course. The final score is a weighted average of the scores given for three exams and the final exam. Karen wants your help in creating the formulas to calculate the final score and to summarize the class scores on all exams. One way to calculate a weighted average is by multiplying each student's exam score by the weight given to the exam, and then totaling the results. For example, consider the following four exam scores:

- Exam 1 = 84
- Exam 2 = 80
- Exam 3 = 83
- Final Exam = 72

If the first three exams are each given a weight of 20% and the final exam is given a weight of 40%, the weighted average of the four scores is:

$84*0.2 + 80*0.2 + 83*0.2 + 72*0.4 = 78.2$

Karen already entered the scores for her students and formatted much of the workbook. She wants you to enter the final formulas and highlight the top 10 overall scores in her class. Figure 3-37 shows the worksheet you'll create.

Figure 3-37

	A	B	C	D	E	F	G	H
1	**Chemistry 303**							
2	**First Semester Scores**							
3	Posted 12/20/2010							
4								
5	Students	36						
6								
7	*Class Summary*	Exam	Weight	Median	Maximum	Minimum	Range	
8		Exam 1	20%	86.0	99.0	52.0	47.0	
9		Exam 2	20%	80.0	99.0	53.0	46.0	
10		Exam 3	20%	83.0	98.0	50.0	48.0	
11		Final Exam	40%	81.5	99.0	51.0	48.0	
12		Overall	100%	80.5	96.8	55.8	41.0	
13								
14								
15	Student Scores				Top Ten Overall Scores			
16	Student ID	Exam 1	Exam 2	Exam 3	Final Exam	Overall		
17	390-120-2	84.0	80.0	83.0	72.0	78.2		
18	390-267-4	98.0	92.0	91.0	99.0	95.8		
19	390-299-8	54.0	56.0	51.0	65.0	58.2		
20	390-354-3	98.0	95.0	90.0	94.0	94.2		

Complete the following:

1. Open the **Chemistry** workbook located in the Tutorial.03\Case1 folder included with your Data Files, and then save the workbook as **Chemistry 303 Final Scores** in the same folder.

2. In the Documentation sheet, enter your name in cell B3 and enter the date in cell B4.

3. In the First Semester Scores worksheet, in cell F17, enter a formula to calculate the weighted average of the first student's four exams. Use the weights found in the range C8:C11, matching each weight with the corresponding exam score. Use absolute cell references for the four weights.

4. Use AutoFill to copy the formula in cell F17 into the range F18:F52.

5. In cell B5, enter a formula to count the number of final scores in the range F17:F52.

 EXPLORE

6. In cell D8, use the MEDIAN function to calculate the median or middle score for the first exam.

7. In cell E8, calculate the maximum score for the first exam.

8. In cell F8, calculate the minimum score for the first exam.

9. In cell G8, calculate the range of scores for the first exam, which is equal to the difference between the maximum and minimum score.

10. Repeat Steps 6 through 9 for each of the other two exams, the final exam, and the overall weighted score.

11. Use conditional formatting to highlight the top 10 scores in the range F17:F52 in a light red fill with dark red text.

12. Insert a page break at cell A14, repeat the first three rows of the worksheet in any printout, and verify that the worksheet is in portrait orientation.

13. Save and close the workbook, and then submit the finished workbook to your instructor, either in printed or electronic form, as requested.

Apply | **Case Problem 2**

Use the skills you learned to create an order form for a fireworks company.

Data File needed for this Case Problem: Wizard.xlsx

WizardWorks   Andrew Howe owns and operates WizardWorks, an online seller of fireworks based in Franklin, Tennessee. Andrew wants you to help him use Excel to develop an order form for his business. The form needs to contain formulas to calculate the charge for each order. The total charge is based on the quantity and type of items ordered plus the shipping charge and the 5% sales tax. Orders can be shipped using standard 3 to 5 day shipping for $4.99 or overnight for $12.99. Andrew is also offering a 3% discount for orders that exceed $200. Both the shipping option and the discount need to be calculated using formulas based on values entered into the worksheet. Figure 3-38 shows a preview of a sample order.

Figure 3-38

Complete the following:

1. Open the **Wizard** workbook located in the Tutorial.03\Case2 folder included with your Data Files, and then save the workbook as **WizardWorks Order Form** in the same folder.
2. In the Documentation sheet, enter your name in cell B3 and enter the date in cell B4.

3. In the Order Form worksheet, in cell C4, enter the customer name, **Kevin Kemper**. In cell C6, enter the order number, **31528**. In the range C9:C13, enter the following address:

Address 1:	**418 Alcorn Lane**
City:	**Greenfield**
State:	**IN**
Zip:	**46140**

⊕ EXPLORE

4. In cell C5, enter a function that displays the current date.

5. In the range B20:E22, enter the following orders:

Item	Name	Price	Qty
BF005	**Bucket of Fireworks**	**$42.50**	**1**
F128	**Nightair Fountain**	**$9.95**	**3**
R315	**Mountain Rockets (Box 20)**	**$49.50**	**3**

6. In cell C15, enter **overnight** to ship this order overnight.

⊕ EXPLORE

7. In cell F20, enter an IF function that tests whether the order quantity in cell E20 is greater than 0 (zero). If it is, return the value of E20 multiplied by D20; otherwise, return no text by entering "". AutoFill this formula into the range F21:F25.

8. In cell F27, calculate the sum of the values in the range F20:F25.

9. In cell F28, enter an IF function that tests whether cell F27 is greater than 200. If it is, return the negative value of F27 multiplied by the discount percentage in cell F12; otherwise, return the value 0 (zero).

10. In cell F29, add the subtotal from cell F27 and the discount value from cell F28.

11. In cell F31, calculate the sales tax by multiplying the after discount value in cell F29 by the sales tax percentage, 0.05.

12. In cell F32, determine the shipping charge by entering an IF function that tests whether cell C15 equals "standard". If it does, return the value in cell F9; otherwise, return the value in cell F10.

13. In cell G32, display the value of cell C15.

14. In cell F34, calculate the total of the after discount value, the sales tax, and the shipping fee.

15. Scale the order form so that it will print on a single page.

16. Reduce the quantity of Mountain Rockets boxes from 3 to **2**, and then verify that the discount is changed to 0 for the order. Change the shipping option from overnight to **standard**, and then verify that the shipping fee is changed to the fee for standard shipping.

17. Save and close the workbook, and then submit the finished workbook to your instructor, either in printed or electronic form, as requested.

Challenge	**Case Problem 3**

Explore how to use relative and absolute references and the PMT function to create a loan table.

Data File needed for this Case Problem: Loan.xlsx

Eason Financial Services Jesse Buchmann is a finance officer at Eason Financial Services in Meridian, Idaho. She works with people who are looking for home mortgages. Most clients want mortgages they can afford, and affordability is determined by the size of the monthly payment. The monthly payment is determined by the interest rate, the total number of payments, and the size of the home loan. Jesse can't change the interest rate, but homebuyers can reduce their monthly payments by increasing the number of years to repay the loan. Jesse wants to give her clients a grid that displays combinations of loan amounts and payment periods so that they can select a loan that best meets their needs and budget. Figure 3-39 shows a preview of the grid that Jesse has in mind.

Figure 3-39

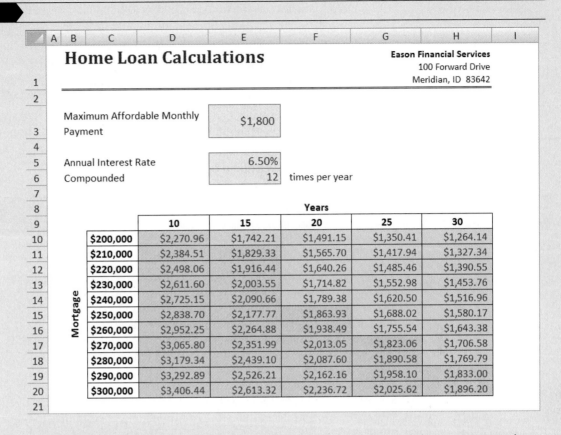

Jesse already entered much of the layout and formatting for the worksheet containing the loan payment grid. She needs your help in entering the PMT function.

Complete the following:

1. Open the **Loan** workbook located in the Tutorial.03\Case3 folder included with your Data Files, and then save the workbook as **Loan Grid** in the same folder.
2. In the Documentation sheet, enter your name and the date.
3. In the Loan Calculation worksheet, in cell E3, enter a monthly payment of **$2,200**.
4. In cell E5, enter the annual interest rate of **6.5%**. In cell E6, enter **12** to indicate that the interest payment is compounded 12 times a year, or monthly.
5. In the range C10:C20, use AutoFill to enter the currency values **$200,000** through **$300,000** in increments of $10,000. In the range D9:H9, use AutoFill to enter the year values **10** through **30** in increments of 5 years.

⊕EXPLORE
6. In cell D10, use the PMT function to calculate the monthly payment required to repay a **$200,000** loan in **10** years at **6.5%** interest compounded monthly. Use absolute references to cells E5 and E6 to enter the annual interest rate and number of payments per year. Use the mixed references D$9 and $C10 to cells D9 and C10, respectively, to reference the number of years to repay the loan and the loan amount. Place a minus symbol before the PMT function so that the value returned by the function is positive rather than negative.

⊕EXPLORE
7. Using AutoFill, copy the formula in cell D10 into the range D11:H10, and then copy that range of formulas into the range D11:H20. Verify that the values entered in those cells match the values shown in Figure 3-39.

⊕ EXPLORE

8. Conditionally format the range D10:H20 to highlight all of the values in the range that are less than the value in cell E3 in a dark green font on a green fill.

9. Add a second conditional format to the range D10:H20 to highlight all of the values in the range that are greater than the value in cell E3 in a dark red font on a red fill.

⊕ EXPLORE

10. Change the value in cell E3 from $2,200 to **$1,800**. If this represents the maximum affordable monthly payment, use the values in the grid to determine the largest mortgage for payment schedules lasting 15 through 30 years. Can any of the home loan values displayed in the grid be repaid in 10 years at $1,800 per month?

11. Save and close the workbook, and then submit the finished workbook to your instructor, either in printed or electronic form, as requested.

| Create | Case Problem 4 |

Create a workbook that automatically grades a driving exam.

Data File needed for this Case Problem: V6.xlsx

V-6 Driving Academy   Sebastian Villanueva owns and operates the V-6 Driving Academy, a driving school located in Pine Hills, Florida. In addition to driving, students must take multiple-choice tests offered by the Florida Department of Motor Vehicles. Students must answer at least 80% of the questions correctly to pass each test. Sebastian has to grade these tests himself. Sebastian realizes that he can save a lot of time if the test questions were in a workbook and Excel totaled the test results. He asks you to help create the workbook.

Sebastian already entered a 20-question test into a workbook. He needs you to format this workbook and insert the necessary functions and formulas to grade a student's answers.

Complete the following:

1. Open the **V6** workbook located in the Tutorial.03\Case4 folder included with your Data Files, and then save the workbook as **V6 Driving Test** in the same folder.

2. In the Documentation sheet, enter your name in cell B3 and enter the date in cell B4.

3. In the Exam1 worksheet, format the questions and possible answers so that the worksheet is easy to read. The format is up to you. At the top of the worksheet, enter a title that describes the exam and then enter a function that returns the current date.

4. Add a section somewhere on the Exam1 worksheet where Sebastian can enter the student's name and answers to each question.

⊕ EXPLORE

5. The answers for the 20 questions are listed below. Use this information to write functions that will grade each answer, giving 1 point for a correct answer and 0 otherwise. Assume that all answers are in lowercase letters; therefore, the function that tests the answer to the first question should check for a "c" rather than a "C".

Question	Answer	Question	Answer	Question	Answer
1	c	8	a	15	b
2	a	9	c	16	b
3	b	10	b	17	b
4	a	11	c	18	b
5	c	12	b	19	b
6	b	13	b	20	c
7	c	14	a		

6. At the top of the worksheet, insert a formula to calculate the total number of correct answers.

7. Insert another formula that divides the total number of correct answers by the total number of exam questions on the worksheet. Display this value as a percentage.

8. Enter a logical function that displays the message "PASS" on the exam if the percentage of correct answers is greater than or equal to 80%; otherwise, the logical function displays the message "FAIL".

Test your worksheet on the following student exams. Which students passed and which failed? What score did each student receive on the exam?

Juan Marquez

Question	Answer	Question	Answer	Question	Answer
1	b	8	a	15	b
2	a	9	c	16	b
3	b	10	b	17	a
4	a	11	c	18	b
5	c	12	c	19	b
6	b	13	b	20	a
7	c	14	a		

Kurt Bessette

Question	Answer	Question	Answer	Question	Answer
1	c	8	b	15	c
2	c	9	c	16	b
3	b	10	b	17	a
4	a	11	c	18	b
5	c	12	a	19	b
6	b	13	b	20	b
7	c	14	a		

Rebecca Pena

Question	Answer	Question	Answer	Question	Answer
1	c	8	a	15	b
2	a	9	c	16	c
3	b	10	a	17	b
4	a	11	c	18	b
5	c	12	b	19	b
6	b	13	b	20	c
7	c	14	a		

9. Save and close the workbook, and then submit the finished workbook to your instructor, either in printed or electronic form, as requested.

Research | Internet Assignments

Use the Internet to find and work with data related to the topics presented in this tutorial.

The purpose of the Internet Assignments is to challenge you to find information on the Internet that you can use to work effectively with this software. The actual assignments are updated and maintained on the Course Technology Web site. Log on to the Internet and use your Web browser to go to the Student Online Companion for New Perspectives Office 2007 at **www.course.com/np/office2007**. Then navigate to the Internet Assignments for this tutorial.

Review | **Quick Check Answers**

Session 3.1

1. Absolute cell reference is $B$21. Mixed cell references are $B21 and B$21.
2. =C11+C12
3. =$B11+C$2
4. =AVERAGE($A11:$A15)
5. Optional arguments are not required in a function. If not included, Excel assumes a default value for the argument.
6. =SUM(B1:B10)
7. =MAX(B1:B10)–MIN(B1:B10)
8. =MAX(B1:B10)/MIN(B1:B10)

Session 3.2

1. Drag the fill handle over the selected range, click the AutoFill Options button, and then click Fill Without Formatting.
2. 12, 15, 18
3. Cell A6 displays the text Tue, cell A7 displays Wed, and cell A8 displays Thu.
4. =IF(A3 > A4, "OK", "RETRY")
5. =TODAY()
6. =NOW()
7. =PMT(0.05/12, 12*20, 130000)
8. NPER

Ending Data Files

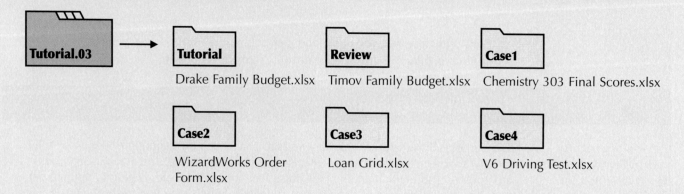

Tutorial.03

Tutorial — Drake Family Budget.xlsx

Review — Timov Family Budget.xlsx

Case1 — Chemistry 303 Final Scores.xlsx

Case2 — WizardWorks Order Form.xlsx

Case3 — Loan Grid.xlsx

Case4 — V6 Driving Test.xlsx

Working with Charts and Graphics

Charting Financial Data

Case | Seaborg Group

Ajita Jindal is a financial assistant for the Seaborg Group, a financial consulting agency located in Providence, Rhode Island. One of her duties is to prepare financial reports on the investments the Seaborg Group makes for its clients. These reports go into a binder containing the financial status of the client's different investments. The client receives the binder at annual meetings with his or her financial advisor, and receives updates on the status of the investments periodically throughout the year.

Many of the company's clients invest in the New Century Fund, a large growth/large risk mutual fund that has been operating for the past 10 years. Ajita needs to create a one-page report that summarizes the fund's financial holdings as well as its 10-year performance record. She already entered the financial data into an Excel workbook, but needs some help in finishing the report. Because many clients are overwhelmed by tables of numbers, Ajita wants to include charts and graphs in the report that display the current and past performance of the New Century Fund. She asks you to help create these charts.

Starting Data Files

Tutorial.04

Tutorial

Fund.xlsx

Review

Crockett.xlsx

Case1

Kenai.xlsx

Case2

Cloud.jpg
Tornado.xlsx

Mitchell.xlsx

Case3

Case4

Basketball.xlsx

Session 4.1

Creating Charts

Ajita already created a workbook in which she entered and formatted data that describes the New Century Fund. You'll begin by opening this workbook.

To open Ajita's workbook:

▶ **1.** Open the **Fund** workbook located in the **Tutorial.04\Tutorial** folder included with your Data Files, and then save the workbook as **New Century Fund** in the same folder.

▶ **2.** In the Documentation sheet, enter your name in cell B3 and the date in cell B4.

▶ **3.** Review the contents of the workbook.

Ajita's workbook contains the following four worksheets in addition to the Documentation sheet:

• The Summary Report worksheet includes summary data and facts about the New Century Fund.
• The Assets worksheet lists the assets of the New Century Fund grouped by investment categories.
• The Sector Weightings worksheet shows the economic sectors in which the New Century Fund invests.
• The Performance History worksheet provides a table that shows how well the New Century Fund performed over the past 10 years compared to two similar funds.

Ajita wants financial data from the Assets, Sector Weightings, and Performance History worksheets placed in the Summary Report worksheet as charts, or graphs. A **chart**, or **graph**, is a visual representation of a set of data. Charts show trends or relationships in data that are more difficult to see by simply looking at numbers, such as the range of months in which the New Century Fund performed exceptionally well.

Figure 4-1 shows Ajita's sketch of how she wants the final Summary Report worksheet to look. In the summary report, she wants one chart that shows the performance of the New Century Fund compared to two similar funds, and she wants two charts that show how money in the New Century Fund is currently invested. The final Summary Report worksheet will be a single page that includes all of the information Ajita wants her clients to see.

Ajita's proposed summary report Figure 4-1

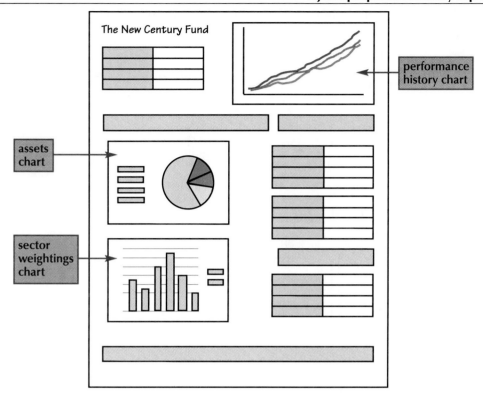

Inserting a Chart | Reference Window

- Select the data source with the range of data you want to chart.
- In the Charts group on the Insert tab, click a chart type, and then click a chart subtype in the Chart gallery.
- In the Location group on the Chart Tools Design tab, click the Move Chart button to place the chart in a chart sheet or embed it into a worksheet.

Selecting a Data Source

Each chart must have a data source. The **data source** is the range that contains the data you want to display in the chart. Each data source is a collection of one or more data series, where each **data series** is a range of values that is plotted as a single unit on the chart. Each data series has three components: the **series name** identifies the data series, the **series values** are the actual data displayed in the chart, and the **category values** are the groups or categories that the series values belong to. After you select the data source, Excel determines the series name, series values, and category values based on that data source. Sometimes, you might need to edit the data series Excel selects.

You'll select the data source for the chart that shows how the money in the New Century Fund is divided among investment categories. This data is located on the Assets worksheet.

To select the data source for the assets chart:

▶ **1.** Click the **Assets** sheet tab to make the Assets worksheet active. You'll select one data series that shows the assets for five investment categories.

▶ **2.** Select the range **A3:B8**. See Figure 4-2.

Figure 4-2 ▶ **Data source selected for the assets chart**

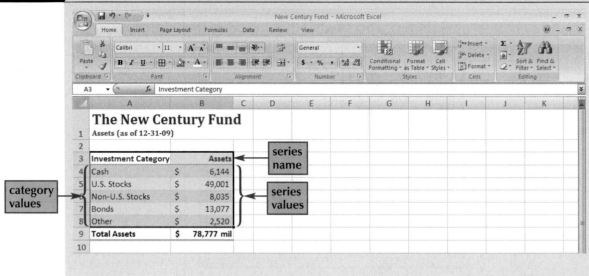

The range you selected for the data source, A3:B8, has a single data series. Excel uses the first row of the selected range as the series name, the first column as the category values, and the remaining columns as the series values. This data source has only one data series, the Assets data series. Its category values in the range A4:A8 list the different asset categories, and its series values in the range B4:B8 contain the data.

If the data source is organized in rows rather than in columns, the first row contains the category values, the remaining rows contain the data values for each data series, and the first column of each series row contains the series names. If your data is organized differently, you can specify a layout for the data source. You'll look at the tools to do this later in this tutorial.

Selecting a Chart Type

Next, you select the type of chart you want to create. Excel supports 73 built-in charts organized into 11 categories. Figure 4-3 describes the different chart type categories. You can also create custom chart types based on the built-in charts.

Categories of Excel chart types ◄ Figure 4-3

Chart Type	Description
Column	Compares values from different categories. Values are indicated by the height of the columns.
Line	Compares values from different categories. Values are indicated by the height of the line. Often used to show trends and changes over time.
Pie	Compares relative values of different categories to the whole. Values are indicated by the areas of the pie slices.
Bar	Compares values from different categories. Values are indicated by the length of the bars.
Area	Compares values from different categories. Similar to the line chart except that areas under the lines contain a fill color.
XY (Scatter)	Shows the patterns or relationship between two or more sets of values. Often used in scientific studies and statistical analyses.
Stock	Displays stock market data, including the high, low, opening, and closing prices of a stock.
Surface	Compares three sets of values in a three-dimensional chart.
Doughnut	Compares relative values of different categories to the whole. Similar to the pie chart except that it can display multiple sets of data.
Bubble	Shows the patterns or relationship between two or more sets of values. Similar to the XY (Scatter) chart except the size of the data marker is determined by a third value.
Radar	Compares a collection of values from several different data sets.

Ajita wants you to create a pie chart of the assets data. A **pie chart** is a chart in the shape of a circle (like a pie) that shows data values as a percentage of the whole. Each value in the data series represents a slice of the pie. The larger the value, the larger the pie slice. For the assets data, each slice will represent the percentage of the total assets from each investment category in the New Century Fund.

Pie charts are most effective with six or fewer slices, and when each slice is large enough to view. The pie chart you are creating for Ajita has five large slices, representing each of the five asset categories—Cash, U.S. Stocks, Non-U.S. Stocks, Bonds, and Other. Notice in Figure 4-2 that you did not select the Total Assets row. The Total Assets row is not an asset category and should not be included in a pie chart.

> **Tip**
>
> Do not include a totals row or column in the data source for a pie chart. Only select the rows or columns that contain the data values and the individual categories.

To insert a pie chart:

► **1.** Click the **Insert** tab on the Ribbon. The Ribbon displays the insert options.

► **2.** In the Charts group, click the **Pie** button to open the Charts gallery, and then click **Pie** (the first pie chart) in the 2-D Pie section. The pie chart is inserted in the Assets sheet, and three new tabs appear on the Ribbon with a label identifying them as Chart Tools contextual tabs. See Figure 4-4.

Figure 4-4	Pie chart inserted in the Assets sheet

Each slice in the pie chart you just created is a different size based on its value in the data series. The biggest slice of the pie represents the U.S. stocks, because that category has the largest value in the data series. The smallest slice of pie represents the Other category, which has the smallest value in the data series.

When you create or select a chart, three Chart Tools contextual tabs appear on the Ribbon. The Design, Layout, and Format tabs provide additional commands to work with the chart's content and appearance. On the Design tab, you set the chart's overall design. On the Layout tab, you work with individual elements of the chart, such as the chart's title. On the Format tab, you format graphic shapes found in the chart, such as the chart's border or markers placed in the chart. When you select a worksheet cell or another object that is not a chart, the Chart Tools contextual tabs disappear until you reselect the chart.

Moving and Resizing Charts

By default, a chart is inserted as an **embedded chart**, which means the chart is placed in a worksheet next to its data source. The advantage of an embedded chart is that you can display the chart alongside any text or figures that can explain the chart's meaning and purpose. An embedded chart covers worksheet cells, which might contain data and formulas.

You can also place a chart in a **chart sheet**, so that the entire sheet contains only the chart and no worksheet cells. Chart sheets are helpful for detailed charts that need more space to be seen clearly or when you want to show a chart without any worksheet text or data. For now, you'll leave Ajita's pie chart as an embedded chart. You'll work with chart sheets later in this tutorial.

Right now, the pie chart is embedded in the Assets worksheet. However, Ajita wants the chart embedded in the Summary Report worksheet. You can move an embedded chart to a different worksheet in the workbook or you can move it into a chart sheet. Likewise, you can move a chart from a chart sheet and embed it in any worksheet you select. The Move Chart dialog box provides options for moving charts between worksheets and chart sheets. You can also cut and paste a chart to a new location in the workbook.

To move the embedded pie chart to the Summary Report worksheet:

▶ **1.** In the Location group on the Chart Tools Design tab, click the **Move Chart** button. The Move Chart dialog box opens.

   Trouble? If you don't see the Chart Tools Design tab on the Ribbon, the chart is probably not selected. Click the chart in the Assets sheet to select it, and then repeat Step 1.

▶ **2.** Click the **Object in** arrow to display a list of worksheets in the active workbook, and then click **Summary Report**. See Figure 4-5.

Move Chart dialog box   **Figure 4-5**

places the chart in a chart sheet

embeds the chart in the selected worksheet

▶ **3.** Click the **OK** button. The embedded pie chart moves from the Assets worksheet to the Summary Report worksheet, and remains selected.

The pie chart is now in the correct worksheet, but its location and size obscures other content in the Summary Report worksheet. You move or resize an embedded chart by first selecting the chart, which displays a **selection box** around the chart, and then dragging the selection box to a new location in the worksheet. You can also drag a **resizing handle** on the selection box to change the chart's width and height.

To move and resize the pie chart:

▶ **1.** Move the pointer over an empty area of the selected chart until the pointer changes to ⇖ and you see the ScreenTip "Chart Area."

▶ **2.** Drag the chart so its upper-left corner is within cell **A13**, and then release the mouse button. The chart's upper-left corner is in cell A13, but it still overlaps some data.

   Trouble? If the pie chart resizes or does not move to the new location, you probably didn't drag the chart from the chart area. Press the Ctrl+Z keys to undo your last action, and then repeat Steps 1 and 2, being sure to drag the pie chart from the chart area.

▶ **3.** Move the pointer over the resizing handle in the lower-right corner of the chart until the pointer changes to ⬂, and then drag the resizing handle up to cell **E21**. The chart resizes to cover the range A13:E21 and remains selected. See Figure 4-6.

Figure 4-6 **Moved and resized pie chart**

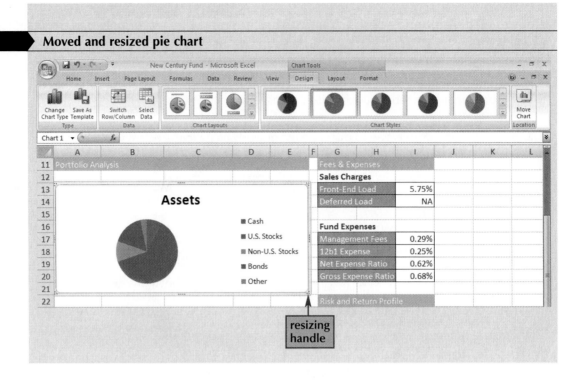

Working on Chart Design

The assets pie chart you have just resized includes a lot of empty space. Also, it's unclear how the different asset categories are related. For example, you can easily see that the largest slice represents the U.S. Stocks category, but it's difficult to tell whether the non-U.S. stocks slice is bigger than the Cash slice. To clarify the relationship between the pie slices, Ajita wants each slice to display its percentage of the whole. She also wants less empty space within the chart.

Selecting Chart Elements

Pie charts have five elements that are common to most charts. The **chart area** is the rectangular box containing the chart and all of the other chart elements. The **chart title** is a descriptive label or name for the chart, and usually appears at the top of the chart area. The **plot area** is the part of the chart that contains the graphical representation of all the data series in the chart. Each data value or data series is represented by a **data marker**. For pie charts, the data markers are the individual pie slices, which represent the data values. The **legend** is a rectangular area that labels the markers or symbols used in the chart. If the chart contains several data series, the legend identifies the markers used for each series. Pie charts, having only one data series, use the legend to identify the different pie slices. Figure 4-7 identifies each of these elements on the pie chart you just created for the assets data.

Common chart elements ◄ Figure 4-7

You can select and format any chart element individually or you can apply a built-in style or chart layout to format all of these elements at once. To select a chart element, you click that element or select it from a list of chart elements on the Chart Tools Layout tab. As you move your pointer over a chart element, its name appears in a ScreenTip. When you click that element, its name appears in the Chart Elements button in the Current Selection group on the Chart Tools Layout tab.

To select elements of the pie chart:

▶ 1. Move your pointer over the chart title until you see the ScreenTip "Chart Title," and then click the chart title. A selection box appears around the chart title.

▶ 2. Click the **Chart Tools Layout** tab on the Ribbon. The Ribbon displays the layout options for charts.

▶ 3. In the Current Selection group, click the **Chart Elements arrow** to display an alphabetical list of all the chart elements in the active chart. In this case, the Chart Elements box shows "Chart Title," indicating that this element is currently selected.

▶ 4. Click **Legend**. The legend is selected in the chart.

▶ 5. In the Current Selection group, click the **Chart Elements arrow**, and then click **Plot Area**. The chart's plot area is selected.

▶ 6. Click the chart area in the chart. The chart area is selected.

Choosing a Chart Style and Layout

The assets pie chart uses the default style for the different slices. A chart style is similar to a cell style or a table style in that it formats several chart elements at one time. You can change the color and appearance of the slices by selecting a different chart style from the Chart Styles gallery on the Chart Tools Design tab. Ajita wants a chart style that gives the slices a rounded, shaded look.

To apply a different chart style to the assets pie chart:

▶ 1. Click the **Chart Tools Design** tab on the Ribbon. The Ribbon displays the design options for charts.

▶ 2. In the Chart Styles group, click the **More** button to open the Chart Styles gallery, and then click **Style 26** (the fourth row, second column). Each pie slice now has a rounded, raised look. See Figure 4-8.

Figure 4-8 | **Style 26 chart style applied**

Trouble? If a dialog box opens, indicating that complex formatting applied to the selected chart may take awhile to display, click the Yes button to continue using the formatting.

You can also use a chart layout to choose which chart elements are displayed and how they are formatted. The chart layouts include some of the most common ways of displaying different charts. Each chart type has its own collection of layouts. Figure 4-9 shows the available layouts for pie charts. Depending on the pie chart layout you choose, you can hide or display the chart title, display a chart legend or place legend labels in the pie slices, and add percentages to the pie slices.

Figure 4-9 | **Pie chart layouts**

Layout	Name	Pie chart with
	Layout 1	Chart title, labels, and percentages
	Layout 2	Chart title, percentages, and legend above the pie
	Layout 3	Legend below the pie
	Layout 4	Labels in pie slices
	Layout 5	Chart title and labels in pie slices
	Layout 6	Chart title, percentages, and legend to the right of the pie
	Layout 7	Legend to the right of the pie

Ajita wants you to apply a layout that shows percentages for the pie slices so her clients can tell exactly how large each asset category is relative to the whole. She also wants to the chart title to remain displayed above the chart and the legend to remain displayed to the side of the chart. Layout 6 does all of these things.

To apply Layout 6 to the assets pie chart:

▶ **1.** In the Chart Layouts group on the Chart Tools Design tab, click the **More** button to open the Chart Layouts gallery.

▶ **2.** Click **Layout 6** in the second row, third column. Percentages appear on or next to the slices in the pie chart. See Figure 4-10.

Layout 6 chart layout applied ◀ | **Figure 4-10**

Tip

Percentages appear on pie slices large enough to fit the number; otherwise, percentages appear next to the slices in the chart area.

Trouble? Depending on your monitor size and resolution, your chart might look different from that shown in Figure 4-10. This does not affect your work with the pie chart.

The percentages on the pie chart will enable clients to quickly see how the assets of the New Century Fund are allocated. For example, 62% of the New Century Fund is invested in U.S. stocks and 10% in non-U.S. stocks. To fit the percentages, Excel reduced the size of the pie chart in the plot area. Ajita wants the pie chart larger, so you'll format some of the other chart elements smaller to make more space for the pie.

Working with the Chart Title

Ajita thinks that the chart title is too large and not descriptive enough. The chart title uses the heading from the column of asset values in the Assets worksheet. You'll change the title to "Allocation of Assets" and reduce its font size to 12 points.

To format the chart title:

▶ **1.** Click the chart title to select it. A selection box appears around the chart title.

▶ **2.** Type **Allocation of Assets**, and then press the **Enter** key. The chart title is updated with your typed entry, and remains selected.

▶ **3.** Click the **Home** tab on the Ribbon.

Tip

You can revise the title text rather than replace it by double-clicking the chart title to place the insertion point in the text, and then editing the text as needed.

4. In the Font group, click the **Font Size arrow**, and then click **12**. The chart title shrinks from 18 points to 12 points, and the pie chart increases in size to fill in the extra space. See Figure 4-11.

Figure 4-11   **Chart title updated and formatted**

Trouble? Depending on your monitor size and resolution, your chart might look slightly different from that shown in Figure 4-11. This does not affect your work with the pie chart.

Working with the Chart Legend

Ajita wants the legend moved to the left side of the chart and an orange border added around the legend text to distinguish it from the rest of the chart. You'll use the tools on the Chart Tools Layout tab to format the legend.

To format the chart legend:

1. Click the **Chart Tools Layout** tab on the Ribbon.

2. In the Labels group, click the **Legend** button, and then click **Show Legend at Left**. The legend moves to the left side of the chart.

3. In the Labels group, click the **Legend** button, and then click **More Legend Options**. The Format Legend dialog box opens. Every chart element has a corresponding dialog box from which you can select more advanced options to format the element's appearance.

4. Click **Border Color** in the list on the left side of the dialog box. The Border Color options appear on the right side of the dialog box.

5. Click the **Solid line** option button. Two more options related to border colors appear.

6. Click the **Color** button ![color button] to open the color palette, and then click **Orange, Accent 6, Lighter 40%** (the fourth row, last column) in the Theme Colors section. See Figure 4-12.

Border Color options set in the Format Legend dialog box | Figure 4-12

7. Click the **Close** button, and then click cell **A23** to deselect the chart. The legend now has a light orange border. See Figure 4-13.

Chart legend moved and formatted | Figure 4-13

Formatting a Pie Chart

Chart titles and legends are common to almost all types of charts. Another common element is a **data label**, which is text associated with a data value. In pie charts, data labels are added to the slices. You already created data labels for the assets chart when you selected Layout 6 to add percentages to the slices. These labels were placed where they best fit in relation to the pie slices. For some asset categories, the label appears within the pie slice; for others, the label appears alongside the slice. Labels placed outside of the pie might appear farther from their slices than is easily read due to space limitations. In those cases, **leader lines** might be added to the labels to connect them to their corresponding slices. For example, a leader line connects the Cash slice and its label in Figure 4-13. Note that a leader line will disappear when enough space exists in the pie chart to place a label next to its slice.

For consistency, Ajita wants all the data labels to appear outside the pie chart. This will make the text for the dark blue and red pie slices easier to read. You'll show leader lines for the labels, which means the leader lines will appear only when the chart area does not have enough space for the labels to appear close to their pie slices.

To format the pie chart's data labels:

▶ **1.** Click the chart to select it.

▶ **2.** In the Labels group on the Chart Tools Layout tab, click the **Data Labels** button, and then click **More Data Label Options**. The Format Data Labels dialog box opens with the the Label Options displayed.

▶ **3.** In the Label Position section, click the **Outside End** option button. In the Label Contains section, the Percentage check box and the Show Leader Lines check box are already checked because these were included in the chart layout you applied earlier. See Figure 4-14.

| Figure 4-14 | Label Options in the Format Data Labels dialog box |

These options set the data labels to display percentages outside the pie chart and use leader lines when needed to connect the labels with their corresponding pie slices. Next, you'll change the percentage values to show two decimal places for more accuracy.

▶ **4.** Click **Number** in the list on the left side of the dialog box.

▶ **5.** Click **Percentage** in the Category list, and then verify that **2** appears in the Decimal places box.

▶ **6.** Click the **Close** button to close the Format Data Labels dialog box, and then click cell **A23** to deselect the chart. See Figure 4-15. Leader lines don't appear in the pie chart shown in Figure 4-15 because the chart area has enough space to place the labels close to their slices.

Pie chart data labels formatted ◀ **Figure 4-15**

Setting the Pie Slice Colors

The pie slices for Cash, Bonds, and Other have similar colors. Depending on the printer quality or the monitor resolution, these slices might be difficult to distinguish in the final report. In pie charts with legends, it's best to make the slice colors as distinct as possible to avoid confusion, especially slices adjacent to each other in the pie. You'll change the fill color of the Other slice to yellow and the Cash slice to light blue. Because each slice represents a different value in the series, you must format each slice rather than the entire data series.

To select and format pie slices in the assets pie chart:

▶ **1.** Click the pie to select the entire data series.

▶ **2.** Click the light blue **Other** slice, which represents 3.20% of the pie. Only that value, or slice, is selected.

▶ **3.** Click the **Home** tab on the Ribbon.

▶ **4.** In the Font group, click the **Fill Color button arrow** 🖌️▾, and then click **Yellow**, the fourth color in the Standard Colors section. The Other slice and legend marker change to yellow.

▶ **5.** Click the dark blue **Cash** slice, which covers 7.80% of the pie.

▶ **6.** In the Font group, click the **Fill Color button arrow** 🖌️▾, and then click **Light Blue**, the seventh color in the Standard Colors section. The Cash slice and legend marker change to light blue. Each slice of the pie is now a distinct color. See Figure 4-16.

Figure 4-16 **Pie slices with new colors**

Pie slices do not need to be fixed in place. An **exploded pie chart** moves one slice away from the pie as if someone were taking the piece out of the pie. To explode a pie slice, select that slice and then drag it away from the pie. To explode all of the slices, select the entire pie and drag the pointer away from the center of the pie. Exploded pie charts are useful when you want to emphasize one category above all of the others. Although you can explode more than one slice, the resulting pie chart is rarely effective.

Creating a 3D Pie Chart

Ajita thinks the pie chart will look better as a three-dimensional (3D) figure. Although 3D charts are visually attractive, they can obscure the relationship between the values in the chart. For example, it is unclear which slice—red or yellow—is bigger in the pie chart shown in Figure 4-17. Actually, they are the same size, each representing 20% of the whole. The yellow slice appears bigger because the 3D effect brings that slice closer to the viewer.

Figure 4-17 **Misleading 3D pie chart**

the yellow and red slices are the same size

Because you already added data labels to the assets pie chart, Ajita thinks her clients will not misinterpret a 3D pie chart. She thinks that making the assets pie chart 3D will provide visual interest to the report while maintaining the pie chart's effectiveness.

To change the assets pie chart to 3D:

▶ **1.** Click the chart area to select the chart, and then click the **Chart Tools Design** tab on the Ribbon.

▶ **2.** In the Type group, click the **Change Chart Type** button. The Change Chart Type dialog box opens.

▶ **3.** Click **Pie in 3-D** (the second chart type in the Pie section).

▶ **4.** Click the **OK** button. The pie chart is now a 3D chart.

Creating Effective 3D Charts | InSight

Because of the visual distortion that can result with 3D representations, you should include data labels with all 3D charts. Also, try to avoid extreme viewing angles that elongate the chart and misrepresent the data. Although 3D charts can be eye-catching, do not use this effect if it overrides the main purpose of a chart, which is data interpretation.

Working with 3D Options

The 3D pie chart does not look very different from the 2D version because you are looking straight down on the chart from "above." To increase the 3D effect, you need to rotate the chart. You can rotate the chart in two directions: horizontally along the x-axis and vertically along the y-axis. Increasing the rotation along the x-axis spins the chart clockwise. Increasing the rotation along the y-axis raises the viewpoint higher above the chart. All 3D charts have a third axis that corresponds to the depth of the chart. Depth values can range from 0 to 2000. The larger the value, the thicker the chart appears. You can also change the chart's **perspective**, which controls how fast the chart appears to recede from the viewer's eye. Perspective values range from 0° to 90°. A 90° perspective value exaggerates the 3D effect, making distant objects appear very small, whereas perspective values near 0° minimize this effect. Try different values for depth and perspective to determine which work best for your chart.

You'll orient the pie chart so that the viewer's eye level is slightly above the chart. You'll also rotate the chart along the horizontal axis so that the largest slice is on the left side of the pie. Often you'll need to experiment to find the right angles for a 3D chart by rotating the chart in different directions until it looks correct without distorting the data. In this case, you'll rotate the chart 90° along the horizontal axis and place the viewer's eye at an angle of 20° above the chart. You will not change the chart's perspective or depth.

To rotate the 3D pie chart:

▶ **1.** Click the **Chart Tools Layout** tab on the Ribbon, and then, in the Background group, click the **3-D Rotation** button. The Format Chart Area dialog box opens with the 3-D Rotation options displayed.

▶ **2.** In the Rotation section, type **90** in the X box and type **20** in the Y box. See Figure 4-18.

Figure 4-18 ▸ **Format Chart Area dialog box**

3. Click the **Close** button. The pie chart rotates based on the new x-axis and y-axis values. See Figure 4-19.

Figure 4-19 ▸ **3D assets pie chart**

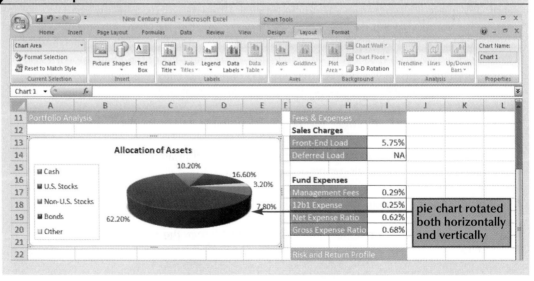

The new x-axis and y-axis values have a significant impact on the way the chart looks. The new x-axis value shifted the pie chart clockwise one quarter of the way around the circle so the largest slice, the red U.S Stocks slice, is in the front. The new y-axis value turned the pie chart so the viewer is looking down on the chart. Ajita is pleased with the 3D effect you added.

The Format Chart Area dialog box shown in Figure 4-18 also includes options to change the 3-D Format of the chart. These options allow you to add drop shadows, raised or beveled corners, and textured surfaces that give the illusion of light reflecting off the chart elements. You saw an example of such a surface in Figure 4-13 when you added a shaded, rounded chart style to the pie chart. You will not use the 3-D Format options for the assets pie chart.

Editing Chart Data

Charts remain linked or connected to their data sources, even if they appear in different worksheets. If you change any values or labels in the data source, the chart is automatically updated to show the new content. For example, if the Other assets increase from $2,520 to $4,520 and the remaining assets are unchanged, the Other slice becomes bigger to reflect its larger percentage of the whole and the remaining slices shrink to reflect their smaller percentage of the whole.

Ajita wants you to edit the data source for the assets pie chart. She thinks the Other category would be better titled as Other Assets and she wants you to correct the assets value for that category. You'll make both of these changes to the data in the Assets worksheet.

To edit the data source for the assets pie chart:

▶ **1.** Click the **Assets** sheet tab to make it the active worksheet.

▶ **2.** Edit the text in cell A8 to **Other Assets**, and then change the value in cell B8 to **4520**.

▶ **3.** Click the **Summary Report** sheet tab, and then verify that the pie chart was updated with the new data value and category name. See Figure 4-20. Note that the percentage values for each category are recalculated based on the new data. As a result, the Other Assets slice increased in size to reflect its larger percentage of the whole, and the remaining slices decreased in size.

Updated pie chart based on revised data   Figure 4-20

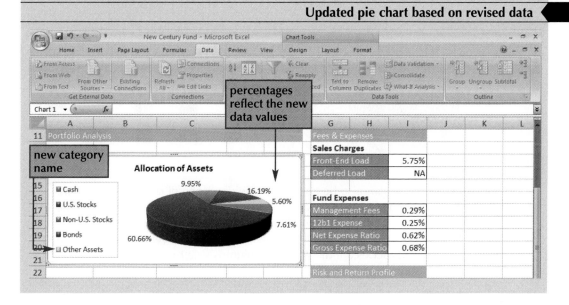

Occasionally, you will not want a chart to reflect new values in the data source, such as when a chart shows a "snapshot" of the data at a certain time. You can do this by copying and pasting the chart as a picture. Select the chart, copy it as usual, click the Paste button arrow, point to As Picture, and then click Paste as Picture. The chart is pasted as a picture without any connection to its data source and cannot be edited or formatted in any way.

Working with Column Charts

The pie chart in the summary report clearly shows that most assets of the New Century Fund are allocated toward U.S. stocks. The next part of the summary report lists the type of stocks being purchased by the fund. Each mutual fund invests in different kinds of stocks. Some funds are heavily invested in information technology, others in the service industry, and still others in manufacturing. Diversification (the distribution of investments among a variety of companies or sectors to limit losses in the event one company or sector has an economic downturn) is important, so all funds are invested to some degree in multiple economic sectors. The New Century Fund is invested in 12 different economic sectors, organized into categories of information, services, and manufacturing.

Creating a Column Chart

Twelve categories are too many for an effective pie chart, so Ajita wants you to create a column chart to display this economic sector data. A **column chart** displays values in different categories as columns; the height of each column is based on its value. Related to the column chart is the **bar chart**, which is a column chart turned on its side, so each bar length is based on its value.

Column and bar charts are superior to pie charts when the number of categories is large or the categories are close in value. It is easier to compare height or length than area. Figure 4-21 displays the same data as a pie chart and a column chart. As you can see, it's difficult to determine which pie slice has the largest area and by how much. This is much simpler to determine in the column chart.

Figure 4-21	Same data displayed as a pie chart and a column chart

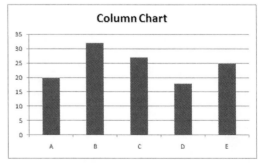

Column and bar charts can also be applied to a wider range of data than pie charts. For example, you can demonstrate how a set of values changes over time, such as the value of the New Century Fund over several years. You can also include several data series in a column or bar chart, such as the value of three funds over several years. The values from different data series are displayed in columns side by side. Pie charts usually show only one data series.

Ajita wants you to create a column chart that shows how the the New Century Fund is distributed among the 12 sectors in which it is invested. The columns will represent only one data series, so you'll use the 2D Clustered Columns chart type. A clustered columns chart uses vertical rectangles to compare values across categories.

To create a column chart from the sector data:

▶ **1.** Click the **Sector Weightings** sheet tab, and then select the range **A3:C15**.

▶ **2.** Click the **Insert** tab on the Ribbon.

▶ **3.** In the Charts group, click the **Column** button, and then click the **Clustered Column** chart, the first chart in the 2-D Column section. The column chart is inserted in the Sector Weightings worksheet, and the Chart Tools Design tab on the Ribbon is selected.

▶ **4.** In the Location group on the Chart Tools Design tab, click the **Move Chart** button. The Move Chart dialog box opens. You'll move the chart to the Summary Report worksheet.

▶ **5.** Click the **Object in** arrow, click **Summary Report**, and then click the **OK** button. The column chart moves to the Summary Report worksheet.

▶ **6.** In the Summary Report worksheet, click a blank spot in the chart area of the column chart, and then drag the chart down so its upper-left corner is in cell **A23**.

▶ **7.** Drag the resizing handle in the lower-right corner of the chart until the chart covers the range **A23:E37**. See Figure 4-22.

Column chart moved and resized in the Summary Report worksheet	Figure 4-22

The column chart shows that the New Century Fund is most heavily invested in health care and consumer services, hardware information technology, and energy manufacturing. On the other hand, the fund does not invest much in telecommunications, software, and media.

Formatting Column Chart Elements

Similar to the pie chart, the column chart has a chart title and a legend that identifies different data series rather than values within a data series. Because this column chart contains only one data series, the sector weightings of the New Century Fund, the legend has only one entry. The column chart also has a few new elements, which are identified in Figure 4-23.

Figure 4-23   **Elements of the column chart**

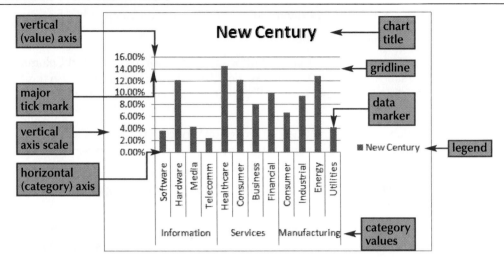

The **vertical**, or **value, axis** displays the values associated with the heights of each column. You can use two value axes to plot different types of data on a chart, such as the number of units sold and the revenue generated from the sale of a group of products. One axis (usually the axis on the left) is called the **primary value axis**, and the other axis is called the **secondary value axis**. The chart shown in Figure 4-23 has a primary value axis but not the optional secondary value axis.

Excel selects the scale that best displays the values in the chart. A **scale** is a range of values that spans the vertical axis, which is 0% to 16% in Figure 4-23. Each value has a **major tick mark** that acts like the lines on a ruler, making it easier to read the scale. In Figure 4-23, major tick marks appear every 2% along the scale. Some axes also use **minor tick marks** to further divide the space between the major tick marks. Figure 4-23 does not display minor tick marks.

Many charts use **gridlines** to extend the tick marks across the plot area. As you can see in Figure 4-23, gridlines make it easier to determine the value of a column. For example, little more than 14% of the stocks from the New Century Fund are invested in healthcare services. A chart can also have vertical gridlines, though none are shown here.

The **horizontal**, or **category, axis** displays the categories associated with each data value. This column chart has two levels of category values: one for the sector category and one for the sector name. You can include as many levels as you need to clearly define the category values; Excel will fit as many as possible below the category axis. In this chart, Excel rotated the sector names to fit them in the space. You can format the axes text, rotate and align the text entries, or select which entries to display in the chart.

The data markers in the column chart are the individual columns. The same data marker (a column) is used for an entire data series; only the columns' heights differ from one data value to another. When a chart has only one data series—such as the column chart you just created—the chart title and legend are redundant. Ajita asks you to remove the legend, and then edit and format the chart title.

To format the legend and chart title of the column chart:

▶   **1.** Click the **Chart Tools Layout** tab on the Ribbon.

▶   **2.** In the Labels group, click the **Legend** button, and then click **None**. The chart legend no longer appears in the chart, and the column chart is resized to fill the available space.

▶   **3.** Click the chart title to select it, and then click the **Home** tab on the Ribbon.

▶   **4.** In the Font group, click the **Font Size arrow**, and then click **12**. The chart title is reduced to 12 points, and remains selected.

▶ **5.** Type **Sector Weightings** as the new chart title, and then press the **Enter** key.

Formatting the Chart Axes

Ajita thinks that the font used in both the value axis and the category axis is too large, and that the value axis scale looks crowded. She asks you to reduce the font size of the axes, place the major tick marks at 5% intervals, and display the percentages without any decimal places.

To format the chart axes:

▶ **1.** Click the **category axis** to select it.

▶ **2.** In the Font group on the Home tab, click the **Font Size arrow**, and then click **8**. The category axis labels are smaller.

▶ **3.** Click the **value axis** to select it, and repeat Step 2 to change the axis font size to **8** points.

▶ **4.** Click the **Chart Tools Layout** tab on the Ribbon.

▶ **5.** In the Axes group, click the **Axes** button, point to **Primary Vertical Axis**, and then click **More Primary Vertical Axis Options**. The Format Axis dialog box opens with the Axis Options displayed. The value axis options are set to Auto, which tells Excel to set the values. You'll modify these so that the major tick marks appear at 5% intervals on the vertical axis to make the chart less cluttered and easier to read.

▶ **6.** Click the **Major unit Fixed** option button, press the **Tab** key, and then type **0.05** for the size of the major tick mark. Major tick marks will now appear on the value axis in 5% increments. See Figure 4-24.

Axis Options in the Format Axis dialog box | Figure 4-24

7. Click **Number** on the left side of the dialog box, type **0** in the Decimal places box, and then click the **Close** button. The percentages on the value axis show no decimal places. See Figure 4-25.

Figure 4-25
Formatted chart axes

The value axis now ranges from 0% to 20% rather than 16%, and the percentages no longer show any decimal places. These changes make the value axis easier to read. Also, the smaller font size used for the value and category axes left more room for the data series. No titles appear next to the value and category axes. This isn't a problem for the category axis because the chart title and the axis labels are self-explanatory. Ajita wants you to add the title "Stock Percentages" to the value axis and rotate it to save space.

To add a rotated title to the value axis:

1. In the Labels group on the Chart Tools Layout tab, click the **Axis Titles** button, point to **Primary Vertical Axis Title**, and then click **Rotated Title**. The text "Axis Title" appears rotated to the left of the vertical axis in a selection box.

2. Type **Stock Percentages**, and then press the **Enter** key. The title is added to the vertical axis.

As with other chart text in the chart, you can format an axis title. Ajita is pleased with the current format of the vertical axis title, so no further changes are needed.

Formatting the Chart Columns

Ajita thinks that the columns are spaced too widely and wants you to reduce the gap between them. Also, she wants you to change the fill color of the columns to a lighter blue and add a shaded appearance to make the columns stand out. To modify the appearance of a data series, you first select the data markers for that series and then apply formatting to selected markers.

To format the chart columns:

▶ **1.** Click any column in the Sector Weightings chart. A selection box surrounds each column in the chart, indicating that the entire series is selected.

Trouble? If only the column you clicked is selected, you selected only a single data value rather than the entire data series. Click a blank spot in the chart area, and then repeat Step 1 to select the entire series.

▶ **2.** In the Current Selection group on the Chart Tools Layout tab, click **Format Selection**. The Format Data Series dialog box opens with the Series Options displayed.

▶ **3.** Drag the Gap width slider to **50%** to reduce the gap between adjacent columns. The columns become wider to fill the space.

Trouble? If you cannot drag the Gap width slider to exactly 50%, type the value 50 in the Gap width box below the slider.

▶ **4.** Click **Fill** on the left side of the dialog box, and then click the **Gradient fill** option button to fill the columns with a gradually changing mix of colors.

▶ **5.** Click the **Direction** button ▣▾ to open a gallery of fill directions, and then click **Linear Right** (the fourth fill direction in the first row). The columns have a gradient fill that blends to the right. See Figure 4-26.

> **Tip**
>
> You can also highlight a data value by formatting one column in a column chart; select the data series and then click the column you want to format. Any formatting applies only to that data marker.

Fill options set in the Format Data Series dialog box ◀ **Figure 4-26**

▶ **6.** Click the **Close** button, and then click cell **A38** to deselect the chart. See Figure 4-27.

Figure 4-27 **Formatted chart columns**

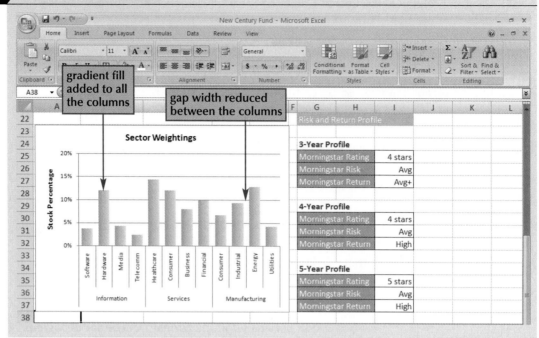

Ajita is pleased with the two charts you've created for the Summary Report worksheet. In the next session, you'll add a chart that describes the performance of the New Century Fund over the past 10 years and work with drawing objects.

InSight | **Designing Effective Charts**

A well-designed chart can illuminate facts that might be hidden by viewing only the numbers. However, poorly designed charts can mislead readers and make it more difficult to interpret data. Keep in mind the following tips for creating more effective and useful charts:

- Keep it simple. Do not clutter a chart with too many graphic elements. Focus attention on the data rather than on decorative elements that do not inform.
- Limit the number of data series used in the chart. Line charts and column charts should display no more than three or four data series. Pie charts should have no more than six slices.
- Use gridlines in moderation. Gridlines should be used to provide only approximate values for the data markers. Too many gridlines can obscure the data being graphed.
- Choose colors carefully. Display different data series in contrasting colors to make it easier to distinguish one series from another. Do not always accept the default color choices. When printing charts, make sure the colors are distinct in the printed copy.
- Limit the use of different text styles to no more than two. Too many text styles in one chart can distract attention from the data.
- Analyze whether you need a chart in the first place. Remember, not all data is meant to be charted. Some data is presented more effectively in a table or as part of a narrative.

Session 4.1 Quick Check | Review

1. What are the three components of a data series?
2. In what two locations can a chart be placed?
3. What is the difference between the chart area and the plot area?
4. A data series contains values divided into 10 categories. Which chart would be better for displaying this data: a pie chart or a column chart? Why?
5. Explain how 3D charts can lead to a false interpretation of the data. What can you do to correct this problem?
6. What are major tick marks, minor tick marks, and gridlines?
7. What is a bar chart?
8. How do you rescale a chart axis?

Session 4.2

Creating a Line Chart

Ajita will include the performance history of the New Century Fund in the summary report because her clients always want to know how well their investments are doing. Clients also want to compare different investments, so Ajita has other data that provides a standard of comparison, or benchmark, to the performance of the New Century Fund. One benchmark is the average performance of other large growth funds, and the other benchmark is the S&P 500 (or Standard and Poor's 500, which is an index of 500 blue chip stocks that is commonly used to measure the performance of stocks and funds).

Ajita entered this data in the Performance History worksheet. She calculated the quarterly returns for the past 10 years from an initial investment of $10,000. Because there are 40 data points for each of the three data series, you'll create a line chart. A **line chart** compares values from several categories with a sequential order, such as dates and times that occur at evenly spaced intervals. The values are indicated by the height of the line. In this case, you'll plot the quarterly value of each investment on the vertical axis and the date on the horizontal axis.

To create the line chart:

▶ 1. If you took a break after the previous session, make sure the New Century Fund workbook located in the Tutorial.04\Tutorial folder is open.

▶ 2. Click the **Performance History** sheet tab to make it the active worksheet, and then select the range **A4:D44**. This range contains the data for the value of the New Century Fund, the average value of large growth funds, and the value of the S&P 500 for each quarter of 2000 through 2009.

▶ 3. Click the **Insert** tab on the Ribbon.

▶ 4. In the Charts group, click the **Line** button, and then click the **Line** chart (the first chart in the 2-D Line section). A line chart is embedded in the Performance History worksheet.

▶ 5. In the Location group on the Chart Tools Design tab, click the **Move Chart** button to open the Move Chart dialog box, click **Summary Report** in the Object in list, and then click the **OK** button. The line chart moves to the Summary Report worksheet.

▶ 6. Move and resize the chart to cover the range **D1:I9**. See Figure 4-28.

Figure 4-28 Moved and resized line chart

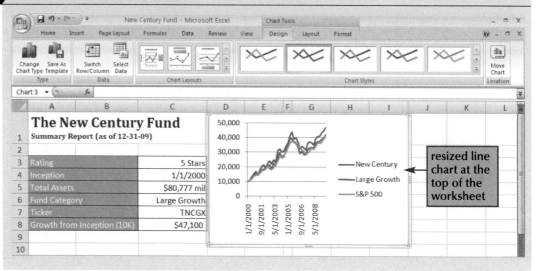

This chart includes three data series—the New Century Fund, the average of large growth funds, and the S&P 500. Each series has a different line color, which is identified in the legend on the right side of the chart area. However, the line chart has little blank space in the chart area and seems crowded by the legend and the date labels on the category axis. You'll reduce the font size of the axis and legend labels, and then add a chart title that clearly identifies the chart's content—the growth of $10,000 for the New Century Fund and the two benchmarks.

To edit the line chart:

▶ 1. Click the **Chart Tools Layout** tab on the Ribbon.

▶ 2. In the Labels group, click the **Chart Title** button, and then click **Above Chart**. A chart title appears above the line chart surrounded by a selection box.

▶ 3. Type **Growth of $10,000** and then press the **Enter** key. The new, descriptive title appears above the chart.

▶ 4. Click the **Home** tab on the Ribbon.

▶ 5. In the Font group, click the **Font Size arrow**, and then click **10**. The chart title is reduced to 10 points.

▶ 6. Click the **value axis** to select it, and then set its font size to **8** points.

▶ 7. Click the **category axis** to select it, and then set its font size to **8** points.

▶ 8. Click the **chart legend** to select it, and then set its font size to **8** points. The line chart resizes to fill the space left by the smaller chart titles, axes, and chart legend.

Formatting Date Labels

Reducing the font size of the different chart elements helps the layout, but the chart still needs work. The most awkward part of the chart is the list of dates. Ajita is more interested in the general trend from year to year, than the exact date on which the different fund values were calculated. She wants the labels to show only years. You can save space by showing the labels only every other year. To do this, you have to set the major tick marks to appear at two-year intervals. You'll also set the minor tick marks to appear at one-year intervals, even though you won't display the minor tick marks on the chart until later.

To format the category axis labels:

▶ 1. Click the **Chart Tools Layout** tab on the Ribbon.

▶ 2. In the Axes group, click the **Axes** button, point to **Primary Horizontal Axis**, and then click **More Primary Horizontal Axis Options**. The Format Axis dialog box opens with the Axis Options displayed.

   Because the horizontal axis contains date values, its scale is based on dates rather than on numbers. This means you can set the tick mark intervals in terms of months and years. You'll display the major tick marks (and their labels) every two years. You'll set the interval for minor tick marks to one year.

▶ 3. Click the **Major unit Fixed** option button, type **2** in the box, press the **Tab** key, select **Years** in the list. The major tick marks are set to every two years.

▶ 4. Click the **Minor unit Fixed** option button, verify that **1** is entered in the box, select **Years** in the list, and then press the **Tab** key. The minor tick marks are set to every year. See Figure 4-29.

Date intervals for tick marks ◀ **Figure 4-29**

Next, you'll format the category labels to show the four-digit year value rather than the complete date. Excel does not have a built-in format to display four-digit year values, but you can create a custom format. Custom date formats use combinations of the letters *m*, *d*, and *y* for months, days, and years. The number of each letter controls how Excel displays the date. Use *m* or *mm* to display the month number, *mmm* to display the month's three-letter abbreviation, and *mmmm* to display the month's full name. For days, use *dd* to display a two-digit day value and *dddd* to display the day's full name. For example, a custom format of *mmm-dd* shows a three-letter month abbreviation followed by a hyphen and a two-digit day number (such as Apr-05). If you don't want to display the month or day but only the year, use the custom format *yy* for a two-digit year or *yyyy* for a four-digit year.

To create a custom format for the four-digit year:

▶ **1.** Click **Number** on the left side of the Format Axis dialog box.

▶ **2.** Type **yyyy** in the Format Code box, which is the code for displaying only years. See Figure 4-30.

Figure 4-30 ▶ **Number options**

custom format to display the four-digit year

built-in date formats

▶ **3.** Click the **Add** button. This format code is added to the list of custom formats.

▶ **4.** Click the **Close** button. The Format Axis dialog box closes and the category axis labels show values for every other year on the major tick marks. See Figure 4-31.

Formatted date labels   Figure 4-31

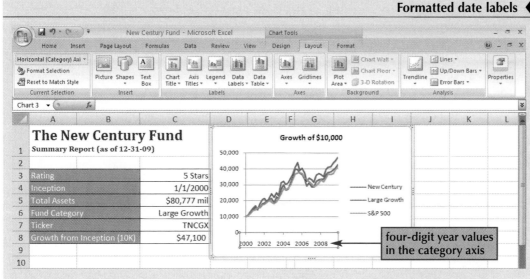

The category axis shows four-digit year values for 2000, 2002, 2004, 2006, and 2008. Because fewer years are included on the axis, there is enough room to display the labels horizontally instead of rotated.

Setting Label Units

Changing the format and tick mark intervals for the category axis has made the text easier to read. Ajita wants you to do something similar for value axis labels. Rather than displaying a large value such as "20,000," she wants to save space by displaying numbers in units of one thousand.

To format the value axis labels:

1. In the Axes group on the Chart Tools Layout tab, click the **Axes** button, point to **Primary Vertical Axis**, and then click **More Primary Vertical Axis Options**. The Format Axis dialog box opens, displaying the Axis Options.

2. Click the **Display units** arrow, click **Thousands**, and then move the dialog box so you can see the chart. The scale of the value axis changes from 10,000 to 50,000 in intervals of 10,000 to 0 through 50 in intervals of 10. The title "Thousands" is added to the axis to indicate that the values are expressed in units of one thousand. To save space, you'll remove this title from the chart.

3. Click the **Show display units label on chart** check box to remove the check mark.

Without the Thousands title, there is no indication what the numbers of the value axis mean. Ajita suggests you add the letter *k* to each number, displaying the numbers as 10k, 20k, and so forth. To do this, you need to create another custom format. In this custom format, you specify the text you want to appear at the end of number. The text must be placed in quotation marks. So, to display the letter *k* after the number you use the custom format #,##0"k". The first part of the custom format specifies that the number should include a thousands separator, and the second part indicates that the number should be followed by the the letter *k*. Next, you'll create the custom format to add the letter *k* after the number.

To create a custom format showing the thousandths unit:

▶ **1.** Click **Number** on the left side of the Format Axis dialog box.

▶ **2.** Click in the Format Code box after the number format, and then type **"k"** to make the format code #,##0"k". The quotation marks surround the text you want to add after the number, which, in this case, is the letter *k*.

▶ **3.** Click the **Add** button. This format code is added to the list of custom formats.

▶ **4.** Click the **Close** button. The Format Axis dialog box closes, and the value axis labels are revised. See Figure 4-32.

Figure 4-32 ▶ **Formatted labels in the vertical axis**

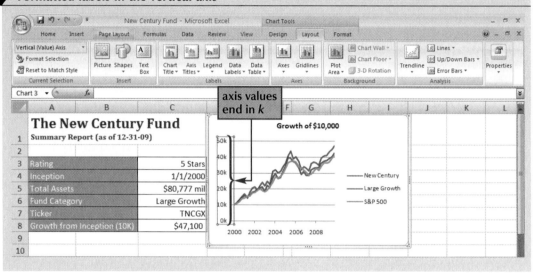

Overlaying a Legend

The modified value axis labels freed space in the chart area. The only other place where you can save space is the chart legend. Rather than displaying the chart legend on the right, you can overlay the legend. There seems to be enough space in the lower-right corner for a legend that will not obscure any of the data lines in the chart.

You can also overlay chart titles on surrounding chart elements to save space, but be aware that overlapping elements might obscure some of the chart content.

To format and overlay the chart legend:

▶ **1.** In the Labels group on the Chart Tools Layout tab, click the **Legend** button, and then click **More Legend Options**. The Format Legend dialog box opens, displaying Legend Options.

▶ **2.** Click the **Show the legend without overlapping the chart** check box to remove the check mark. The legend moves left, overlaying the chart. Because the plot and the legend now intersect, you'll add a fill color and border to the legend to make it easier to read.

▶ **3.** Click **Fill** on the left side of the Format Legend dialog box, and then click the **Solid fill** option button.

▶ **4.** Click the **Color** button 🎨▾ , and then click **white** (the first color) in the Theme Colors section.

5. Click **Border Color** on the left side of the Format Legend dialog box, and then click the **Solid line** option button.

6. Click the **Color** button, and then click **Blue** (the eighth color) in the Standard Colors section.

7. Click the **Close** button. The Format Legend dialog box closes, and the reformatted legend overlays the chart.

An overlaid chart element floats in the chart area and is not fixed to a particular position. This means you can drag the chart element to a new location. You'll drag the overlaid legend down a bit so it doesn't obscure any of the data in the line chart.

To move the chart legend:

1. Position the pointer over a blank spot in the chart legend so the pointer changes to and "Legend" appears in a ScreenTip.

2. Drag the legend to the lower-right corner of the plot area so the bottom of the legend is on the horizontal axis. The legend no longer covers the data lines.

   The chart has many horizontal lines from the horizontal gridlines and the chart legend; the chart would look better with vertical gridlines at each minor tick mark.

3. In the Axes group on the Chart Tools Layout tab, click the **Gridlines** button, point to **Primary Vertical Gridlines**, and then click **Minor Gridlines**. Vertical gridlines appear on the chart at each minor tick mark (recall that minor tick marks appear every year).

4. Click cell **J2** to deselect the chart. See Figure 4-33.

Final line chart | **Figure 4-33**

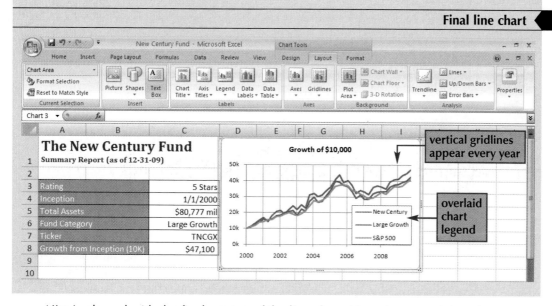

Ajita is pleased with the final version of the line chart. It's easier to read than the unformatted version, and it highlights how well the New Century Fund has performed in the past 10 years compared to the two benchmarks.

Adding a Data Series to an Existing Chart

Ajita wonders how the distribution of stocks owned by the New Century Fund compares to the S&P 500. For example, does the New Century Fund invest more in the information sector, and is that why it outperformed the S&P 500 for the past 10 years? Ajita researched the sector weightings for the S&P 500. She wants you to enter this data in the Sector Weightings worksheet and then add it to the Sector Weightings column chart you already created.

To enter data on the S&P 500 to the Sector Weightings worksheet:

▶ **1.** Click the **Sector Weightings** sheet tab to make that the active worksheet, and then select the range **C3:C15**. You'll copy these formats from the New Century Fund data and paste them in column D for the S&P 500 data.

▶ **2.** Click the **Home** tab on the Ribbon, and then, in the Clipboard group, click the **Format Painter** button .

▶ **3.** Select the range **D3:D15** to paste the formats. Now, you'll enter the S&P data in the range you just formatted.

▶ **4.** In the range **D3:D15**, enter the data shown in Figure 4-34.

| Figure 4-34 | Sector weightings for the S&P 500 |

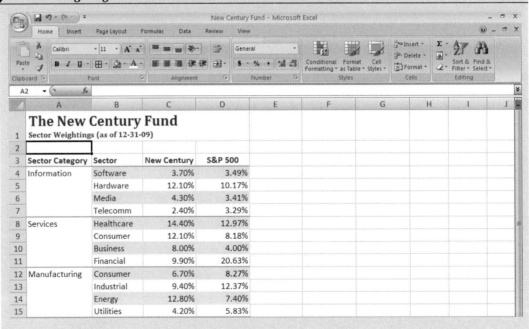

Adding the data to the table in the Sector Weightings worksheet does not add the data to the chart you already created. You must explicitly add the new data series to the chart. A new data series will have the same style and format as the existing data series in the chart.

Adding a Data Series to a Chart | Reference Window

- Select the chart to which you want to add a data series.
- In the Data group on the Chart Tools Design tab, click the Select Data button.
- Click the Add button in the Select Data Source dialog box.
- Select the range with the series name and series values you want for the new data series.
- Click the OK button in each dialog box.

You'll add the sector weightings data for the S&P 500 to the column chart in the Summary Report worksheet.

To add a data series to the existing column chart:

▶ 1. Click the **Summary Report** sheet tab, and then click the chart area of the column chart to select it.

▶ 2. Click the **Chart Tools Design** tab on the Ribbon, and then, in the Data group, click the **Select Data** button. The Select Data Source dialog box opens. The left side lists all of the data series displayed in the chart. The right side lists the category axis labels associated with each data series. You can add, edit, or remove any of these data series from the chart.

▶ 3. Click the **Add** button. The Edit Series dialog box opens. In this dialog box, you specify the name of the new data series and its range of data values.

▶ 4. With the insertion point in the Series name box, click the **Sector Weightings** sheet tab, click cell **D3**, and then press the **Tab** key. The cell with the series name is entered and the insertion point is in the Series values box.

▶ 5. Click the **Sector Weightings** sheet tab, and then select the range **D4:D15**. See Figure 4-35.

Edit Series dialog box ◀ Figure 4-35

▶ 6. Click the **OK** button. In the Select Data Source dialog box, you can see that the S&P 500 data is added to the list of data series in the chart. See Figure 4-36.

Figure 4-36 **Select Data Source dialog box**

7. Click the **OK** button. The S&P 500 sector values appear as red columns in the chart. See Figure 4-37.

Figure 4-37 **Column chart with added series**

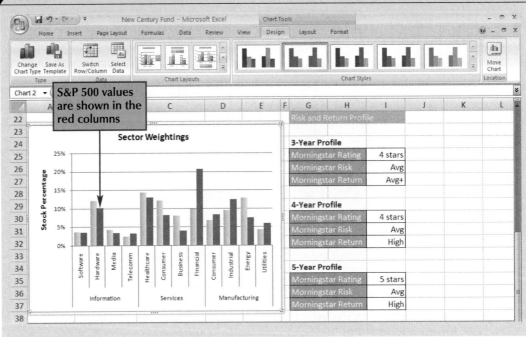

With so many columns, the data is difficult to read and interpret. Ajita suggests you separate the S&P 500 values from the New Century Fund values by plotting them as lines rather than columns.

Creating a Combination Chart

> **Tip**
>
> Combination charts can only be two-dimensional. You cannot create 3-D combination charts.

The type of chart that Ajita wants you to create is a **combination chart**, which is a chart that combines two or more chart types in a single graph. To create a combination chart, you select a data series in an existing chart, and then apply a new chart type to that series, leaving the other data series in its original format.

Creating a Combination Chart | Reference Window

- Select a data series in an existing chart that you want to appear as another chart type.
- In the Type group on the Chart Tools Design tab, click the Change Chart Type button, and then click the chart type you want.
- Click the OK button.

You'll display the S&P 500 values as a line chart so that it's easier to distinguish between the two data series.

To apply the line chart type to a data series:

▶ 1. Click any red column to select the entire S&P 500 data series.

▶ 2. In the Type group on the Chart Tools Design tab, click the **Change Chart Type** button. The Change Chart Type dialog box opens.

▶ 3. In the Line section, click **Line with Markers** (the fourth Line chart type).

▶ 4. Click the **OK** button. The S&P 500 values change to a line chart with markers. See Figure 4-38.

Combination chart ◀ Figure 4-38

As noted earlier, line charts are best for categories that follow some sequential order, such as the performance history chart in which the categories represented dates. In this case, the sector categories do not have a sequential order and the lines between sectors have no meaning. You'll remove these lines from the chart to avoid confusing Ajita's clients. Also, you'll change the square markers to horizontal line markers at each data point.

To remove the lines and edit the markers in the line chart:

▶ **1.** Click the red line in the S&P 500 line chart to select it.

▶ **2.** Click the **Chart Tools Layout** tab on the Ribbon, and then, in the Current Selection group, click **Format Selection**. The Format Data Series dialog box opens.

▶ **3.** Click **Line Color** on the left side of the dialog box, and then click the **No line** option button to remove the line from the line chart.

▶ **4.** Click **Marker Options** on the left side of the dialog box, and then click the **Built-in** option button.

▶ **5.** Click the **Type** arrow and click the horizontal line marker (the seventh marker in the list), and then click the **Size** up arrow until **10** appears in the box. See Figure 4-39.

Figure 4-39	Marker Options in the Format Data Series dialog box

▶ **6.** Click the **Close** button. The S&P 500 values appear only as data markers.

Because the chart now has two data series, you'll add a legend to the top of the chart to identify them.

▶ **7.** In the Labels group, click the **Legend** button, and then click **Show Legend at Top**. The legend appears above the chart.

▶ **8.** Click the **legend** to select it, click the **Home** tab on the Ribbon, and then reduce the font size of the legend to **8** points.

▶ **9.** Click cell **A38** to deselect the chart. See Figure 4-40.

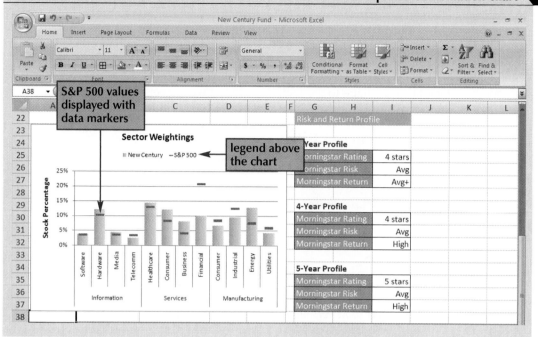

Completed combination chart   Figure 4-40

The combination chart effectively shows that the New Century Fund invests less than the S&P 500 in sectors from the financial service industry, and invests more in other sectors such as energy, consumer services, and hardware. This might account for the higher performance of the New Century Fund.

Choosing the Right Type of Chart | InSight

How do you know which type of chart to use with your data? In general, pie charts should be used only when the number of categories is small and the relative sizes of the different slices can be easily determined. If you have several categories, use a column or bar chart.

Line charts are best for categories that follow a sequential order. Be aware, however, that the time intervals must be a constant length if used in a line chart. Line charts will distort data that occurs in irregular time intervals, making it appear that the data values occurred at regular intervals when they did not.

Pie, column, bar, and line charts assume that numbers are plotted against categories. In science and engineering applications, you will often want to plot two numeric values against one another. For that data, use **XY scatter charts**, which show the patterns or relationship between two or more sets of values. XY scatter charts are also good for data recorded at irregular time intervals.

If you still can't find the right chart to meet your needs, you can create a custom chart based on the built-in chart types. Third-party vendors also sell software to allow Excel to create charts not built into the software.

Working with Shapes

Financial analysts give the New Century Fund a five-star rating based on its performance history. In cell C3, Ajita entered this rating as text. She wants you to replace the text with five stars.

Inserting a Shape

Excel, like all Office programs, includes a gallery of 160 different shapes organized into eight categories. These shapes range from simple squares and circles to more complex objects such as flowchart symbols, block arrows, and banners. After you insert a shape into a chart or worksheet, you can resize and move it, set its fill color and border color, and apply 3D effects to make it stand out on the page.

You'll add the first star shape to the Summary Report worksheet.

To insert a star shape in cell C3:

1. Right-click cell **C3**, and then click **Clear Contents** on the shortcut menu. The text "5 Stars" is erased from the cell.

2. Click the **Insert** tab on the Ribbon.

3. In the Illustrations group, click the **Shapes** button to display the Shapes gallery, and then click **5-Point Star** (the fourth star) in the Stars and Banners section. The pointer changes to ✛.

4. Drag the pointer over cell C3 to create a star shape. The embedded star shape is selected and the Format tab appears on the Ribbon with a label identifying it as Drawing Tools. The Drawing Tools Format tab appears whenever you select a shape. See Figure 4-41.

Figure 4-41 ▸ **Star shape embedded in cell C3**

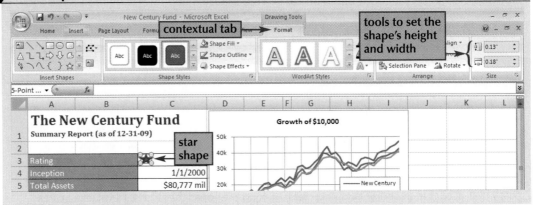

Resizing, Moving, and Copying a Shape

Shapes, like embedded charts, are objects you can move and resize. To set a shape's size more exactly, you enter the width and height you want in the Size group on the Drawing Tools Format tab. You'll match the star's height and width to the cell's height and width so it fills the cell.

To resize the star shape:

1. In the Size group on the Drawing Tools Format tab, click the **Shape Height** down arrow to set the height to **0.1"**.

2. In the Size group, click the **Shape Width** down arrow to set the width to **0.1"**.

3. Drag the star to the left edge of cell C3 and center it within the height of the cell.

The first star is embedded and positioned in cell C3. Next, you'll copy the star shape and paste four copies into cell C3 so that the contains a total of five stars.

To copy and paste the star shape:

▶ 1. With the star selected, click the **Home** tab on the Ribbon, and then, in the Clipboard group, click the **Copy** button 🗎.

▶ 2. In the Clipboard group, click the **Paste** button to paste the star shape. The new star shape is pasted to the lower-right of the first star.

▶ 3. Drag the star to the right of the star already in cell C3.

▶ 4. Repeat Steps 2 and 3 until you have five stars next to each other in cell C3. The stars do not have to align exactly. You'll align them next.

Aligning and Grouping Shapes

Placing shapes by dragging is inexact and can be frustrating. Instead of dragging and dropping shapes, you can line them up neatly using the tools on the Drawing Tools Format tab. You can horizontally align selected shapes in several ways: by their tops, by their bottoms, or by their middles. If you're aligning the shapes vertically, you can align them along their left edges, their right edges, or their centers. In this case, you'll line up the stars by their middles, and then distribute them horizontally so that they are evenly spaced from each other.

To horizontally and vertically align the five star shapes:

▶ 1. Click the first star in cell C3 to select it.

▶ 2. Hold down the **Shift** key, click each of the four remaining stars, and then release the **Shift** key. Each star you click is added to the selected shapes.

▶ 3. Click the **Drawing Tools Format** tab on the Ribbon.

▶ 4. In the Arrange group, click the **Align** button, and then click **Align Middle**. The stars align along their middles. You also want the stars evenly spaced in the cell.

▶ 5. In the Arrange group, click the **Align** button and then click **Distribute Horizontally**. The five stars are evenly spaced within the cell.

When you have several shapes that you want to treat as one unit, you can **group** them. You can move and resize grouped shapes as one, which makes it easier to develop interesting graphical shapes composed of several smaller parts. It also frees you from having to realign and redistribute the shapes if you move or copy them to a new location in the worksheet. You'll group the five stars in cell C3 so that they always remain together and aligned properly.

To group several shapes into a single unit:

▶ 1. With all five stars selected, in the Arrange group on the Drawing Tools Format tab, click the **Group** button, and then click **Group**. A single selection box surrounds the five stars, indicating that they are grouped. The grouped stars can be moved together if needed without losing their relative alignment.

▶ 2. Click cell **A2** to deselect the group of stars. See Figure 4-42.

Figure 4-42 **Grouped and aligned star shapes**

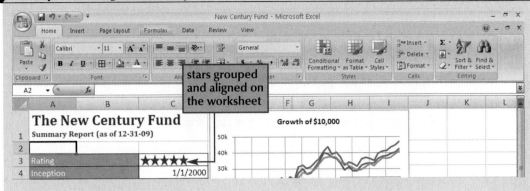

Creating a Chart Sheet

Ajita asks you to create a cover sheet for the workbook that shows a 3D image of the performance of the New Century Fund over the past 10 years. Because this chart is purely decorative, you can make a visually interesting chart without concern about easily reading its data. The cover sheet will contain only the chart and no other data or text, so you'll create a chart sheet. Recall that chart sheets show only charts and no worksheet data.

To create a chart sheet:

1. Click the **Performance History** sheet tab, and then select the range **A4:B44**, if necessary. This range contains the data you want to use in the chart.

2. Click the **Insert** tab on the Ribbon.

3. In the Charts group, click the **Line** button, and then click the **3-D Line** chart type. The 3D line chart is embedded in the Performance History worksheet. You'll move this chart to its own chart sheet.

4. In the Location group on the Chart Tools Design tab, click the **Move Chart** button. The Move Chart dialog box opens.

5. Click the **New sheet** option button, type **Cover Sheet** in the box, and then click the **OK** button. A chart sheet named "Cover Sheet" that contains the 3D line chart is inserted in the workbook.

6. Drag the **Cover Sheet** sheet tab to the right of the Documentation sheet tab. See Figure 4-43.

Chart sheet with the 3D line chart | Figure 4-43

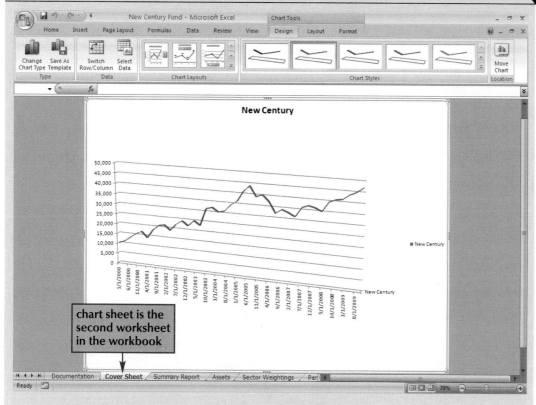

chart sheet is the
second worksheet
in the workbook

The Cover Sheet appears before Summary Report worksheet and the worksheets that contain the detailed data used to create the summary report. Next, you'll remove the axes labels and legend from the chart and rotate the chart in three dimensions. To increase the 3D effect, you'll widen the chart's base from 100 to 1000 points.

To format the chart sheet:

▶ **1.** If necessary, click the chart area to select it.

▶ **2.** In the Chart Styles group on the Chart Tools Design tab, click the **More** button, and then click **Style 40** (the fifth row, last column) of the Chart Styles gallery.

▶ **3.** Click the **Chart Tools Layout** tab on the Ribbon.

▶ **4.** In the Labels group, click the **Legend** button, and then click **None** to turn off the legend.

▶ **5.** In the Axes group, click the **Axes** button, point to **Primary Horizontal Axis**, and then click **None** to remove the horizontal axis.

▶ **6.** In the Axes group, click the **Axes** button, point to **Primary Vertical Axis**, and then click **None** to remove the vertical axis from the chart.

▶ **7.** In the Axes group, click the **Axes** button, point to **Depth Axis**, and then click **None** to remove the depth axis.

▶ **8.** In the Background section, click the **3-D Rotation** button. The Format Chart Area dialog box opens, displaying the 3-D Rotation options.

▶ **9.** In the Rotation section, set X to **60°**, Y to **20°**, and Perspective to **80°**, and then, in the Chart Scale section, set the Depth (% of base) to **1000**.

These settings rotate the chart, exaggerate the 3D effect, and make the chart appear thicker. Next, you'll change the background color of the chart area to a gradient fill.

▶ **10.** Click **Fill** on the left side of the dialog box, and then click the **Gradient fill** option button.

▶ **11.** Click the **Preset colors** button, and then click **Daybreak**, the fourth color in the first row.

▶ **12.** Click the **Direction** button, and then click **Linear Down**, the second direction in the first row.

▶ **13.** Click the **Close** button. See Figure 4-44.

Figure 4-44 ▶ **Formatted chart sheet**

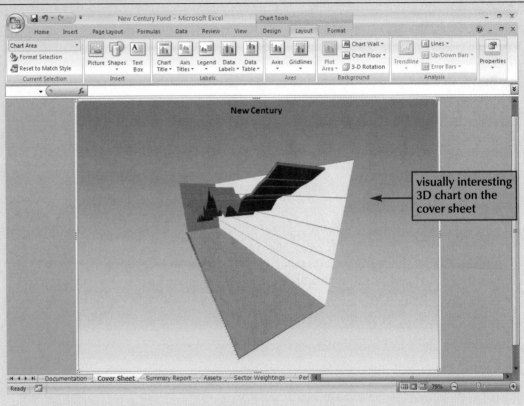

visually interesting 3D chart on the cover sheet

To complete the chart sheet, you'll overlay the chart title "The New Century Fund," and format it in a 48-point white font.

To overlay and format the chart title:

▶ **1.** In the Labels group on the Chart Tools Layout tab, click the **Chart Title** button, and then click **Centered Overlay Title**. The chart title is overlaid above the chart.

▶ **2.** Type **The New Century Fund**, and then press the **Enter** key. The new title is entered.

▶ **3.** Click the **Home** tab on the Ribbon, and then set the font size to **48** points and the font color to **white**.

▶ **4.** Click outside of the chart to deselect it. The cover sheet is final. See Figure 4-45.

Final cover sheet | Figure 4-45

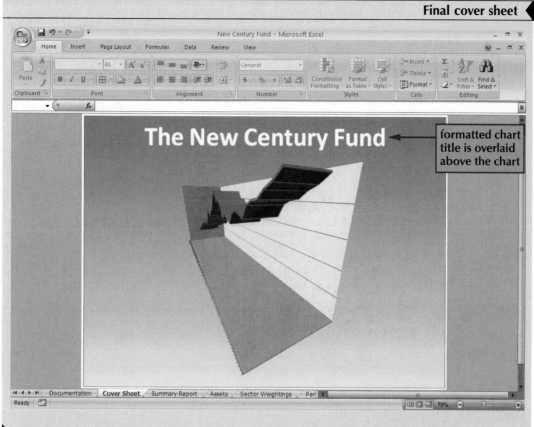

5. Save your changes to the workbook, and then close it.

You show the final version of the cover sheet and the workbook to Ajita. She is pleased with the work you've done adding charts and graphics to the workbook. Ajita will present the Summary Report worksheet, with the embedded charts, to her clients to provide them a concise report on the performance of the New Century Fund. The cover sheet you've created adds visual interest to the report.

Session 4.2 Quick Check | Review

1. When should you use a line chart in place of a column chart?
2. How do you overlay a chart legend?
3. How do you add a data series to an already existing chart?
4. What is a combination chart? Describe how you create a combination chart.
5. How do you insert a shape into a worksheet?
6. Describe how to set the exact height and width of a shape.
7. Describe how to horizontally align the tops of three shapes in Excel.
8. How do you create a chart sheet?

In this tutorial, you learned how to work with charts and graphics. You reviewed the different parts of a chart and the relationship between charts and data sources. Then, you inserted an embedded chart and reviewed the different types of chart, chart layouts, and chart styles supported by Excel. The first chart you created was a pie chart. You worked with the pie chart legend and formatted individual slices. Next, you made the pie chart a 3D chart and learned about some limitations of 3D charts. The second chart you created and formatted was a column chart. The third chart you created and formatted was a line chart. You also learned when line charts are preferable to column charts. The fourth chart you created was a combination chart that combined the column and line charts. You then inserted shapes into a worksheet, and aligned and grouped them. Finally, you created a chart sheet as a cover sheet for the entire workbook.

Key Terms

bar chart	embedded chart	pie chart
category values	exploded pie chart	plot area
chart	graph	primary value axis
chart area	gridlines	resizing handle
chart sheet	group	scale
chart title	horizontal (category) axis	secondary value axis
column chart	leader line	selection box
combination chart	legend	series name
data label	line chart	series values
data marker	major tick mark	vertical (value) axis
data series	minor tick mark	XY scatter chart
data source	perspective	

| Practice | **Review Assignments** |

Practice the skills you learned in the tutorial using the same case scenario.

Data File needed for the Review Assignments: Crockett.xlsx

Ajita asks you to help on a new project. She has to create a report on the investment portfolio for Brian and Tammy Crockett. She wants to add charts that display where the couple's money is currently being invested and how their portfolio has performed in recent years. She's already entered the data. She needs you to complete the report by adding the charts and a decorative cover sheet.

Complete the following:

1. Open the **Crockett** workbook located in the Tutorial.04\Review folder included with your Data Files, and then save the workbook as **Crockett Portfolio** in the same folder. In the Documentation sheet, enter your name in cell B3 and the date in cell B4.

2. In the Composition worksheet, select the range A3:B8, and then insert a 2D pie chart. Move and resize the embedded pie chart to cover the range D1:G9 in the Portfolio Report worksheet.

3. Move the legend to the left side of the chart area. Change the chart title to **Composition** and set its font size to 12 points. Change the fill color of the Cash slice to yellow. Add data labels that show the percentage of each pie slice to two decimal places outside of the pie chart, and then set the font size of the labels to 8 points.

4. Change the pie chart to a 3D pie chart and set the 3D rotation of the x-axis to 230° and the y-axis to 40°.

5. In the Sector Weightings worksheet, select the range A3:D15, and then insert a 2D clustered column chart. Move and resize the embedded chart to cover the range A12:D25 in the Portfolio Report worksheet.

6. Change the font size of the axis labels and legend to 8 points. Insert the chart title **Sector Weightings** over the plot and set its font size to 12 points. Change the format of the percentages in the vertical axis to display no decimal places. Overlay the legend at the top of the chart, and then change its fill color to white and insert a solid border around the legend.

7. Change the chart type of the S&P 500 series to a line chart, remove the line connecting the markers in the chart, and then change the marker type to a solid horizontal line of size 10.

8. Change the fill color of the columns for the Portfolio data series to the theme color Purple, Accent 4, Lighter 60%. Set the gap width of the columns in the Portfolio data series to 30%.

9. In the Portfolio Value worksheet, select the range A3:B127, and then insert a 2D area chart. Move and resize the chart to cover the range D28:G42 in the Portfolio Report worksheet. (*Hint:* You will need to scroll down the Portfolio Report worksheet to locate the chart when you move it from the Portfolio Value worksheet.)

10. Remove the chart legend. Set the font size of the chart title to 11 points, and then set the font size of the axis labels to 8 points. Change the fill color of the data series to the theme color Purple, Accent 4, Lighter 60%.

11. Modify the category axis so that the vertical axis crosses the maximum date. (*Hint:* Use the Axis Options in the Format Axis dialog box.)

12. Set the major tick mark interval at two years and the minor tick mark interval at one year. Use a custom format that displays the category axis date values as four-digit year values. Insert vertical gridlines for the minor tick marks.

13. In the Portfolio Value worksheet, select the range A3:B127, and insert a 3D area chart. Move the embedded chart into a new chart sheet named **Cover Sheet**. Move the Cover Sheet worksheet directly after the Documentation sheet.

14. Change the chart style to Style 34, located in the fifth row and second column of the Chart Styles gallery. Remove the display of the horizontal, vertical, and depth axes. Remove the chart legend.

15. For the 3D rotation, set the x-axis to 60°, the y-axis to 10°, the perspective to 40°, and the depth of the base to 2000.

16. Change the chart title to **Crockett Family Portfolio**. Set the font size of the chart title to 40 points.

17. Insert two 5-pointed stars, one directly to the left and the other directly to the right of the chart title. Set the height and width of each star to 0.3". Align the middle of the two stars and then group them into a single object.

18. Save and close your workbook, and then submit the finished workbook to your instructor, either in printed or electronic form, as requested.

| Apply | | **Case Problem 1** |

Use the skills you learned to create 3D charts of usage data for a national park.

Data File needed for this Case Problem: Kenai.xlsx

Kenai Fjords National Park Maria Sanford is the chief of interpretation at Kenai Fjords National Park. Part of her job is to report on park usage at each visitor center and all visitor centers. She has recorded last year's usage data in an Excel workbook. She asks you to present this data in a 3D column chart for an upcoming meeting with her supervisor. She wants the chart to show the monthly usage totals organized by visitor center. Figure 4-46 shows a preview of the 3D column chart you'll create for Maria.

Figure 4-46

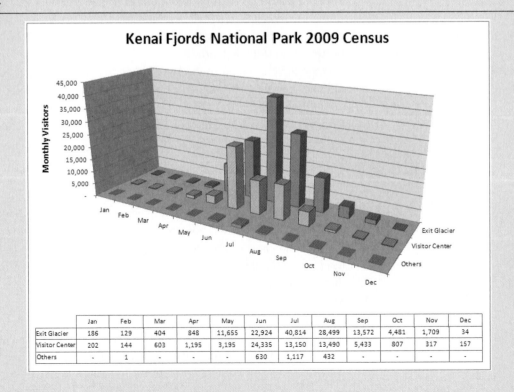

	Jan	Feb	Mar	Apr	May	Jun	Jul	Aug	Sep	Oct	Nov	Dec
Exit Glacier	186	129	404	848	11,655	22,924	40,814	28,499	13,572	4,481	1,709	34
Visitor Center	202	144	603	1,195	3,195	24,335	13,150	13,490	5,433	807	317	157
Others	-	1	-	-	-	630	1,117	432	-	-	-	-

Complete the following:

1. Open the **Kenai** workbook located in the Tutorial.04\Case1 folder included with your Data Files, and then save the workbook as **Kenai Fjords Park** in the folder. In the Documentation sheet, enter your name in cell B3 and the date in cell B4.

2. In the Park Usage Data worksheet, select the range A4:D16, and then insert the 3-D Column chart (the last chart in the 3-D Column section in the Charts gallery).

3. Move the chart to a chart sheet named **Monthly Visits**. Place the Monthly Visits chart sheet directly after the Documentation sheet.

4. Change the style of the chart to Style 34 (the fifth style in the second column in the Chart Styles gallery).

5. Insert the chart title **Kenai Fjords National Park 2009 Census** at the top of the chart area, and then set its font size to 24 points. Remove the legend from the chart.

6. Add the title **Monthly Visitors** to the vertical axis. Rotate the title 90° and set the font size to 14 points.

7. Rotate the 3D chart using the following parameters: x-axis rotation 30°, y-axis rotation 20°, perspective 25°, and base width 130. Modify the depth axis so that the values are displayed in reverse order.

⊕ EXPLORE

8. Insert a data table without legend keys below the 3-D chart to provide data values so that the reader is not confused about the relative sizes of the different columns. (*Hint:* Use the Data Table button in the Labels group on the Chart Tools Layout tab.)

9. Change the fill color of the Exit Glacier series to light blue. Change the fill color of the Visitor Center series to orange.

10. In the Park Usage Data worksheet, select the range B4:D4;B17:D17, and then insert a 3D pie chart. Move the embedded chart to a chart sheet named **Center Visits**. Place the Center Visits sheet directly after the Monthly Visits chart sheet.

11. Insert the chart title **Kenai Fjords National Park: Visits by Center** above the pie chart, and set its font size to 24 points.

12. Move the chart legend below the pie chart, and change its font size to 18 points.

13. Change the fill color of the Exit Glacier slice to light blue. Change the fill color of the Visitor Center slice to orange.

14. Add data labels to the outside end of the pie chart showing the values (not percentages) of each slice. Set the font size of the labels to 18 points.

15. Save and close your workbook, and then submit the finished workbook to your instructor, either in printed or electronic form, as requested.

Apply | **Case Problem 2**

Use the skills you learned to create a combination chart describing the occurrence of tornados in the twentieth century.

Data Files needed for this Case Problem: Cloud.jpg, Tornado.xlsx

Midwest Tornado Institute   Joyce Bishop is a meteorologist at the Midwest Tornado Institute located in Decatur, Illinois. Joyce is preparing for a talk she is giving to a local civic group on the possible effects of global warming on tornados. She's collected data on minor, moderate, and major tornado sightings in five-year periods during the second half of the twentieth century and wants to create a graph for her talk showing her data. She's already entered her data into an Excel workbook; she needs your help in creating the chart. Figure 4-47 shows a preview of the chart you'll create for Joyce.

Figure 4-47

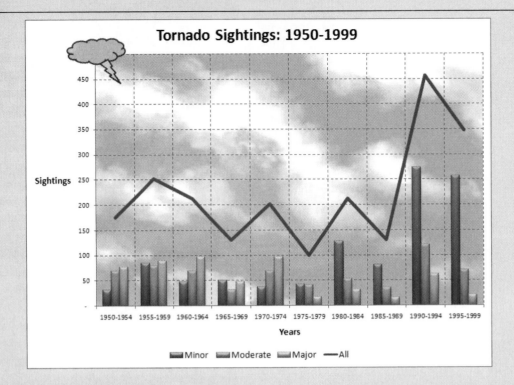

Complete the following:

1. Open the **Tornado** workbook located in the Tutorial.04\Case2 folder included with your Data Files, and then save the workbook as **Tornado Sightings** in the same folder. In the Documentation sheet, enter your name in cell B3 and the date in cell B4.

2. In the Sightings History worksheet, select the range A3:E13, and then insert a 2D clustered column chart. Move the embedded chart to a chart sheet named **Sightings Chart**.

3. Change the chart style to Style 32 (the last chart style in the fourth row of the Chart Styles gallery).

4. Insert the chart title **Tornado Sightings: 1950 – 1999** at the top of the chart in a 24-point font.

5. Add the vertical axis title **Sightings** in a 14-point font with horizontal orientation. Add the horizontal axis title **Years** in a 14-point font.

6. Move the legend to the bottom of the chart, and then set its font size to 14 points.

⊕ EXPLORE

7. Change the line style of the horizontal gridline from a solid line to a dashed line. (*Hint:* Use the Dash type list in the Line Style group in the Format Major Gridlines dialog box.)

8. Add vertical gridlines to the major tick marks in the chart. Display the gridlines as dashed lines.

9. Change the chart type of the All data series from a column chart to a 2D line chart. Change the color of the line to a standard blue.

10. In the upper-left corner of the chart, insert a cloud shape. Set the width of the cloud to 1.2". Set the height to 0.5". Set the fill color of the cloud shape to a light gray.

11. Adjacent to the cloud shape, insert a lightning bolt shape with a height of 0.48" and a width of 0.42". Set the fill color of the shape to yellow.

12. Group the cloud and lightning bolt shapes.

EXPLORE   13. Select the plot area and change the fill to a picture fill, using the **Cloud.jpg** file located in the Tutorial.04\Case2 folder included with your Data Files. (*Hint:* Click the Shape Fill button in the Shape Styles group on the Drawing Tools Format tab, click Picture, and then locate and select the picture file.)

14. Save and close your workbook, and then submit the finished workbook to your instructor, either in printed or electronic form, as requested.

| Challenge | **Case Problem 3** |

Explore how to use Excel to chart stock market data.

Data File needed for this Case Problem: Mitchell.xlsx

Hardin Financial   Kurt Lee is a financial analyst for Hardin Financial, a consulting firm in Owatonna, Minnesota. As part of his job, he records stock market activity in Excel workbooks. One of his workbooks contains the recent stock market activity of Mitchell Oil. He wants your help in creating a chart displaying the stock values. The chart should display the stock's opening, high, low, and closing values and number of shares traded for each day of the past few weeks. The volume of shares traded should be expressed in terms of millions of shares.

Excel includes several chart types specially designed for displaying stock market activity. A preview of the chart you'll create for Kurt is shown in Figure 4-48.

Figure 4-48

Complete the following:

1. Open the **Mitchell** workbook located in the Tutorial.04\Case3 folder included with your Data Files, and then save the workbook as **Mitchell Oil** in the same folder. In the Documentation sheet, enter your name and the date.

EXPLORE
2. In the Stock Values worksheet, select the range A3:F33, and then insert a Volume-Open-High-Low-Close stock chart. Move the embedded chart to the chart sheet named **Stock History**.

3. Insert the chart title **Mitchell Oil** above the plot area. Remove the chart legend.

4. Add the title **Date** to the primary horizontal axis, and then set its font size to 14 points. Add the title **Shares Traded** to the primary vertical axis, set its font size to 14 points, and then rotate the title 270°, as shown in Figure 4-48.

EXPLORE
5. Add the title **Stock Value** to the secondary vertical axis, set its font size to 14 points, and rotate the title 90°, as shown in Figure 4-48. (*Hint:* Open the Format Axis Title dialog box for the secondary vertical axis and use the Text Direction button found in the Alignment category.)

6. Set the font size of all of the axes values to 12 points.

7. Display the horizontal gridlines using a dashed line style. Set the interval between major tick marks on the primary horizontal axis to 7 days.

8. For the primary vertical axis, display the values in units of one million, change the number format to two decimal place accuracy, and then set the maximum value of the axis scale to 2,000,000.

9. For the secondary vertical axis, set the minimum value of the scale to 10.

10. Decrease the gap width between the columns in the plot to 30% and change the fill color to light blue.

EXPLORE
11. In a stock market chart, the daily chart values will either show an increase or a decrease from the previous day. Increases are shown with an up bar displayed in white and decreases are shown in a down bar displayed in black. Select the data series for the up bars and change their fill colors to light green. Select the data series for the down bars and change their fill colors to red.

12. Save and close your workbook, and then submit the finished workbook to your instructor, either in printed or electronic form, as requested.

Create | **Case Problem 4**

Create an Excel workbook to provide a graphical report on a sporting event.

Data File needed for this Case Problem: Basketball.xlsx

Blowout Sports   Steve Eagan is the owner and operator of Blowout Sports, a sports information and scouting company located in Lexington, Kentucky. One of Steve's jobs is to provide detailed graphical reports and analysis of college basketball games for the media, coaches, and interested fans. Steve has been placing box score data and game logs into an Excel workbook. He wants to summarize this data in one worksheet using charts and graphs. He's asked you to help develop the workbook. Steve has a sample workbook containing the results of a recent basketball game for you to work on.

Complete the following:

1. Open the **Basketball** workbook located in the Tutorial.04\Case4 folder included with your Data Files, and then save the workbook as **Basketball Report** in the same folder. In the Documentation sheet, enter your name and the date.

2. The Game Report worksheet contains some basic information about a recent basketball game. Supplement this information with charts and graphs. The final format of the sheet is up to you and you may insert additional information if you desire.

3. The Game Log worksheet contains the minute-by-minute score of the game. Use the data in this worksheet to create a line chart describing the ebb and flow of the game that is embedded in the Game Report worksheet. The format of the chart is up to you, but should include titles for the chart and the axes, a chart legend overlay, vertical gridlines spaced at 4-minute intervals, and horizontal gridlines at 5-point intervals. (*Hint:* To display vertical gridlines at 4-minute intervals, you must turn off the multi-level category labels.)

4. The Box Score worksheet contains statistical summaries of the game. Use the data in this worksheet to create two column charts describing the points scored by each player on the two teams. Embed the charts in the Game Report worksheet. The format of the charts is up to you, but should include titles for the chart and axes and fill colors for the columns that employ a fill gradient.

5. The Box Score worksheet also contains team statistics. Use this data to create several pie charts that compare the two teams. Embed the pie charts in the Game Report worksheet. The final pie charts should include data labels for the pie slices and slice colors that match the team's colors (red for Wisconsin, gold for Iowa).

6. Create a chart sheet for the report that will be a cover sheet. The cover sheet should include a 3D chart from some of the data in the workbook. The format of the chart and chart sheet is up to you.

7. Save and close your workbook, and then submit the finished workbook to your instructor, either in printed or electronic form, as requested.

Use the Internet to find and work with data related to the topics presented in this tutorial.

The purpose of the Internet Assignments is to challenge you to find information on the Internet that you can use to work effectively with this software. The actual assignments are updated and maintained on the Course Technology Web site. Log on to the Internet and use your Web browser to go to the Student Online Companion for New Perspectives Office 2007 at **www.course.com/np/office2007**. Then navigate to the Internet Assignments for this tutorial.

| Assess | **SAM Assessment and Training** |

If you have a SAM user profile, you may have access to hands-on instruction, practice, and assessment of the skills covered in this tutorial. Log in to your SAM account (**http://sam2007.course.com**) to launch any assigned training activities or exams that relate to the skills covered in this tutorial.

| Review | **Quick Check Answers** |

Session 4.1

1. the series name, series values, and category values
2. in a chart sheet or embedded in a worksheet
3. The chart area contains the entire chart, including the plot area. The plot area contains the region of the chart in which the data values are plotted.
4. A column chart is more appropriate because there are so many categories; pie charts make it difficult to compare one category to another.

5. Objects that are rendered as more distant from the eye will appear smaller, reducing their significance in the chart. To avoid confusion, 3D charts should include data labels explicitly identifying the values associated with different data markers.

6. A major tick mark matches each entry on the chart axis. Minor tick marks further divide the space between the major tick marks. Gridlines extend the tick marks into the plot area.

7. A bar chart is similar to a column chart except that the length of the bars, rather than the height of the columns, is used to indicate the data value.

8. Click the Axes button in the Axes group on the Chart Tools Layout tab, select the axis you want to rescale, and then click the More Options button. Enter the new axis scale in the Axis Options of the Format Axis dialog box, specifying the minimum and maximum value of the new scale and the space between the minor and major tick marks.

Session 4.2

1. Use line charts in place of column charts when the number of categories is so large that the columns will be forced to be too small to read, and the categories have a natural, sequential order (such as time and dates) that you want to show in the chart.

2. Click the Legend button in the Labels group on the Chart Tools Layout tab and select one of the overlay options, or open the Format Legend dialog box and deselect the check box to show the legend without overlaying the chart.

3. Click the Select Date button in the Date group on the Data tab. Click the Add button in the Select Data Source dialog box and select the range with the new data series.

4. A combination chart combines two or more of the Excel chart types. To create a combination chart, select a data series from the chart and apply a chart type to that series.

5. Click the Shapes button in the Illustrations group on the Insert tab, and then select a shape from the gallery.

6. Select the shape, and then enter the exact height and width in the Shape Height and Shape Width boxes in the Size group on the Drawing Tools Format tab.

7. Select all of the shapes by holding down the Shift key and clicking each of the shapes. Click the Align button in the Arrange group on the Drawing Tools Format tab, and then click Align Top.

8. Select a chart, and then click the Move Chart button in the Location group on the Chart Tools Design tab. Specify the name of the chart sheet in the Move Chart dialog box.

Ending Data Files

Tutorial.04

Tutorial
New Century Fund.xlsx

Review
Crockett Portfolio.xlsx

Case1
Kenai Fjords Park.xlsx

Case2
Tornado Sightings.xlsx

Case3
Mitchell Oil.xlsx

Case4
Basketball Report.xlsx

Reality Check

Excel is valuable to a wide audience of users: from accountants of *Fortune 500* companies to homeowners managing their budgets. An Excel workbook can be complex, recording data from thousands of financial transactions, or it can simply track a few monthly expenses. Everyone who has to balance a budget, track expenses, or project future income can make use of the financial tools in Excel. In this exercise, you'll use Excel to create a sample budget workbook that will contain information of your choice, using Excel skills and features presented in Tutorials 1 through 4. Use the following steps as a guide to completing your workbook.

Note: Please be sure *not* to include any personal information of a sensitive nature in any workbooks you create to be submitted to your instructor for this exercise. Later, you can update the workbooks with such information for your personal use.

1. Create a new workbook for the sample financial data. Use the first worksheet as a documentation sheet that includes your name, the date on which you start creating the workbook, and a brief description of the workbook's purpose.
2. In a second worksheet, enter realistic monthly earnings for each month of the year. Use formulas to calculate the total earnings each month, the average monthly earnings, and the total earnings for the entire year.
3. On the same worksheet, enter realistic personal expenses for each month. Divide the expenses into at least three categories, providing subtotals for each category and a grand total of all the monthly expenses. Calculate the average monthly expenses and total expenses for the year.
4. Calculate the monthly net cash flow (the value of total income minus total expenses).
5. Use the cash flow values to track the savings throughout the year. Use a realistic amount for savings at the beginning of the year. Use the monthly net cash flow values to add or subtract from this value. Project the end-of-year balance in the savings account under your proposed budget.
6. Format the worksheet's contents using appropriate text and number formats. Add colors and line borders to make the content easier to read and interpret. Use cell styles and themes to provide your worksheet with a uniform appearance.
7. Use conditional formatting to automatically highlight negative net cash flow calculated in Step 4.
8. Insert a pie chart that compares the monthly expenses for the categories.
9. Insert a column chart that charts all of the monthly expenses regardless of the category.
10. Insert a line chart that shows the change in the savings balance throughout the 12 months of the year.
11. Insert new rows at the top of the worksheet and enter titles that describe the worksheet's contents.

12. Think of a major purchase you might want to make—for example, a car. Determine the amount of the purchase and the current annual interest rate charged by your local bank. Provide a reasonable length of time to repay the loan, such as five years for a car loan or 20 to 30 years for a home loan. Use the PMT function to determine how much you would have to spend each month on the payments for your purchase. Add this information to your monthly budget. If the payment exceeds your budget, reduce the estimated price of the item you're thinking of purchasing until you determine the monthly payment you can afford under the conditions of the loan.

13. Format the worksheets for your printer. Include headers and footers that display the filename of your workbook, the workbook's author, and the date on which the report is printed. If the report extends across several pages, repeat appropriate print titles on all of the pages and include page numbers and the total number of pages on every printed page.

14. Save and close your workbook, and then submit the completed workbook to your instructor, in printed or electronic form, as requested.

Objectives

Working with Excel Tables, PivotTables, and PivotCharts

Tracking Museum Art Objects

Case | LaFouch Museum

Henry LaFouch, a rancher in Missoula, Montana, amassed a huge collection of North American art, particularly art of the West. Henry was a well-respected, active member of the community, and he often donated art to the town. Similarly, he loaned the town artwork to place in public locations and community centers. Upon his death, Henry donated his art collection to the town of Missoula and its people. They established an art museum in his name.

Mary Littlefield was recently hired as the curator and director of the LaFouch Museum. She is responsible for assessing the current holdings and using the endowment set aside by Henry to purchase additional art in keeping with his vision for the collection. One of Mary's first tasks was to establish an accurate inventory of the museum's holdings. For each piece of artwork, she identified the title, the artist, the date acquired, the type of art, and other pertinent facts such as its location in the museum, its condition, and its appraised value. Then, she entered all this data in an Excel worksheet.

Mary asks you to help her maintain this data so she can provide current and accurate information to the administration and board of directors about the art objects. You'll work with the data using Excel table features. You will sort the data and add, modify, and delete the data to ensure it is current. You'll also filter the information to display only data that meets certain criteria. Finally, you'll summarize the data using a PivotTable and a PivotChart.

Starting Data Files

Tutorial	Review	Case1	Case2
Museum.xlsx	Art.xlsx	Pledges.xlsx	Ring.xlsx

Case3	Case4
CustLoans.xlsx	Bowls.xlsx

Session 5.1

Planning a Structured Range of Data

One of the more common uses of a worksheet is to manage data, such as lists of clients, products, and transactions. Using Excel, you can store and update data, sort data, search for and retrieve subsets of data, summarize data, and create reports. In Excel, a collection of similar data can be structured in a range of rows and columns. Each column in the range represents a **field** that describes some attribute or characteristic of a person, place, or thing, such as a last name, address, city, or state. Each row in the range represents a **record**, or a collection of related fields that are grouped together. The first row of the range contains column headers that describe the data fields in each column. Figure 5-1 shows a portion of the data Mary compiled for the LaFouch Museum's art objects. In this data, the ArtID, Artist, and Title columns are the first three fields. Each row is a record that stores the data for each art object—art ID, artist name, title, date acquired, category, condition, location, and appraised value. All the art object records make up the structured range of data. A structured range of data is commonly referred to as a list or table.

Figure 5-1   LaFouch Museum art objects data

The Importance of Planning | InSight

Before you create a structured range of data, you should do some planning. Spend time thinking about how you will use the data. Consider what reports you want to create for different audiences (supervisors, customers, directors, and so forth) and the fields needed to produce those reports. Also consider the various questions, or queries, you want answered and the fields needed to create these results. The end results you want to achieve will help you determine the kind of data to include in each record and how to divide that data into fields. Careful and thorough planning will help to prevent having to redesign a structured range of data later on.

Before creating the list of art objects, Mary carefully planned what information she needs and how she wants to use it. Mary plans to use the data to track where each art object is located in the museum, its condition, the date it was acquired, its art category, and its appraised value. She wants to be able to create reports that show specific lists of art objects, such as all the objects by a specific artist or all the objects that are paintings. Based on her needs, Mary developed a **data definition table**, which is documentation that lists the fields to be maintained for each record (in this case, each art object) and a description of the information each field will include. Figure 5-2 shows Mary's completed data definition table.

Data definition table for the art objects | Figure 5-2

Field	Description
ArtID	Unique number
Artist	Name of artist
Title	Title of art object
Date Acquired	Date of purchase or donation of art object
Category	Painting, Sculpture, Installation, Textile
Condition	Excellent, Good, Fair, Poor
Location	Location of art object
Appraised Value	Appraised value of art object

After you determine the fields and records you need, you can enter the data in a blank worksheet or use a range of data that is already entered in a worksheet. You can then work with the data in many ways. The following is a list of common operations you can perform on a structured range of data:

- Add, edit, and delete data in the range
- Sort the data range
- Filter to display only rows that meet specified criteria
- Insert formulas to calculate subtotals
- Create summary tables based on the data in the range (usually with PivotTables)
- Add data validation to ensure the integrity of the data
- Apply conditional formatting

You'll perform many of these operations on the art objects data.

InSight | **Creating an Effective Structured Range of Data**

For a range of data to be used effectively, it must have the same structure throughout. Keep in mind the following guidelines:

- Enter field names in the top row of the range. A **field name** (also called a **column header**) is a unique label that describes the contents of the data in that column. The row of field names is called the **header row**. Although the header row often is row 1, it can be any row.
- Use short, descriptive field names. Shorter field names are easier to remember and enable more fields to appear in the workbook window at once.
- Format field names to distinguish the header row from the data. For example, apply bold, color, and a different font size.
- Enter the same kind of data for a field in each record.
- Separate the data from other information in the worksheet by *at least* one blank row and one blank column. The blank row and column enable Excel to accurately determine the range of the data.

You'll open the workbook in which Mary entered the art objects data according to the data definition table.

To open and review the Museum workbook:

▶ **1.** Open the **Museum** workbook located in the **Tutorial.05\Tutorial** folder included with your Data Files, and then save the workbook as **LaFouch Museum** in the same folder.

▶ **2.** In the Documentation worksheet, enter your name in cell B3 and the current date in cell B4.

▶ **3.** Switch to the **Art Collection** worksheet. This worksheet (which is shown in Figure 5-1) contains data about the museum's art objects. Currently, the worksheet lists 115 art objects. Each art object record is a separate row (rows 2 through 116) and contains eight fields (columns A through H). The top row, the header row, contains labels that describe the data in each column. The field names are boldface to make it easier to distinguish them from the data.

▶ **4.** Scroll the worksheet to row 116, the last record. The column headers, in the top row, are no longer visible.

▶ **5.** Press the **Ctrl+Home** keys to return to cell A1.

Freezing Rows and Columns

You want to see the column headers as you scroll the art objects data. Without the column headers visible, it is difficult to know what the data entered in each column represents. You can select rows and columns to remain visible in the workbook window as you scroll around the worksheet. **Freezing** a row or column lets you keep headings visible as you work with the data in a large worksheet. To freeze a row or column, you select the cell immediately below the row(s) and to the right of the column(s) you want to freeze. For example, if you want to keep only the column headers in the top row displayed on the screen, you click cell A2 (first column, second row), and then freeze the panes. As you scroll the data, the first row remains on the screen so the column headers are visible, making it easier to identify the data in each record.

You'll freeze the first row, which contains the column headers, so that they remain on the screen as you scroll the data.

To freeze the top row in the worksheet:

▶ **1.** Click the **View** tab on the Ribbon. The Ribbon changes to display the View options.

▶ **2.** In the Window group, click the **Freeze Panes** button, and then click **Freeze Top Row**. A dark, horizontal line appears below the column headers to indicate which row is frozen.

▶ **3.** Scroll the worksheet to row 116. This time, the column headers remain visible as you scroll. See Figure 5-3.

Freezing the top row of the worksheet ◀ **Figure 5-3**

▶ **4.** Press the **Ctrl+Home** keys to return to cell A2, the cell directly below the frozen row.

After you freeze panes, the first option on the Freeze Panes menu changes to Unfreeze Panes. This option unlocks all the rows and columns so you can scroll the entire worksheet. You will use a different method to keep the column headers visible, so you will unfreeze the top row of the worksheet.

To unfreeze the top row of the worksheet:

▶ **1.** In the Window group on the View tab, click the **Freeze Panes** button. The first Freeze Panes option is now Unfreeze Panes.

▶ **2.** Click **Unfreeze Panes**. The dark, horizontal line below the column headers is removed, and you can scroll all the rows and columns in the worksheet.

Creating an Excel Table

You can convert a structured range of data, such as the art objects data in the range A1:H116, to an Excel table. Recall that an Excel table is a range of related data that is managed independently from the data in other rows and columns in the worksheet. An Excel table uses features designed to make it easier to identify, manage, and analyze the groups of related data. You can create more than one Excel table in a worksheet.

InSight		Saving Time with Excel Table Features

Excel tables provide many advantages to structured ranges of data. When you create an Excel table, you can perform the same operations as you can for a structured range of data. In addition, you can do the following:

- Format the Excel table quickly using a table style.
- Add new rows and columns to the Excel table that automatically expand the range.
- Add a Total row to calculate the summary function you select, such as SUM, AVERAGE, COUNT, MIN, and MAX.
- Enter a formula in one table cell that is automatically copied to all other cells in that table column.
- Create formulas that reference cells in a table by using table and column names instead of cell addresses.

These Excel table features let you focus on analyzing and understanding the data, letting the program perform the more time-consuming tasks. You will use these Excel table features in this and other tutorials.

Next, you'll create an Excel table from the art objects data in the Art Collection worksheet. By doing so, you'll be able to take advantage of the many features and tools for working with Excel tables to analyze data effectively.

Tip

If your data does not contain column headers, Excel adds headers with the default names Column1, Column2, and so forth to the table.

To create an Excel table from the art objects data:

1. Verify that the active cell is cell **A2**, which is in the range of art objects data.

2. Click the **Insert** tab on the Ribbon, and then, in the Tables group, click the **Table** button. The Create Table dialog box opens. The range of data for the table is entered in the dialog box. See Figure 5-4.

Figure 5-4	Create Table dialog box

range reference for the art objects table data

option checked because the art objects table includes column headers

3. Click the **OK** button. The dialog box closes, and the range of data is converted to an Excel table. Filter arrows appear in the header row, the table is formatted with a predefined table style, and the Table Tools Design contextual tab appears on the Ribbon. See Figure 5-5.

Excel table created for the art objects data ◄ **Figure 5-5**

4. Scroll the table down. The text of the header row replaces the standard lettered column headings (A, B, C, and so on) as you scroll so that you don't need to freeze panes to keep the header row visible. See Figure 5-6.

Art objects table scrolled ◄ **Figure 5-6**

5. Press the **Ctrl+Home** keys to make cell A1 active. The column headings return to the standard display, and the header row scrolls back into view as row 1.

Renaming an Excel Table

Excel assigns the name Table1 to the first Excel table created in a workbook. Any additional Excel tables you create in the workbook are named consecutively, Table2, Table3, and so forth. You can assign a more descriptive name to a table, which makes it easier to identify a particular table by its content. Descriptive names are especially useful when you create more than one Excel table in the same workbook. Table names must start with a letter or an underscore and can use any combination of letters, numbers, and under-scores for the rest of the name. Table names cannot include spaces.

Mary asks you to change the name of the Excel table you just created from the art objects data to ArtObjects.

To rename the Table1 table:

▶ 1. In the Properties group on the Table Tools Design tab, select **Table1** in the Table Name box. See Figure 5-7.

Figure 5-7 ▶ Table Name box

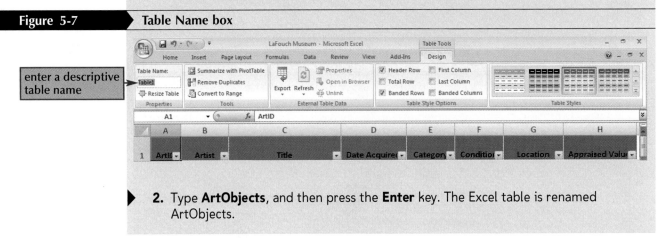

enter a descriptive table name

▶ 2. Type **ArtObjects**, and then press the **Enter** key. The Excel table is renamed ArtObjects.

Formatting an Excel Table

Refer to Figure 5-7 and note the check boxes in the Table Style Options group on the Table Tools Design tab. These check boxes enable you to quickly and easily add or remove table elements or change the format of the table elements. For example, you can choose to remove the header row in a table by deselecting the Header Row check box; you can easily toggle back to display the header row by clicking to select this check box. Similarly, you can change the appearance of a table from banded rows to banded columns by deselecting the Banded Rows check box and then clicking to select the Banded Columns check box. With these options readily available on the Table Tools Design tab, it's easy to achieve the exact content and look for a table.

Mary likes the default table style applied to the Excel table, but asks you to make a few modifications to improve the table's appearance. She wants the ArtID values in the first column of the table highlighted for emphasis. She also wants the width in the Date Acquired and Appraised Value columns reduced to better fit the values.

To format the ArtObjects table:

▶ 1. In the Table Style Options group on the Table Tools Design tab, click the **First Column** check box to insert a check mark. The text in the ArtID column is bold, and the fill color is the same as the header row.

▶ 2. Change the width of column D to **12**. The Date Acquired column width better fits the dates.

▶ 3. Change the width of column H to **12**. The Appraised Value column better fits the monetary values.

▶ 4. Click cell **A1**, if necessary.

Maintaining an Excel Table

Mary has several changes that need to be reflected in the ArtObjects table. First, the museum acquired a new painting and received a sculpture from an anonymous donor; both art objects need to be added to the table. Second, Mary just learned that the Moonlight painting needs to be repaired as its condition has deteriorated; the condition of this art object needs to be changed from Fair to Poor. Finally, one of the paintings has been sold to raise money for new acquisitions; the record for this art object needs to be deleted from the table. Mary asks you to update the ArtObjects table to reflect these changes.

Adding Records

As you maintain an Excel table, you often need to add new records. You add a record to an Excel table in a blank row. The simplest and most convenient way to add a record to an Excel table is to enter the data in the first blank row below the last record. You can then sort the data to arrange the table in the order you want. You can also insert a row within the table for the new record, if you want the record in a specific location.

Next, you'll add records for the new painting and sculpture to the ArtObjects table.

To add two records to the ArtObjects table:

1. Press the **End+↓** keys to make cell A116 the active cell. This cell is in the last row of the table.

2. Press the **↓** key to move the active cell to cell A117. This is the first blank row below the table.

3. Type **116** in cell A117, and then press the **Tab** key. Cell B117 in the Artist column becomes the active cell. The table expands to include a new row in the table structure with the same formatting as the rest of the table. The AutoCorrect Options button appears so you can undo the table formatting if you hadn't intended the new data to be part of the existing table. The sizing handle in the lower-right corner of the table indicates the last row and column in the table. You can use the sizing handle to add columns or rows to the Excel table to expand it or remove them to make the table smaller. See Figure 5-8.

New row added to the ArtObjects table ◄ Figure 5-8

Tip

As you type in a cell, Auto-Complete displays any existing entry in the column that matches the characters you typed. Press the Tab key to accept the entry or continue typing to replace it.

Trouble? If cell A118 is the active cell, you probably pressed the Enter key instead of the Tab key. Click cell B117 and then continue entering the data in Step 4.

4. In the range B117:H117, enter **Giama**, **Starry Night**, **4/3/2010**, **Painting**, **Excellent**, **South Pavilion**, and **8500** for the Artist, Title, Date Acquired, Category, Condition, Location, and Appraised Value fields, pressing the **Tab** key to move from cell to cell, and pressing the **Tab** key after you enter all the data for the record. Cell A118 becomes the active cell and the table expands to incorporate row 118.

   Next, you'll enter the second record.

5. In the range A118:H118, enter **117**, **Higgins**, **Apache Warrior**, **4/5/2010**, **Sculpture**, **Excellent**, **Garden**, and **23000**, and then click cell **A119** after the last entry. The record for the sculpture is added to the table. See Figure 5-9.

Figure 5-9	Two records added to the ArtObjects table

115	114	Mogan	Shadow House	5/5/2005	Painting	Good	East Pavilion	$	5,500
116	115	Mogan	Storytelling at the Campfire	3/19/2005	Painting	Excellent	East Pavilion	$	18,000
117	116	Giama	Starry Night	4/3/2010	Painting	Excellent	South Pavilion	$	8,500
118	117	Higgins	Apache Warrior	4/5/2010	Sculpture	Excellent	Garden	$	23,000
119									

two new records

Documentation | Art Collection | Sheet3

Ready

Trouble? If a new row is added to the table, you probably pressed the Tab key instead of the Enter key after the last entry in the record. On the Quick Access Toolbar, click the Undo button to remove the extra row.

Finding and Editing Records

You need to update the condition for the art object with the title Moonlight. Although you can manually scroll through the table to find a specific record, a quicker and more accurate way to locate a record is to use the Find command. You edit the data in a field the same way as you edit data in a worksheet cell. You'll use the Find command to locate the record for the Moonlight painting, which has deteriorated to poor condition. Then, you'll edit the record in the table to change the condition to "Poor."

To find and edit the record for the Moonlight painting:

1. Press the **Ctrl+Home** keys to move to the top of the worksheet, and then click cell **C2** to make it the active cell.

2. In the Editing group on the Home tab, click the **Find & Select** button, and then click **Find**. The Find and Replace dialog box opens.

3. Type **Moonlight** in the Find what box, and then click the **Find Next** button. Cell C69, which contains the title Moonlight, is selected. This is the record you want. If it weren't, you would click the Find Next button again to display the next record that meets the search criteria.

4. Click the **Close** button. The Find and Replace dialog box closes.

5. Press the **Tab** key three times to move the active cell to the Condition column, and then type **P**. AutoComplete displays Poor in the cell, which is the condition text you want to enter.

▶ **6.** Press the **Tab** key to enter the AutoComplete entry. The painting's condition is changed in the table.

▶ **7.** Press the **Ctrl+Home** keys to make cell A1 active.

Deleting a Record

The final update you need to make to the ArtObjects table is to delete the record for the Trappers painting (art ID 90), which is the art object that was sold. You'll use the Find command to locate the painting's record. Then, you'll delete the record from the table.

To find and delete the Trappers painting record:

▶ **1.** In the Editing group on the Home tab, click the **Find & Select** button, and then click **Find**. The Find and Replace dialog box opens.

▶ **2.** Type **90** in the Find what box, and then click the **Find Next** button. Because Excel searches the entire worksheet (not just the current column), and because it finds the search value even if it is part of another value, the appraised value $1,900 is selected. This is not the record you want to delete.

▶ **3.** Click the **Find Next** button to highlight the appraised value $1,900 for a different record, and then click the **Find Next** button again to highlight the value 90 in the ArtID column. This is the record you need to delete.

▶ **4.** Click the **Close** button. The Find and Replace dialog box closes.

Next, you'll delete the record for the Trappers painting.

▶ **5.** In the Cells group on the Home tab, click the **Delete button arrow**, and then click **Delete Table Rows**. The record for the Trappers painting is deleted from the table.

Trouble? If a different record was deleted, the active cell was not in the record for the Trappers painting. On the Quick Access Toolbar, click the Undo button 🔄 to restore the record, and then repeat Steps 1 through 5.

▶ **6.** Press the **Ctrl+Home** keys to make cell A1 active.

Sorting Data

The records in the ArtObjects table appear in the order that Mary entered them. As you work with tables, however, you'll want to view the same records in a different order, such as by the artist name or by the art object's location in the museum. You can rearrange, or **sort**, the records in a table or range based on the data in one or more fields. The fields you use to order the data are called **sort fields**. For example, to arrange the art objects by artist name, you can sort the data using the Artist column as the sort field.

You can sort data in ascending or descending order. **Ascending order** arranges text alphabetically from A to Z, numbers from smallest to largest, and dates from oldest to newest. **Descending order** arranges text in reverse alphabetical order from Z to A, numbers from largest to smallest, and dates from newest to oldest. In both ascending and descending order, blank fields are placed at the end of the table.

Sorting One Column Using the Sort Buttons

The simplest way to sort data with one sort field is to use the ▲↓ or ▼↓ button. Mary wants you to sort the art objects in ascending order by the artist. This will rearrange the table data so that the records appear in alphabetical order by the artist name.

To sort the art objects table in ascending order by the artist name:

1. Click any cell in the Artist column. You do not need to select the entire ArtObjects table, which consists of the range A1:H117. Excel determines the table's range when you click any cell in the table.

2. Click the **Data** tab on the Ribbon, and then, in the Sort & Filter group, click the **Sort A to Z** button ▲↓. The data is sorted in ascending order by Artist. The Artist filter arrow indicates the data is sorted by that column. See Figure 5-10.

Figure 5-10 ▶ ArtObjects table sorted by Artist

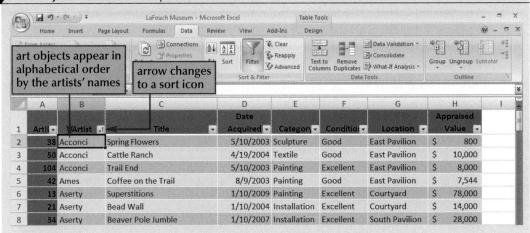

Trouble? If the data is sorted in the wrong order, you might have clicked in a different column than the Artist column. Repeat Steps 1 and 2.

Sorting Multiple Columns Using the Sort Dialog Box

Sometimes, sorting by one sort field is not adequate for your needs. For example, Mary wants you to arrange the ArtObjects table so that all the art objects in each location are together, and then all the objects for each artist within each location are together, and then each artist's work is arranged by the date acquired. You must sort on more than one column to accomplish this. The first sort field is called the **primary sort field**, the second sort field is called the **secondary sort field**, and so forth. You can use up to 64 sort fields in a single sort. In this case, the Location field is the primary sort field, the Artist field is the secondary sort field, and the Date Acquired field is the tertiary sort field. When you have more than one sort field, you should use the Sort dialog box to specify the sort criteria.

Sorting Data Using Multiple Sort Fields | Reference Window

- Click any cell in a table or range.
- In the Sort & Filter group on the Data tab, click the Sort button to open the Sort dialog box.
- If the Sort by row exists, modify the primary sort by selections; otherwise, click the Add Level button to insert the Sort by row.
- Click the Sort by arrow, select the column heading that you want to specify as the primary sort field, click the Sort On arrow to select the type of data, and then click the Order arrow to select the sort order.
- To sort by a second column, click the Add Level button to add the first Then by row. Click the Sort by arrow, select the column heading that you want to specify as the secondary sort field, click the Sort On arrow to select the type of data, and then click the Order arrow to select the sort order.
- To sort by additional columns, click the Add Level button and select appropriate Then by, Sort On, and Order values.
- Click the OK button.

Mary wants you to sort the art objects by location, and then within location by artist, and then within artist by date acquired with the most recently acquired objects for the artist appearing before the older ones. This will make it faster for her to find information about the location and the creator of the art objects in each location.

To sort the art objects table by location, then by artist, and then by date acquired:

▶ **1.** Click cell **A1** in the ArtObjects table. Cell A1 is the active cell, although you can click any cell in the table to sort the table data.

▶ **2.** In the Sort & Filter group on the Data tab, click the **Sort** button. The Sort dialog box opens. Any sort specifications (sort field, type of data sorted on, and sort order) from the last sort appear in the dialog box.

You'll set the primary sort field—Location.

▶ **3.** Click the **Sort by** arrow to display the list of the column headers in the ArtObjects table, and then click **Location**.

▶ **4.** If necessary, click the **Sort On** arrow to display the type of sort, and then click **Values**. Typically, you want to sort by the numbers, text, or dates stored in the cells, which are all values. However, you can also sort by formats, such as cell color, font color, and cell icon (a graphic that appears in a cell as a result of applying a conditional format).

▶ **5.** If necessary, click the **Order** arrow to display sort order options, and then click **A to Z**. The sort order is set to ascending.

The specification for the primary sort field are complete. Next, you will specify the secondary sort field—Artist. First, you need to insert a blank sort level.

▶ **6.** Click the **Add Level** button. A Then by row is added below the primary sort field.

▶ **7.** Click the **Then by** arrow and click **Artist**, and then verify that **Values** appears in the Sort On box and **A to Z** appears in the Order box.

The second sort field is specified. You'll add the third sort field—Date Acquired.

▶ **8.** Click the **Add Level** button to add a second Then by row.

▶ **9.** Click the second **Then by** arrow and click **Date Acquired**, verify that **Values** appears in the Sort On box, click the **Order** arrow, and then click **Newest to Oldest** to specify a descending sort order for the Date Acquired values. See Figure 5-11.

Figure 5-11	Sort dialog box with complete sort specifications

10. Click the **OK** button. Excel sorts the table records first in ascending order by Location, then within each location by Artist (again, in ascending order), and then within each artist by Date Acquired. For example, notice the three works by Acconci located in the East Pavilion; the works are arranged in descending order by the value in the Date Acquired column, so that the newer works appear before the older works. See Figure 5-12.

Figure 5-12	Art objects sorted by Location, then by Artist, and then by Date Acquired

11. Scroll the table to view the sorted table data.

Mary wants to review the condition of each art object to determine how many objects need repairs. To do this more easily, she asks you to sort the objects by Condition. Because she wants to sort by only one field, you'll use the Sort A to Z button.

To sort the table by condition:

▶ **1.** Click any cell in the **Condition** column.

▶ **2.** In the Sort & Filter group on the Data tab, click the **Sort A to Z** button ![Sort A to Z icon]. The previous sort is removed and the art objects are now sorted in ascending order by Condition.

▶ **3.** Scroll the table to see the reordered art objects.

As Mary reviews the sorted table, she realizes that the data is sorted in alphabetical order by the condition of the art objects: Excellent, Fair, Good, and Poor. This default sort order for fields with text values is not appropriate for the condition ratings. Instead, Mary wants you to base the sort on quality ranking rather than alphabetical. You'll use a custom sort list to set up the sort order Mary wants.

Sorting Using a Custom List

Text is sorted in ascending or descending alphabetical order unless you specify a different order using a custom list. A **custom list** indicates the sequence in which you want data ordered. Excel provides four predefined custom sort lists. Two days-of-the-week custom lists (Sun, Mon, Tues, ... and Sunday, Monday, Tuesday, ...) and two months-of-the-year custom lists (Jan, Feb, Mar, Apr, ... and January, February, March, April, ...). If a column consists of day or month labels, you can sort them in their correct chronological order using one of these predefined custom lists. You can also create custom lists to sort records in a sequence you define. In this case, you want to create a custom list to arrange the art objects based on their condition, with the top-quality condition appearing first, as follows: Excellent, Good, Fair, Poor.

Creating a Custom List | Reference Window

- In the Sort & Filter group on the Data tab, click the Sort button.
- Click the Order arrow, and then click Custom List.
- In the List entries box, type each entry for the custom list, pressing the Enter key after each entry.
- Click the Add button.
- Click the OK button.

You'll create a custom list that Mary can use to sort the records by the Condition field.

To create the custom list based on the Condition field:

▶ **1.** Make sure the active cell is in the table, and then, in the Sort & Filter group on the Data tab, click the **Sort** button. The Sort dialog box opens, showing the sort specifications from the previous sort.

▶ **2.** Click the **Sort by** arrow, click **Condition** to select the sort field (if necessary), and then verify that **Values** appears in the Sort On box.

▶ **3.** Click the **Order** arrow to display the sort order options, and then click **Custom List**. The Custom Lists dialog box opens.

▶ **4.** Click **NEW LIST** in the Custom lists box to place the insertion point in the List entries box.

Next, you'll enter the condition values in the order you want them sorted. You must press the Enter key after each entry.

▶ **5.** Type **Excellent**, press the **Enter** key to move the insertion point to the next line, type **Good**, press the **Enter** key, type **Fair**, press the **Enter** key, type **Poor**, and then press the **Enter** key. The four items appear in the List entries box.

▶ **6.** Click the **Add** button. The custom list entries are added to the Custom lists box. See Figure 5-13.

Figure 5-13 ▶ **Custom Lists dialog box with custom list defined**

click to add the list entries as a custom list

custom list with art object condition values

click to permanently remove the selected custom list

▶ **7.** Click the **OK** button to return to the Sort dialog box. The custom sort list—Excellent, Good, Fair, Poor—appears in the Order box.

▶ **8.** Click the **OK** button. The table is sorted based on the custom list.

▶ **9.** Scroll the sorted table to verify that the art objects are sorted by their condition rankings: Excellent, Good, Fair, and Poor. Note that there are six art objects in poor condition.

In this session, you created an Excel table for the art objects, and then named and formatted the table. Next, you updated the table by adding records, editing a record, and deleting a record. You sorted the records by one field and then by three fields. Finally, you created a custom list to sort the Condition field by its quality ratings. In the next session, you will filter the ArtObjects table to retrieve specific information on some of the art objects.

Review | **Session 5.1 Quick Check**

1. What is the purpose of the Freeze Panes button in the Window group on the View tab? Why is this feature helpful?

2. What three elements indicate an Excel table has been created in the worksheet?

3. What fields do you use to order data?
4. An Excel table of college students tracks each student's first name, last name, major, and year of graduation. How can you order the table so students graduating the same year appear together in alphabetical order by the student's last name?
5. How do you enter a new record in an Excel table?
6. An Excel table of faculty data includes the Rank field with the values Full, Associate, Assistant, and Instructor. How can you sort the data by rank in the following order: Full, Associate, Assistant, and Instructor?
7. If you sort table data from the most recent purchase date to the oldest purchase date, in what order have you sorted the data?

Session 5.2

Filtering Data

Mary is working on her budget for the upcoming year. She needs to determine which art objects the museum can afford to repair this year. She asks you to prepare a list of all paintings in poor condition. Mary will then examine these paintings, estimate the repair costs, and decide which ones to place on the upcoming year's repairs list.

Although you could sort the list of paintings by condition to group those in poor condition, you are still working with the entire table. A better solution is to display only the specific records you want. The process of displaying a subset of rows in the table that meets the criteria you specify is called **filtering**. Filtering, rather than rearranging the data as sorting does, temporarily hides any records that do not meet the specified criteria. After data is filtered, you can sort, copy, format, chart, and print it.

Filtering Using One Column

When you create an Excel table, filter arrows appear in each of the column headers. You can see these filter arrows in the ArtObjects table you created for Mary. You click a filter arrow to open the Filter menu for that field. You can use options on the Filter menu to create three types of filters. You can filter a column of data by its cell colors or font colors; by a specific text, number, or date filter, although the specific choices depend on the type of data in the column; or by selecting one or more of the exact values by which you want to filter in the column. After you filter a column, the Clear Filter command becomes available so you can remove the filter and redisplay all the records.

Mary wants to see only paintings in poor condition. First, you need to filter the ArtObjects table to show only those records with the value "Paintings" in the Category column. Remember, filtering the data only hides some of the records.

> **Tip**
>
> You can display or hide filter arrows for an Excel table or a range of data by using the Filter button in the Sort & Filter group on the Data tab.

To filter the ArtObjects table to show only paintings:

▶ 1. If you took a break after the previous session, make sure the LaFouch Museum workbook is open, the Art Collection worksheet is active, and the ArtObjects table is active.

▶ 2. Click the **Category filter arrow**. The Filter menu opens, as shown in Figure 5-14, listing the unique entries in the Category column: Installation, Painting, Sculpture, and Textile. Initially, all the items are selected, but you can select which items you want to use to filter the data. In this case, you want to select the Painting item.

| Figure 5-14 | Filter menu for the Category column |

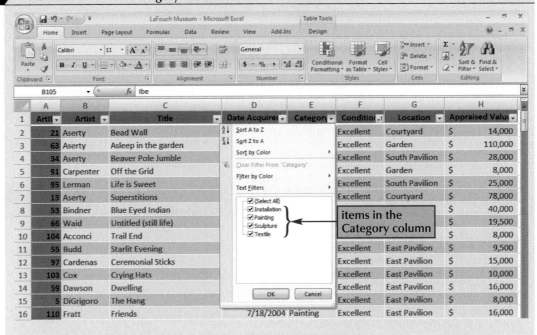

Notice the **Sort by Color** and **Filter by Color** options in the filter menu. These options enable you to filter and sort data using color, one of many cell attributes. Suppose that Mary used specific cell background colors for certain works of art in the ArtObjects table. For example, she might want to highlight those works given to the museum by its two most generous donors, using yellow for one and red for the other. So, the cells in the Title column for the two donors would be formatted with these colors. You could then click the Sort by Color option in the filter menu to display a list of available colors by which to sort, and then click the specific color so that all the records for the first donor (formatted with yellow) would appear together, and all the records for the second donor (formatted with red) would appear together. Similarly, you could click the Filter by Color option to display a submenu with the available colors by which to filter, and then click a color. In this example, if you selected yellow, only the records for the first donor would be displayed in the table, allowing you to focus on just those records.

▶ **3.** Click the **(Select All)** check box to remove the check marks from all the Category items, and then click the **Painting** check box to insert a check mark. The filter will show only those records that match the checked item and hide records that contain the unchecked items.

▶ **4.** Click the **OK** button. The filter is applied. The status bar lists the number of paintings found in the entire table. Fifty-seven of the 116 records in the table are displayed. See Figure 5-15.

ArtObjects table filtered to show only paintings | Figure 5-15

5. Review the records to verify that only records with a value equal to Painting in the Category column are visible. All records that do not have the value Painting in this column are hidden. Notice the gaps in the row numbers in the worksheet. As a reminder that the records are filtered, the row numbers of the filtered records are blue and the Category filter arrow changes to indicate that this column is being used to filter the table.

6. Point to the **Category filter arrow**. A ScreenTip—Category: Equals "Painting"—describes the filter applied to the column.

InSight		**Exploring Text Filters**

You can use different text filters to display the records you want. If you know only part of a text value or want to match a certain pattern, you can use the Begins With, Ends With, and Contains operators to filter a text field to match the pattern you specify.

The following examples are based on a student directory table that includes First Name, Last Name, Address, City, State, and Zip fields:

- To find a student named Smith, Smithe, or Smythe, create a text filter using the Begins With operator. In this example, use Begins With *Sm* to display all records that have *Sm* at the beginning of the text value.
- To Find anyone whose Last Name ends in "son" (such as Robertson, Anderson, Dawson, Gibson, and so forth), create a text filter using the Ends With operator. In this example, use Ends With *son* to display all records that have *son* as the last characters in the text value.
- To find anyone whose street address includes *Central* (such as 101 Central Ave, 1024 Central Road, or 457 Avenue De Central), create a text filter using the Contains operator. In this example, use Contains *Central* to display all records that have *Central* anywhere in the text value.

When you create a text filter, think about the results you want. Then, consider what text filter you can use to best achieve those results.

Filtering Using Multiple Columns

If you need to further restrict the records that appear in a filtered table, you can filter by one or more of the other columns. Each additional filter is applied to the currently filtered data and further reduces the records that are displayed. Mary wants to see only paintings that are in poor condition, rather than all the paintings in the ArtObjects table. To do this, you need to filter the paintings records to display only those with the value "Poor" in the Condition column. You'll use the filter arrow in the Condition column to add this second filter criterion to the filtered data.

To filter the painting records to show only those in poor condition:

▶ 1. Click the **Condition filter arrow**. The Filter menu opens.

▶ 2. Click the **Excellent**, **Good**, and **Fair** check boxes to remove the check marks. The Poor check box remains checked, so only paintings in poor condition will be displayed.

▶ 3. Click the **OK** button. The ArtObjects table is further filtered and shows the three paintings that are in poor condition. See Figure 5-16.

ArtObjects table filtered to show only paintings in poor condition | Figure 5-16

Clearing Filters

When you want to see all the data in a filtered table, you can **clear** (or remove) the filters. When you clear a filter from a column, any other filters are still applied. For example, in the ArtObjects table, you would see all the paintings in the table if you cleared the filter from the Condition field, or you would see all the art objects in poor condition if you cleared the filter from the Category field. To redisplay all the art objects in the table, you need to clear both the Condition filter and the Category filter. You will do this now to restore the entire table of art objects.

> **To clear the filters to show all the records in the ArtObjects table:**
>
> ▶ 1. Click the **Condition filter arrow**, and then click **Clear Filter From "Condition"**. The Condition filter is removed from the table. The table shows only paintings because the Category filter is still in effect.
>
> ▶ 2. Click the **Category filter arrow**, and then click **Clear Filter From "Category"**. The Category condition is removed, and all the records in the ArtObjects table are displayed again.

Selecting Multiple Filter Items

You can often find the information you need by selecting a single filter item from a list of filter items. Sometimes, however, you need to specify a more complex set of criteria to find the records you want. Earlier, you selected one filter item for the Category column and one filter item for the Condition column to display the records whose Category field value equals Painting AND whose Condition field value equals Poor. The records had to have both values to be displayed. The AND condition requires that all of the selected criteria be true for the record to be displayed. Now you want to select two filter items for the Category column to display records whose Category field value equals Installation OR whose Category field value equals Sculpture. The records must have at least one of these values to be displayed. A filter that selects more than one item from the list of items uses the OR condition, which requires that only one of the selected criteria be true for a record to be displayed. For example, if you check the Installation and Sculpture check boxes in the Category filter items, you create the filter condition "*Category equal to installation*" OR "*Category equal to sculpture*."

The museum's board of directors wants a list of all installations or sculptures valued above $20,000. Mary asks you to create a list of these holdings.

To select multiple filter items:

▶   **1.** Click the **Category filter arrow**, and then click the **Painting** and **Textile** check boxes to remove the check marks.

▶   **2.** Verify that the **Installation** and **Sculpture** check boxes remain checked. When you select more than one item, you create a multiselect filter.

▶   **3.** Click the **OK** button. The ArtObjects table is filtered, and the status bar indicates that 51 out of 116 records are either an installation or a sculpture.

Creating Criteria Filters to Specify More Complex Criteria

Filter items enable you to filter a range of data or an Excel table based on exact values in a column. However, many times you need broader criteria. **Criteria filters** enable you to specify various conditions in addition to those that are based on an "equals" criterion. For example, you might want to find all art objects with an appraised value greater than $20,000 or acquired after 7/1/2009. You use criteria filters to create these conditions.

The type of criteria filters available change depending on whether the data in a column contains text, numbers, or dates. Figure 5-17 shows some of the options for text, number, and date criteria filters.

Figure 5-17 ▷   **Options for text, number, and date criteria filters**

Filter	Criteria	Records displayed
Text	Equals	Exactly match the specified text string
	Does Not Equal	Do not exactly match the specified text string
	Begins With	Begin with the specified text spring
	Ends With	End with the specified text string
	Contains	Have the specified text string anywhere
	Does Not Contain	Do not have the specified text string anywhere
Number	Equals	Exactly match the specified number
	Greater Than or Equal to	Are greater than or equal to the specified number
	Less Than	Are less than the specified number
	Between	Are greater than or equal to and less than or equal to the specified numbers
	Top 10	Are the top or bottom 10 (or the specified number)
	Above Average	Are greater than the average
Date	Today	Have the current date
	Last Week	Are in the prior week
	Next Month	Are in the month following the current month
	Last Quarter	Are in the previous quarter of the year (quarters defined Jan, Feb, Mar; Apr, May, June; and so on)
	Year to Date	Are since January 1 of the current year to the current date
	Last Year	Are in the previous year (based on the current date)

You will modify the filtered ArtObjects table to add a criteria filter that includes only objects valued greater than $20,000.

To create a number criteria filter:

▶ **1.** Click the **Appraised Value filter arrow**, and then point to **Number Filters**. A menu opens displaying the comparison operators available for columns of numbers.

▶ **2.** Click **Greater Than**. The Custom AutoFilter dialog box opens. The upper-left box lists *is greater than*, the comparison operator you want to use to filter the Appraised Value column. You enter the value you want to use for the filter criteria in the upper-right box, which, in this case, is 20,000.

▶ **3.** Type **20000** in the upper-right box. See Figure 5-18. You use the lower set of boxes if you want the filter to meet a second condition. You click the And option button to display rows that meet both criteria. You click the Or option button to display rows that meet either of the two criteria. You only want to set one criteria for this filter, so you'll leave the lower boxes empty.

Custom AutoFilter dialog box   Figure 5-18

▶ **4.** Click the **OK** button. The status bar indicates that 7 of 116 records were found. The seven records that appear in the ArtObjects table are either installations or sculptures and have an appraised value greater than $20,000.

Before Mary sends this list to the board of directors, you'll sort the filtered data to show the largest appraised value first. Although you can sort the data using Sort buttons, as you did earlier, these sort options are also available on the Filter menu for your convenience. If you want to perform a more complex sort, you still need to use the Sort dialog box.

To sort the filtered table data:

▶ **1.** Click the **Appraised Value filter arrow**. The Filter menu opens. The sort options are at the top of the menu.

▶ **2.** Click **Sort Largest to Smallest**. The filtered table now displays installations and sculptures with an appraised valued above $20,000 sorted in descending order. See Figure 5-19.

| Figure 5-19 | Filtered ArtObjects table |

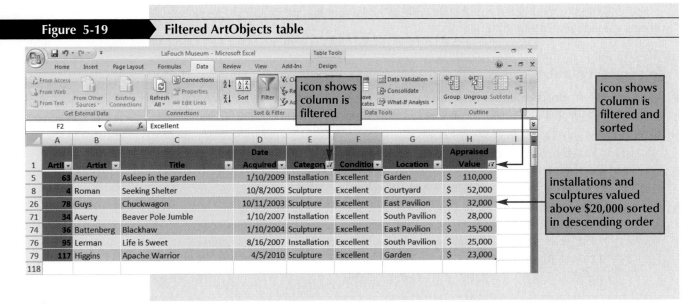

Mary will send this list to the board of directors. You need to restore the entire table of art objects, which you can do by clearing all the filters at one time.

To clear all the filters from the ArtObjects table:

▶ **1.** Click the **Data** tab on the Ribbon, if necessary.

▶ **2.** In the Sort & Filter group, click the **Clear** button. All the records appear in the table.

Using the Total Row to Calculate Summary Statistics

You can calculate summary statistics (including sum, average, count, maximum, and minimum) on all the columns in an Excel table or on a filtered table in a Total row. A **Total row**, which you can display at the end of the table, is used to calculate summary statistics for the columns in an Excel table. When you click in each cell in the Total row, an arrow appears that you can click to open a list of the most commonly used functions.

Mary is creating a brochure for an upcoming fund-raising event, and wants to know the number and value of the items in the current museum collection, excluding art objects in poor condition. She asks you to filter the table to display art objects that are in excellent, good, and fair condition. Then, you will display the Total row for the ArtObjects table to count the number of art objects and add their total appraised value.

To add a Total row and select summary statistics:

▶ **1.** Click the **Condition filter arrow**, click the **Poor** check box to remove the check mark, and then click the **OK** button. The ArtObjects table displays objects that are in excellent, good, or fair condition. The status bar indicates that 110 of 116 records remain in the filtered table.

Next, you will display the Total row.

▶ **2.** Click the **Table Tools Design** tab on the Ribbon, and then, in the Table Style Options group, click the **Total Row** check box to insert a check mark.

3. Scroll to the end of the table. The Total row is the last row of the table, the word "Total" appears in the leftmost cell, and the total appraised value $1,118,723 appears in the rightmost cell. By default, the Total row adds the numbers in the last column of the Excel table or counts the number of records if the data in the last column contains text. See Figure 5-20.

Total row added to the ArtObjects table ◄ **Figure 5-20**

In the Artist cell of the Total row, you want to count the number of records whose Appraised Values were added in the last column.

4. Click cell **B118** (the Artist cell in the Total row), and then click the **arrow button** to display a list of functions. None is the default function in all columns except the last column. See Figure 5-21.

Total row functions ◄ **Figure 5-21**

Tip

You can click the More Functions command to open the Insert Function dialog box and select any available function.

5. Click **Count**. The number 110 appears in the cell, which is the number of records in the filtered ArtObjects table. See Figure 5-22.

| Figure 5-22 | Count of records in the filtered table |

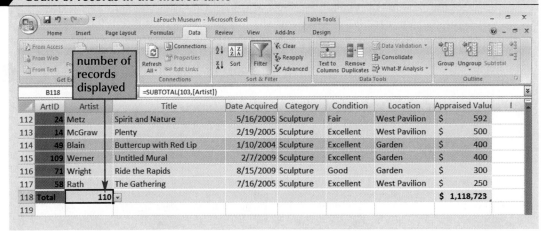

Mary will include this information in her fund-raising brochure. You will remove the Total row and clear the filter.

To remove the Total row and clear the filter from the ArtObjects table:

1. In the Table Style Options group on the Table Tools Design tab, click the **Total Row** check box to remove the check mark. The Total row is no longer visible.

2. Scroll to the top of the table, click the **Condition filter arrow**, and then click **Clear Filter From "Condition"**. The ArtObjects table displays all the art objects.

The board of directors asked Mary to create a report that shows all the museum's art objects sorted by Category with the total appraised value of the art objects in each category. The board also wants to see the total appraised value for each category after the last item of that category. Although you could use the Total row in the Excel table to calculate the results, you would need to filter, total, and print the data for each category separately. A faster way to provide the information Mary needs is to use the Subtotal command.

Inserting Subtotals

You can summarize data in a range of data by inserting subtotals. The Subtotal command offers many kinds of summary information, including counts, sums, averages, minimums, and maximums. The Subtotal command inserts a subtotal row into the range for each group of data and adds a grand total row below the last row of data. Because Excel inserts subtotals whenever the value in a specified field changes, you need to sort the data so that records with the same value in a specified field are grouped together *before* you use the Subtotal command. The Subtotal command cannot be used in an Excel table, so you must first convert the Excel table to a range.

Calculating Subtotals for a Range of Data | Reference Window

- Sort the data by the column for which you want a subtotal.
- If the data is in an Excel table, in the Tools group on the Table Tools Design tab, click the Convert to Range button, and then click the Yes button to convert the Excel table to a range.
- In the Outline group on the Data tab, click the Subtotal button.
- Click the At each change in arrow, and then click the column that contains the group you want to subtotal.
- Click the Use function arrow, and then click the function you want to use to summarize the data.
- In the Add subtotal to box, click the check box for each column that contains the values you want to summarize.
- To calculate another category of subtotals, click the Replace current subtotals check box to remove the check mark, and then repeat the previous three steps.
- Click the OK button.

To produce the results Mary needs, you will sort the art objects by category and calculate subtotals in the Appraised Value column for each category grouping.

To calculate appraised values subtotals for each category of art object:

▶ **1.** Click the **Category filter** arrow, and then click **Sort A to Z** on the Filter menu. The ArtObjects table is sorted in ascending order by the Category field. This ensures one subtotal is created for each category.

▶ **2.** In the Tools group on the Table Tools Design tab, click the **Convert to Range** button. A dialog box opens, asking if you want to convert the table to a normal range.

▶ **3.** Click the **Yes** button. The Excel table is converted to a range. You can tell this because the filter arrows and the Table Tools Design tab disappear, and the Home tab on the Ribbon is selected.

Next, you'll calculate the subtotals. The active cell needs to be in the header row so you can select the correct column.

▶ **4.** Press the **Ctrl+Home** keys to make cell A1 the active cell, click the **Data** tab on the Ribbon, and then, in the Outline group, click the **Subtotal** button. The Subtotal dialog box opens. See Figure 5-23.

Subtotal dialog box | **Figure 5-23**

▶ **5.** Click the **At each change in** arrow, and then click **Category**. This is the column you want Excel to use to determine where to insert the subtotals; it's the column you sorted. A subtotal will be calculated at every change in the Category value.

▶ **6.** If necessary, click the **Use function** arrow, and then click **Sum**. The Use function list provides several options for subtotaling data, including counts, averages, minimums, maximums, and products.

▶ **7.** In the Add subtotal to list box, make sure only the **Appraised Value** check box is checked. This specifies the Appraised Value field as the field to be subtotaled. If the data already included subtotals, you would check the Replace current subtotals check box to replace the existing subtotals or uncheck the option to display the new subtotals on separate rows above the existing subtotals. Because the data has no subtotals, it makes no difference whether you select this option.

▶ **8.** Make sure the **Summary below data** check box is checked. This option places the subtotals below each group of data, instead of above the first entry in each group, and places the grand total at the end of the data, instead of at the top of the column just below the row of column headings.

▶ **9.** Click the **OK** button to insert subtotals into the data. Excel inserts rows below each category group and displays the subtotals for the appraised value of each art category. A series of Outline buttons appears to the left of the worksheet so you can display or hide the detail rows within each subtotal.

Trouble? If each item has a subtotal following it, you probably forgot to sort the data by Category. Repeat Steps 1 through 9.

▶ **10.** Scroll through the data to see the subtotals below each category and the grand total at the end of the data. See Figure 5-24.

| Figure 5-24 | Subtotals and grand total added to the art objects data |

Trouble? If necessary, increase the column width so you can view the subtotal values.

Using the Subtotal Outline View

In addition to displaying subtotals, the Subtotal feature "outlines" your worksheet so you can control the level of detail that is displayed. The three Outline buttons at the top of the outline area, as shown in Figure 5-24, allow you to show or hide different levels of detail in the worksheet. By default, the highest level is active, in this case, Level 3. Level 3 displays the most detail—the individual art object records, the subtotals, and the grand total. Level 2 displays the subtotals and the grand total, but not the individual records. Level 1 displays only the grand total.

The subtotals are useful, but Mary wants you to isolate the different subtotal sections so that she can focus on them individually. You will use the Outline buttons to prepare a report for Mary that includes only subtotals and the grand total.

To use the Outline buttons to hide records:

▶ 1. Click the **Level 2 Outline** button. The individual art object records are hidden, and you see only the subtotals for each category and the grand total. See Figure 5-25.

Table displaying only subtotals and grand total ◀ **Figure 5-25**

Trouble? If necessary, scroll the worksheet up to see the complete Level 2 list.

▶ 2. Click the **Level 1 Outline** button. The individual art object records and the subtotals for each category are hidden. Only the grand total remains visible.

▶ 3. Click the **Level 3 Outline** button. All the records along with the subtotals and the grand total are visible.

Mary has all the information she needs for her meeting with the board to review financial plans for the next fiscal cycle. So you can remove the subtotals from the data.

To remove the subtotals from the art objects data:

▶ **1.** In the Outline group on the Data tab, click the **Subtotal** button. The Subtotal dialog box opens.

▶ **2.** Click the **Remove All** button to remove the subtotals from the data. Only the records appear in the worksheet.

You'll reset the art objects data as an Excel table.

▶ **3.** Make sure the active cell is a cell within the structured range of data.

▶ **4.** Click the **Insert** tab on the Ribbon, and then, in the Tables group, click the **Table** button. The Create Table dialog box opens.

▶ **5.** Click the **OK** button to create the Excel table, and then click any cell in the table. The table structure is active.

You need to rename the table as ArtObjects.

▶ **6.** In the Properties group on the Table Tools Design tab, type **ArtObjects** in the Table Name box, and then press the **Enter** key. The Excel table is again named ArtObjects.

Mary needs to generate some information for a meeting with the budget director to review financial plans for the next fiscal cycle. You will work with the art objects data in the next session to gather the information she needs for that meeting.

Review | **Session 5.2 Quick Check**

1. Explain the relationship between the Sort and Subtotal commands.
2. An Excel table includes records for 500 employees. What can you use to calculate the average salary of employees in the finance department?
3. How can you display a list of marketing majors with a GPA of 3.0 or greater from an Excel table with records for 300 students?
4. After you display subtotals, how can you change the amount of detail displayed?
5. True or False: The Count function is a valid subtotal function when using the Subtotal command.
6. An Excel table of major league baseball players includes the column Position (pitchers, catchers, infielders, outfielders, and so forth). What feature can you use to display only pitchers and catchers in the table?
7. If you have a list of employees that includes fields for gender and salary, among others, how can you determine the average salary for females using the Total row feature?

Session 5.3

Analyzing Data with PivotTables

An Excel table can contain a wealth of information, but the large amounts of detailed data often make it difficult to form a clear, overall view of that information. You can use a PivotTable to help organize the data into a meaningful summary. A **PivotTable** is an interactive table that enables you to group and summarize either a range of data or an Excel table into a concise, tabular format for easier reporting and analysis. A PivotTable summarizes data into categories using functions such as COUNT, SUM, AVERAGE, MAX, and MIN. For example, Mary is preparing a presentation for the museum's board of directors that will include a report of the appraised value of the museum's art objects by location, category, and condition. A PivotTable can generate the information she needs.

To create a PivotTable report, you need to specify which fields in your data source you want to summarize. In the ArtObjects table, the Appraised Value field is the most likely field to summarize. In other applications, fields such as salaries, sales, and costs are frequently summarized fields for PivotTables. In PivotTable terminology, the fields that contain summary data are known as **value fields**. **Category fields** group the values in a PivotTable by fields, such as condition, location, and year acquired. Category fields appear in PivotTables as row labels, column labels, and report filters, which allows you to focus on a subset of the PivotTable by displaying one, several, or all items. Figure 5-26 shows the PivotTable you will create.

Sample PivotTable | **Figure 5-26**

	A	B	C	D	E	F
1	Location	(All)				
2						
3	Sum of Appraised Value	Column Labels				
4	Row Labels	Excellent	Good	Fair	Poor	Grand Total
5	Installation	$185,000	$2,500			$187,500
6	Painting	$611,520	$41,669	$10,500	$18,450	$682,139
7	Sculpture	$194,292	$16,300	$3,942	$3,950	$218,484
8	Textile	$7,400	$18,100	$27,500		$53,000
9	Grand Total	$998,212	$78,569	$41,942	$22,400	$1,141,123

You can easily rearrange, hide, and display different category fields in the PivotTable to provide alternative views of the data. This ability to "pivot" the table—for example, change row headings to column positions and vice versa—gives the PivotTable its name and makes it a powerful analytical tool. The PivotTable in Figure 5-26 could be rearranged so that the Condition items appear as row labels and the Category items appear as column labels.

To conceptualize the layout of a PivotTable and convey your ideas to others who might implement them, a useful first step in creating a PivotTable is to sketch its layout. Mary's sketch, shown in Figure 5-27, illustrates the PivotTable you will create to show the appraised value of the art objects organized by location, category, and condition.

PivotTable sketch | **Figure 5-27**

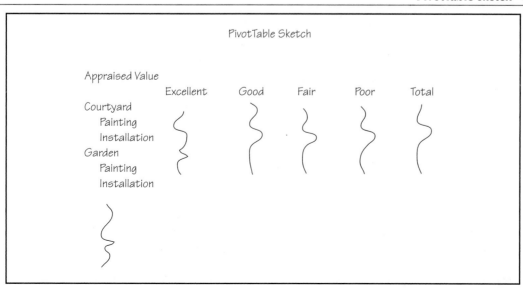

You are ready to create a PivotTable summarizing the total appraised value of art objects by location, category, and condition.

PivotTables are a great way to summarize data in a professional looking report when you do not want to see detailed data and you have many variables you want to summarize.

Although PivotTables most frequently show results using the SUM function, you can use many other functions to summarize the data, including COUNT, AVERAGE, MIN, MAX, PRODUCT, COUNT NUMBERS, STDEV, STDEVP, VAR, and VARP.

You can also display the values of a PivotTable in different views. If you want to compare one item to another item in the PivotTable, you can show the values as a percentage of a total. You can display the data in each row as a percentage of the total for the row. You can display the data in each column as a percentage of the total for the column. You can display the data as a percentage of the grand total of all the data in the PivotTable. Viewing data as a percentage of total is useful for analyses such as comparing product sales with total sales within a region or expense categories compared to total expenses for the year.

Creating a PivotTable

To create the PivotTable that will provide Mary with the information she needs, you will use the PivotTable dialog box to select the data to analyze and the location of the Pivot-Table report. Often when creating a PivotTable, you begin with data stored in a worksheet, although a PivotTable can also be created using data stored in an external database file, such as one in Access. In this case, you will use the ArtObjects table to create the PivotTable and place the PivotTable in a new worksheet.

- Click in the Excel table or select the range of data for the PivotTable.
- In the Tables group on the Insert tab, click the PivotTable button.
- Click the Select a table or range option button and verify the reference in the Table/Range box.
- Click the New Worksheet option button or click the Existing Worksheet option button and specify a cell.
- Click the OK button.
- Click the check boxes for the fields you want to add to the PivotTable (or drag fields to the appropriate box in the layout section).
- If needed, drag fields to different boxes in the layout section.

To create a PivotTable using the ArtObjects table:

▶ **1.** If you took a break after the previous session, make sure the LaFouch Museum workbook is open, the Art Collection worksheet is active, and the Excel table is active.

▶ **2.** Click the **Insert** tab on the Ribbon, and then, in the Tables group, click the **PivotTable** button. The Create PivotTable dialog box opens. See Figure 5-28.

Create PivotTable dialog box ◀ **Figure 5-28**

In this dialog box, you specify where to find the data for the PivotTable. The data can be an Excel table or range in the current workbook or an external data source such as an Access database file. You also specify whether to place the PivotTable in a new or existing worksheet. If you place the PivotTable in an existing worksheet, you must also specify the cell in which you want the upper-left corner of the Pivot-Table to appear. For the appraised value PivotTable report, you will use the ArtObjects table and place the PivotTable in a new worksheet.

▶ **3.** Make sure the **Select a table or range** option button is selected and **ArtObjects** appears in the Table/Range box.

▶ **4.** Click the **New Worksheet** option button, if necessary. This sets the PivotTable report to be placed in a new worksheet.

▶ **5.** Click the **OK** button. A new worksheet, Sheet1, is inserted to the left of the Art Collection worksheet and the PivotTable Tools contextual tabs appear on the Ribbon. The left side of Sheet1 shows an empty PivotTable report area, which is where the finished PivotTable will be placed. On the right is the PivotTable Field List, which you use to build the PivotTable by adding, removing, and arranging fields, or columns. See Figure 5-29.

Tip

You can also create a PivotTable by clicking the Summarize with Pivot-Table button in the Tools group on the Table Tools Design tab.

| Figure 5-29 | PivotTable report area and PivotTable Field List |

The PivotTable Field List is divided into two sections. The upper field list section displays the names of each field in the ArtObjects table. You check a field check box to add that field to the PivotTable. The lower layout section includes boxes for the four areas in which you can place fields: Report Filter, Row Labels, Column Labels, and Values. Figure 5-30 describes the function of each area.

| Figure 5-30 | Layout areas for a PivotTable |

Layout Area	Description
Row Labels	The fields you want to display as the rows in the PivotTable. One row is displayed for each unique item in this area. You can have nested row fields.
Column Labels	The fields you want to display as columns at the top of the PivotTable. One column is displayed for each unique item in this area. You can have nested column fields.
Report Filter	A field used to filter the report by selecting one or more items, enabling you to display a subset of data in a PivotTable report.
Values	The fields you want to summarize.

Initially, selected fields with numeric data are placed in the Values area and the SUM function is used to summarize the PivotTable. Fields with nonnumeric data are placed in the Row Labels area. You can always change these default placements of fields in the PivotTable by dragging them to other layout areas to better suit your needs.

Adding Fields to a PivotTable

You need to calculate the total appraised value of art objects by location, within location by category, and within category by condition. In the PivotTable, you'll begin by adding the Location, Category, and Condition fields to appear as row labels, and the data in the Appraised Value field to be summarized. First, you will create a PivotTable summarizing Appraised Value by Location. Then, you'll expand the PivotTable report by adding the Category and Condition fields.

To add fields to the PivotTable:

▶ 1. In the PivotTable Field List, click the **Location** check box. The Location field is added to the Row Labels box and the unique values in the Location field—Courtyard, East Pavilion, Garden, South Pavilion, and West Pavilion—appear in the PivotTable report area. See Figure 5-31.

PivotTable with the Location field items as row labels ◀ Figure 5-31

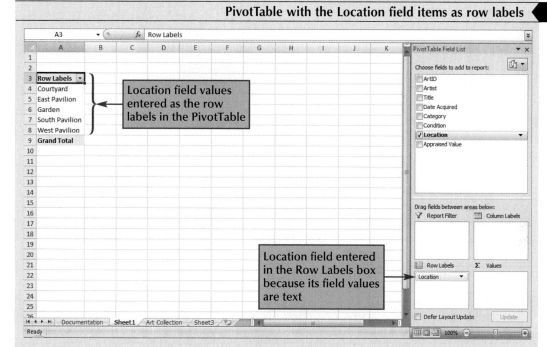

▶ 2. Click the **Appraised Value** check box in the PivotTable Field List. The Sum of Appraised Value button appears in the Values box. The PivotTable groups the items from the ArtObjects table by Location, and calculates the total appraised value for each location. The grand total appears at the bottom of the PivotTable. See Figure 5-32.

Figure 5-32 PivotTable of the appraised value of art objects by location

3. Rename the worksheet as **Appraised Value Summary**.

By default, the PivotTable report uses the SUM function for numbers in the Values area and the COUNT function for text and other nonnumeric values. If you want a different summary function, such as average, maximum, or minimum, click the appropriate button in the Values box (in this case, the button is called Sum of Appraised Value) in the Pivot-Table Field List, and then click Value Field Settings. The Value Field Settings dialog box opens. You can then select the type of calculation you want from the list of available functions, and then click the OK button.

Next, you'll add the Category and Condition fields to the PivotTable.

To add the Category and Condition fields to the PivotTable:

1. In the PivotTable Field List, click the **Category** check box. The Category field appears in the Row Labels box below the Location field and the unique items in the Category field are indented below each location field item in the PivotTable.

2. In the PivotTable Field List, click the **Condition** check box. The Condition field appears in the Row Labels box below the Category field and its unique items are indented below the Location and Category fields already in the PivotTable. See Figure 5-33.

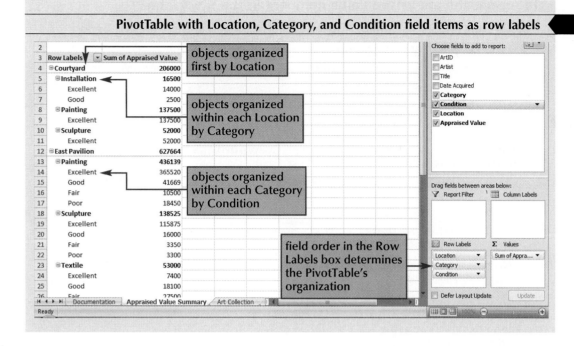

Applying PivotTable Styles

As with worksheet cells and Excel tables, you can quickly format a PivotTable report using a preset style. You can choose from a gallery of PivotTable styles similar to Table styles. Remember that you can point to any style in the gallery to see a Live Preview of the PivotTable with that style applied. You also can modify the appearance of PivotTables using PivotTable Style Options by adding or removing Banded Rows, Banded Columns, Row Headers, and Column Headers.

Mary wants you to apply the Medium 3 Style, which makes each group in the Pivot-Table stand out and subtotals in the report easier to find.

To apply a PivotTable style to the PivotTable report:

► **1.** Make sure the active cell is in the PivotTable, and then click the **PivotTable Tools Design** tab on the Ribbon.

► **2.** In the PivotTable Styles group, click the **More** button to open the PivotTable Styles gallery.

► **3.** Move the pointer over each style to preview the PivotTable report with that style.

► **4.** Click the **Pivot Style Medium 3** style (the third style in the Medium section). The style is applied to the PivotTable.

Formatting PivotTable Value Fields

Applying PivotTable styles does not change the numeric formatting in the PivotTable. Mary wants the numbers in the PivotTable to be quickly recognized as currency. You can format cells in a PivotTable the same way as you do cells in the worksheet. You'll change the total appraised values in the PivotTable to Currency style.

To format the appraised value numbers in the PivotTable:

▶ **1.** Click any cell in the **Sum of Appraised Value** column of the PivotTable report.

▶ **2.** Click the **PivotTable Tools Options** tab on the Ribbon, and then, in the Active Field group, click the **Field Settings** button. The Value Field Settings dialog box opens. See Figure 5-34.

| Figure 5-34 | Value Field Settings dialog box |

settings affect this component of the PivotTable →

enter the label you want to appear on the PivotTable

click to view other ways to view the values

select a summary calculation

click to format the PivotTable values

If you want to change "Sum of Appraised Value" (cell B3), the name used to describe the calculations in the PivotTable report, use the Custom Name box in the Value Field Settings dialog box.

▶ **3.** Click the **Number Format** button. The Format Cells dialog box opens. This is the same dialog box you've used before to format numbers in worksheet cells.

▶ **4.** Click **Currency** in the Category list, and then type **0** in the Decimal places box.

▶ **5.** Click the **OK** button in each dialog box. The numbers in the PivotTable are formatted as currency with no decimal places.

With the style applied and the numbers formatted as currency, the data in the Pivot-Table is much easier to interpret.

Rearranging a PivotTable

Although you cannot change the values within a PivotTable, you can add, remove, and rearrange fields to change the PivotTable's layout. Recall that the benefit of a PivotTable is that it summarizes large amounts of data into a readable format. After you create a PivotTable, you can view the same data in different ways. The PivotTable Field List enables you to change, or pivot, the view of the data in the PivotTable by dragging the field buttons to different areas in the layout section.

Refer back to Mary's PivotTable sketch in Figure 5-27. As illustrated in the sketch, the Condition field items should be positioned as column labels instead of row labels in the PivotTable. You'll move the Condition field now to produce the format Mary wants.

To move the Condition field:

▶ **1.** In the layout section of the PivotTable Field List, drag the **Condition** field button from the Row Labels box to the Column Labels box. The PivotTable is rearranged so that the Condition field is a column label instead of a row label. See Figure 5-35. Each time you make a change in the PivotTable Field List, the PivotTable layout is rearranged.

PivotTable rearranged with Condition as a column label ◀ **Figure 5-35**

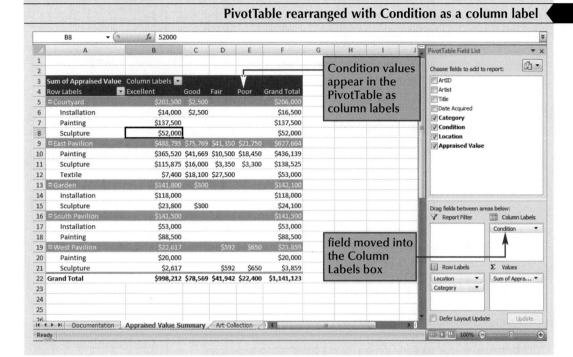

Changing the PivotTable Report Layout Options

The Compact report layout, shown in Figure 5-35, places all fields from the row area in a single column and indents the items from each field below the outer fields. This is the default layout for PivotTable reports. You can choose two other layouts. In the Outline report layout, each field in the row area takes a column in the PivotTable. By default, the outline form shows the subtotals for each group at the top of every group. The Tabular report layout displays one column for each field and leaves space for column headers. A total for each group appears at the bottom of each group. You can find these report layout options on the PivotTable Tools Design tab in the Layout group. Mary asks you to show her how the PivotTable looks in these alternative layouts so she can select the one she prefers.

To display the PivotTable in Outline and Tabular layouts:

▶ **1.** Click the **PivotTable Tools Design** tab on the Ribbon.

▶ **2.** In the Layout group, click the **Report Layout** button, and then click **Show in Outline Form**. The PivotTable layout changes. See Figure 5-36.

Figure 5-36 | Outline PivotTable report layout

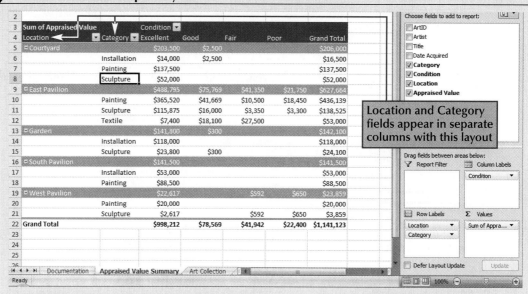

Location and Category fields appear in separate columns with this layout

Next, you'll review the Tabular report layout.

   3. In the Layout group, click the **Report Layout** button, and then click **Show in Tabular Form**. The PivotTable layout changes. See Figure 5-37.

Figure 5-37 | Tabular PivotTable report layout

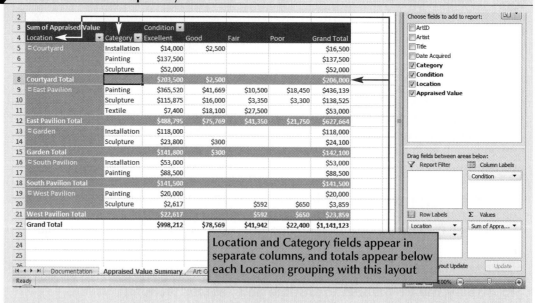

Location and Category fields appear in separate columns, and totals appear below each Location grouping with this layout

Mary prefers the original layout, the Compact form.

   4. In the Layout group, click the **Report Layout** button, and then click **Show in Compact Form**.

Adding a Report Filter to a PivotTable

You can drag a field to the Report Filter area to create a filtered view of the PivotTable report. A **report filter** allows you to filter the PivotTable to display summarized data for one or more field items or all field items in the Report Filter area. For example, creating a report filter for the Location field allows you to view or print the total appraised value for all locations or for specific locations such as the Courtyard.

You will add a report filter for the Location field to see if displaying the information in this way adds value to the report.

To add a report filter for the Location field:

▶ **1.** Drag the **Location** button from the Row Labels box to the Report Filter box. The Report Filter field item shows All to indicate that the PivotTable report displays all the summarized data associated with the Location field. See Figure 5-38.

PivotTable with the Location report filter applied ◀ Figure 5-38

Next, you'll change the summarized report to show only art objects in the East Pavilion.

▶ **2.** Click the **report filter arrow** in cell B1. A filter menu opens, showing the field items displayed.

Mary wants you to filter by a single item.

▶ **3.** Click **East Pavilion** in the filter menu, and then click the **OK** button. The Pivot-Table displays the total appraised value of art objects located in the East Pavilion only. The report filter arrow changes to an icon to indicate the PivotTable is currently filtered. See Figure 5-39.

Figure 5-39 | **Report filter view for art objects in the East Pavilion**

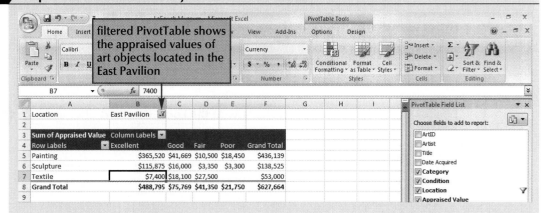

filtered PivotTable shows the appraised values of art objects located in the East Pavilion

After reviewing the PivotTable, Mary decides she prefers the previous layout.

▶ **4.** In the PivotTable Field List, drag the **Location** button from the Report Filter box to the top of the Row Labels box. The Location field is positioned above the Category field, and the PivotTable returns to its previous layout.

Trouble? If the PivotTable report is arranged differently, the Location field is not the top field in the Row Labels box. Drag the Location button in the Row Labels box above the Category button.

Filtering PivotTable Fields

Filtering a field lets you focus on a subset of items in that field. You can filter field items in the PivotTable by clicking the field arrow button in the PivotTable that represents the data you want to hide and then uncheck the check box for each item you want to hide. To show hidden items, you click the field arrow button and check the check box for the item you want to show.

Mary wants to focus her analysis on art objects in excellent, good, and fair condition. She asks you to remove art objects in poor condition from the PivotTable. You will hide the art objects in poor condition from the PivotTable report.

To filter the Condition field items from the PivotTable:

▶ **1.** In the PivotTable, click the **Column Labels filter arrow**. The Filter menu displays the list of items in the Condition field.

▶ **2.** Click the **Poor** check box to remove the check mark. The Select All check box is deselected as well.

▶ **3.** Click the **OK** button. The Poor column is removed from the PivotTable. The PivotTable includes only art objects in excellent, good, and fair condition. See Figure 5-40.

PivotTable report filtered by Condition | **Figure 5-40**

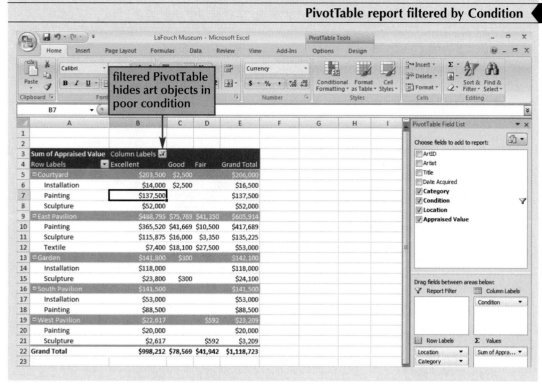

The report contains the art objects data Mary wants to review. Although the art objects in poor condition are hidden, you can show them again by clicking the Column Labels arrow and checking the Poor check box.

Collapsing and Expanding Items

You can expand and collapse items in the row labels of the PivotTable to view fields at different levels of detail. The Expand and Collapse buttons identify where more details exist. The Expand button indicates you can show more details for that item, and the Collapse button indicates you can hide details for that item. The lowest level of the hierarchy does not have Expand and Collapse buttons because there is no data to expand or collapse. These buttons are helpful when you have complex PivotTables where you want to switch quickly between a detailed view and an overview.

Mary wants to see the total appraised value for each location without the Category items in the PivotTable. She asks you to collapse the level of detail so that only the Location items are showing. Currently, all items are expanded.

To collapse the Courtyard items in the PivotTable:

▶ 1. Point to the **Collapse** button ☐ next to Courtyard until the pointer changes to ⬉, and then click the **Collapse** button ☐ next to Courtyard. The detail items below Courtyard are hidden, and the Collapse button changes to an Expand button.

▶ 2. Click the **Collapse** button ☐ next to East Pavilion, Garden, South Pavilion, and West Pavilion. The details for these four locations are hidden, and only the Location items are displayed. The PivotTable provides a higher level summary without displaying the Category details. See Figure 5-41.

Figure 5-41 | **PivotTable with all locations collapsed and categories hidden**

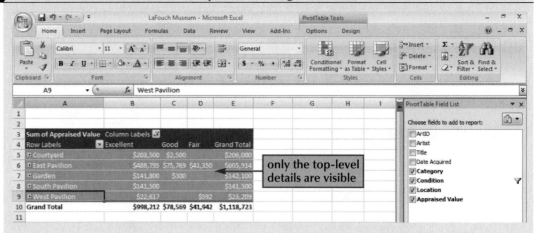

You can collapse or expand all level of detail in a PivotTable at one time. You'll do this to return to the original level of detail.

To expand all items in the PivotTable:

▶ **1.** Click the **PivotTable Tools Options** tab on the Ribbon. The Active Field group has buttons for expanding or collapsing all the details at one time.

▶ **2.** In the Active Field group, click the **Expand Entire Field** button. The detail items for all levels reappear. The lowest level of the hierarchy does not have Expand and Collapse buttons.

Sorting PivotTable Fields

Mary thinks the PivotTable would be more informative if the appraised values in each location were sorted in descending order. You can sort a PivotTable field either by its own items, for example alphabetizing fields such as Location and Category, or on the values in the body of the PivotTable. To sort a PivotTable field, you can use any of the Sort buttons on the Options tab to sort the information in a PivotTable report. These options are similar to the sort options you used earlier in the tutorial.

Mary wants you to sort the PivotTable so that the location with the highest total appraised value is displayed first. You need to sort the PivotTable values in descending order.

To sort the PivotTable to display the Location values in descending order based on their total appraised value amounts:

▶ **1.** Click cell **E5**, which contains the Grand Total for Courtyard. This is the field total you want to sort.

> **2.** In the Sort group on the PivotTable Tools Options tab, click the **Sort Largest to Smallest** button $\frac{Z}{A}\downarrow$. The Location field is sorted based on the total appraised value for each location. Note, for example, that the East Pavilion location appears first in the PivotTable because it has the highest total appraised value, $605,914. The Courtyard location appears next because it has the second highest total appraised value, $206,000, and so on. See Figure 5-42.

PivotTable results sorted by Location   Figure 5-42

Adding a Second Value Field to a PivotTable

You can expand a PivotTable to create a more informative table by adding fields to the Values layout area. For example, Mary believes that a more accurate presentation of the art objects would include the number of objects corresponding to the total value in each cell of the PivotTable. Adding the Title field to the Values box would count the number of art objects in each location-category-condition combination (because the title is a nonnumeric field). Mary thinks the additional information will be useful during her meeting with the board of directors. You will add the Title field to the PivotTable.

To drag and drop the Title field to the Values box:

> **1.** In the PivotTable Field List, drag **Title** from the field list to immediately below the Sum of Appraised Value button in the Values box. The PivotTable displays the number of art objects as well as the total appraised value. The Values box in the layout area includes a second button, Count of Title, and fields from the Values box are added to the Column Labels box. See Figure 5-43.

Figure 5-43 | Count of art objects added to the PivotTable

Part of the PivotTable is hidden behind the PivotTable Field List. You'll hide the Pivot-Table Field List so you can view more of the PivotTable.

▶ **2.** In the Show/Hide group on the PivotTable Tools Options tab, click the **Field List** button. The PivotTable Field List disappears.

Next, you'll change the "Count of Title" label to "Count."

▶ **3.** In the PivotTable, click any of the **Count of Title** labels.

▶ **4.** In the Active Field group on the PivotTable Tools Options tab, click the **Field Settings** button. The Value Field Settings dialog box opens.

▶ **5.** In the Custom Name box, type **Count**, and then click the **OK** button. The Count label appears in the PivotTable instead of Count of Title.

Removing a Field from a PivotTable

The PivotTable report with the Count looks cluttered and is difficult to read. Mary asks you to remove the Count field. If you want to remove a field from a PivotTable, you click the field's check box in the PivotTable Field List. Removing a field from the PivotTable has no effect on the underlying Excel table. You will remove the Title field from the PivotTable.

To remove the Title field from the PivotTable:

▶ 1. In the Show/Hide Group on the PivotTable Tools Options tab, click the **Field List** button. The PivotTable Field List is displayed.

▶ 2. Click the **Title** check box in the field area. The Count column is removed from the PivotTable, which returns to its previous layout. The Title field is still in the ArtObjects table.

The PivotTable is almost complete. Mary asks you to improve the appearance of the PivotTable by removing the field headers (Row Labels and Column Labels) and hiding the Expand/Collapse buttons.

To hide field headers and the Expand/Collapse buttons from the PivotTable:

▶ 1. In the Show/Hide group on the PivotTable Tools Options tab, click the **+/- Buttons** button. The Expand/Collapse buttons disappear from the PivotTable.

▶ 2. In the Show/Hide group, click the **Field Headers** button. The headers Column Labels and Row Labels are hidden. See Figure 5-44.

PivotTable without field headers and Expand/Collapse buttons ◀ Figure 5-44

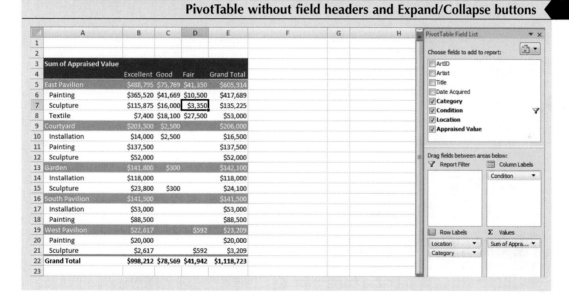

Refreshing a PivotTable

Mary just learned that the art object Dancing in the Light by Cridler has been reappraised and its value is now $4,000 (its value is currently listed as $1,000). You cannot change the data directly in the PivotTable. Instead, you must edit the Excel table, and then **refresh**, or update, the PivotTable to reflect the current state of the art objects list.

You'll edit the record for Dancing in the Light in the ArtObjects table. This sculpture is located in the East Pavilion and is in fair condition. This one change will affect the Pivot-Table in several locations. For example, currently the Total value of objects in the East Pavilion is $605,914; the sculptures in the East Pavilion are valued at $135,225; and sculptures in the East Pavilion in fair condition are valued at $3,350. After you update the appraised value of this art object in the Excel table, all these values in the PivotTable will increase by $3,000.

To update the ArtObjects table:

▶ 1. Switch to the **Art Collection** worksheet, and then find **Cridler, Dancing in the Light** (ArtID 73).

▶ 2. Click the record's Appraised Value cell, and then enter **4000**. The sculpture's value is updated in the table. You'll return to the PivotTable report to see the effect of this change on its values.

▶ 3. Switch to the **Appraised Value Summary** worksheet. The appraised value totals for the East Pavilion are still $605,914, $135,225, and $3,350, respectively.

The PivotTable is not updated when the data in its source table is updated, so you need to refresh the PivotTable manually.

▶ 4. Click any cell in the PivotTable.

▶ 5. Click the **PivotTable Tools Options** tab on the Ribbon, and then, in the Data group, click the **Refresh** button. The PivotTable report is updated. The appraised value totals are now $608,914, $138,225, and $6,350. See Figure 5-45.

Figure 5-45 ▶ **Refreshed PivotTable**

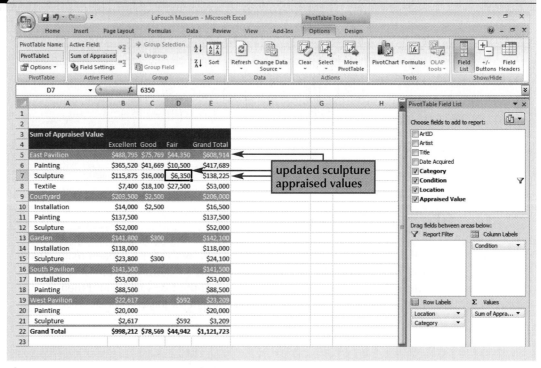

Mary is satisfied with the final version of the PivotTable report.

Grouping PivotTable Items

When a field contains numbers, dates, or times, you can combine items in the rows of a PivotTable and combine them into groups automatically. Mary thinks another PivotTable, one displaying the number of objects acquired each year, would be of interest to the board of directors. This report involves using the Date Acquired field as a row label and ArtID (or other field) as the value field. When using a date field as a row label in a PivotTable, each date initially appears as a separate item. Typically, you want to analyze date data by month, quarter, or year. To do that, you need to group the data in the Date Acquired field. Grouping items combines dates into larger groups such as months, quarters, or years, so that the PivotTable can include the desired level of summarization. You can also group numeric items, typically into equal ranges. For example, you can calculate the number of art objects in appraised value groups based on increments of any amount you specify (for example, 1–25,000, 25,001–50,000, and so on).

You'll add a second PivotTable in a new worksheet.

To create the PivotTable based on the Date Acquired field:

▶ 1. Switch to the **Art Collection** worksheet, and then click any cell in the Excel table. The table is active.

▶ 2. Click the **Insert** tab on the Ribbon, and then, in the Tables group, click the **PivotTable** button. The Create PivotTable dialog box opens.

▶ 3. Verify that the Table/Range box shows **ArtObjects** and the **New Worksheet** option button is selected, and then click the **OK** button. The PivotTable report area and PivotTable Field List appear in a new worksheet.

▶ 4. In the PivotTable Field List, click the **Date Acquired** check box. The Date Acquired field appears in the Row Labels box. Each unique date appears in the PivotTable report area. Mary wants each year to appear as a row label. You will correct that shortly.

Next, you'll add the ArtID field to the PivotTable.

▶ 5. Click the **ArtID** check box in the PivotTable Field List. The Sum of ArtID appears in the Values box in the layout area, because the ArtID field contains numeric data. See Figure 5-46.

Figure 5-46 | **PivotTable with Sum of ArtID for each date**

The PivotTable includes the sum of ArtIDs instead of a count of art objects, as Mary requested. This occurs because fields that contain numbers placed in the Values area are summed. Adding all the ArtIDs together to get a total is meaningless; you need to count the number of ArtIDs in each year. To do this, you need to change the SUM function to the COUNT function so Excel will *count* the number of objects in each group.

▶ **6.** Click any value in the **Sum of ArtID** column, and then, in the Active Field group on the PivotTable Tools Options tab, click the **Field Settings** button. The Value Field Settings dialog box opens.

▶ **7.** Click **Count** in the Summarize value field by box, and then type **Count** in the Custom Name box. The label indicating the type of summary in the PivotTable will be changed to Count.

▶ **8.** Click the **OK** button. The dialog box closes and the PivotTable report displays the number of art objects acquired by date. See Figure 5-47.

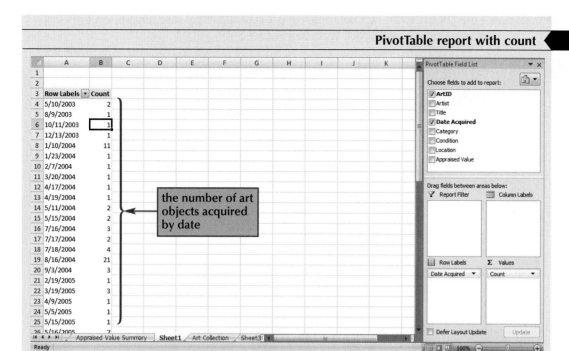

Grouping Date Fields

The layout of this PivotTable is not what Mary would like. Mary wants a count of acquisitions by year, not by date. You can group a range of dates into periods such as months, quarters, or years using the Group Fields command. Mary wants to group the Date Acquired dates by year.

To group Date Acquired by year:

▶ **1.** Click any date value in the Row Labels column of the PivotTable, and then, in the Group group on the PivotTable Tools Options tab, click the **Group Field** button. The Grouping dialog box opens.

▶ **2.** Click **Months** to deselect it, and then click **Years** to select it. See Figure 5-48.

Grouping

Auto

☑ Starting at: 5/10/2003 ◀── earliest date in the ArtObjects table

☑ Ending at: 4/6/2010 ◀── latest date in the ArtObjects table

By

Seconds
Minutes
Hours
Days
Months
Quarters
Years

Number of days: 1

OK   Cancel

▶ **3.** Click the **OK** button. The PivotTable report is grouped by year, displaying the number of art acquisitions in each year. See Figure 5-49.

Figure 5-49   PivotTable report of annual acquisitions

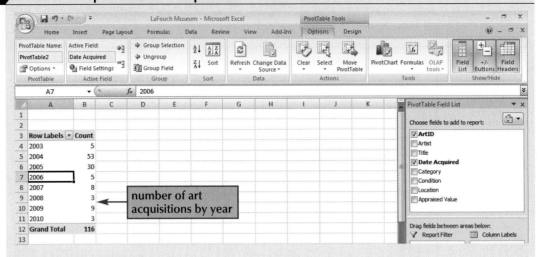

▶ **4.** Rename the worksheet as **Acquired By Year**.

InSight | **Creating Different Types of PivotTable Reports**

This tutorial only touched the surface of the variety of PivotTable reports you can create. Here are a few more examples:

- Most PivotTable summaries are based on numeric data, but PivotTables can also contain only nonnumeric data. You cannot add nonnumeric data, so you must use the COUNT function to produce summaries. For example, you could count the number of art objects by Location and Category.
- You can use PivotTables to combine items into groups. Items that appear as row labels or column labels can be grouped. If items are numbers or dates, they can be grouped automatically using the Grouping dialog box or manually using the Ctrl key to select items in a group and choosing Group from the shortcut menu. For example, you can manually combine the Courtyard and Garden locations into an Outdoor group and combine the three pavilion locations into an Indoor group and then provide counts or total appraised values by these groups within the PivotTable. Being able to combine categories that aren't part of your original data with the grouping feature gives you flexibility to summarize your PivotTables in a way that meets your analysis requirements.
- You can develop PivotTables using the value filter, which allows you to filter one of your row or column fields in the PivotTable based on numbers that appear in the Values area of the PivotTable. For example, a PivotTable can show the total value of art objects for each artist and be filtered to display only artists whose total is greater than $25,000. Filtering provides you with a more precise way to view the PivotTable results by enabling you to include or remove data from the report.

Creating a PivotChart

Now that the PivotTable is complete, Mary asks you to add a PivotChart next to the PivotTable. A **PivotChart** is a graphical representation of the data in a PivotTable. A

PivotChart allows you to interactively add, remove, filter, and refresh data fields in the PivotChart similar to working with a PivotTable. PivotCharts can have all the same formatting as other charts, including layouts and styles. You can move and resize chart elements, or change formatting of individual data points.

Mary asks you to prepare a clustered column chart next to the new PivotTable report. You can create a PivotChart from the PivotTable.

To create the PivotChart:

▶ 1. Click any cell in the PivotTable, and then, in the Tools group on the PivotTable Tools Options tab, click the **PivotChart** button. The Insert Chart dialog box opens.

▶ 2. Click the **Clustered Column** chart (the first chart in the first row of the Column section), if necessary, and then click the **OK** button. A PivotChart appears next to the PivotTable along with the PivotChart Filter Pane, which you use to filter the data shown in the PivotChart.

▶ 3. Close the PivotTable Field List, and then move the PivotChart Filter Pane to the right of the PivotChart.

Because the PivotChart has only one series, you do not need a legend.

▶ 4. In the PivotChart, click the **legend** to select it, and then press the **Delete** key. The legend is removed from the PivotChart.

Next, you'll modify the chart title.

▶ 5. Right-click the **chart title**, and then click **Edit Text**. The insertion point appears in the title so you can edit it.

▶ 6. Select the title, type **Number Acquired By Year** as the new title, and then click the **chart area** to deselect the title.

▶ 7. Move the PivotChart so its upper-left corner is in cell D3. The PivotChart is aligned with the PivotTable. See Figure 5-50.

> **Tip**
>
> You can also create a Pivot-Chart based directly on the Excel table, in which case both a PivotTable and a PivotChart are created.

PivotChart added to the PivotTable report ◀ **Figure 5-50**

The PivotChart Tools contextual tabs enable you to manipulate and format the selected PivotChart the same way as an ordinary chart. A PivotChart and its associated PivotTable are linked. When you modify one, the other also changes. Mary asks you to display only art acquisitions after 2004.

To filter items in the PivotChart:

▶ **1.** Make sure the PivotChart is selected, and then, in the PivotChart Filter Pane, click the **Axis Fields (Categories) filter arrow**. The filter menu opens.

▶ **2.** Click the **<5/10/2003**, **2003**, and **2004** check boxes to remove the check marks.

▶ **3.** Click the **OK** button. The PivotChart displays only art objects acquired after 2004. The PivotTable is also filtered to display the same results.

You have completed your work on the LaFouch Museum workbook.

▶ **4.** Save your changes to the workbook, and then close it.

Mary is pleased with the PivotTable and PivotChart. Both show the number of art objects acquired by year, which will be important information for her upcoming board meeting.

Review | **Session 5.3 Quick Check**

1. What is the default summary function for numeric data in a PivotTable?
2. When creating a PivotTable, what do you use to lay out the fields in the PivotTable report?
3. After you update data in an Excel table, what must you do to a PivotTable based on that table?
4. Fields such as region, state, and country are most likely to appear as _____ in a PivotTable.
5. Fields such as revenue, costs, and profits are most likely to appear as _____ in a PivotTable.
6. A list of college students includes a code to indicate the student's gender (male or female) and a field to identify the student's major. Which tool, Filter or PivotTable, would you use to (a) create a list of all females majoring in history, and (b) count the number of males and females in each major?

Tutorial Summary | Review

In this tutorial, you learned how to create an Excel table, enter, edit, and delete data in the table, and then sort data. You filtered the Excel table to display only data that meets certain criteria. You used the Total row to display detailed rows along with summary results for a filtered table. You inserted subtotals into a structured range of data. Finally, you summarized a table using a PivotTable and PivotChart.

Key Terms

ascending order	field	record
category field	field name	refresh
clear	filter	report filter
column header	freeze	secondary sort field
criteria filter	header row	sort
custom list	PivotChart	sort field
data definition table	PivotTable	Total row
descending order	primary sort field	value field

Practice	**Review Assignments**

Practice the skills you learned in the tutorial using the same case scenario.

Data File needed for the Review Assignments: Art.xlsx

Mary has another art object that needs to be entered in the art objects list. To further understand the information in the workbook, she wants to sort the data by date acquired. She wants to filter data to retrieve all art with the word *cowboy* in the title. She wants to use a PivotTable to determine the average value of artwork for each artist. Mary has asked you to gather the information she needs for further analysis of the museum's art objects.

Complete the following:

1. Open the **Art** workbook located in the Tutorial.05\Review folder included with your Data Files, and then save the workbook as **Art Museum** in the same folder.
2. In the Documentation sheet, enter your name and the date, and then switch to the Art Collection worksheet.
3. Create an Excel table for the art objects data. Change the table style to Medium 25.
4. Rename the Excel table as **Collection**.
5. Sort the art objects by Date Acquired to display the newest objects first. Make a copy of the Art Collection worksheet, rename the copied worksheet as **Q5** (for "Question 5"), and then return to the Art Collection worksheet. (*Hint*: Ctrl + drag the sheet tab to make a copy of the worksheet.)
6. Sort art objects by Category (Z to A), Location (A to Z), Artist (A to Z) in ascending order, and by Date Acquired (showing the oldest first). Make a copy of the Art Collection worksheet, rename the copied worksheet as **Q6** (for "Question 6"), and then return to the Art Collection worksheet.
7. Filter the Collection table to produce a list of art objects with the word *Cowboy* in the title, and then redisplay all the art objects. Make a copy of the Art Collection worksheet, rename the copied worksheet as **Q7**, and then return to the Art Collection worksheet. Display all records.
8. Use the Total row to calculate the average value of objects acquired between 2006 and 2010. Change the label in the Total row from Total to **Average**. Make a copy of the Art Collection worksheet, rename the copied worksheet as **Q8**, and then return to the Art Collection worksheet. Remove the Total row.
9. Use the Subtotal command to count how many art objects there are in each Location, displaying the count in the ArtID column. Make a copy of the Art Collection worksheet, rename the copied worksheet as **Q9**, and then return to the Art Collection worksheet. Remove the subtotals.
10. Create a PivotTable to show the average value of art objects by artist. Format the Value column.
11. Sort the PivotTable showing the artist with highest average value first.
12. Rename the PivotTable sheet as **Q10-15 Artist Summary**.
13. Modify the PivotTable to include Category as a Report filter field, and then filter the report so the average by Artist is based on Paintings.
14. Insert a new record in the Collection Excel table, and then enter the following data:
    ArtID #: **118**   Category: **Painting**
    Artist: **Abonti**   Condition: **Excellent**
    Title: **Trouble Ahead**   Location: **Garden**
    Date Acquired: **4/15/2010**   Appraised Value: **1200**
15. Refresh the PivotTable.
16. Save and close the workbook. Submit the finished workbook to your instructor, either in printed or electronic form, as requested.

| Apply | | Case Problem 1 |

Use the skills you learned to analyze and summarize donation data for a zoo.

Data File needed for this Case Problem: Pledges.xlsx

Hewart Zoo   Marvis Chennard is the director of fund-raising for the Hewart Zoo. The zoo relies on donations to fund operations, temporary exhibits, and special programs. Marvis created an Excel table to track information about donors and their pledges. Marvis asks you to analyze the data in the list.

Complete the following:

1. Open the **Pledges** workbook located in the Tutorial.05\Case1 folder included with your Data Files, and then save the workbook as **Zoo Pledges** in the same folder.
2. In the Documentation worksheet, enter the date and your name, and then switch to the Pledges worksheet.
3. Create an Excel table, and then rename the table as **PledgeData**.
4. Sort the data in ascending order by Donor Type and Fund Name, and in descending order by Amt Pledged (largest first). Make a copy of the Pledges worksheet, rename the copied worksheet as **Q4** (for "Question 4"), and then return to the Pledges worksheet. (*Hint*: Ctrl + drag the sheet tab to make a copy of the worksheet.)
5. Filter the data to display Individual donors whose Amt Owed is over zero. Sort the filtered data by Pledge Date, with the oldest date displayed first. Make a copy of the Pledges worksheet, rename the copied worksheet as **Q5** (for "Question 5"), and then return to the Pledges worksheet. Display all records.
6. Filter the data to display records that have a Pledge Date in October through December. Sort the filtered data by Amt Pledged (largest first). Make a copy of the Pledges worksheet, rename the copied worksheet as **Q6**, and then return to the Pledges worksheet. Display all records.
7. Filter the data to display only records with Amt Received greater than zero. Then use the Subtotal command (SUM) to display the total Amt Received by Fund Name. Make a copy of the Pledges worksheet, rename the copied worksheet as **Q7**, and then return to the Pledges worksheet. Remove the subtotals.
8. Create a PivotTable that displays the total and average Amt Owed by each Donor Type and Fund Name. Place the PivotTable in a new worksheet. Select an appropriate report layout and format, and rename the worksheet with a descriptive name.
9. Using Figure 5-51 as a guide, create a PivotTable on a new worksheet that shows the Amt Pledged by month and Fund Name. Format the PivotTable appropriately, and then rename the worksheet with a descriptive name. Print the PivotTable report.

Figure 5-51

| Sum of Amt Pledged | Column Labels | | | | |
Row Labels	Bird Sanctuary	General Support	Kids Zoo	ZooMobile	Grand Total
Jan		$1,000	$100		$1,100
Feb			$1,100	$150	$1,250
Mar			$100	$1,000	$1,100
Apr	$75	$500	$425		$1,000
Jun			$1,000	$50	$1,050
Jul	$1,000	$1,000			$2,000
Sep	$100	$25	$250	$150	$525
Oct	$200	$200			$400
Nov		$250			$250
Dec			$150	$750	$900
Grand Total	$1,375	$2,975	$3,125	$2,100	$9,575

10. Add the following data to the Pledge table, and then update the PivotTable you created in Step 9.

Pledge #	Donor Name	Donor Type	Fund Name	Pledge Date	Amt Pledged
2129	**Elliot Anderson**	**Individual**	**Kids Zoo**	**12/31/2010**	**1000**

11. Save and close the workbook. Submit the finished workbook to your instructor, either in printed or electronic form, as requested.

Apply		**Case Problem 2**

Use the skills you learned to analyze and summarize expenditure data for a farm.

Data File needed for this Case Problem: Ring.xlsx

Ring Family Farm Fred and Alesia Ring own a small family farm just outside Abita Springs, Louisiana. The couple wants to better organize their financial records for their accountant. They created an Excel workbook to record the various expenses associated with farming. Typical expenses include those associated with hay production (seed, fertilizer, and irrigation), animal husbandry, fence maintenance, veterinary services, self-administered medicines, vehicles and maintenance, and so forth. The workbook includes categories associated with these expenses as well as an area to record how much is spent, the purpose of the expenditure, the check number, and the date paid.

Complete the following:

1. Open the **Ring** workbook located in the Tutorial.05\Case2 folder included with your Data Files, and then save the workbook as **Ring Farm** in the same folder.
2. Insert a new worksheet. Enter the company name, your name, the date, and a purpose statement in the worksheet, and then rename the worksheet as **Documentation**.
3. Create an Excel table in the Expenditures worksheet, and then rename the table as **Checkbook**.
4. Replace the Category code Farm in each record with the more descriptive Category code **Payroll**.
5. Sort the Checkbook table in ascending order by Category, then by Description, and then by Date Paid (newest first). Make a copy of the Expenditures worksheet, rename the copied worksheet as **Q5** (for "Question 5"), and then return to the Expenditures worksheet. (*Hint:* Ctrl + drag the sheet tab to make a copy of the worksheet.)
6. Filter the Checkbook table to display all expenditures for Equipment and Repairs in December, and then sort by Amount (smallest first). Make a copy of the Expenditures worksheet, rename the copied worksheet as **Q6** (for "Question 6"), and then return to the Expenditures worksheet. Display all records.
7. Filter the Checkbook table to display all checks that include the word **vet** in the description. Include the total Amount at the bottom of the table. Make a copy of the Expenditures worksheet, rename the copied worksheet as **Q7**, and then return to the Expenditures worksheet. Remove the filter and totals.
8. Use conditional formatting to apply a Yellow Fill with Dark Yellow text to all Outstanding checks. (*Hint:* "Yes" appears in the Outstanding column.) Make a copy of the Expenditures worksheet, rename the copied worksheet as **Q8**, and then return to the Expenditures worksheet.
9. Use the Subtotal command to display total Amount for each Category, displaying the subtotal in the Amount column. Make a copy of the Expenditures worksheet, rename the copied worksheet as **Q9**, and then return to the Expenditures worksheet. Remove all subtotals.

10. Create a PivotTable that summarizes expenditures by Category and month. Place the PivotTable in a new worksheet. Format the PivotTable appropriately, choose a layout, and then rename the worksheet with a descriptive name.

11. Insert a PivotChart with the Clustered Column chart type on the same sheet as the PivotTable.

⊕ EXPLORE 12. Create the PivotTable shown in Figure 5-52 in a new worksheet. Sort the Amount column in descending order. (*Hint:* Check the Show values as tab in the Value Field Setting dialog box to calculate percent of total.)

Figure 5-52

	A	B	C
1			
2			
3		**Values**	
4	**Row Labels** ▾	**Sum of Amount**	**Pct of Total**
5	Equipment	$6,575.00	37.0%
6	Payroll	$2,638.27	14.9%
7	Vet	$2,320.57	13.1%
8	Repairs	$2,003.44	11.3%
9	Feed	$2,002.24	11.3%
10	Medicine	$1,249.32	7.0%
11	Administration	$958.09	5.4%
12	**Grand Total**	**$17,746.93**	**100.0%**

13. Save and close the workbook. Submit the finished workbook to your instructor, either in printed or electronic form, as requested.

Apply | **Case Problem 3**

Use the skills you learned to analyze and summarize loan data for a bank.

Data File needed for this Case Problem: CustLoans.xlsx

High Desert Bank Eleanor Chimayo, loan manager for High Desert Bank, is getting ready for the bank's quarterly meeting. Eleanor is expected to present data on the status of different types of loans within three New Mexican cities. Eleanor asks you to summarize and analyze the data for her presentation.

Complete the following:

1. Open the **CustLoans** workbook located in the Tutorial.05\Case3 folder included with your Data Files, and then save the workbook as **High Desert Bank** in the same folder.

2. In the Documentation sheet, enter the date and your name.

3. In the Loans worksheet, create an Excel table, and then rename the table as **LoanData**.

4. Format the Amount and Interest Rate fields so it is clear that these fields contain dollars and percentages.

5. Change the table style to one of your choice.

⊕ EXPLORE 6. To the right of the Type column, insert a new column named **Monthly Payment**. Use the PMT function to calculate the monthly payment for each loan. Adjust the formula so each loan is displayed as a positive amount and improve the formatting.

7. Sort the loan data in ascending order by Type, within Type by City, and within City by Last Name.

8. Use conditional formatting to display loans above average using a format that highlights these loans. Make a copy of the Loans worksheet, rename the copied worksheet as **Q3–8**, for ("Question 3–8"), and then return to the Loans worksheet. (*Hint*: Ctrl + drag the sheet tab to make a copy of the worksheet.)

9. Filter the LoanData table to display loans made during March and April of 2010. Include the number of loans, total amount of loans, and average monthly payment for the filtered data at the bottom of the table. Make a copy of the Loans worksheet, rename the copied worksheet as **Q9**, for ("Question 9"), and then return to the Loans worksheet. Then remove the total loans and show all records.

10. Sort the loans in ascending order by City; then by Type of loan; and then by Amount of loan (largest loan first). Insert subtotals (Average) for loan Amount and Monthly Payment by City. Include your name in a custom footer. Make a copy of the Loans worksheet, rename the copied worksheet as **Q10**, and then return to the Loans worksheet. Remove the subtotals.

11. Create a PivotTable that displays the number (Count) and average loan by Type and City. Place the PivotTable in a new worksheet. Remove the Other loan type from the PivotTable. Format the PivotTable appropriately. Rename the PivotTable worksheet as **Q11 Loans-Type And City**.

✥ EXPLORE 12. Create a second PivotTable, shown in Figure 5-53, in a new worksheet. The PivotTable shows three calculations: Number of Loans, total loans (Loan Amount), and total monthly payments (Payment) categorized by Type of loan. Insert a report filter based on Loan Date, grouped so you can filter by month. Filter the PivotTable report for March and April. Rename the PivotTable worksheet as **Q12 Loans-Type and Loan Date**.

Figure 5-53

	A	B		C	D
1	Loan Date	(Multiple Items)	▼		
2					
3		Number of Loans		Loan Amount	Payment
4	Car	5		$157,000	$3,681.77
5	Mortgage	5		$929,000	$7,890.77
6	Other	2		$35,000	$860.49
7	Grand Total	12		$1,121,000	$12,433.03

13. Save and close the workbook. Submit the finished workbook to your instructor, either in printed or electronic form, as requested.

Challenge | Case Problem 4

Explore how to summarize data from a department store by creating more complex subtotals, PivotTables, and PivotCharts.

Data File needed for this Case Problem: Bowls.xlsx

Bowls Department Stores Bowls Department Stores, with corporate headquarters in Portland, Oregon, operates department stores in midsize towns in selected northwestern areas. Although the organization maintains a large computer system for its accounting operations, the sales department often downloads data to complete additional analysis of its operations. Daniel Partner, analyst for the corporate sales department, regularly downloads data by territories and product areas including automotive, electronics, garden centers, and sporting goods. He often presents reports based on his analysis of sales by product areas and territory, best and worst performing product group-periods, and total sales for certain regions and product groups. He asks you to help him compile and summarize the data.

Complete the following:

1. Open the **Bowls** workbook located in the Tutorial.05\Case4 folder included with your Data Files, and then save the workbook as **Bowls Stores** in the same folder.

2. In the Documentation sheet, enter the date and your name and an appropriate purpose statement.

3. In the SalesData worksheet, create an Excel table. Rename the table as **ProductSales**. Format the Sales column in the Currency number format with no decimal places.

4. Sort the table in ascending order by Territories, then by Product Group, then by Year, and then by Month. Month should be sorted in Jan, Feb, Mar, ... order, not alphabetically. Make a copy of the SalesData worksheet, rename the copied worksheet as **Q4**, for ("Question 4"), and then return to the SalesData worksheet. (*Hint*: Ctrl + drag the sheet tab to make a copy of the worksheet.)

EXPLORE

5. Display records for Automotive and Electronic products in 2010, excluding sales in Vancouver. Sort this data by Sales in descending order. Add a Total row and calculate the average sales for the filtered data. Change the label in the Total row to **Average**. Insert a new worksheet and copy this filtered data to the new worksheet. Split the worksheet into two panes. The top pane displays all the rows but the last row on your screen. The bottom pane displays the Total row. (*Hint:* Click the Split button in the Window group on the View tab.) Rename the new worksheet as **Q5 Auto Electronic**. Return to the SalesData worksheet, remove the Total row, and display all the records.

EXPLORE

6. Display subtotals for sales (Sum) by Year, Month (Jan, Feb, Mar, ...), and Territory. Make a copy of the SalesData worksheet, rename the copied worksheet as **Q6**, for ("Question 6"), and then return to the SalesData worksheet. Remove the subtotals.

7. Display the five lowest periods based on sales. Assume each row represents a period. Sort the Sales so lowest sales appears first. Insert a new worksheet and copy this filtered data to the new worksheet. Rename the new worksheet as **Q7 Lowest Periods**. Return to the SalesData worksheet, and then display all the records.

EXPLORE

8. Create a PivotTable similar to the one shown in Figure 5-54, displaying percentage of sales by Product Group, Territories, and Year. Omit the columnar grand totals. Use a tabular layout, inserting subtotals at the bottom of each Product Group and excluding the Sporting product group. Rename the worksheet as **Q8 Percent of Sales**.

Figure 5-54

	A	B	C	D
1				
2				
3	**Pct of Sales**		**Year**	
4	**Product Group**	**Territories**	**2009**	**2010**
5	**Automotive**	Oregon	10.05%	8.85%
6		Vancouver	7.32%	9.71%
7		Washington	6.88%	9.94%
8	**Automotive Total**		**24.25%**	**28.50%**
9	**Electronics**	Oregon	7.53%	8.67%
10		Vancouver	7.61%	6.88%
11		Washington	8.05%	9.22%
12	**Electronics Total**		**23.20%**	**24.78%**
13	**Gardening**	Oregon	8.19%	6.85%
14		Vancouver	8.46%	5.89%
15		Washington	9.77%	9.91%
16	**Gardening Total**		**26.42%**	**22.66%**
17	**Houseware**	Oregon	6.86%	5.01%
18		Vancouver	8.20%	7.67%
19		Washington	11.07%	11.39%
20	**Houseware Total**		**26.14%**	**24.07%**
21	**Grand Total**		**100.00%**	**100.00%**

EXPLORE

9. Using Figure 5-55 as a guide, create a PivotChart of total Sales By Product Group. Create a second PivotChart of total Sales By Territory in the same worksheet. Include only the PivotCharts in the worksheet. Rename the worksheet as **Q9 PivotCharts**.

Figure 5-55

10. Using Figure 5-56 as a guide, create a PivotTable to show four calculations: minimum, maximum, average, and total Sales categorized by Territories and Product Group and filtered by Year. Display the results for 2010. Rename the worksheet as **Q10 Statistical Summary**.

Figure 5-56

	A	B	C	D	E	F
1	Year	2010				
2						
3			Values			
4	Territories	Product Group	Average	Sum	Minimum	Maximum
5	⊟Oregon	Automotive	$ 50,196	$ 602,354	$ 1,825	$ 98,358
6		Electronics	$ 49,175	$ 590,099	$ 7,164	$ 95,985
7		Gardening	$ 38,859	$ 466,305	$ 5,396	$ 95,795
8		Houseware	$ 28,428	$ 341,139	$ 3,374	$ 64,982
9		Sporting	$ 70,243	$ 842,910	$ 26,643	$ 91,786
10	Oregon Total		$ 47,380	$2,842,807	$ 1,825	$ 98,358
11	⊟Vancouver	Automotive	$ 55,074	$ 660,886	$ 865	$ 99,526
12		Electronics	$ 39,033	$ 468,391	$ 2,141	$ 98,044
13		Gardening	$ 33,419	$ 401,027	$ 467	$ 97,793
14		Houseware	$ 43,473	$ 521,678	$ 4,046	$ 80,035
15		Sporting	$ 60,199	$ 722,385	$ 29,824	$ 94,129
16	Vancouver Total		$ 46,239	$2,774,367	$ 467	$ 99,526
17	⊟Washington	Automotive	$ 56,359	$ 676,304	$ 3,893	$ 99,258
18		Electronics	$ 52,307	$ 627,680	$ 15,485	$ 84,624
19		Gardening	$ 56,206	$ 674,471	$ 5,507	$ 94,166
20		Houseware	$ 64,579	$ 774,942	$ 27,164	$ 94,725
21		Sporting	$ 63,189	$ 758,272	$ 17,919	$ 90,879
22	Washington Total		$ 58,528	$3,511,669	$ 3,893	$ 99,258
23	Grand Total		$ 50,716	$9,128,843	$ 467	$ 99,526

11. Save and close the workbook. Submit the finished workbook to your instructor, either in printed or electronic form, as requested.

Research		Internet Assignments

Use the Internet to find and work with data related to the topics presented in this tutorial.

The purpose of the Internet Assignments is to challenge you to find information on the Internet that you can use to work effectively with this software. The actual assignments are updated and maintained on the Course Technology Web site. Log on to the Internet and use your Web browser to go to the Student Online Companion for New Perspectives Office 2007 at **www.course.com/np/office2007**. Then navigate to the Internet Assignments for this tutorial.

Assess		SAM Assessment and Training

If you have a SAM user profile, you may have access to hands-on instruction, practice, and assessment of the skills covered in this tutorial. Log in to your SAM account (**http://sam2007.course.com**) to launch any assigned training activities or exams that relate to the skills covered in this tutorial.

Review		Quick Check Answers

Session 5.1

1. To keep, or freeze, rows and columns so that they don't scroll out of view as you move around the worksheet. Freezing the rows and columns that contain headings makes understanding the data in each record easier.
2. Filter arrows appear in the column headers, a table style format is applied to the table, and the Table Tools Design contextual tab appears on the Ribbon.
3. sort fields
4. Sort by year of graduation and then by last name.
5. Enter the data for the new record in the row immediately following the last row of data in the table.
6. Create a custom list.
7. descending (Newest to Oldest)

Session 5.2

1. You must first sort the data for which you want to calculate subtotals, because subtotals are inserted whenever the value in the specified field changes.
2. Filter the table to show only the finance department, and then use the AVERAGE function in the Total row.
3. Click the Major filter arrow, and then check only the Accounting and Finance check boxes. Click the GPA filter arrow, point to Number Filters, click Greater Than, and then enter the value 3.0 in the Greater Than dialog box to specify the condition for a GPA greater than 3.0.

4. Click the Level Outline buttons.

5. True

6. Multiselect

7. Click the Gender filter arrow, and check only the Female check box. Insert the Total row, click the arrow that appears to the right of the total for the Salary column, and then click Average in the list of functions.

Session 5.3

1. SUM

2. PivotTable Field List box

3. refresh the PivotTable

4. rows labels, column labels, or report filters

5. values

6. (a) Filter; (b) PivotTable

Ending Data Files

Tutorial.05 →

Tutorial
LaFouch
Museum.xlsx

Review
Art
Museum.xlsx

Case1
Zoo
Pledges.xlsx

Case2
Ring
Farm.xlsx

Case3
High Desert
Bank.xlsx

Case4
Bowls
Stores.xlsx